Messianic Church Arising!

Volume Two of
Sons of Zion vs Sons of Greece

Dr. Miles R. Jones

Messianic Church Arising!
Volume Two of Sons of Zion vs Sons of Greece

Dr. Miles R. Jones, author
Rae Lloyd-Jones, editor

ISBN: 978-957488-01-1
© copyright *2022 Miles R. Jones*
First Edition

Great Publishing Company
Benai Emunah Institute
121 Mountain Way
Kerrville, Texas
writingofgod.com

"Yehovah gave the Word;
Great was the company
of those that published it!"
Psalm 68:11

The fabulous cover, **Pirate Battle at Sea**, is used by permission of the fabulous artist, **Christopher Lane** check out his other great work at fineartamerica.com.

Dr. Miles R. Jones is an internationally renowned expert in accelerated learning of languages, mathematics, memory training, historical linguistics, and discoverer of *The Hebrew Gospels*. He is now Director of the Benai Emunah Institute. He was called from teaching CEO's and top executives in Europe, the Middle East, the U.S., and Mexico to teach in inner-city schools in Dallas, Tx. He taught in the inner-city for six years before becoming an education professor at Texas A & M. Dr. Jones has since created an accelerated learning curriculum for home-schoolers which has won international acclaim.

Previous work as director of university English programs in the United Arab Emirates and as a specialist with the U.S. government in Yemen, training military officers, allowed him to begin his research in the field. As an historical linguist, the origin of the alphabet had always captivated him. There had only been one alphabet in history from which all others are derived. That original alphabet appeared in the path of the Exodus at the time of the Exodus. *The Writing of God* is the result of decades of expert research on the origin of the alphabet.

Dr. Jones is now translating the surviving manuscripts of *The Hebrew Gospels*. The history of *The Hebrew Gospels* and the Messianic Church throughout history are detailed in:

***Sons of Zion vs Sons of Greece* - Volume One:** (2019)
Survival of the Hebrew Gospels and the Messianic Church

***Messianic Church Arising!* - Volume Two of**
Sons of Zion vs Sons of Greece (2022)

Dr. Jones received his PhD in Foreign Languages & Linguistics at the University of Texas at Austin in 1985. He has taught worldwide and developed accelerated curriculum in numerous subjects, including Spanish, French, Hebrew, ESL, Mathematics, Speed Reading, & Memory Training. He is a researcher in historical linguistics - writing of ancient Messianic manuscripts.

Messianic Church Arising!

Vol. Two - Sons of Zion vs Sons of Greece

	page:
Introduction	6
Sepharad - The New Jerusalem	15
1 - The New Jerusalem	16
2 - The Golden Age	40
3 - The Neo-Messianic Movement	58
4 - The Underground Church	75
5 - The Age of Chivalry & Crusades	100
6 - Messianic Church in Sepharad	129
The New World	151
7 - The Hammer of the Inquisition	152
8 - Columbus & the New World	175
9 - Messianic Diaspora & the Renaissance	192
10 - Hebrew Pirates of the High Seas	205
11 - Reformation & *The Received Text*	240
12 - Messianic Church Arising!	277
13 - Conclusion - The Schizophrenic Church	313
Appendices: A-328, B-331, C-338, D-346	328
Bibliography pp. 355-373	355

Prologue

Sons of Zion versus Sons of Greece ended with the declaration - **"The new Greco-Roman Church of Constantine became Apostate the moment they cut off and condemned as heretic the original church of the Messiah - the Messianic Church!"** Many of the new churches will say they split off from the Apostate Greco-Roman Church long ago. The Apostasy of the new churches remains upon those who have split off unless they split because of the rejection of the Messiah's Church. One must be prepared to embrace the new churches who repent of the historical sins of persecuting, torturing and executing fellow believers, or non-believers. Sin not confessed and repented comes around again and again. And so it has been for millennia now. **Time to stop the murder!** We are only 75 years out from the last Holocaust - a moment in the sandglass of time. The response to this declaration will be denial, silence, perhaps outrage - and a deep desire to disregard these sins. One is not freed of sin without confession and repentance - even churches. **There is no corporate exception to sin!** What is sin? *"Whoever commits sin transgresses Torah: for sin is the transgression of Torah"* (1st Sam 15:24, Dan 9:11, 1st John 3:4). In the Apostate Church, holding to Torah was *Judaizing*, punishable by death!

The defense of the Apostate Church is that those persecuted, tortured and slain were, after all, *'heretics!'* The *'heresy'* of the Messianic Church was preserving *The Hebrew Gospels*, and imitating Yeshua the Messiah by seeking to understand and obey Yehovah's Word in Torah. It was so long ago, they will say, besides they are a totally different, and better, church now. Agreed, they are. However, a murderer and thief is not sinless because he hasn't murdered or robbed anyone lately. Descendants of murderers and thieves are not sinless if they seek to cover up, deny or defend sins of their fathers. The new churches profited by those sins and have inherited the poisonous fruit of past sin. Unrepentant sin makes certain the repeat of such sin.

True, millions of souls have been saved in these new churches. That doesn't mean the Spanish Inquisition or the Holocaust didn't happen. It simply means **the Church is now - and has always been - a spiritual battleground!** The doing of great evil is a hideous consequence of that battle. Soon, the debate will end at the Christian doctrinal stance: The Gospel was not written in Hebrew (but Greek), Yeshua was not the Messiah (Christ was), and the Torah (Old Testament) is dead and rejected legalism!

At least we are having an honest dialog now…
Shall we begin?

Introduction

In Volume One I related how I was led to the manuscript of *The Hebrew Gospels from Catalonia*. I had been researching *The Hebrew Gospels* for an entire year. It was clearly emphasized in mainstream academia that no manuscript of *The Hebrew Gospels* had survived. When Yehovah told me to go to Israel to find *The Hebrew Gospels* I did so - and they were delivered into my hands! At the time (2014), one could only have found them by going to Israel. Now these Hebrew manuscripts are available online due to the public interest that has arisen about these manuscripts - much of it from our work at Benai Emunah Institute to inform the public - and to translate and publish *The Hebrew Gospels and Brit Hadashah* (New Testament in Hebrew) with analysis and commentary on their importance. However, Yehovah was not done with me yet. Herein lies this new story.

Benai Emunah Research Updates 2019 - Expedition to Save the Underground Bibles

My reason for making this trip sprang from my translation of *The Hebrew Gospels* which revealed many of the differences between the Hebrew and the Greek Gospel manuscripts. Then I became aware of another text - the *Evan Bohan* by Shem Tov (*The Touchstone*) which contained *The Hebrew Gospel of Matthew*. My analysis (pp.48-50) determined that it came from the same original source as *The Hebrew Gospels from Catalonia*, both published in Catalonia, Spain, within the same century. Since I had discovered *The Hebrew Gospels from Catalonia* came from a first century source, that meant the Shem Tov manuscript must have as well. [*Sons of Zion vs Sons of Greece - Volume One* has the detailed analysis.] Then I discovered yet another manuscript of the Gospels in ancient Romaunt which had the markers of being translated from *The Hebrew Gospels*!

The Hebrew Gospels had been targeted for extinction by the Greco-Roman Church starting in the fourth century. In fact, **The Hebrew Gospels are the most forbidden and most targeted book(s) in the history of humankind!** They have been now for almost two millennia. It was a death sentence to possess them! **But *The Hebrew Gospels* survived!** I have three manuscripts on my desk. **If I have three - there must be more!**

The Hebrew Gospels had survived, both in Hebrew and in translation from Hebrew into the early European languages of The Underground Church! The original Messianic-Apostolic Church had morphed over the centuries into the Neo-Messianic movement of the Middle Ages. It was violently and viciously put down, its congregants and their Scriptures burned! But it was not destroyed - it just went underground. Having failed to destroy all the manuscripts of the early Messianic Church, the second line of attack was to discredit and dismiss them. In short, the manuscripts that had escaped destruction were simply being ignored. *The Hebrew Gospels* were deemed a myth, they never existed. They were banned and burned whenever possible. **They were forbidden!** Of course, if they were a myth - forbidding them would not be necessary. When Hebrew manuscripts were uncovered, they were automatically labeled nothing more than a translation from the Greek or Latin - and heretical as well! Again, if they were a translation then they would not be heretical, would they? In any case, the study of *The Hebrew Gospels* was banned. The truth is, *The Hebrew Gospels* had survived and were being ignored! Should I go after them?

I prayed about going after the Underground Bibles and soon received the command I needed, *"I already told you to go find The Hebrew Gospels, so go!"* I put the Expedition to Recover the Underground Bibles out to the members of my email list, which was only about 400 people at the time. In a response, nothing short of miraculous, they contributed $10,000 for me to travel to Europe and purchase digitized copies of the manuscripts I sought to find. Even a digitized copy of a single manuscript can be quite expensive - sometimes running more than a thousand dollars. So I left for Europe in December of 2019 for a 30-day research blitz with only a vague idea of where I would go and what I would do. These are the newsletters I sent that month.

Research Update #1 - Dec 6, 2019 - Manchester, England
Day 3 of a 30-day Expedition to Save the Underground Bibles

I arrived in England Dec. 4th. Despite the jet lag, upon arrival I met with Wayne Krantz a wonderful Hebraic Roots congregant who had offered assistance. We drove north to meet with Dr. Richard Harvey, an expert Messianic who has worked all of his life to reconcile mainstream Christianity with the Messianic Church. We did a great interview (posted on writingofgod.com).

It was clear to me *The Hebrew Gospels* were being ignored because of the foundational Christian belief in Greek primacy of the Bible. In other words, Greek primacists' central belief is that God has provided - by divine providence - the most authoritative Scripture in Greek. All Hebrew manuscripts must not be inspired by the Holy Spirit, did not exist, or can be ignored as translations from the Greek. Jewish scholars were no better since *The Hebrew Gospels* were forbidden to them as well - considered to be the source of their oppression by Christians and a corruption of their beliefs. Considering this prohibition from both sides of the aisle, the only scribes and scholars preserving and recopying *The Hebrew Gospels* were Messianics. Who else would risk burning at the stake to preserve them? **Whenever we find a Gospel in Hebrew it marks the presence of a Messianic community for which it was preserved!**

As the Messianic Movement spread throughout Europe the new converts were mostly Gentile now but - always and everywhere - they were devoted to the restoration of the first century Messianic-Apostolic Church of the Messiah. So *The Hebrew Gospels* were translated into the common languages of early Europe: Romaunt, Catalan, and Occitan, etc. My premise was correct. There is much more evidence of *The Hebrew Gospels* than anyone expected. Of course, mainstream Christian theologians believe there is none at all. That is a pretty low bar.

On the first full day of the Expedition we found the following manuscripts at Cambridge Library. I had no idea these manuscripts were there. I went there for a totally different reason. Here are the manuscripts found on the first day:

1) The New Testament in Hebrew (Cambridge MS Oo.1.32)
2) Acts & Epistles Cor, Gal, Eph. in Hebrew (MS Oo.1.16.1)
3) Revelation in Hebrew (Cambridge MS Oo.1.16.2)
4) The Gospel of John in Hebrew (MS Add.170)

Two days later we discovered a fifth manuscript at Rylands Library in Manchester, #5) Gaster MS 1616, another complete manuscript *of The Hebrew Gospels and Brit Hadashah!* All five manuscripts were recovered from Cochin, India - documents from the St. Thomas Christians - the first of which, quite probably, was brought there by the Apostle Thomas in the first century.

This is a sensational find if it can be authenticated!

These manuscripts were recovered by Claudius Buchanan in 1806 from the synagogue of the Black Jews of Cochin. The first historical attestation to them was by Eusebius, *"The Gospel according to Matthew had been taken to India by the Apostle Bartholomew* [first century]... *written in 'Hebrew script' and preserved there until the visit of Pantaenus (circa 190 AD)... Pantaenus brought* [a copy of] *Hebrew Matthew with him on his return from India to Alexandria."* [brackets mine] There it was available to Origin (in the 3rd century AD). Origin compiled his famous *Hexapla* - a comparison of the Hebrew and Greek Old Testament[1] extant at the time, also having *The Hebrew Gospels from Cochin* to aid the analysis. Pantaenus was head of the Christian exegetical school in Alexandria, as was Origin, his successor.

The Cochin Hebrew Gospels were preserved and expanded upon as the Epistles became available and were translated into Hebrew. Historical evidence indicates that some; the Epistles of Hebrews, James, John, Peter, Jude, and Revelation; were originally written in Hebrew. The Epistles of Paul in Greek were translated into Hebrew in order to make a compilation of *The Hebrew Gospels & Brit Hadashah* for Hebrew-speaking Messianics, who were still the majority of believers until later in the 2nd century.

Matthew and Luke were originally written in Hebrew. When Luke was translated into Greek more material was added, doubling it in size, so Luke is a hybrid. Since Luke and Acts were written as a two-part letter by Luke to Theophilus, it is probable that Acts was a Hebrew original as well. Mark and John appear to be originally written in Greek but early church fathers cite Hebrew *'translations'* of both John and Acts in the library at Caesaria in the 4th century, where many Jews studied them and were converted. Keep in mind that all Hebrew N.T. manuscripts are automatically assumed to be *translations* due to Greek primacy. So these manuscripts may be from Hebrew originals. One thing is not in doubt, there was a very early compilation of *the Hebrew Gospels & Brit Hadashah*. The entire early Church was Hebrew-speaking and they continued to be predominant for centuries. A compilation was certain - **but unproven until now! We now have those compilations of** *The Hebrew Gospels and Brit Hadashah* **- from The Cochin manuscripts!** They should give us some answers to those very important questions.[2]

---

[1] Most of the New Testament, comes from the Old Testament, so it would be of use in Origin's analysis in the *Hexapla*. [2] Evidence of this compilation is given at length in Vol. One, and summarized in chapter 11 of this volume.

At John Rylands Library in Manchester I recovered the fifth manuscript in the Cochin Collection. My friends Wayne and Judith Kranz had contacted the curator so we knew of this Hebrew manuscript of the Gospels from the early 1800s. It was a truly amazing day when I opened it up and discovered not only a complete set of *The Hebrew Gospels* but the entire *Brit Hadashah* as well! We now had two compilations of the New Testament in Hebrew. It was a fabulous moment and a beautiful manuscript in a calligraphy so fine it looked like a printed book. This sort of care indicates the importance of the manuscript to those who preserved it. Keep in mind The Cochin Gospels discovered at Rylands Library (Gaster MS 1616) was not digitized nor even listed in the catalogue. **That means that practically no one had ever seen *The Cochin Gospels*!** In Cambridge we took high resolution photographs of each page of the manuscripts avoiding the expense and delay of having the library do it. These manuscripts would not have been recovered if we had not gone there.

We also obtained copies from the British Museum of the Hebrew Epistles of 2nd Peter, James, Jude, and the Hazon Hebrew manuscript of Revelation. The Hazon MS was incomplete - only the first seven pages - up to Rev 2:12. However, we had just recovered two manuscripts of *The Brit Hadashah*, **the first *complete* Hebrew manuscripts of Revelation ever found!**

Thanks to my initial translation of ***The Hebrew Gospels from Catalonia*** (Matthew, Mark, Luke & John), which I had been working on the previous two years, I knew how *The Hebrew Gospels* differ from *The Greek Gospels*. I had also proven that they came from a first century source.[3] Now we can compare these new manuscripts to see if they match the markers of *The Hebrew Gospels from Catalonia* which I have already translated.

Research Update #2 - Dec 13, 2019 - Paris, France
Day 10 of a 30-day Expedition to Save Underground Bibles

In Paris, I purchased a digital copy of one of the most beautiful manuscripts I have ever seen. It is the New Testament in Catalan, the Pieresc Manuscript. The colorful illumination is gorgeous! **This manuscript was definitely translated from *The Hebrew Gospels*!** I know this because I know its history and the markers - what is different in the Hebrew vs the Greek![4]

---

[3]See review of the proof in chapter 11, pp.260-3. [4]Markers - in chapter 2, p.51.

There is plenty of historical attestation and analysis to prove the Pieresc MS came from Hebrew. Such a conclusion has been dismissed by Greek primacists. Now we have both *The Hebrew Gospels* and *The Pieresc Catalan N.T.* to examine - making it much harder to ignore or dismiss. That is the primary importance of this Expedition. **We have discovered a Hebrew Manuscript Tradition of the New Testament!** Not simply one manuscript has survived but numerous manuscripts in Hebrew as well as translations into the early languages of southern Europe.

You may remember in my fund-raising letter I bemoaned the fact than an entire collection of the most ancient manuscripts of the Waldensians, held at Cambridge Library, had disappeared! One of the manuscripts lost was the oldest Waldensian Gospels. It was for this reason that I went first to Cambridge to investigate the story of what might have happened to this priceless collection.

The Waldensians were the oldest Messianic-Apostolic Church on the continent of Europe. For this reason the new Church of Rome declared them heretic and expelled them from Rome. The Waldensians were never part of the Roman Church. They opposed Rome, so they moved *en masse* to northern Italy, to the area of Lombardy. They took their *Hebrew Gospels* with them. **The preface to *The Hebrew Gospels from Catalonia* stated *The Hebrew Gospel of Matthew* was already in Lombardy!** This is an early and extraordinary witness to the Waldensians' devotion to *The Hebrew Gospels*!

They took *The Hebrew Gospels* with them to Lombardy along with the oldest compilation of the entire Bible, *The Itala* Bible in Latin. It was compiled about 150 AD and later put into Greek by Lucian of Antioch about 280 AD. Lucian's Greek Bible is called *The Received Text* because it was received - accepted - by all the Christian churches in the known world as the true Word. It was not until the 4th century that Rome began to produce its own versions, Eusebius' Greek Bible in 320 AD and Jerome's Latin Vulgate Bible in 380 AD. **For 2000 years there has been this standoff between the original Messianic-Apostolic Church versus the Roman Church!** Neo-Messianics inhabited Northern Italy, Southern France, Spain, the Celts of Ireland, Scotland, and England etc. - all of whom had Lucian's *Received Text* derived from *The Hebrew Gospels* and *The Itala*.

The Roman Church did everything in its power to erase the Waldensians, and other Neo-Messianic groups like the Cathars of France and Conversos in Spain - and destroy their Scriptures! The survival of these manuscripts tells the Neo-Messianics' story of faith and sacrifice. It was the Neo-Messianics who preserved *The Received Text* of the Bible throughout many centuries of massacre and martyrdom. **It is the greatest story never told!**

Finding out about the missing Waldensian manuscript collection was at the top of my list. The disappearance of this crucial collection had been widely published by Alexis Muston, and others. I wanted to know what had happened to them if I could possibly find out. There must be some clues. I searched out the Cambridge Manuscript Curator, Frank Bowles, and finally got the whole story.

There is reason for great joy! Although it was not widely known, the Waldensian collection, missing for centuries, had been found! A previous Curator, Henry Bradshaw, found them. Because of their larger binding they were placed on different shelves in the archives than the rest of the collection, and were apparently forgotten. Many readers have lamented their loss but only a few librarians knew of their recovery! One of these manuscripts is the oldest surviving New Testament to be found anywhere in the scattered Waldensian archives! It is in ancient Romaunt. It has never been digitized. This means that no one has seen it for centuries! After all, it had disappeared. I have now had it reproduced for the archives of the Benai Emunah Institute and it is presently being translated. You are all responsible for that happening! It would not have happened without you!

The oldest New Testament of the Waldensians has been recovered!

Click on *free downloads* on the writingofgod.com website to receive the Research Updates Newsletter. Benai Emunah Institute has organized a team of translators - we have more than 2000+ pages of *Hebrew Gospels*, plus texts in other languages. If you were getting your first job when the Dead Sea Scrolls were discovered - you would have been retired by the time they were all published! That cannot be allowed to happen with these priceless *Hebrew Gospels*! To avoid that outcome:

I need your support!

---

[5] Since this book was first published we have located a total of 61 manuscripts, six are complete texts of the entire Brit Hadashah (New Testament) in Hebrew.

Research Update #3 - Dec 18, 2019 - on a train from Rome to Venice
Day 15 of the Expedition to Save the Underground Bibles

I have spent the last few days at the Vatican Library in Rome where some momentous things have happened. I was able to examine the original manuscript of *The Hebrew Gospels from Catalonia* (Vat. Ebr. 100) which I had spent the last two years translating from a digital copy. There is much you can tell from the original manuscript. There are sometimes notes that were not included with the reproduction. The binding is important for dating purposes. It was very useful to me as I will demonstrate.

I got to examine the latest find of a new *Hebrew Gospels* manuscript, first discovered by Nehemia Gordon in the famous Vatican junk box. Loose manuscript pages flutter to the floor all the time in old libraries. Not knowing where to put them, they get shoved into a catch-all category. In this case, it is called Vat. Ebr. 530, not a manuscript but a miscellaneous collection of loose pages. Fragment #11 is approximately an 11 x 17 inch large sheet of parchment folded down the middle with a page printed on all four sides. **The four pages of Vat. Ebr. 530 fragment 11, are in Hebrew and contain the title pages to Luke and John! These pages are not from an already known manuscript!**

<u>This is a new manuscript of *The Hebrew Gospels*</u>!

We know this is a complete text from only four pages because it is part of a *quire*, a method of binding ancient texts. *Quire* is Latin for five, so for example, take five 11 x 17 inch parchment sheets, fold them in half and write your manuscript pages - then do a preliminary binding. You make two pin holes through all five pages at the fold and pull a string through it to tie the quire together. You put a number on the first page of the quire. There will be various quires before you are done but they are all numbered so you simply stack them in order for the final binding. This one large parchment sheet of MS. Vat. Ebr. 530 fragment 11, has the pin holes for a quire binding - meaning that it is part of a complete manuscript. **A manuscript that I consider the most important in the entire Vatican Hebrew text collection!** There are 652 ancient Hebrew texts in the collection. I reviewed all 652 to make sure I did not miss anything of value. The original text of Vat. Ebr. 530 fragment 11 is not there.

Why is Vat. Ebr. 530 fragment 11, a part of the most important manuscript at the Vatican? Number One, it consistently uses the name of God - Yehovah - with the correct vowel pointing throughout all four pages. Number Two, it contains markers of the Hebrew Manuscript Tradition, so it is not a translation from Latin or Greek. It is a new and previously unknown manuscript of the family of Hebrew texts surviving from the first century! Number Three, the manuscript of which fragment 11 is a part - must be somewhere in the Vatican archives!

The staff of the Vatican Library had been helpful beyond expectations and very interested in new information on their holdings. They referred my questions to one of their manuscript experts and I found myself speaking to a small group of their staff on this particular fragment 11, what it contains, and the significance of it. There was one gentleman who was particularly interested and I asked his name. I was rather stunned when he told me he was Dr. Delio Proverbio. There are only a handful of experts worldwide who have studied *The Hebrew Gospels*. I know them all either from personal contact or reading their work. Dr. Proverbio is one of them! I had read his article *Vangeli Hebraico (Hebrew Gospels)*. He fully agreed with me that there must be other manuscripts of *The Hebrew Gospels* which have survived and I shared with him the discovery of *The Cochin Gospels*.

Dr. Proverbio and I met the next day to go through all the other fragments of Vat. Ebr. 530 and found nothing else. I brought up the possibility it might be in the Secret Archives of the Vatican. Yes, they exist! Nor is their existence a secret anymore. I said they might be there because they were considered heretical. Dr. Proverbio said, with a wry smile, *"They still are!"* There is a new policy of openness in the Vatican. However, if Yehovah wants those documents released and he has paved the way, then the one he sends to knock on that huge Vatican door and ask for them will receive them. I asked Dr. Proverbio if he considered finding the manuscript belonging to fragment 11 important enough to go into the Secret Archives and he said, *"Definitely!"* When I return I will ask Dr. Proverbio to accompany me into those Archives. Security is extreme, nonetheless, it is possible to get things released from the Secret Archives.

We will see what comes of marching up and knocking on the Vatican door asking to release *The Hebrew Gospels*!

Part 3
Sepharad:
The New Jerusalem

*Who has established all the ends of the earth?
What is His name, and what is the name of His Son?
Surely you know... Every word of God is tested!*

Proverbs 30:4-5

Part 1: In the Beginning
Part 2: The Messianic Church
are in *Volume One - Sons of Zion vs Sons of Greece*

***Please note the most important sentence(s)
or phrase(s) are highlighted on each page.**

Chapter One
The New Jerusalem

*The captivity of Jerusalem, which is in Sepharad,
shall possess the cities of the south.*
Obadiah 1:20

Rome fell in 410 AD to Alaric's Visigoths. The Classical Age had come to an end. *"As the Western Empire died, it left behind it empty cities with marble ruins lying like great skeletons at their centres."*[1] The pagan Greeks (and Romans) had many faults but a lack of curiosity of the mind was not one of them. Despite their superstition, the light of reason shone brightly, creating the Western model of science and civilization - but their white marble cities are now skeletons. The Dark Ages have begun.

The Roman Church had many good qualities, but freedom of thought was not one of them. Scripture in Greek and Hebrew were banned. As a result, the study of those languages withered away. Many priceless classics of the Greeks were lost. For a millennium, the rare scholar who studied Hebrew hastened to declare his intent was solely to expose the lies and perfidy of the Jews. Simply to challenge the dogma of the Church was to court death.

The light came from the East - and it came through Sepharad. The Hebrew word '*Sepharad*' means '*land of the Book.*' The Sephardim were, therefore, the '*people of the Book.*' It is true that the diaspora Jews were more Hellenized, **but it was those diaspora Jews who would keep both Hebrew language and Greek literature alive for the next thousand years - along with Hebrew Scriptures - including** *The Hebrew Gospels*!

In 1971, excavators of the Church of the Holy Sepulcher in Jerusalem broke through a wall and discovered a room dated to the early second century - when the Messianic Church was still predominate in Israel - but was being forced to emigrate! Excavators discovered a *"red and black drawing of a... sailing vessel with the inscription* **'Domine Ivimus - Latin for 'Lord, we went'.**"[2] Where did they go? **They went across the sea to Sepharad - '*the New Jerusalem*' - where the largest and most prosperous community of Jews, and Messianics, was a refuge for Hebrew emigrants from a century and a half of Roman war against Israel.**

[1] John Romer, 1988:p.244, *Testament: The Bible and History*. [2] E. M. Meyers, 1988:p.77, "*Early Judaism and Christianity*", Biblical Archaology v.51(2).

Sepharad - Land of the Book

Colonies of Hebrews in Spain stretch back to the earliest history of that region - to Solomon's trading outposts during the time of the first temple in the 7th century BC. In 587 BC, Nebuchadnezzar's capture of Jerusalem and destruction of the first temple sent huge numbers of captives to Spain. Nebuchadnezzar had powerful princes as allies, among them were Hispanus and his cousin Pyrrhus. One early name for Spain *"Hispania"* was derived from Hispanus, and Pyrrhus is cited as a prince of Merida in the region of Andalusia, in ancient Sepharad (Spain). When Nebuchadnezzar conquered Jerusalem, Hispanus and Pyrrhus were given a large share of the captives - so great that when they returned them to the city of Toledo in Andalusia, the region was unable to contain so many captives. Many of these were royal descendants and were resettled in Granada. This was related by R. Solomon ben Virga, who adds *"that the numbers were afterwards increased by the fugitives from Jerusalem, at the overthrow by Titus."*[3] This refers to the destruction of the second temple in 70 AD by the Romans.

Toledo was recaptured from the Moors in 1080 AD by Alfonso VI. The Jews living there assured him they were the descendants of the first captivity from the time of the Chaldean king Nebuchadnezzar.[4] Again, in 1492 when the Jews were expelled, they protested - citing an ancient inscription in the city square by an early Christian bishop that the Jews had lived in Toledo during the entire period of the second temple.[5] **Jewish arrival in the 7th century BC is confirmed in Obadiah 1:20, *"The captivity of Jerusalem which is in Sepharad."***

So many Hebrew captives - turned colonists in the barely populated region - would be reflected in place names. For example, the name *"Iberia"* comes from the word *"Ibri"* - Hebrew. Strabo cited it as the land southwest of the *"Iberos"* River, the region known as *"Hiberos"* in Latin, from which Spain was known as *"Hiberia,"* all from *"Ibri."* Other place names originating from Hebrew are *"Escalona from Ascalon, Noves from Nove, Magueda from Megiddo, Yepes or Jepes from Joppa, and Toledo from Toledoth (generations), because the exiles reviewed their family genealogies when they assembled to... found the city."*[5]

---

[3] R. Solomon ben Virga, 13th century, *Sceptre of Judah.* [4] Sandoval, *Historia de los Reyes de Castilla y de Leon.* [5] James Finn, 1841:p.18, *Sephardim.*

Certainly one can contend against all these things, however there is more solid evidence. In 1480, it was first published that a large stone inscription of an ancient sepulcher existed in the town of Murviedro among the ruins of the originally Greek Zacynthian colony, '*Saguntum*' in Latin. In ancient Hebrew characters it read: "*This is the tomb of Adoniram, The servant of king Solomon; Who came to collect the tribute, And died...*"[6] In 1st Kings 4:6 where the officers of Solomon are recorded, it states "*Adoniram the son of Abda was over the tribute.*" Nearby, another inscription in ancient Hebrew reads, "*Of Oran Hebahh the President - Who rebelled against his prince, The Lord has taken him... And his glory to Amaziah.*"[6] Amaziah was king of Judah 150 years after Solomon's reign. **According to these inscriptions, a large, ancient, and continuous settlement of Jews in Spain existed from the time of Solomon and the first Temple!**

The Phoenicians' colony at Carthage just across from Iberia, traded extensively with Spain, as did Solomon who also had a great navy... "*a fleet of Tarshish*" it is called in 1st Kings 10:22. Tarshish (Jonah 1:3), later called Tartessos, is on the Atlantic coast of Spain just outside the '*Pillars of Hercules*' - the narrow exit of the Mediterranean as it spills into the Atlantic. The spread of sea-faring and ship-building from the Greek Sea Peoples to the Celt-Iberians caused ships to be built for the higher waves and turbulence of the Atlantic ocean. Ships became larger with deeper keels and decks high above the surface of the water, carrying more sail and cargo. These great "*ships of Tarshish*" were prized! These superior ships of the Celts and Carthaginians almost defeated Rome centuries before the Visigoths did!

Many historians deny that Nebuchadnezzar, and Solomon, established any outposts beyond their boundaries. This ignores a main purpose of naval power, which was, in fact, precisely to further extend their military, commercial and colonial reach far beyond their current borders! Jonah speaks of Hebrew travel to Spain.

"*Ships of Tarshish*" aka *Tartessos*

---

[6] These inscriptions were copied by Luis de San Francisco, into the *Globus Arcanorum Linguae Sanctae*, p.709; & Fabricius' *Bibliotheca Graeca*, v14, p166.

The Roman historian Strabo (in Liber XV), stated that Nebuchadnezzar *"traversed as far as the Pillars* [of Hercules]... *and returned with his armies from Iberia."* **It was these Chaldeans, after all, whom the Bible states captured and resettled the ten *"lost"* tribes of Israel throughout their empire beginning even before Nebuchadnezzar became their king.**

The Jews in Sepharad were of such large numbers and such cohesion in their culture that their synagogues multiplied rapidly throughout the land. They were connected to the east under the rule of the Patriarchs - first from Jerusalem, then Jamnia, then Tiberius. Their synagogues welcomed emigrants and traveling Hebrew teachers - including the Apostles and their followers. In Jerusalem 70 AD, Vespasian ordered Titus - his son, prince and general to destroy *"the temple, and remove many families in the house of David and Judah into Aspamia, which is Spain."*[7] The same citation was made by Josephus - who was an eye-witness - *"Now the number of those that were carried captive during the whole war, was collected to be 97,000..."*[8]

> Whether the apostle James, or Paul, or Eugenius the missionary from France, had first preached the gospel of redemption in Spain, it is asserted that this Eugenius had very early a church in Toledo, which thus became the... center of its Christianity.[9]

In the same year as the Council of Nicea, 324 AD; another Council at Elvira, Spain, was convened by Constantine to involve the western extent of the Empire. The canons coming out of this Council included, Canon XVI - *"The daughters of Catholics shall not be given in marriage to heretics... also decreed of Jews and Schismatics."* Canon L - *"If any person... shall take food with the Jews, he is to abstain from communion."* Canon LXXVIII - *"If any one of the faithful... shall commit adultery with a Jewess, or a Pagan, he is to be cast out from our communion."*[10] Nonetheless, the Hebrews were long-settled in Spain at the time of the Council of Elvira and *"during their subsequent eventful history... Their book-learning talents for business served to elevate them above the surrounding ignorance, and afforded them security amid political convulsions."*[11]

---

[7] R. Jose ben Hilpetha, 3-4th century, *Order of Time*. [8] Josephus, *The Jewish War*. [9] James Finn, *Sephardim*, 1841: pp.35. [10] *Canons of the Council of Elvira*.
[11] James Finn, 1841: pp.28-29.

Barbarians at the Gate

The Western Roman Empire soon fell to the barbarians, as it says in every book of church history. **It is rarely mentioned that the barbarians were Christians - Arian Christians!** Arians believed in the divine origin of the Son but not his preeminence. Yehovah was in the beginning, then he created Yeshua, who created the universe. They assaulted the walls of Rome with the battle cry, *"The Father is greater than the son!"*

"Although Alaric and his Visigoths were Christians, their sack of Rome is usually depicted in history and art as the act of barbarians… Historical personages who were Arians are frequently presented as if they were not Christians at all."[12] The story of the Arians revolves around the tale of the second Eusebius. This was not Eusebius bishop of Caesarea, but his contemporary, the Eusebius who became bishop of Nicomedia which was the capital of the Roman Empire under Constantine.

At the Council of Nicea it was decreed God and his Son were of the same substance, as was also the Holy Spirit. **The 'mystery' of the Trinity has been controversial since its inception and is hotly debated even unto this day. Logical it is not - at least not within the framework of monotheism!** Many Christians believed in Arianism, unable to reconcile monotheism with the Trinity of divinity, *'three gods in one!'*

Arius of Alexandria did not believe the essence of God was divisible as if it were mashed potatoes. His protagonist Athanasius argued otherwise, arguing that if Christ did not have the exalted status of God Himself then the Gospels were defunct - for salvation was given by God alone. Both men had powerful intellects, personalities and followers - for decades church doctrine hung in the balance. Both, at times, were exiled. *"Constantine in 335 AD ordered the first of Athanasius' five exiles - the same year Arius regained the favor of the Roman emperor."*[13] After Nicea, Constantine wrote a harsh letter condemning Arian Christianity, ordering *"that Arius' works be… burnt, and anyone who does not surrender copies in his possession is to be executed."*[13] However, *"Within ten years of the Council of Nicaea… Constantine became convinced that Arius' ideas fell within the pale of orthodoxy."*[13]

---

[12] M. Maddox, *"Alaric the Visigoth was Christian,"* americanenglishdoctor.com
[13] C. Hall, *"How Arianism Almost Won,"* in Christianity Today, issue 85.

The man who changed Constantine's mind was Eusebius of Nicomedia. This Eusebius was a cousin of Constantine.

> Like Arius, he [Eusebius] was a pupil of Lucian of Antioch, and it is probable that he held the same views as Arius from the very beginning; he was also one of Arius' most fervent supporters... Eusebius was powerful enough that Arius was able to put his theology down in writing... At the First Council of Nicaea, 325, he [Eusebius] signed the Confession, but only after a long and desperate opposition in which he *"subscribed with hand only, not heart"* according to ancient sources. It was a huge blow to the Arian party since... the participants in the First Council of Nicaea were evenly split between non-Arians and Arians.[14]

Eusebius of Nicomedia strongly defended the Arian way - and in so doing angered Constantine - who believed far more in unity than doctrine. Eusebius was exiled but after three years regained favor with the emperor, convincing him Arius' doctrine did not conflict with the Nicene Creed. That is a stretch perhaps - but Constantine was playing politics. Eusebius had brought into the Arian priesthood an extraordinary star named Ulfias. Eusebius sent him unto the German Goths who received him with open arms. Ulfias devised an alphabet for the Gothic language and translated the Bible. **With this new Gothic Bible, Arian Christianity spread like wildfire throughout the West! The Roman Church soon lost this catalyst of the Word when it was decreed that Latin must be the only language of Scripture!** Few citizens of the era were literate, even fewer knew Latin.

On his deathbed May 22, 337 AD, Constantine was baptized by Bishop Eusebius of Nicomedia **as an Arian**! It was a belief that his sons Constantine II, Constantius II and Constans shared. *"In 350, the empire was consolidated under the rule of Constantius. It appeared the entire Christian world had fallen into Arian hands."*[14] This crucial fact of Constantine's life was left out of the writings of Eusebius of Caesarea. Later emperors were Arian (Constantius), pagan (Julian), or Nicean (Theodosius). *"Thus, if a Roman emperor was disposed favorably toward Arian ideas - as Constantius and Valens were - bishops supporting the creed formulated at Nicaea could be severely punished, most often by being deposed and exiled. If an emperor favoring Nicaea was in power, Arian believers would suffer."*[15]

[14] Samuel Jackson, 1914, *"Eusebius of Nicomedia,"* Schaff-Herzog Encyclopedia.
[15] Christopher Hall, *"How Arianism Almost Won,"* in Christianity Today, # 85.

Emperor Julian the Apostate tried to end Christianity as the state religion and reinstate pagan worship. He reigned from 361-363 AD, but was soon killed in an invasion of Persia.

> It was only after Julian, through the successive reigns of the emperors Valentinian and Theodosius, that the empire came to be formally declared Christian; only then that Christian heresy was pronounced a capital crime; only then that pagan worship was officially banned; only then that the authority of the Jewish patriarchate was abolished forever. **And it was then that they questioned what to do about the Jews who refused either to yield or to disappear...**[16]

"Once church and state had agreed that it was righteous and legal to execute those Christians - Docetists, Donatists, Nestorians, Arians who dissented from defined dogma on relatively arcane matters of theology, why in the world should stiff-necked Jews who openly rejected the entire Christian proclamation be permitted to live?"[16] Bishop Ambrose of Milan issued a call to burn synagogues *"that there might not be a place where Christ is denied."* He called them *"a hiding place of madmen, under the damnation of God Himself."*[17] Ambrose declared destroying synagogues to be a righteous act. Not only should this act be exempt from punishment but to rebuild a synagogue was described by Ambrose as *"an act of treason to the Faith!"*

Saint Augustine Trembled

Augustine (354-430 AD) is considered the father of Christian theology. His masterpiece of theology was *The Trinity*, completed in 410 AD, the same year Alaric's Gothic hordes sacked Rome. The Goths' strategy was simplicity itself. They destroyed the aqueducts that brought water to the city. Practically overnight Rome shrank from a city of one million to a few thousand. It was a turning point in Augustine's worldview. The shaken and sobered Augustine wrote, not without qualms, in justification of force to defend and propagate the orthodox faith. Punitive laws against pagans and heretics were now approved by the master theologian who argued for a policy of *'correctio,'* some must be *"compelled by fear or pain, so that they might afterwards be influenced by teaching... What trembling we feel in these things!"*[18]

[16] James Carroll, 2001:p.206, *Constantine's Sword.* [17] *Ibid*, p.207. [18] p.211.

The Last Gasp of Rome

In 410 AD, Alaric did not stay to rule over Rome. After three days of sacking and burning the city, the Romans gave in to his demands and emptied their meager treasury to pay him to leave - which he did. Rome limped along like a wounded animal for more than a half century. The tribes of Europe, pushed south and west by the invasion of Attila's Huns, quickly encircled the dying Western Roman Empire and tore it to pieces. The Angles and Saxons took Britain. The Franks pushed south taking Gaul (France). Vandals devastated Spain, then were pushed out into North Africa by the Visigoths, who burned and destroyed any cities untouched by the Vandals. The Vandals ravaged North Africa leaving us the word '*vandalize,*' before invading the south of Italy. The entire Western "*Roman Empire had stalled under the cumulative weight of plague, barbarian invasion, inflation, over-taxation, over-extended military commitments, and inept leadership.*"[19] Rome had lost its territories, revenues, and worse - its will to fight! Its leaders were weak and ineffective, its soldiers unpaid, its peasantry enslaved and oppressed. **The truth is - Romans no longer felt Rome worth fighting for!**

In the year **476 AD**, "*On the last day of the empire, a barbarian commander... entered the city unopposed.* Odovacar easily dethroned the sixteen-year-old emperor Romulus Augustalus.... By the time he entered the city, the Roman control of Britain, Spain, Gaul, and North Africa had already been lost to the Goths and Vandals.*"[20]

The Arian Visigoths led by Theodoric kicked the Vandals out of Spain in 456 AD. The Visigoths' "*résumé - long on marauding and pillage - was short on any skill relevant to reviving an Iberian economy that had been deteriorating during the empire's centuries-long death throes. The Visigoths had seized a few shards of an empire they themselves helped shatter, and they had no clue how to reassemble the pieces.*" Later, in 589 AD, "*the Visigoth king Recared, motivated by genuine faith, political savvy, or more likely some combination of both, led Visigoth Arian bishops in confessing*"[20] the Nicene Creed. **The Roman Church had picked up the reigns of** the fallen Roman Empire!

---

[19] Chris Lowney, 2006: pp.23-25, *A Vanished World*, Oxford Univ. Press, N.Y.
[20] Don Wasson, 2015, "*Fall of the Roman Empire*," *Ancient History Encyclopedia*.

The Last Mathematician

"By this time... Christianity had developed an ugly face: the formerly persecuted were all too ready to become the persecutors, and 'pagans,' those who were neither Christian nor Jew, were also likely to be targets of violence."[22]

This book is not only the narrative of the Messianic Church. We must also know what the new Greek Church was becoming - because it will resonate far into the future! Hypatia's murder was a harbinger of what was to come. As the Classical Age came to an end, Alexandria - *'the city of the mind'* - rapidly degenerated. Alexandria had ruled the intellectual world for seven centuries. Now the will and the resources to support the famous Alexandrian Library and Museum were waning. During the third century AD there were a series of civil wars and due to looting, and burning, many of the libraries' collections were destroyed.

The last known member of the Museum was Theon of Alexandria, a mathematician and astronomer. It was Theon who schooled his precocious daughter Hypatia (370-415 AD), forever to be known as *"the last mathematician of Alexandria."*

Hypatia is the first woman mathematician of whom we have reasonably detailed knowledge... She wrote at least two books on mathematics and one on astronomy and she gave public lectures in philosophy. She had a large following and was a popular teacher, much admired by her students.[23]

The most renowned mathematicians of the Alexandrian school were Euclid and Ptolemy. Euclid (365-300 BC), is considered the greatest mathematician of the classical age of Greece. He was a student of Plato and is known as the father of geometry. His 13 volume series on geometry (also algebra and number theory) is called *The Elements*. Ptolemy (100-170 AD) wrote *The Almagest*, also in 13 volumes, which set out the theory of the solar system, motion of the planets and the mathematics necessary to calculate their orbits - allowing the ancients to remove the planets from the realm of superstition and the supernatural.

[22] Michael Deakin, 2007:p.21, *Hypatia of Alexandria.* [23] Deakin, 2007, p.15-16.

By the time Ptolemy had completed his work, not only were the motions of the sun and moon utterly predictable, but they were predictable with such accuracy that eclipses (formerly strange and frightening aberrations) had become explicable and could be foretold… [and] planetary positions could be calculated in advance.[24]

These foundational works of mathematics were developed and elaborated by later Alexandrians such as Apollonius (240-160 BC) and Diophantus (201-285 AD). Apollonius was born in Perga but studied in Alexandria. Theon wrote three commentaries of Euclid and Ptolemy's work, part of which he credited to "*my philosopher-daughter Hypatia.*"[25] Theon's great work was to "*preserve and to adapt for student use the great classics of Alexandrian mathematics - Euclid and Ptolemy… Hypatia continued this work with the later and more demanding classics by Apollonius and Diophantus.*"[26] Hesychius, a former student of Hypatia who became governor of upper Libya, "*mentions three works from her pen: a commentary on Diophantus, another on the 'astronomical table'* [possibly Ptolemy's *Handy Tables*], *and a commentary on Apollonius's Conics*"[26] [brackets mine].

Hypatia was described by Damascius as "*exceedingly beautiful and fair of form.*" Socrates Scholasticus stated she was admired due to her "*self-possession of manner, which she had acquired in consequence of the cultivation of her mind… [and] on account of her extraordinary dignity and virtue.*" Hypatia embraced celibacy throughout her lifetime although she did not lack for suitors. When one such bedazzled student declared his love for her, it is said she removed her menstrual napkin and thrust it at him, saying "*It is this you love, young man, not beauty!*"[26] In the Greek society of Hypatia's era, once married, a woman gave up all her inheritance and her independence.

Hypatia… lived in a time when her intellectual heritage, a 700 year old tradition, was crumbling… **Almost alone, virtually the last academic, she stood for intellectual values, for rigorous mathematics, ascetic Neoplatonism, the crucial role of the mind, and the voice of temperance and moderation in civic life…**
Her lectures and charismatic presence drew multitudes.[26]

---

[24] Deakin, 2007: p.61. [25] The 2nd edition of Theon's *Commentary on Book III of Ptolemy's Almagest,* notes Hypatia's contribution. [26] Deakin, pp.59, 62 66.

Cyril of Alexandria

"Early in the fifth century, in 412, Theophilus was succeeded in the archbishopric by his nephew Cyril (Saint Cyril of Alexandria)."[27] Cyril was the epitome of the new Constantinian Christian, now in charge and willing to flex his muscles to force others to conform to the Greco-Roman Church's proscribed beliefs. *"Cyril was much at loggerheads with the civil governor Orestes. Orestes was a Christian but a much more tolerant one than Cyril...* [who was] *personally a most intemperate man. In, possibly 414* [AD], *Cyril unilaterally took it upon himself to expel the Jews from Alexandria, and this he did, much to Orestes displeasure. The ensuing riots and* **the feud between the two men were the direct cause of Hypatia's death!**"[27] [brackets mine]

Cyril was a key figure in the development and enforcement of orthodox belief, the main reason he was exalted to sainthood. *"He supported these orthodox views not only by reasoning and debate but also by means of a military and full-frontal 'muscular Christianity'... During his life, Cyril waged mighty war against... heretics... The contention between orthodoxy and the various heresies was conducted with a violence and bitterness that will hardly be apparent in the bare outlines of doctrinal divergence... that few people understood anyway."*[27] **The difference between 'orthodoxy' and 'heresy' was determined by who won the doctrine wars. It was about power not salvation!**

Cyril was under authority from distant Constantinople, established by Constantine as the power center of the Greco-Roman Church. Cyril, following in the footsteps of his uncle Theophilus before him, armed a large community of Nitrian monks who served as *"a powerful militia owing allegiance to him rather than being under the control of the legitimate imperial authority."*[28] These armed monks were responsible for *"savage intercommunal violence"* at Cyril's behest - against Jews, pagans and those of differing Christian beliefs. One of his henchmen, named Hierax, incited a riot on the Sabbath at a Jewish dance exhibition. Orestes, the governor and rival of Cyril, had Hierax arrested and tortured. Cyril blamed the Jews and incited violence, in which the Jews gained the upper hand killing many Christians.

---

[27] Michael Deakin, 2007, pp.21-22, 33-34, *Hypatia of Alexandria.* [28] *Ibid.* p.69.

Creating such a pretext may indeed have been the plan all along. Cyril then proceeded to call out his storm troopers. *"Accompanied by a large and angry mob of Christians he marched on the synagogues, seized them, and systematically expelled the Jews from Alexandria, further motivating his followers by encouraging them to loot Jewish homes and synagogues."*[29] Orestes was angered and appealed to the Emperor in Constantinople for redress of grievances, as did Cyril in return.

Cyril, displayed a pugnacious and violent aggression that seemed to characterize all his interactions, escalating every confrontation. *"The Nitrian monks… who manifested 'a very fiery disposition' were once more called upon, and some five hundred of them left their monasteries and headed for Alexandria… These new arrivals quickly confronted Orestes himself."*[29] Surrounding and taunting Orestes, the mob soon turned into a melee. One Nitrian monk named Ammonius stoned Orestes, gashing his head. The mob was dispersed and Ammonius was seized. The monk was publicly tortured to death. Cyril canonized Ammonius as a saint, declaring him a martyr for the Christian cause.

Cyril had overreached. Many Christian citizens of Alexandria pointedly disagreed with the bestowal of martyr status, and sainthood, upon Ammonius. Never called upon to renounce his faith, Ammonius had viciously attacked another Christian over political differences. By canonizing Ammonius, Cyril had clearly implicated himself in the attack on Orestes, although - of course - Cyril claimed not to have known about it until it was over.

Things did not look good for Cyril. A more temperate man might have retreated and taken a more civil path - not Cyril!

Another attack was called for and this time against a somewhat easier target. That target became Hypatia. She was close to Orestes without being Orestes. She was genuinely a pagan and… less likely to be protected by armed men… She publicly expounded Neoplatonist philosophy - a set of teachings that rivaled those of Christianity - and indeed had influenced Christian thinkers… whose views were more tolerant than those of the invincibly self-righteous Cyril.[30]

---

[29] Michael Deakin, 2007, pp.70-72, *Hypatia of Alexandria*.   [30] *Ibid.*, p.73.

The Murder of Hypatia

> Thus it happened that a crowd of Christian zealots, led by one Peter the Lector, blocked the homeward path of the carriage in which Hypatia was riding, dragged her from it, and (as if to seek divine sanction for their act) hauled the hapless woman into a church where they stripped her naked and battered her to death with roofing tiles. This done, they continued their frenzy by tearing her corpse limb from limb, orgiastically transporting her body out through the church portals and burning its fragments.[31]

Cyril's biggest defender was perhaps the 7th century Coptic bishop John of Nikiu, who claimed that after Hypatia's death *"all the people surrounded the patriarch Cyril and proclaimed him 'the new Theophilus' - because he had destroyed the last remnants of idolatry in the city."*[32]

Hypatia's *"life became forfeit to the bloodlust of those who would claim... access to a higher morality."*[33] **In a bizarre twist to the death of Hypatia by a Christian mob, her charismatic story took root in folklore. It is probable that Hypatia was the basis for the legend of Saint Catherine of Alexandria!**

> We have the wondrous beauty, the learning, the standing among philosophers, the dedicated virginity, the wheel (Hypatia was dragged down from her chariot), and the martyrdom. The inconvenient fact that Hypatia was killed by Christians, a martyr to her pagan faith, is thus quietly overlooked.[34]

Her cult began in the 8th century and was well-established by the 10th century. Saint Catherine's monastery in the Sinai Peninsula was built to house her '*discovered*' remains and to venerate her legend. She was one of the most celebrated saints of the Christian calendar for a thousand years, listed as one of the most saintly Christian women who ever lived. She was painted by Carravaggio, Durer, Raphael, Rubens, Titian and Tintoretto. She became, however, a profound embarrassment for the Roman Church as it became clear there was no historical evidence for her existence. In 1969 the Catholic Church repudiated her cult.

---

[31] Michael Deakin, 2007, p. 73, *Hypatia of Alexandria.* [32] p.76. [33] p.66. [34] p.136.

The Nestorian Schism

Cyril's next opponent - or victim - was Nestorius, the archbishop and patriarch of Constantinople. There is little doubt that Cyril was making a power play for leadership of the Church. He had extended his influence by means of currying favor with other bishops and by paying, or bribing, agents in various cities of the Empire, especially Constantinople - its center. Within a year of Nestorius' rise to power as bishop of Constantinople, trouble began. The disputes of the Church in the early centuries were all about the nature of Christ. Nestorius was of the Antiochian School, said to have been mentored by Theodore of Mopsuestia.

A controversy arose and its opponents brought it before Nestorius. Some called Mary, "*Mother of God*" - '*theotokos*' in Greek meaning "*bearer of God.*" Nestorius expressed the idea that a woman could not be the mother of a god. This was a pagan practice in Egypt where humans were consecrated as gods. He suggested she be called '*Christotokos*' or "*bearer of Christ.*" In doing so he sided with the Antiochian School of thought that Christ had two natures, being both totally human and totally divine. Nestorius' views actually reflect modern theological thought. Whether it was orthodox at the time became more of a political decision than a doctrinal one. Nestorius was criticized as portraying Christ as "*a mere man.*"

Ugly accusations were also brought against those who held to the opposite view, in particular, Cyril of Alexandria. Both men were called heretics by the opposing side. By appearing to support one side of the argument, Nestorius had placed himself in the ranks of Cyril's enemies. Cyril replied "*I had till now no quarrel with him and wish him betterment; but for supporting my enemies he shall give answer before God… that wretched man shall not hope that he can be my judge. I will withstand him, if I come hither, and it is he who shall answer for error.*"[35] There is consensus among historians that "*the real cause of the controversy is to be found in the intrigues of Cyril of Alexandria.*"[35] Cyril then proceeded to make war against Nestorius. He wrote a five volume series, *Against Nestorius*, which denounced him for 43 '*heretical*' quotations taken from his sermons.

---

[35] Friedrich Loofs, 1914: p.33-34, *Nestorius and His Place in Christian Doctrine*.

In hindsight, the humble Nestorius was ill-matched to counter the junkyard-dog aggressiveness of Cyril. Cyril enlisted the support of the bishop of Rome, Pope Celestine, via *"a letter that was as untrue as it was clever."*[36] His paid agents began a campaign of agitation against Nestorius. Nestorius, in turn, sought the support of Emperor Theodosius, who had appointed him. He asked for an ecumenical synod to discuss the issue and resolve it. Nestorius even offered to step down and return to his monastery if he was shown to be the cause of the uproar which was threatening the unity of the Church. The Emperor ordered that a council be held in Ephesus in June, 431 AD.

Cyril and the bishops supporting him arrived early and convened the council before Nestorius' supporters could arrive. Nestorius refused to attend before the eastern bishops could participate and was declared a heretic, *in absentia*. Cyril's agents then proceeded to provoke the people of Ephesus to outrage over the '*heretical*' bishop Nestorius. Once informed of these events, the Emperor sent a confidant, Count John, as commissioner. John took both Nestorius and Cyril into custody until the issue was resolved. Nestorius accepted custody with grace. **Cyril reportedly bribed Count John to take his side of the issue with the Emperor and '*escaped*' custody, returning to his power base in Alexandria. His ploy evidently worked and Nestorius was anathematized and exiled.**

> However, a number of churches, particularly those associated with the School of Edessa in Assyria and northern Mesopotamia, supported Nestorius, though not necessarily the doctrine ascribed to him, and broke with the churches of the Roman and Byzantine Empires. Many of Nestorius' supporters relocated to Sasanian Persia.
> **These events are known as the Nestorian Schism.**[37]

Outraged by this arrogant manipulation, the Church of the East (called the Assyrian Church) embraced Nestorius - an act more political than doctrinal. *"As Wilhelm Baum and Dietmar W. Winkler said, "Nestorius himself was no Nestorian" in terms of doctrine. Even from the beginning, not all churches called "Nestorian" adhered to the Nestorian doctrine; in China, it has been noted that none of the various sources for the local Nestorian church refer to Christ as having two natures."*

---

[36] Friedrich Loofs, 1914, pp.41-42. [37]*"Nestorius"*, in *Encyclopaedia Britannica*.

Some modern scholars, such as Bethune-Baker, have argued that Nestorius was indeed orthodox.[38] After all, in the fifth century, "the *Nicene Creed, when brought to the attention of the [Nestorians], was accepted.*" Some have pointed out his doctrine of the dual nature of the Son of God is orthodox today. I will leave it to others to argue these theologies. The crucial question remains - **is there room within Christ's salvation for sincere differences of opinion** - or must all variance from political orthodoxy be purged by exile, torture or burning at the stake? "*The Byzantine Emperor Marcion decided to pardon and release him, but the news arrived as Nestorius was laying in his deathbed.*"[39]

> The real issue in the struggle was no issue of the Person of Christ, but one of rivalry between the sees of Antioch and Alexandria. In its final phase **this controversy developed into a clash between Semitic thought and Greek philosophy**… tension between these opposing parties became so great it shook the very foundations of the Church throughout the Christian Empire.[38]

Nestorius and the Nestorians continued to be reviled by Rome. "*Friar Odoric… went out to the Far East as a world traveler and… missionary… between 1316-1318… He refers to the Nestorians as 'vile and pestilent… schismatics and heretics.*'"[40] It was common practice for the Roman Church to indiscriminately accuse heretics of all types of evil-doing - sexual immorality, perverse practices, demonic behaviors, blasphemy, etc. So much so that most all of their reports on their opponents must be discounted as biased. Often, all we know about other Christian beliefs come from the slander in the official record of Rome since they destroyed all Scripture and manuscripts of their opponents. **The truth is a different story - but it is that story which is critical to our narrative!**

In the case of the Nestorians, the Greco-Roman Church did not have the reach to destroy all Nestorian documents and history. The Nestorians took large collections of books with them at the time of the schism, religious texts in Syriac (Aramaic), Greek and Hebrew. **Many others were classics of the Greeks in mathematics, astronomy, medicine, etc. It is due to the Nestorians that many of these masterpieces survived and were returned to the West later on!**

---

[38]Bethune-Baker, 1908, *Nestorius & His Teaching.* [39]Jeffrey Hays, 2008, p.4, *Christianity and the Mongols.* [40]Friar Odoric, 1330, *Eastern Parts of the World.*

The Nestorian Church

Because they sided with Nestorius, the Church of the East, aka the Assyrian Church, became known as the Nestorian Church. They called themselves *"the oldest Christian people."* Although they did not predate the Messianic Church - they existed before the Roman Church. Now split from the West, they spread to the East. ***"While the Western Church devoted itself to dogmatic discussion, the East undertook the spreading of the Gospel."***[41]

By the fifth century they had established bishoprics in Teheran (Iran), Ispahan, Khorasan, Merv and Herat. Moving East into India, by the sixth century they were recorded in Bombay, Ceylon and Malabar. In the seventh century they opened up China, and by the eighth had become established in Egypt and Cyprus. Later they are cited in Afghanistan, Turkestan and Siberia. Their missionaries contributed to opening trading routes to the Far East. *"Marco Polo tells us that in his day the trade routes from Bagdad to Peking were lined with Nestorian chapels."*[42] There were 70 Nestorian Christian bishoprics in the Asian provinces by 1265 AD.[43] **The Nestorian Church had become the largest Christian Church in the world!**

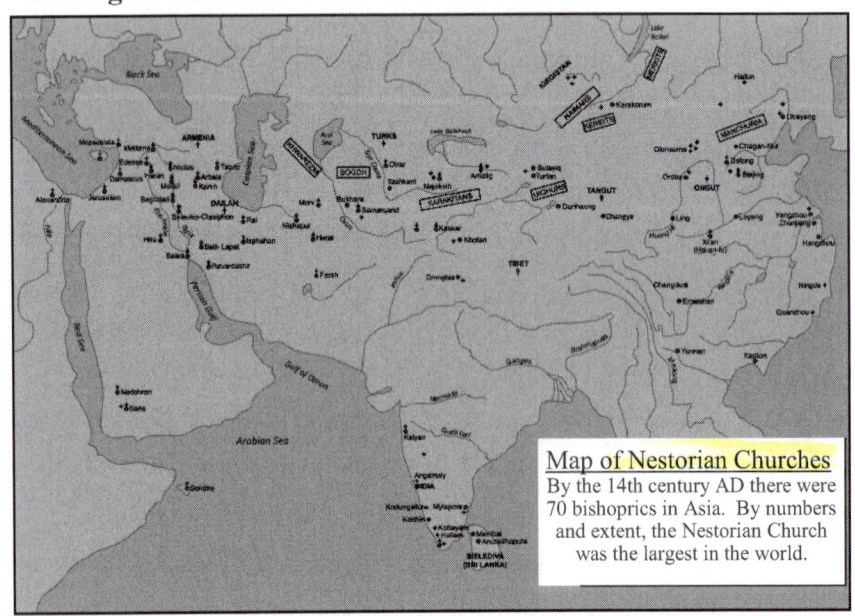

Map of Nestorian Churches
By the 14th century AD there were 70 bishoprics in Asia. By numbers and extent, the Nestorian Church was the largest in the world.

---

[41] William Emhardt & George Lamsa, 1926, p.52, *The Oldest Christian People.*
[42] *Ibid.*, in the same place, pp.64-65.   [43] *Ibid.,* p.76.

"*For several centuries brave Assyrian* [Nestorian] *Christians traversed the entire breadth of the Silk Road. Before the year 600, the Assyrians had sent missionaries and established Christian communities throughout the Far East... It was estimated that around the end of the first millennium AD, there were more Nestorians than Catholics and Orthodox Christians combined.*"[44] Many of my readers have never heard of the Nestorian Church and their heroic accomplishments in saving millions and spreading the Gospel to the ends of the earth. Nestorians were far more akin to the Hebrew Messianic ideal than the Greek one.

"*Nestorians were employed to translate into Arabic the works of the Greek philosophers which were current in Syriac. Schools of philosophy and medicine were opened in many of the large cities. Most of the teachers were Nestorian Christians.*"[44] The Greco-Roman Church of Constantine later split into the Greek Orthodox and the Roman Catholic. **The Roman Church banned Greek - thus isolating the West from Greek science!** The Roman Church succeeded in controlling the historical narrative in the West. They wrote church history. All other denominations were competitors for power and were declared heretical. If you do an internet search of maps of the spread of Christianity, most will record only the history of the Roman Church.

> Between the 9th and 14th centuries, at its height, the [Nestorian] Church of the East represented the world's largest Christian church in terms of geographical extent, with dioceses stretching from its heartland in Upper Mesopotamia, from the Mediterranean Sea to as far afield as China, Mongolia, Central Asia, Anatolia, the Arabian Peninsula and India.[44]

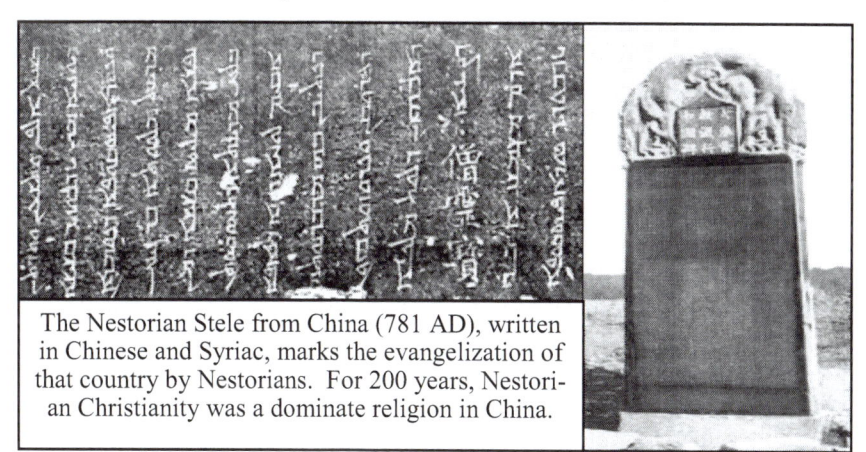

The Nestorian Stele from China (781 AD), written in Chinese and Syriac, marks the evangelization of that country by Nestorians. For 200 years, Nestorian Christianity was a dominate religion in China.

[44] William Emhardt & George Lamsa, 1926, p.52, *The Oldest Christian People*.

Meanwhile, in the West, the Roman Church was busily shutting down intellectual inquiry in favor of imposing their own framework of belief. Rome was committed to amassing the power of a *'Universal,'* aka *'Catholic,'* Church. The Church banned the study of Hebrew and Greek, burnt heretics and their manuscripts, as well as threatening anyone who defied the Church in all things religious, intellectual and artistic. *"The famous Academy of Athens that had been founded by Plato in 387 B.C.E. [was] shut down in 529 C.E. by the Roman emperor Justinian, anxious to stamp out Greek philosophy and all pagan ideas."*[45]

The Nestorian Awakening

At this period the Nestorian libraries contained more manuscripts of classical and scientific learning than any others throughout the world... Greek thought was transformed by the Nestorians, given to the Arabs, and through the genius of the Arabian empire carried to the far corners of Africa, **Spain and Europe... Most scholars will admit that as far as the beginnings of modern chemistry, gun-powder, the compass, medicine, philosophy... are concerned, much is due to the combined labors of the Nestorians and the Arabs.**[46]

Nestorians brought the alphabet to the Uighurs and Mongols turning them into literate cultures. Nestorian books, translations, and teaching helped spark a Golden Age of Islamic learning and science, spreading through the Mideast to Spain. In 1268 AD, the Mongols under Hulagu Khan conquered the Middle East. Favored by the Mongols, the Nestorians underwent their last great expansion. *"The golden days under the Khans marked wonderful expansion and success in the Nestorian Church. Nestorian missionaries went among the Mongols, Tartars and Chinese, establishing schools and other Christianizing centers."*[46]

Arabic translations of Greek texts... made by non-Muslims, made their way from the Islamic East... to the Iberian Peninsula in the Islamic West where some were translated by **Jews and Christians, for instance in the multilingual city of Toledo in Spain**, to Latin. It is true that some ancient Greek texts were reintroduced to the West via Arabic, sometimes **passing via Syriac or Hebrew along the way.**[47]

---

[45] Chris Lowney, 2005, p.187, *A Vanished World: Muslims, Christians & Jews.*
[46] William Emhardt & George Lamsa, 1926:p.76-8, *The Oldest Christian People.*
[47] B. Fjordman, 2012, *Assyrian Contributions to Islamic Civilization.*

"The translators of Greek and other non-Muslim scientific works to Arabic were never Muslims. They were [Nestorian] *Christians... The language of... these Christians was Syriac (Eastern Aramaic)... Cultivated Christians were often bilingual, even trilingual: they used Arabic for daily life, Syriac for liturgy, and Greek for cultural purposes"*[48] [brackets mine]. **This illustrates a stark contrast between the educated Nestorians of the East and the regressive Roman Church in Europe at the time**!

By 1394, the Mongol leader Tamerlane had conquered the Middle East. Tamerlane converted to Islam and began a slaughter of Christians. Periodic slaughter by the Muslims was to decimate the Nestorian Church over the coming centuries - culminating in the Armenian Christian Genocide by the Turks during World War I, which destroyed the last large remnant of the ancient Assyrian, or Nestorian, Church. Turkey has yet to acknowledge this as mass murder in which 1.5 million Armenian Christians died!

In 711, a ragtag army of Muslims arrived from North Africa and encountered little resistance in taking all of the Iberian Peninsula and more, later extending their conquest deep into France. It took Spain more than seven centuries to accomplish the *Reconquista* (Reconquest). In 1492, King Ferdinand and Queen Isabella finally took the Moors' last stronghold at Granada. That same year they expelled the Jews from Spain and launched an expedition by Christopher Columbus to the New World.

La Convivencia

The *Convivencia* (co-existence) refers to that epoch in Medieval Spain when Muslims, Jews, and Christians - at times - lived in relative harmony, and their cooperation birthed one of the most productive intellectual movements in human history, known as '*The Golden Age!*'

---

[48] Remi Brague, 2011:p.164, *The Legend of the Middle Ages*.

Charlemagne (742-814 AD)

It was Charlemagne (Charles the Great) who restored the Roman marriage of the Church and State. After the death of his father, Charlemagne became king of half the Frankish kingdom along with his brother who ruled the other half. In 771, his brother died mysteriously, making Charlemagne, at 24, king of all the Franks.

Over a reign of 48 years, Charlemagne and his armies waged constant war, eventually uniting most of Europe under one rule. From the North Sea to the Mediterranean; from France to Germany and Poland; from the Netherlands to the tip of Italy - **it was later declared to be the new Holy Roman Empire!** If nothing else, it had certainly inherited Roman brutality.

In his role as a zealous defender of Christianity, Charlemagne gave money and land to the Christian church and protected the popes. As a way to acknowledge Charlemagne's power and reinforce his relationship with the church, Pope Leo III crowned Charlemagne emperor of the Romans on December 25, 800, at St. Peter's Basilica in Rome. [21]

In turn, Charlemagne demanded that all the tribes he conquered be baptized into the Roman Catholic faith - or die! He slaughtered many thousands to enforce his will. Celtic Christianity had been peacefully making great inroads into the pagan tribes via the Celtic Bible since 687 AD, now, however, they were all forced to bow to the iron fist of the Holy Roman Empire.

Charlemagne saved the Roman Church from possible extinction twice over. Not only did he impose their faith by military force but he also established schools throughout his vast domain. This prompted the Carolingian Renaissance - reviving once more the Roman Church - **as most of their priests had fallen into illiteracy and ignorance.**

Charlemagne's domains

[21] https://www.history.com/topics/middle-ages/charlemagne

Paper & the Printing Press

The invention of paper helped spark the Golden Age in Spain, which in turn sparked the Renaissance in Europe. The manufacture of paper was first passed to the Arabs by the Chinese in the 8th century. Paper played a huge part in the growth of Islam which mandated the proliferation of literacy and the Koran! **At a time when the Roman Church was still prohibiting reproduction of the Bible in the vernacular - Islam taught it was the spiritual duty of Muslims to read the Koran in Arabic.** As a result, Islam exploded throughout the Middle East to North Africa, India and China - a conquest as much intellectual, and spiritual, as military.

Arabs learned the technology [to make paper] from Chinese prisoners captured in an eighth-century battle (751) near Talas, a remote region of present-day Turkestan not far from the Chinese border... **Within Europe, the process remained Muslim Spain's more or less proprietary craft, centered in the small enclave of Játiva**, which fell into Christendom's orbit when 13th century Crusaders overran Muslim Valencia[49] [brackets mine].

The proliferation of paper spurred on another critical innovation, the printing press. In 1452 - Johannes Gutenberg of Mainz, Germany adapted the Chinese technique of woodblock printing by *"devising an alloy of lead, tin and antimony that would melt at low temperature, cast well in the die, and be durable in the press."*[50] Now these *'lead'* typeface letters could be re-arranged to publish any text. By 1500 AD there were 2500 printing presses in Europe. **It caused the Roman Church's prohibition on reading the Bible in the vernacular to crumble! The Reformation followed.** By 1600, printing had exploded and Bibles, as well as other books, were being printed in the languages of every major culture in the known world!

---

[49] Chris Lowney, 2005:p.75.   [50] Steven Kreis, 2016, *The History Guide*.

> The Jewish community spawned talented merchants and administrators, adept go-betweens who assimilated the cultural and language skills needed to thrive in the dominant Muslim or Christian society. Steeped in their law's mandate to study Torah, devout Jewish families educated their children... and in the process blessed Spain's broader society with a disproportionate share of literate citizens... well-educated Jews were valuable and safe additions to the civil service. **The prominent presence of Jews at Muslim and Christian courts inevitably embroiled the wider Jewish community in broader cultural struggles...**[49]

The population of Jews in Sepharad was to grow to a half-million by the 15th century, about half of which were Messianic Jews. Many Jews became followers of Yeshua by their own choice. The Sephardim *'people of the book'* were true to their name, renowned for their Hebrew Bibles - also for translations from Greek, Hebrew and Arabic - **and for *The Hebrew Gospels*! Messianic Jewish Christians had their own Yeshiva schools, churches and literature.** They shared the educational tradition of the Jews and, as converts, had the trust of native Christians.

> Many Jews found a niche in the new Christian society by virtue of their mastery of the language [Arabic] and Islamic culture. Because these intellectuals were also at home in Latin as well as all of the Spanish regional vernaculars - Castilian, Catalan, Navarrese - they could provide very specialized services to their monarchs... successful interpreters frequently moved on to become diplomats for the Christian kings, serving as ambassadors to the various Muslim kingdoms...[51]

Jewish intellectuals living in the Muslim domains served the same diplomatic and translation function. *"Muslim diplomats were loathe to go to the 'lands of the infidels,' and the notion of enduring the politesse and rituals of negotiating with 'infidels' was anathema... Consequently, Jews negotiated treaties..."*[51] Something similar can be said about the attitudes of devout Christians toward Islam at the time. **That left Jews as the critical and continuous intermediaries between the two civilizations.** *"Because they were politically neutral they were generally trusted... after all... they were in no position to revolt."*[51]

---

[49]Lowney, 2005:p.101. [51]Jane Gerber, 1992: p.98. [51] bid, p.163. [51] *Ibid*, p.94.

"Few Christian scholars read Arabic [but] *Muslims and many Jewish scholars did..."*[52] Catholic scholars of Spain seldom mastered Arabic or Greek, much less Hebrew. That left it to the Jews and Messianics to do the lion's share of translation and diplomacy between Muslims and Christians.

> We have never yet repaid our debt of grateful acknowledgment to the illustrious Hebrew schools of Cordova, Seville, Toledo and Granada... **There were twelve thousand Jewish students in the Toledo school** [alone].[53] [brackets mine]

Of course, the barriers against Muslim contact with infidels were broken, especially among those of an intellectual or creative mindset, which was what made the Convivencia so unique. *"Abd al-Rahman III from 912 to 961 came the closest to achieving the full realization of this coexistence."*[54] He implemented a *"policy of reconciliation of the Berbers, Arabs, Jews and Christians of the Iberio-Hispanic population."* All were allowed to practice their religion without persecution, including Jews and Christians. *"Intrinsic to the success of Convivencia during his reign was the political figure Hasdai Ibn Shapmut, the Jewish Vizier of Abd al-Rahman."* Together, they promoted *"the importance of Greek Philosophy, particularly the work of Aristotle which was translated into many languages"*[54] through their efforts... **Arabs were at the peak of their enlightened civilization and because of this, by the end of the tenth century Spain** *"was at least 80% Muslim...* [due to] *the steady stream of Spaniards deserting Christianity for Islam."* The Spanish cleric Eulogius bemoaned *"a Cordoba transformed by Islamic rule, 'expanded in glory, piled full of riches, and with great energy, filled with an abundance of all the delights of the world.'"*[55]

---

[52] Remi Brague, 2011, p.164. [53] *The Hebrew Christian Witness*, 1873:p.313.
[54] Sarah Thomas, 2013:p.2, *The Convivencia*. [55] Cited in Lowney, 2005:p.63.

Chapter Two
The Golden Age

Remember Yehovah your God, for it is He who gives you the ability to produce wealth, and so confirms His covenant, which He swore to your ancestors, as it is today.
Deuteronomy 8:18

Control of Iberia see-sawed between the Arabs and the Christians. Like two opponents who fight, then shake hands and feast together, periods of coexistence still bloomed under both Muslim and Christian rule. The 13th century Christian king Alfonso X *"generously supported Jewish scholars who helped bring the world's wisdom to his Spanish kingdom, from Aristotle and astronomical treatises to the Talmud and Quran."* [1]

Even the Roman Church was charmed by the advances in knowledge coming out of Spain. In 12th century Toledo, Archbishop Raymond *"resolved to sponsor the retranslation into Latin of Arabic translations of Greek classics by Aristotle, Galen, and others. Gerard of Cremona emerged as the most prolific translator-scholar of the whole medieval era... he learned the Arabic language. The indefatigable Italian ferreted through Toledo's libraries, churning out translations of at least 70 major works previously unavailable in the Latin-speaking West"* [12] One of his greatest accomplishments was the translation of *The Canon of Medicine* by Avicenna. This renowned text was still used 500 years later, which *"speaks less to Avicenna's undoubted genius than to the abysmal pace of progress in Western science."* [3]

> Christian Europe's so-called doctors were mired in a swamp of ignorance and sinking deeper each passing generation.... No medical writer of note emerged for nearly a millennium after Galen [the Greek]; worse yet, most volumes of classical authors had been lost in barbarian rampages. Absent any stimulus to progress, European medicine regressed.[4] [brackets mine]

After Gerard tapped into Toledo's treasure trove of Greco-Arabic scientific texts, **"*a long procession of European scholars - drawn by Spain's intellectual riches - journeyed to Toledo and found the libraries and intellectual stimulus... sought.*"**[5]

---

[1]Lowney, 2005, *A Vanished World*, pp.10. [2]*Ibid.* p.150. [3]p.151. [4]p.148. [5]p.149.

> Scholars were swarming into… Toledo, the continent's entryway for the knowledge that had come from the East in mathematics, philosophy, medicine, botany, astronomy, and practical geometry... being translated from the Arabic.[6]

One of these intrepid intellectual explorers was Gerbert of Aurillac. Count Borrell of Barcelona discovered the young genius at the Benedictine monastery in Aurillac. The Count financed Gerbert's way to Spain in 966 where he mastered Hindu-Arabic numerals a century before their acceptance in Europe. This system of the numerals 1-9 was a vast improvement over the Roman numerals still in use at that time, for example transforming CCCLXXXVIII into 388. Gerbert was even accused of black magic - as the new system allowed him to do rapid mathematical calculations in his head. If you ever try to multiply using Roman numerals you will understand what an advance this was. Although Gerbert did not succeed in converting Europe to the new numeral system - that had to await the innovation of the zero - he did succeed in becoming Pope Sylvester, the first French Pope.

> Nestorians attained unlikely yet vital prominence on civilization's stage when a ninth-century caliph founded the House of Wisdom in Baghdad. **Scholars flocked from across the Islamic world to hear Nestorians teach Greek wisdom. The texts they once translated into their native Syriac were retranslated into Arabic….** Baghdad-based scholars nurtured a revival of classical learning just when Dark Ages Europe had lost almost all touch with it.[7]

"One of the first directors of the House of Wisdom in Baghdad in the early 9th century was an outstanding Persian mathematician called Muhammad Al-Khwarizmi."[8] He wrote Kitab *al-Jabr*, *'Book of Reckonings,'* rendered as *'Book of Algebra'* - making Al-Khwarizmi *'the Father of Algebra.'* **He brought the zero into the West which makes the decimal system (0-10) so efficient.** *"When nothing is left over, write the little circle so that the place does not remain empty."*[9]

[6] Gerber, p.99. [7] Lowney, p.186. [8] Mastin, 2010, *Story of Math...* [9] *Kitab al-Jabr.*

Al-Khwarizmi advocated for the Hindu-Arabic numeral system, which he recognized as having the power and efficiency to revolutionize mathematics. A 12th century Italian, Leonardo of Pisa, called **Fibonacci**, picked up **this Hindu-Arabic number system** traveling in North Africa and wrote *Liber Abaci - 'Book of Calculation'* in 1202 - with so many practical applications of its use that it finally caught hold in Europe.

Muhammad Al-Khwarizmi circa 780-850 AD

Ideas wound some five thousand miles and eight centuries through Greece, Egypt, Turkey, Syria, Iraq, and North Africa before blossoming in Spain... Such was the unlikely preservation and transmission of some of humanity's most precious intellectual heritage: pagan Greek thought, suppressed by Christian emperors, preserved by heretic Nestorians, promoted by Baghdad's caliphs, welcomed by the Muslim successors of those who wrested Spanish rule from Visigoth Christians.[10]

"Toledo was one of the earliest towns of Spain to embrace Christianity. It is said that St. Peter and St. James passed here, and some add St. Paul, preaching the Gospel and creating bishops. St. Eugenius... was the first."[12]

"How have the Jews conferred benefits on Europe in general by their studies? At a time when the Greek language and its whole valuable literature lay buried to the Western nations, the Hebrews were reading in their own language works of Aristotle, Plato, Ptolemy, Apollonius, Hippocrates, Galen, and Euclid, derived from the Arabic of the Moors."[11]

Support of the Jews by the Muslims eventually swung in the other direction. *"In Muslim Spain, support failed when the breakup of the caliphate made it vulnerable to invasion by fundamentalist tribes from North Africa [in 1086 AD] that were intolerant of Jews. The Jews were forced to flee to Christian Spain."*[13] There, they became famous for their Hebrew Bibles.

[10] Chris Lowney, 2010:p.188. [11] James Finn, 2012:pp.227-8, *Sephardim*.
[12] Hannah Lynch, 2014, *Toledo - The Story of an Old Spanish Capital*.
[13] Martinez-Davila, Diaz & Hart, 2016:p.17, *Fractured Faiths*, Fresco Books.

Puig i Tarrech proposes that **the most likely translators for the 14th century Bibles were converted Jews**, well-versed in Latin but also naturally familiar with certain aspects of Jewish tradition. Catalan translations seem to be following rabbinical traditions, adding details found in the *Targum* or *Midrash* that do not appear in either the Vulgate or the Hebrew text. Such a hypothesis is tantalizing, it suggests these biblical texts might also shed light on Christian-Jewish relations in 14th century Catalonia.[14]

Shem Tov's Hebrew Matthew

It was during the 14th century that Shem Tov Ibn Shaprut defied the Jewish prohibition against the propagation of the New Testament in Hebrew. Shem Tov's monumental work was called the *Even Bohan*, or in English, '*The Touchstone*.' The original work consisted of 11 chapters, only one of which contained the complete text of Hebrew Matthew. Of the other chapters, "*nine deal with passages in the Bible disputed by Jews and Christians*."[15]

Shem Tov copied Hebrew Matthew *circa* 1380 in Spain

Spanish Bishops were forcibly converting Jews by compelling Jewish leaders to debate the Gospels. "*While still a young man he [Shem Tov] was compelled to debate in public, on original sin and redemption, with Cardinal Pedro de Luna, afterward Pope Benedict XIII. This disputation took place in Pamplona, Dec. 26, 1375, in the presence of bishops and learned theologians.*"[16] If the Christian judges determined the Jews had lost the debate - they and their community - were required (forced) to convert. Shem Tov's debate was a case of a Jewish triumph. For this reason Shem Tov reproduced Hebrew Matthew in order to include polemical arguments for Jews forced to debate. "*I have chosen to complete my treatise... Evan Bohan by **transcribing the books of the gospel** in spite of the fact that the **books are forbidden for us to read**... to answer the Christians from them... in this way glory will come to the Jew who debates with them.*"[15]

[14] Jaume, Casanellas & Tarrech, 2004, *Catalan Bibles of 14th century Spain*.
[15] George Howard, 1995:p.xi, *Hebrew Gospel of Matthew*, Mercer Univ. Press.
[16] Richard Gottheil & Meyer Kayserling, 1906, *Jewish Encyclopedia*.

The Hebrew Gospels in Spain

Note the use of the plural in regard to reproducing "*the books of the gospel*" in Hebrew. Shem Tov made revisions to the *Even Bohan* text over the years and mentioned his plans to reproduce Mark, Luke and John from the Hebrew in the same polemical fashion. Although Shem Tov never completed this task it was a clear statement that a complete compilation of the Gospels in Hebrew was extant in 14th century Spain.

George Howard did an-depth and thorough linguistic analysis of Shem Tov's Hebrew Matthew, concluding *"The gospel text incorporated into the Even Bohan was not a freshly made translation… but was a reproduction… of an already existing literary Hebrew tradition that had been in the process of evolution for some time."*[17] Nor was George Howard the first to say such a thing. *"From the gospel quotations from the Pugio Fidei by Raymund Martini, written about 1278 and based on Hebrew manuscripts confiscated earlier from the Jews in Aragon, Alexander Marx concludes;* **'we learn that a Hebrew translation of the Gospels already existed in thirteenth-century Spain.'** [18] *The existence of Hebrew gospels in the fourteenth century is thus a probability."*[17]

> The Hebrew Matthew of Shem-Tob… **the basic text pre-dates the fourteenth century, in some instances going back to very early times. Our evidence for this is its connection with quotations of Matthew in early Jewish polemical treatises and in one case the Talmud.** Assuming that the basic text of Shem Tob's Hebrew Matthew is a primitive Hebrew text, we have in this case what one might expect, a writing composed primarily in BH [biblical Hebrew] with a mixture of MH [Mishnaic Hebrew] elements, but which has undergone scribal modification… to make it conform more closely to the standard Greek and Latin texts of the Gospel during the Middle Ages… Nevertheless, **enough of the original text is left intact to observe its primitive nature.**[17] [brackets mine]
> (George Howard, 1995, vol. II, p.22)

---

[17]George Howard, 1995, pp.19-22, *Hebrew Gospel of Matthew*, Mercer U. Press.
[18] Marx, *The Polemical Manuscripts*, Jewish Theological Seminary of America.

The Hebrew Bibles of Catalonia

Almost a fourth of the Vatican Library's holdings of ancient Hebrew manuscripts are Hebrew Bibles - or Hebrew commentaries on books of the Bible - from one small area of the world, during a relatively brief era. Those Hebrew Scriptures came from Medieval Spain, much of it from Catalonia... not counting the many translations of Scripture, done in the other languages of Spain such as Latin, Castilian, or Catalan. Jewish and Messianic translators were renowned for using Hebrew sources in scriptural translation - often to the chagrin of their Gentile clients. Manuscripts *"show occasional influence from the Hebrew text - influence which Puig i Tarrech calls 'undeniable,' ...many specific examples... such as when the translation matches the Hebrew but not any known Vulgate versions..."*[19]

The Peiresc Manuscript

Two events crucial to our story occurred during the 14th century in Medieval Spain. **One, Shem Tov defied the Jewish prohibition to reproduce Matthew in Hebrew from the extant *Hebrew Gospels*.**[20] **Two, these same *Hebrew Gospels* were translated into Catalan** - which come down to us in a document now known as the Peiresc Manuscript - due to its purchase and preservation by Nicolas Claude Fabri de Peiresc (1580-1637). *"Peiresc, who pursued all disciplines... was lionized and beloved by virtually the entire learned world.... The true greatness of Peiresc... lay in the selfless manner with which he forever collaborated and contributed, lent learning, and traded in research, put one scholar or scientist in touch with another, carried the news, and in general served tirelessly, by travel and correspondence, as a link between alien disciplines, distant places, and separated personalities."*[21]

Pause for a moment to reflect upon how difficult the advancement of science was before the internet. Peiresc was the internet of his day! From his great fortune - and greater love of knowledge - he bought, translated, recopied and restored thousands of manuscripts, *"to withstand the normal wear and tear of use as well as the normal risk of subsequent destruction."*[21]

---

[19] Jaume, Casanellas & Tarrech, 2004, *Catalan Bibles of 14th century Spain*.
[20] George Howard, 1995, *Hebrew Gospel of Matthew*, Mercer Univ. Press.
[21] Pierre Gassendi, (*circa* 1640) reprinted 1970, *Peiresc & his Books*, Godine.

Peiresc was equally generous in giving away his restored works to those authors and experts who could most benefit from them. As a result, it is impossible to estimate just how many priceless manuscripts this one man saved from oblivion. *"For he could never endure that the least invention or observation of any man should be lost, being always in hopes that either himself, or some other, would be advantaged thereby."*[21] He recopied worn manuscripts from the regional languages of his day, or from Latin, Greek, Arabic, Turkish or *"any other language."* At his death, his remaining collection of 5400 manuscripts was donated to the College of Navarre in Paris.

It is Peiresc we must thank for preserving *The Catalan Gospels*, precursor of the *Hebrew Gospels of Catalonia*. **As the Spanish Inquisition drew Spain into its death grip, the extant *Hebrew Gospels* of 14th century Spain disappeared - driven underground or destroyed. The Messianic Church of 15th century Spain took *The Catalan Gospels* and retranslated them back into Hebrew!**

The *Hebrew Gospels from Catalonia* [HGC] occasionally use Catalan words written in Hebrew letters. It was common among Jews of the diaspora to write other languages using Hebrew letters. Some examples, in the HGC, are the following words:

'*capitulo*' - chapter
'*evangelistas*' - disciples
'*evangele*' - gospel
'*san*' - saint
'*peseta*' -weight of silver
'*escandalist*' - to offend
'*diumenge*' - Sunday

THE HEBREW GOSPELS
The First Gospels in Hebrew
Manuscript
Vat. 100 Ebr.

Chief Editor
Miles R. Jones, PhD.

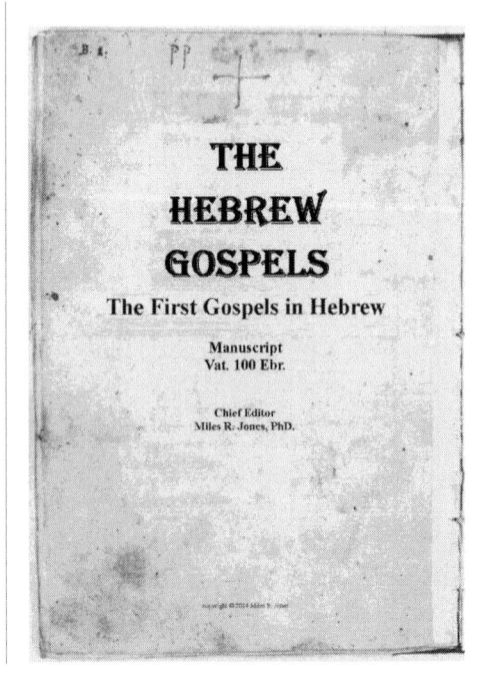

[21] Pierre Gassendi, (*circa* 1640) reprinted 1970, *Peiresc & his Books*, Godine.

The Hebrew Gospels, still extant, in 14th century Spain, spawned both the *Hebrew Matthew* of Shem Tov and *The Catalan Gospels* of the Peiresc manuscript. Although there is still much work to be done in the study of these *Catalan Gospels*, one example, out of many, should suffice to illustrate how they are linked, as the precursor, to the *Hebrew Gospels of Catalonia.*

Each of the first three Gospels began with a preface by St. Jerome who, in the 4th century, translated *The Hebrew Gospel* from Hebrew into Latin and Greek. It was at that time that he composed these prefaces in Hebrew. These prefaces are reproduced in both *The Catalan Gospels* and *The Hebrew Gospels from Catalonia.* In the Hebrew preface to Luke it says:

> Luke, according to the genealogy was from Syria and **<u>sat in Antioch</u>**, was a great doctor in the art of medicine. He was a disciple of the apostles and after that he did not separate from the company of St. Paul...
> The Gospel was already written in Judea by Matthew.

In Catalan, it also reads "*sat in Antioch,*" "*Sant Luch, sagons nació, fonch de Círia, e <u>**stech**</u> en Antiotza.*" The context is crystal clear, Luke was from Syria and dwelt in Antioch. However, the use of the curious phrase "<u>*sat in Antioch*</u>" can only be explained by the subtext, the original language from which it was translated. In *The Hebrew Gospels* the word used is '*yashav*' which means **to sit** or **to dwell**. In translating *The Hebrew Gospels* into Catalan the word was mistranslated as '*sat*' but when *The Catalan Gospels* were translated back into Hebrew a century later, it once again became '*yashav*' - in this case - *he dwelt.*

The Catalan Gospels were translated back into Hebrew by Messianic scribes precisely because they had originally come from Hebrew. If they had wanted the Roman version they would have translated the Gospels from the *Latin Vulgate.* **Two things are certain about *The Hebrew Gospels from Catalonia.* One, they were written by Messianic scribes. Only Messianics would risk death at the stake to preserve *The Hebrew Gospels*! Two, despite their detour through Catalan, the original language of these Gospels was Hebrew from the same extant *Hebrew Gospels* as the Shem Tov manuscript!**

How can we be so sure the *Shem Tov Manuscript* [STM] and *The Hebrew Gospels from Catalonia* [HGC] come from the same source - *The Hebrew Gospels* still extant in the 14th century? Because there are too many similarities to be a coincidence!

Correspondences between *Hebrew Gospels from Catalonia* (HGC) and the Shem Tov *Hebrew Matthew* (STM):
[The King James Version (KJV) is used as a comparison.]

Matthew 1:19
KJV says Joseph is concerned Mary will be put to shame for becoming pregnant, the HGC & STM say Joseph is worried about Myriam being put to death, the ultimate penalty for adultery.

Mathew 1:21
KJV "You shall call his name Jesus for he shall save his people from their sins." HGC & STM *"You shall call his name YeSHua because he will save* (YoSHia) *my people from their sins."*
Note the Hebrew internal rhyme is preserved in the HGC & STM.

Matthew 2:2
KJV "*We are come to worship him.*" HGC & STM say "*We are come to worship him with gifts.*"

Matthew 5:13
KJV "*You are the salt of the earth.*" in HGC & STM "*And then Yeshua said to his disciples, you are the salt of the earth.*"

Matthew 5:35
KJV "*Jerusalem... city of the great King.*" HGC "*Yerushalaym.. city of El* [Elohim]," STM "*city of Elokim* [Elohim]." In the margin of the *Codex Sinaiticus*, the oldest copy of the Bible we have in Greek, a '*scholia*' note confirms that in the *Gospel according to the Hebrews*, in Matt 5:35, it says "*city of God.*"

Matthew 5:41
KJV "Whoever compels you to walk a mile with him, go with him two miles." HGC & STM *"He who asks you to go 1000 steps with him, go 2000 steps."*

Matthew 6:1-4
KJV "*Do not do your alms before men.*" HGC "*Do not do your good acts* (HaToViM) *before men.*" STM "*Do not display your righteousness* (TSaDiKiM)."

Matthew 6:13 Lord's Prayer Doxology:
KJV "**For thine is the kingdom, and the power, and the glory, forever.**" HGC has no doxology. STM has no doxology. The doxology was added to the New Testament after becoming a part of the Greek liturgy. It is not in the early manuscripts of the New Testament, either in Greek or Hebrew.

Matthew 8:5-6
KJV "*a centurion beseeched him… saying my servant lies at home sick..*" HGC & STM "*my son (BeNaY) lies at home sick.*"

Matthew 8:13
KJV "*and his servant was healed at that hour.*" HGC "*and the lad (YeLeD) was healed at that time.*" STM "*the boy (NAR) was healed at that hour.*"

Matthew 8:29
KJV "*They cried out, saying, what have we to do with you, Jesus, son of God.*" HGC "*They cried out, saying, what have we to do with you, son of David, Yeshua Ha Mashiach.*" STM "*They cried out saying, what is between you and us, Yeshua, (with 'gershayim'), son of God (BeN ELoKiM).*" *Gershayim* are hashmarks used to accent the divine name of God.

Matthew 10:2-4
KJV lists the order of Jesus' disciples. The HGC & STM have a different order of Yeshua's disciples, but both are in agreement.

Matthew 10:12
KJV "*When you come into a house, salute it.*" The HGC & STM say, "*When you come into a house give shalom to it.*"

Matthew 10:18
KJV "*You shall be brought before kings… for a testimony against them and against the Gentiles.*" HGC "*to testify for me before the nations.*" STM "*to bear witness on my behalf to them and to the Gentiles.*"

Matthew 10:35
KJV "*For I am come to set a man at variance against his father, and the daughter against her mother, and the daughter-in-law against her mother-in-law.*" The HGC & STM do not have the underlined phrase '*daughter-in-law against her mother-in-law.*'

Matthew 11:17
KJV *"We have piped unto you, and you have not danced."* HGC & STM *"We have sung unto you, and you have not danced."*

Matthew 12:42
KJV *"The queen of the south shall rise up in judgement."*
HGC & STM *"The queen of Sheba... will rise up in judgement."*

Matthew 13:55
KJV *"son of the carpenter"* HGC & STM *"son of the smith"* - (BeN NaPaCH). Note: The word used was NaPaCH, *'smith.'* In the KJV, Matt 13:55 says the "*son of the carpenter*" but in Mark 6:3 where the same quote is used it says "*Is this not the carpenter.*" The HGC is consistent saying "BeN NaPaCH," "*son of the smith*" in both Matt 13:55 and Mark 6:3. In the Greek it says *technon"* which means *'builder.'*

Matthew 28:9
KJV *"Jesus met them saying, All Hail!"*
HGC "[May] *El save you."* STM *"HaSHeM deliver you."*

These correspondences between the HGC and the STM are not found in any other versions of the text of Matthew. The correspondences between the HGC and the STM are far too many for it to be a coincidence, and far too few for it to be a copy. There are numerous differences between the HGC and the STM. The only conclusion possible is that both the HGC and STM, although changed somewhat over time, come from a common Hebrew source. Shem Tov stated it was copied from the Hebrew.

I have chosen to complete this my treatise, which I have called, *Even Bohan* by transcribing the books of the gospel in spite of the fact that the books are forbidden for us to read.[22]

In the preface to Matthew by Jerome in the HGC it says, *"The first Evangelist wrote this in the Holy Tongue from memory to his brothers..."* The *'Holy Tongue'* always referred to Hebrew. In the preface to Luke by Jerome in the HGC, *"The Gospel was already written for those in Judea."* Luke 1:1-4 in the Greek, says it is a copy of what Luke was sent by the Apostles. Luke 1:1-4 is not in the HGC, nor *The Catalan Gospels*, a clear statement the HGC Luke was not from Greek - but of Hebrew origin!

---

[22] Cited from George Howard, 1995, p.177, *Hebrew Gospel of Matthew*.

"*In Jerome's Commentary on Matthew… the name of <u>Bar Abbas</u>* [is cited as] '*son of the teacher,*' [Bar Raban] *in the Gospel that is written 'according to the Hebrews,'*" so says Saint Jerome. In *The Hebrew Gospels* [HGC] he is referred to as "*Bar Raban.*"

Markers of the Hebrew Manuscript Tradition:

The HGC and the STM are examples of a Hebrew Manuscript Tradition that survived outside of the grasp of the Roman Church. Are there other examples of the Hebrew Manuscript Tradition? I have found one other in my rather preliminary search, the Waldensian Bible. The Waldensians were warred upon and martyred by the Roman Church for centuries for not accepting Rome's interpretation of Scripture. The Waldensian Bible predates the Latin Vulgate according to their oral tradition. Their Scripture is called the Roumant Bible. Here are the markers:

1) The name of the Messiah is derived from Hebrew - Yeshua, Yeshuas or Yeshu.

2) Where it says "<u>*son of Man*</u>" in the Vulgate etc., it often says "*son of the virgin*" in the HGC and Roumant Bible.

3) KJV John 1:1 "*In the beginning was the <u>Word</u>, and the <u>Word</u> was with God, and the <u>Word</u> was God…*"
HGC "*In the beginning was the Son Eloah, and the Son of El was with El.*" In the Roumant book of John, **"*In the beginning was the Son, and the Son was with God, and the Son was God.*"**

What is the importance of *The Hebrew Gospels*? In so many passages it gives us the authentic Hebrew perspective of Yehovah and Yeshua rather than the Hellenized version. For example, In Exodus 25:31 "*And you shall make a **Menorah** of pure gold…*" The word "*Menorah*" in Hebrew Scripture is always changed to "*candlesticks*" in Christian texts to avoid using the Hebrew icon - *Menorah* - created by Yehovah Himself (Ex 25:31-40). **In the HGC Matthew 5:15 - Yeshua teaches on the Menorah - "Neither do men light a candle and put it under a bushel - but on a Menorah - so that it gives light to all." Does this not convey a deeper, more true, Hebraic meaning!**

Return to the Garden

The Age of Enlightenment in Europe was due to the intellectual and artistic achievements of the Golden Age - planted and propagated in Sepharad. Much artistic focus came from recreating the paradise of *'the garden'* - a common refrain among the Sephardic poets. Garden soirees showcased the arts such as poetry, literature, music, song and story-telling. They are germane to our narrative primarily because they illustrate the priceless transfer of knowledge between East and West. *"Among the Arabs, evening meetings were held in rose-gardens, beside the fountains - warriors became poets..."*[23]

> A poem would... be introduced to guests after a leisurely meal... while a charming youth, male or female, served goblets of wine throughout the evening's entertainment, which would normally include dancers and musicians. The resulting mixture... sometimes glistens through the lines of a sensual courtly poem.[24]

The Golden Age of the Arabs, Persians and Sephardim overlapped - sparking and sharing inspiration, innovation, ideas and information!

"Wine was a favorite topic for improvisation."[24] Since antiquity wine has symbolized the essence of life. In Egypt, *"the walls of the tombs show vintners pressing new wine... a metaphor for spiritual processes... also in the biblical wine symbolism."*[25] The Hebrew word for man is *'adam'*, and the word *'dam'* for blood - also inferring wine, sap, juice, essence - comes from the same Hebrew root, *"the life of the flesh is in the blood"* (Lev 17:11).

> A book of verse, a loaf of bread
> A jug of wine, and thou
> beside me singing
> In the wilderness, and
> wilderness were paradise enou.
>
> Omar Khayyam - The Rubaiyat

---

[23]James Finn, 1841, reprint 2012:p.155, *Sephardim*. [24]Gerber, 1992:pp.66-67, *Jews of Spain*. [25]Moustafa Gadalla, 1996:p.237, *Untold Story of Ancient Egypt*.

The master of the wine metaphor was Omar Khayyam (*circa* 1200 AD). Khayyam was the most brilliant scholar of the Golden Age of Persia. He created a new calendar more accurate than any used before, discovered irrational numbers, did proofs of Euclid and published advanced calculations of cubic equations and conic sections. **Despite this, Khayyam is better known for his timeless poetry of *The Rubaiyat* than for his mathematics. His story is fascinating and encompasses a perfect illustration of the transfer of knowledge, culture and ideas from East to West.** If the reader will indulge me - the story will be worth it!

> You know, my Friends, how bravely in my House
> For a new Marriage I did make Carouse;
> Divorced old barren Reason from my Bed,
> And took the Daughter of the Vine to Spouse.[26]

Omar Khayyam was born in Naishapur, where his father sent him to study under the great wise man Imam Mowaffak. The Imam's wisdom and knowledge were of such renown it was considered a certainty that anyone who studied with him would attain to ambition, honor and happiness. Under Imam Mowaffak's tutelage, Khayyam became fast friends with two other students; Nizam ul-Mulk and Hassan Ben Sabbah. They were three brilliant young men who were each to rise to the pinnacle of power.

[26] Edward Fitzgerald, translator, 1952, *The Rubaiyat of Omar Khayyam*.

As Nizam ul-Mulk relates the story, one day Ben Sabbah said to his two friends, *"It is a universal belief that the pupils of the Imam Mowaffak will attain to fortune. Now, even if we all do not attain thereto, without doubt one of us will - what shall be our mutual pledge and bond?... Well, he said,* **let us make a vow that to whomsoever this fortune falls, he shall share it equally with the rest...** *'Be it so' we replied."*[27] It was Nizam ul-Mulk who eventually rose to be the Grand Vizier of the Seljuk Sultan Alp Arslan who reigned over the entire Middle East in his day, making Nizam ul-Mulk practically the most powerful man in the world!

Muezzin - caller to prayer

Eventually, both of Nizam's old friends came to ask a share in his great fortune. Khayyam did not ask for treasure but only his patronage to help continue his studies in mathematics and astronomy. Ul-Mulk - once he realized Khayyam's refusal of fortune was sincere - granted him a yearly pension. Khayyam became the paragon of his age. He was praised for his knowledge of mathematics, science and reform of the calendar - gaining the laurels and favor of Sultan Arslan.

Hassan Ben Sabbah also came to his old friend to demand a place in the government, which Nizam ul-Mulk granted him. Ben Sabbah became seduced by the power and intrigue of the court. Not satisfied with rising by his own efforts he attempted a coup to supplant his benefactor Nizam ul-Mulk as Grand Vizier. Ben Sabbah was found out - yet instead of being slain was only disgraced and banished due to the mercy of his old friend.

In time, Ben Sabbah became the leader of the Ismailians, a fanatical sect of assassins.[27] Ben Sabbah seized the remote fortress of Alamut south of the Caspian Sea. Famed as the *'Old Man of the Mountain'* he spread terror throughout the kingdoms of Islam and the Christian crusaders. He brought his recruits to Alamut and plied them with wine and hashish until they passed out - awakening in a gorgeous garden where beautiful young women were eager to serve their every need!

[27] Edward Fitzgerald, translator, 1952, *The Rubaiyat of Omar Khayyam*.

After again drugging the recruit until he was unconscious, the young man would reawaken in the cold, rugged, remote fortress of Alamut. He was told he had had a vision of paradise where 72 virgins awaited him should he die serving Allah by assassinating his enemies. The Ismalians were called '*hashishim*' for the hash they smoked, a word which comes down to us as '*assassin.*' The *Old Man of the Mountain* was universally feared! One of Hassan Ben Sabah's victims was the Grand Vizier Nizam ul-Mulk, his loyal, kind, and merciful boyhood friend.

The Troubadours

The crusades brought traveling troubadours who followed the armies and returned with books, stories, poetry, song and innovation passed on, in turn, wherever they went. They performed before the elite of all nations and everywhere people were hungry for knowledge of the places they had been. Many valuable accounts, concepts, and manuscripts, passed through their hands into the West. One of the most documented of these is the story of Scheherazade.

For those who may not know the story, Shah Rivar goes out from his castle on a hunting trip. Returning early he finds his beautiful young queen having sex with her serving men. The Shah is so totally devastated by this betrayal that he orders her put to death. And to insure it never happens again, he takes a new wife each night then has her executed at dawn! It falls to the Shah's Vizier to find him a new wife daily.

Caught in the middle of all this angst was the Vizier of the Shah who had to obtain a new woman for him daily only to see her die the next morning. Finally, the Vizier's brilliant and beautiful daughter, Scheherazade, persuaded him to let her be the Shah's bride. Scheherazade had a plan.

After the Shah weds and beds her, Scheherazade begins to tell him a tale. Fatigue overcomes him before she ends the story and the Shah grants her a reprieve of one day to finish the tale. The next night she finishes the tale and begins another story which, once again, is left hanging as the Shah grants her yet another day of reprieve. These unfinished tales go on night after night, for months, then years, until finally the Shah admits he is so deeply in love with Scheherazade he could not bear her death. The stories are famed as the '*Thousand and One Arabian Nights.*'

It may surprise the reader that these stories and others like them caused a revolution in Western thought. Troubadours and other story-tellers, including poets such as Khayyam, promoted romantic love over the arranged marriages of convenience usually determined by parents. This movement of '*Courtly Love*' invaded the West with a will - promoted by the verses of troubadours in the early Middle Ages. It was picked up by knights and courtiers who came to typify it as '***Chivalry***' - fealty to one's beloved as to higher ideals of truth, justice, honor. **Gallantry towards women was as big a part of this new warriors' code as courage in combat. Before this, women - even noble born - were considered little more than property.**

The story of Scheherazade has always been considered fiction - because the Shah and his Vizier - have never been found in the history books. In my research into Khayyam's boy-hood friend Nizam ul-Mulk, I located a rare copy of his book *Rules for Kings*. In it he related that his Sultan assigned him for some time to aid a crucial ally in need, to serve as his Vizier in arranging his affairs. **That ally was none other than Shah Rhiyar!**[28] During this sojourn, Nizam ul-Mulk wrote the story of his friends Khayyam and Ben-Sabbah and his book *Rules for Kings*. So there may be truth in the legendary account of Scheherazade - the love story which infused the passion of romantic love into the West!

---

[28] Nizam ul-Mulk, *The Book of Government or Rules for Kings*, reprinted 1960, p.248, New Haven, Yale University Press, translated by Hubert Darke.

Much of this cultural exchange between East and West was carried by the traveling troubadours who sparked the social movement known as *'Courtly Love,'* better known to us as *'Chivalry.'* Interestingly enough, the center of the troubadour movement was at Fanjeaux in the south of France. Fanjeaux was also the center of the Cathar religion during the same era. Troubadours spreading a great social movement of amorous love were rubbing shoulders with an equally dynamic religious movement whose spiritual leaders, called *'perfecti,'* practiced and promoted celibacy as the highest level of spiritual attainment.

These movements of Cathars, Conversos and Waldenses (Vaudois) were Neo-Messianic! We know because they left witnesses - their Scriptures and other writings. These movements not only had a pivotal effect on the people of Europe in the Middle Ages, they also later helped spark the Reformation. All of their writings, gospels, beliefs, reputations and their very lives have been destroyed, burned or buried in the crusade for dominance by the Roman Church.

> Of the Vaudois documents… the highest authority [belongs] to the poems called *La Nobla Leyzon, La Barea, Lo Novel Sermon, Lo Novel Confort, Lo Peyre Eternal, Lo Despreczi del mont,* and *L'Avangeli de li quatre scemencz and to the prose compositions called La Potesta dona a li Vicaris de Xrist, Sermon del Judyei, Epistola amicus, Epistola fideli, De la temor del Segnor, De las Tribulacions,* and *Glosa Paternoster…*
> **written… with the language of the Troubadours.**[29]

[29] Alexis Muston, 1875, reprint 2017:p.516, *The Israel of the Alps*, vol. II.

Chapter Three
The Neo-Messianic Movement

There appeared a great wonder in heaven, a woman clothed in the sun... and upon her head a crown of twelve stars... And she was with child...and the woman fled into the wilderness.
Revelation 12:1-6

Civilization spread around the rim of the Mediterranean - that great waterway of cultural contact, catalyst, and commerce between East and West, North and South. Churches established by the twelve Apostles had sprung up from Jerusalem to India and China - from Anatolia to Africa and Spain, in Italy and all along the Rhine into Germany, among the Celtic tribes in France, Britain, Scotland and Ireland. Although persecuted by pagans at times - for a millennium they were mostly free to pursue their beliefs. In Europe, the Roman Church gradually consolidated its doctrine and power. What to do about these primitive churches going their own way? Some were gathered into the fold. Others refused. When they rejected Rome's persuasions, Rome demanded - when they rejected Rome's demands - Rome turned to force. If they would not see reason - they would convert to Roman Catholicism or die! The Crusade and the Inquisition were born.

Their opponent was the Neo-Messianic Movement, mostly Gentile now, but still the continuation of the original primitive Church! **The original church of the Messiah still thrived!** In the second millennium, the Neo-Messianic Movement was forced underground when Rome initiated the Crusades and the Inquisition to consolidate its power. Neo-Messianics were labeled by different names; Waldensians in Italy, Cathars in France, and Conversos of Spain. They were but a few of the many moveable players in the ever-shifting mosaic of the Underground Church.

The Neo-Messianics continued to proselytize and spread. Persecuted and extinguished in places, survivors fled to neighboring regions where they became part of a new version of the Underground Church. They were all uniform in holding to the original Messianic-Apostolic Church as typified in the Gospels. In *The Key of Truth - Manual of the Paulician Church* - **the new '*Messianic*' was defined, not as a Jew, but one who is committed to imitate the Messiah and restore his Messianic Church!**

In 1891, Fred Conybeare went to Armenia looking for a rare manuscript of the *Book of Enoch*. What he found instead was *The Key of Truth*, the manual "*of the Paulicians. For I found in it the same rejection of image-worship, of Mariolatry, and of the cult of saints and holy crosses,* [the rejection of] *which was characteristic of the Paulicians*"[2] [brackets mine]. Fortunately, Conybeare was not only knowledgeable of the early church but also a linguist of the Armenian language. "*The date at which the book was written in its present form cannot be put later than the ninth century, nor earlier than the seventh. But we can no more argue that the prayers and teaching and rites preserved in it are not older.*"[1] Cornybeare, from his impressive in-depth knowledge gives us a guide to the odyssey of the original church:

> Driven out of the Roman Empire, we find it at the beginning of the fourth century and later encamped along the borders of the Greek and Latin worlds, in Mesopotamia, in Armenia **and in Spain**, in Bavaria... in Britain. It would seem also to have lingered on in the ancient Church of Phyrgia. Perhaps it was the pressure from behind of the advancing tide of Islam, both in Spain and in the Taurus, which... hurled it back into the Roman Empire... it was not there that it really bore fruit. **Yet it was not stamped out, but only driven underground.** It still lurked all over Europe, but especially in the Balkans, **in Lombardy**, in Gascony, and along the Rhine. In these hiding places it seems to have gathered its forces together in secret, in order to emerge once more into daylight when opportunity presented itself. **That opportunity was the European reformation, in which... this leaven of the early Apostolic Church is found freely mingling with and modifying other forms of faith in engendering this great religious movement... partly imbibed from Paulician missionaries.**[1]

The Paulicians gained their name from Paul of Tarsus. They spread the Word throughout the world with Gospels that pre-dated those of the Roman Church. Among these were *The Hebrew Gospels*. "*The Gospel first went to the Jews. It is easy to forget that almost every hero of the Bible was a Jew and that every book of the Sacred Scriptures was written by a Hebrew. Jesus Christ himself was an Israelite... For a long time... the bulk of the early Church members [were] descendants of Israel.*"[2]

---

[1] Conybeare, 1898, 2012: pp. vi & cxcvi, *The Key of Truth: The Manual of the Paulician Church*, Forgotten Books. [2] Wilkinson, *Truth Triumphant*, 1944:19.

The Messianic Movement of Jewish Christianity morphed over time into the Neo-Messianic Movement, predominately Gentile, but dedicated to restoring the original first century church of the Hebrew Messiah. Over the centuries they were labeled with different names, declared heretics, attacked, and groups were often exterminated. It was not until the 12th century that the Roman Church had consolidated and extended its power sufficiently to seriously challenge the Neo-Messianic Movement.

A leader had arisen among the Neo-Messianics, a prosperous merchant from Lyons who had given his fortune away to the poor. He also had the original version of the Bible, the *Itala*, preserved by the Messianics, and translated into ancient Romaunt. His name was Peter Waldo. The Roman Church branded the Neo-Messianic Movement as Waldensians and heretics. It was always the tactic of Rome to isolate a competing church and brand them as heretical followers of a cult leader. Although many Neo-Messianic congregations were exterminated or forced to flee to other countries - the Waldensians of the Alps - although subjected to nearly constant attack and martyrdom, were never eliminated. The Waldensian Bible became the core text of the Reformation Bibles which converted two-thirds of Europe, within a few decades, into Protestant reformers.

> The old Waldensians were not seceders from the Church of Rome, for neither themselves nor their ancestors had ever embraced its faith. Claudius Seyssel, a popish archbishop, declares that the **Waldensian heresy originated from one Leo**, who, in the days of Constantine the Great, led a party of heretics from Rome into the valleys. Pope Gregory the VIII observes that it is well known that in the days of Constantine the Great, **some assemblies of Jewish Christians being persecuted at Rome, because they persisted in obedience to the law of Moses, wandered off into the valleys where their descendants remain to this day.**
>
> Reiner Sacco, declares that, in the opinion of many authors of note, their antiquity could be traced to the apostolic age. He also observes that never, within the memory of man, have they acknowledged allegiance to the papal see.[3]

---

[3] Tamar Davis, 1851:pp. 66-69, *The General History of the Sabbatarians*, Lindsay & Blakiston, Philadelphia, USA.

After Israel was devastated in the revolts of 70 & 135 AD, many Jewish-Christians emigrated to Syria, especially Antioch. There, **Lucian of Antioch compiled the first Greek Bible which came to be called the *Textus Receptus*, or *Received Text*,** which was not only the Bible of Eastern Christianity but most of the West as well. Rome did not send missionaries to the West before 250 AD. The first Christians reached France and Britain from Asia Minor. The Galatians - an early church established by Paul - were Gauls, who were *"of the same family, and spoke the same languages as the Irish, Scotch, British, Welsh, and French."*[4]

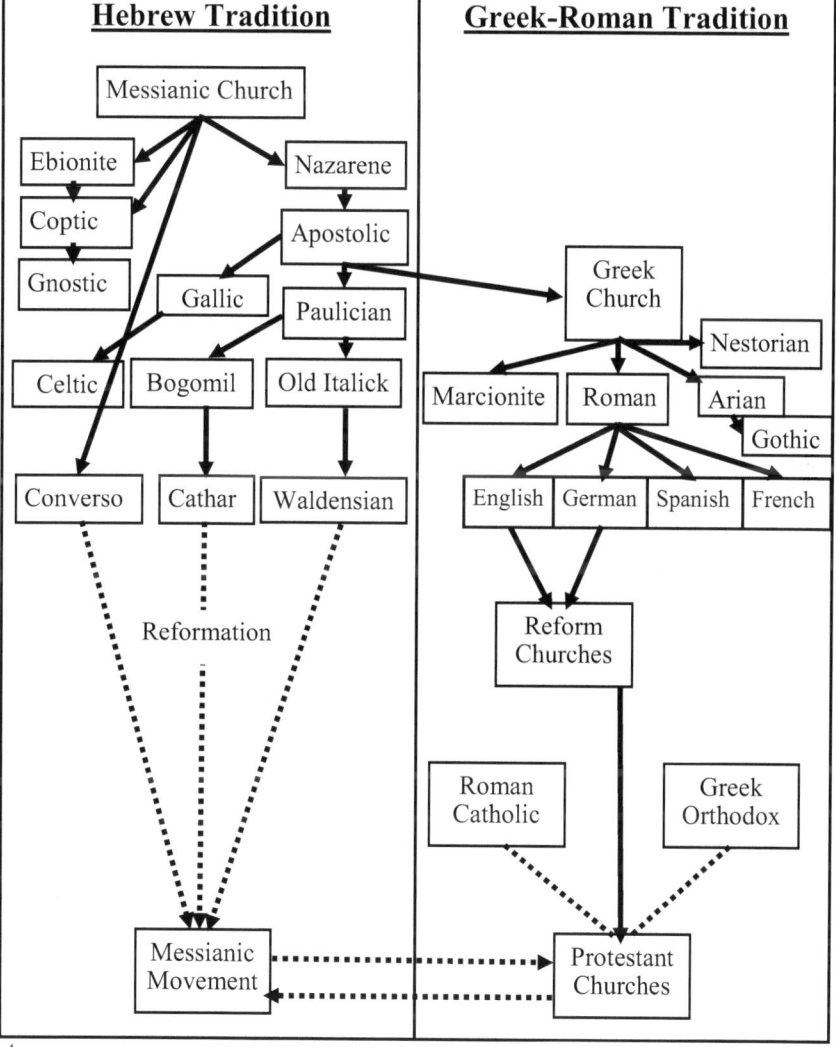

Hebrew Tradition	**Greek-Roman Tradition**
Messianic Church → Ebionite, Nazarene, Coptic, Gnostic, Apostolic, Gallic, Paulician, Celtic, Bogomil, Old Italick, Converso, Cathar, Waldensian	Greek Church → Nestorian, Marcionite, Roman, Arian, Gothic; Roman → English, German, Spanish, French → Reform Churches
Reformation → Messianic Movement	Roman Catholic, Greek Orthodox → Protestant Churches

[4] B. G. Wilkinson, 1944:p.23, *Truth Triumphant: Church in the Wilderness.*

It was Lucian of Antioch who first wrote of the two movements in Christianity, *"one loose in doctrine and affiliating itself with heathenism - the other based on the deep foundations of the Christian faith."*[5] These two have become crystal clear by the Middle ages. The Roman Church, full of power-lust, was incorporating pagan holidays and practices into its doctrine - and the Neo-Messianic Church preserving the faith of the Messiah and his Apostles, keepers of the original Church. The Roman Church, however, controlled the historical narrative in the West - making much of some Bible scholars and Bible texts and erasing others.

About 150 AD, the first compilation of the Old and New Testaments was translated into Latin by authors unknown to us but to whom we owe a debt of profound gratitude. **The '*Itala*' was the first complete Bible as we know it today - translated when the original manuscripts in Hebrew and Greek were still available!** By all accounts it was an inspired and beautiful text of the Bible! The primary goal of the New Testament exegete, like myself, is to find the original most authentic manuscript. Second to *The Hebrew Gospels* that would be the *Itala* [aka Old Italick, Italic or Old Latin Bible]. The *Itala* manuscript tradition is well established from Bibles translated or copied from that source. Its authenticity is beyond any doubt:

> The earliest evidence we have for the Bible in Latin seems to be a quotation from 1 Tim. 6:15 in the *Acts of the Scillitan Martyrs* of AD 180 which also echo several New Testament phrases.
> Tertullian [150-230 AD] used an already existing Latin translation in some of his quotations. We may infer from this and other evidence that the Bible was translated into Latin by the mid-second century... For the Gospels this state of affairs is represented by *Itala* **which gives the text of the principal pre-Vulgate manuscripts in a clear and usable form... a consensus line of text, if we may call it so, is present.**[6]

The *Itala* is the most ancient, authentic and inspired complete Old and New Testament but it is seldom mentioned in the research literature. Instead, all roads lead to Rome and the translation of Jerome's Vulgate Bible centuries later. Western history was written by the Roman Church and its institutions.

---

[5] Benjamin Wilkinson, 1944:p.41, *Truth Triumphant.* [6] G.D. Kilpatrick, 1978, p.56, "*The Itala*", in *The Classical Review,* vol.28, no.1.

If we wish to know the earliest, most authoritative texts of the Bible we must learn about Lucian of Antioch (250-312 AD). Even before Constantine and Eusebius, Lucian, before 300 AD, compiled the first complete Greek Bible. *"Lucian, in an hour when documentary confusion was threatening chaos, defended, preserved and passed on the true text of the Holy Scripture."*[7] Lucian was a Messianic Jew, and Hebrew scholar, able to compare and correct the Greek versions of the Old Testament from the Hebrew text of the Tanakh - using *The Hebrew Gospels* and the *Itala*! The churches of Syria and Asia Minor adopted his version. The Lucian Greek Bible became *The Received Text* of the Greek Church in the East and much of the West - except Rome and Alexandria.

Only three decades later, Eusebius was commissioned by Constantine to compile Scripture **into a brand new Greek Bible**. Jerome, a few decades after Eusebius, was commissioned by Pope Damasus to compile Scripture **into a brand new Latin Bible**. Viewed through the perspective of Catholic Church history these are the earliest and most authentic Bibles. Despite that spin, they were neither the first nor the most authentic. Why did the Roman Church need a new Latin (and Greek) translation? It seems clear they were written, first, to canonize the narrative of Constantine - second, to canonize the doctrine of the Church of Rome.

There are marked differences between the Greek and Latin manuscript traditions of Rome and the texts of Lucian and the *Itala* which came before them. **Lucian's Greek Bible is called the *Received Text*, the *Textus Receptus*, firmly based on the *Itala*. It is - without a doubt - the closest text to *The Hebrew Gospels* which were still extant at the time!**

We will tackle some crucial examples. However, we must first convey the context - the big picture - so the agendas at work in the creation of the Bible text can be clearly understood. We are justly horrified that someone would purposefully alter a sacred text to advance their own doctrinal agenda. Yet this is a constant danger we must be vigilant about in arriving at the true Scripture. With patience, knowledge and divine guidance - we will recover *The Received Text*!

---

[7] Benjamin Wilkenson, 1944:p.40, *Truth Triumphant*.

Paul of Tarsus

After his dramatic conversion on the road to Damascus, Paul of Tarsus lived and taught in Antioch for eight years creating a strong early church in that city. After his arrest in Jerusalem he was in Rome for two years awaiting his appeal to Caesar. During that time he wrote his Epistles, preached and taught - evangelizing many in Rome. Paul was released from prison - returning a few years later when Nero came to power. Nero blamed Christians for the fire, in 64 AD, that destroyed much of Rome and began a horrendous persecution. It was extensive and bloody, with many burned at the stake, torn apart by beasts in the arena, or otherwise tortured and executed. It was during that intense, but brief, persecution that Paul was martyred - Nero died in 68. **Christians were steadfast in their faith. Those who escaped fled - many to northern Italy - taking their Gospels with them.**

> The Vaudois (Waldensians) are in fact descended from these refugees from Italy, who, after St. Paul had there preached the gospel, abandoned their beautiful country and fled like **the woman mentioned in the Apocalypse**, to these wild mountains, where they have to this day handed down the gospel from father to son in the same purity and simplicity as it was preached by St. Paul.[8]

The reference to *'the woman'* is from Revelation 12:6, *"And the woman fled into the wilderness, where she had a place prepared by God, that they should feed her there a thousand two hundred and threescore days ['years']."* The woman, *"a great wonder in heaven... **a woman clothed in the sun**... and upon her head a crown of twelve stars"* (Rev 12:1) **is the bride of Christ - his original Messianic Church!** She gives birth to a son [the body of Christ] as the dragon [Satan] awaits - to devour it as soon as it is born (Rev 12:4). So, a period of 1260 years of persecution was prophesized as *"the dragon was enraged at the woman, and went to make war with the remnant of her seed which kept the commandments of God and have the testimony of Yeshua Maschiach"* (Rev 12:17). **The *'woman,'* therefore, is the Messianic-Apostolic Church... *'in the wilderness!'*** The apostate counterfeit church is also prophesized... pompous, living in luxury - fornicating with kings and princes - clothed in the blood of those martyred for the Word of God and the Messiah.

---

[8]Henri Arnaud, 1827:p.xiv, *Glorious Recovery by the Vaudois*, Murray, London.

Waldensians of the Alps

The Waldensians were located in the Alpine regions of northern Italy (the Piedmont & Lombardy) and southern France. Any disciple going to or from Rome on foot would pass through northern Italy. Acts speaks of the Apostle Paul (and others) spreading the Gospel throughout Greece and Italy - in all directions. Not only Paul, but the Apostle Andrew, brother of Peter, evangelized from Greece to Rome including northern Italy. Long before the Roman Church extended its power out from Rome there were congregations throughout the country - in the Piedmont and Lombardy - unto Lyons on the other side of the Alps in France. To claim that all of these churches sprang from or bowed to the Church of Rome - defies both logic and history.

Nonetheless, Rome has tried to paint the Waldensians as a Medieval movement of the late 12th century. On this question hangs an important issue. **If the Waldensians' claim to a first century origin are true - it highlights the fact that Rome was not the original church but only one of many.** Waldensians fled Rome in 64 AD. Later, in the time of Emperor Constantine and Pope Sylvester in the fourth century, many others followed who had rejected the doctrine of Rome over the issue of idolatry.

B.C.	Hebrew Tanakh*	Old Testament	Greek Septuagint
A.D.	**Hebrew Gospels**	**New Testament**	**Greek Gospels**
100	Itala Bible-Old Latin		
200	Lucian Greek Bible		
300	Waldensian Bible		Eusebius Greek Bible
			Jerome Latin Vulgate
Two Streams of Bible traditions - Hebrew vs Greco-Roman			

Torah is only the first five books, the *Tanakh* is the entire Hebrew O.T.

Early on, Antioch became the center of Christianity after Jerusalem was destroyed by the Romans. It continued to be a prominent center of faith for six and a half centuries. Tens of thousands of Messianic Jewish-Christians fled to neighboring Syria during the Roman persecution of the Jewish revolts in 70 and 135 AD. Very little has been acknowledged of the truly great civilization the Messianic Church created in Syria:

> These exiles were to populate with beautiful cities, and with institutions of unsurpassed scholarship, a section of country northward beyond the bounds of Canaan. They would furnish an evangelical grasp of Christianity's greatest doctrines which their background of Jewish history enabled them to appreciate more profoundly than could Gentile converts.[9]

The language of the Jews was Hebrew - the Syrians, Aramaic - a closely related sister language. *"Jerusalem's fall produced its greatest moral effect upon the millions of Jews who did not reside in Palestine. Stunned by this event, they listened to the gospel - and untold numbers turned to Christ!"*[9] **For many centuries their Scripture was the Hebrew Tanakh [O.T.] and *The Hebrew Gospels*! They called themselves '*Nazarenes.*'** The Bible was soon translated into Aramaic - called the *Peshitta*.

Paul and Barnabas went forth from their base at Antioch to evangelize. As was the practice of all the Apostles, they went first unto the Jewish communities wherever they traveled. Two thousand years of devotion to the Word had made the Jews ready to accept their Messiah as prophesized in the Tanakh. The Jews converted in droves, in stark contrast to the utter failure of the Roman Church to appeal to Jews in later years by preaching invective-laced sermons filled with anti-Semitism!

"Syria... was the richest and most prosperous province of the Roman Empire. It was also famed for culture and learning."[10] *"The school of Antioch at that time surpassed almost every other in scientific and literary repute, and its methods dominated all the East."*[11] **Now its cities are silent, their remains unexcavated, their achievements unsung - in part - due to the bias that minimizes the Messianic Church and its primary role in spreading Christianity throughout the world!**

---

[9] Wilkinson, 1944:pp.20 & 31, *Truth Triumphant*. [10] O'Leary, 1909:p.34, *Syriac Church and Fathers*. [11] G.T. Stokes, 1892:p.242, *Ireland and the Celtic Church*.

It was Lucian who founded the college of Antioch. He studied Scripture for many years while translating the Hebrew into Greek. Lucian developed a method of theology based on what was written in Scripture, avoiding tradition as a basis for doctrine - dismissing texts lacking in the rigorous tenets of truth - such as the Apocryphal texts Lucian opposed adding to the Bible.

Mutilations of the Sacred Scripture abounded. There were at least eighty heretical sects all striving for supremacy. Each took unwarranted license in removing or adding pages to Bible manuscripts.[12]

Lucian of Antioch
250-312 AD

Most especially, Lucian fought against the influence of pagan religion and philosophy being incorporated into Scripture - *'Philosophy'* meaning that of the Greeks. The *'sons of Greece'* were so intellectually dominant that **many Christians, such as Clement of Alexandria,[13] felt no sacred book would be viable long-term without framing Christian thought in Greek garments**! We will analyze that Greek framework in this book.

Rome and Alexandria were allied in these ecclesiastical wars against Antioch. **They held that Church tradition was as important a basis for theology as Scripture.** Church tradition was declared equal to Scripture at the Council of Trent in 1563. This was the same thinking that had brought the Judaic religion to Rabbinicalism. The opinions and interpretations of Rabbis established a multitude of new laws for believers to follow. This plethora of new religious laws were considered as binding as those of Yehovah. Now, the decrees of the bishops of Rome and her councils would determine belief for Christian congregants. Heaven forbid that believers should disagree.

> Rome and Alexandria well knew that most of the churches throughout the world sanctified Saturdays as the Sabbath of the fourth commandment... when Victor I [in 190 AD] pronounced excommunication on all the churches of the East who would not... make Easter always on Sunday... Lucian opposed... [these] policies and for this has been bitterly hated and his name kept in the background.[14]

---
[12] Eusebius, *Ecclesiastical History*, b.5, ch.28, in *Nicene & Post-Nicene Fathers*.
[13] John Mosheim, 1856, *Historical Commentaries on the Church Converse*, NY.
[14] Wilkinson, 1944:p.42, *Truth Triumphant: Church in the Wilderness*.

In 352 AD, emperor Justinian decreed that all subjects of the Roman Empire would embrace imperial Christianity or else. The '*or else*' led to a split with the Church of the East and eventually with the Greek Orthodox Church. Those who would not subject themselves to tampering with the commandments of Yehovah - many devout and productive citizens - were driven out of the Roman Empire. Modern Christianity still reflects this rupture.

> Now the Scriptures alone do not contain all the truths which a Christian is bound to believe... is not every Christian obliged to sanctify Sunday... Is not the observance of this law among the most prominent of our sacred duties? But you may read the Bible from Genesis to Revelation, and you will not find a single line authorizing the sanctification of Sunday. The Scriptures enforce the religious observance of Saturday, a day which we never sanctify.[15]

Clearly, theological *"speculation within the church was tearing to pieces the faith once delivered to the saints. The very foundations of the gospel itself was as stake...* **In that time God raised up a tireless champion of truth - Lucian!"**[16] **For this reason, Lucian was condemned by many in the Church as a 'Judaizer' - one exalting the forbidden Hebrew Scriptures above those of the Roman [and Alexandrian Greek] Church.** Church historians of the era, such as Socrates Scholasticus and Salminius Sozomen confirm that *"almost all churches throughout the world celebrate the sacred mysteries on the Sabbath every week...* **yet the Christians of Alexandria and at Rome, on account of some ancient tradition, have ceased to do this.***"*[17]

Lucian took a brave stance against those who taught that the laws of Yehovah were not binding to Christians. Lucian was martyred in 312 AD during the last Roman persecution. To the end he encouraged his brothers to hold to the faith. In 365 AD, at the Synod of Laodicea the Roman Church decreed, *"Christians must not Judaize by resting on the Sabbath, but must work on that day... **if any shall be found to be Judaizers, let them be anathema to Christ!**"*[18] What was this ancient tradition justifying not only altering the Sabbath to the *'Lord's Day,'* but speculating that all God's commandments were non-binding upon Christians?

---

[15] Cardinal James Gibbons, 1876, *The Faith of Our Fathers*, Baltimore, MD.
[16] Benjamin Wilkinson, 1944:p.47, *Truth Triumphant: Church in the Wilderness*.
[17] Socrates, *"Ecclesiastical History,"* b.5, ch.22, *Nicene & Post-Nicene Fathers*.
[18] Council of Laodicea, Canon 29, Scribner's Nicene... Fathers, vol.14, p.148.

How to Alter Sacred Writ

<u>**One**</u>, create a new version including your desired changes.

<u>**Two**</u>, announce it - with as much hoopla as possible - **as the new -official-best-most- authoritative version ever!**

<u>**Three**</u>, destroy or minimize all competing versions. Always refer **only** to the new revised rendition forevermore. Any competing versions will soon be dismissed, neglected, and forgotten.

"The Church [changed] the day of rest from the Jewish Sabbath, or seventh day of the week, to the first... Sunday - as the day to be kept holy... the Lord's Day. The Council of Trent [1545 AD]... condemns those who deny that the Ten Commandments are binding on Christians."[19] As if to say, '*Just this one small change - the other nine are still good!*' Protestant religion followed in the footsteps of Rome on this issue. So, where did this authoritative ancient tradition come from? To answer that - we must revisit a debate in Volume One, chapter 6 - the insertion of John 6:4.

That ancient tradition and authority was provided by Eusebius' 3½ year ministry of Jesus Christ! That is why there was a new Greek compilation of the Bible - only thirty years after Lucian's superb Greek Bible. The new Greek Bible created the theological pillars of the new Church of Constantine. The '*preterist*' [meaning '*past*'] position on prophecy was established - declaring all prophecy has now been fulfilled in the past. **Eusebius' insertion of "*Passover was nigh*" into John 6:4, made possible this 3½ year ministry** which prophetically culminates in the '*end of prophecy*' (Daniel 9:24) heralding the return of the "*conquering-king Messiah*" who will end the persecution of the saints and rule over all the nations of the world. Constantine was proclaimed as the "*conquering-king Messiah!*"

The '*divine right of kings*' to rule had now been Christianized, uniting the church and Roman state into an ungodly alliance! The power of armies, secret police and the stake were all in the hands of the Roman Church. John 6:4 redated the crucifixion by two years to Friday 33 AD... sanctifying the '*Good Friday - Easter Sunday - Lord's Day*' tradition. The Lord's Day Sunday Sabbath and the 3½ year ministry of Christ, were **the two major doctrinal hammers used to force other churches to their will - both depend upon the insertion of John 6:4.**

[19] *The Catholic Encyclopedia*, 1908, vol.4 - article on "*Commandments of God*," Robert Appleton Co., online edition 1999, p. 153.

Critique of John 6:4

There is a manuscript tradition that does not include the insertion of John 6:4. The Nestle-Aland 27th [1998] edition of the New Testament in Greek annotates those manuscripts that do not include John 6:4. One of these is MS 472 preserved in Lambeth Palace in London. Labeled MS 511 in Schrivener, who declared it, *"for valuable readings by far the most important at Lambeth."*[20] It reads, *"And Jesus went up into a mountain, and there he sat with his disciples. When Jesus then lifted up his eyes, and saw a great company come unto him, he said unto Philip. 'Where shall we buy bread that these may eat?'"* (John 6:3-5). No *"passover... was nigh!"* There are similar manuscripts, such as MS 1634 from the Lavra Monastery in Athos, Greece.

These MSS are 13th & 14th century, not very old - certainly not the oldest - and therefore seen as not very authoritative. However, **they are later only when using dates of surviving copies instead of the source text(s).** The MS 472 from Lambeth palace [21] *"according to the Claremont Profile Method... has a mixture of Byzantine..."* The manuscript was originally from Constantinople, which used the Lucian *Received Text* in Greek. There is now new evidence that bears on that source.

Supporters of Eusebius cite two manuscripts, P66 & P75 [aka P. Bodmer II & XV], which contain John 6:4. These manuscripts - discovered in 1952, and dated around 200 AD - seem to make a great argument for the Eusebius version, *circa* 330 AD. Are those early dates justified? Recently P66 & P75 were reassessed by a specialist named Brent Nongbri. P66 had been assigned a date by comparing its handwriting to some fragments of Homer, which were also **paleographically dated - which is ultimately a best guess!** As Nongbri put it - **guessing a date based on another paleographic guess is** *"only jelly propped up with jelly."*[21] So he reanalyzed P. Bodmer II [P66] based on dated manuscripts rather than guesses based on guesses. *"Within the same cache of manuscripts purchased with P. Bodmer II, there is a more firmly datable papyrus that bears many striking resemblances to P. Bodmer II, namely P. Bodmer XX."*[21] **These papyri are...** *remains of the library of the Pachomian monastic order, founded in the fourth century."*[21]

[20]Schrivener, 1894:p.355, *Criticism of the NT.* [20] *Ibid.,* labeled MS 511 in Schrivener, 1894:p.355, *Criticism of the NT.* [21] Brent Nongbri, 2014:pp.4,13,21, *"Date and Provenance of P. Bodmer II (P66),"* in *Museum Helveticum*, vol.71.

Manuscripts	Contents	Date estimated
P Bodmer II - MS P 66	**Gospel of John**	2nd-3rd cent.*
P. Bodmer V, X, XI, VII, XIII, XII, XX, IX, VIII "Miscellaneous" Codex	Genesis of Mary, Corinthians Ode of Solomon, Jude, Melito, Phileas, Psalms 33-4, 1-2 Peter	3rd-4th cent.
P. Bodmer XIV-XV	**Gospels of Luke and John**	2nd.-3rd cent.*
P. Bodmer XXIV	Psalms 17-118	3rd-4th cent.
P. Bodmer XLV, XLVI, XLVII, XXVII	Susanna, Daniel, Moral exhortations, Thucydides	3rd-4th cent.
P. Bod. XXIX-XXXVIII	Hermas, Doroteheos, hexameters	4th-5th cent.
P.Monts.Roca.inv.126-78	Cicero, hexameters on Alcestis	4th cent.
Bodmer Collection of papyri of same origin as P. Bodmer II & XV		

As Nongbri noted, "*The bulk of the pieces have been assigned dates in the fourth & fifth centuries.*"[22] Comparing P. Bodmer II [P66] & XV [P75] to the other papyri in that collection that are also Coptic Bible manuscripts does not change the result.

Manuscripts	Contents	Date estimated
P. Bodmer III	John and Genesis	4th cent.
P. Bodmer VI	Proverbs	4th-5th cent.
P. Bodmer XVI	Exodus	5th-(6th) cent.
P. Bodmer XVIII	Deuteronomy	4th cent.
P. Bodmer XIX	Matthew and Tobit	4th-5th cent.
P. Bodmer XXI	Joshua and Tobit	5th cent.
P. Bodmer XXII	Lamentations, Jeremiah	4th cent.
P. Bodmer XXIII	Isaiah	4th cent.
P. Bodmer XL	Song of Songs	5th cent.
P. Bodmer XLI	Acts of Paul	4th cent.
Crosby-Schoyen Codex	2 Macc., Peter, Jonah	4th cent.

[22] Brent Nongbri, 2014:pp.22-23, "*Date and Provenance of P. Bodmer II (P66),*" in *Museum Helveticum*, vol. 71.

At several points in the P66 manuscript the *tau* and *rho* were combined to form a *'staurogram'* the sign of the cross. This was not in common use until the time of Constantine in the fourth century. The binding on the manuscript was a type not used until the mid to late fourth century. **"The combined weight of these considerations point to a date for the production of P. Bodmer II in the early or mid part of the fourth century."**[23]

Fig. 22: Detail of P. Bodmer II P.137, line 3, abbreviation of tau rho staurogram:

After P. Bodmer II [P66], Nongbri took on the analysis of P. Bodmer XIV-XV [P75], the other outlier - finding that it, *"fits comfortably in a fourth-century context, along with the bulk of the other 'Bodmer papyri' with which it was... discovered."*[24] Here, a major issue raises its head, *"the text of P. Bodmer XIV-XV so closely matches that of Vaticanus - a codex widely acknowledged to be a product of the fourth century - suggests that **P.Bodmer XIV-XV was also itself produced in the fourth century!**"*[24]

Eusebius' manuscript of the Greek Bible done in the fourth century did not survive. There are two manuscripts which are considered to be copies of Eusebius. They are the *Codex Sinaiticus* and the *Codex Vaticanus*, considered the oldest, mostly complete copies of the Greek Bible, and therefore hailed as the most authoritative. They were discovered in the mid 1800s. **By the late 1800's a great revision of the Bible was initiated making more than 30,000 changes to the King James Version of the Bible based on these texts!** Eventually all modern Bible translations followed suit.

So the validity of the Bible you hold in your hand today hinges on these two copies of Eusebius' Greek Bible. Even so, the two copies themselves do not agree more than 75% of the time. However, the P75 [P. Bodmer XIV-XV] agrees with Vaticanus 90-94% of the time, making it a 4th century text, *"'the most significant' N.T. papyrus... come to light in the 20th century."*[24]

---

[23] Brent Nongbri, 2014: p.35, *"Date... of P. Bodmer II (P66)," Museum Helveticum*, vol..71. [24] Brent Nongbri, 2016,"*Reconsidering the Place of Papyrus Bodmer XIV-SV (P75) in Text Criticism of the N.T.*," JBL, 135, no.2, pp. 405-437.
[24] Nongbri, *Ibid.*, p.405. [24] Nongbri, *Ibid.*, p.406.

This establishes the P75 text as a fourth-century text, not an *'exceptionally early'* second-century manuscript. Nonetheless, it has been hailed as the opposite - an attempt to prove *Vaticanus* was not a re-interpretation of Scripture - but a faithful preservation of what had come before! Therefore a major revision of the Bible was considered justified. Fenton Hort, who came under serious criticism as the prime mover on the revision committee, said that *Vaticanus* "*must be regarded as having preserved not only a very ancient text, but a very pure line of very ancient text.*"[24] I am sure the reader recognizes spin. Absent any evidence, how would Hort know either the antiquity or purity of the ancestry of the *Vaticanus*? Certainly not from the P75 manuscript. The misdating of this document is an intensely political issue!

We must judge by the greatest probability. "*This early date was established solely on the basis of paleography (the analysis of handwriting), which cannot reliably produce such a narrow window of possible dates...* **The actual evidence used to establish that date was not strong...** *In fact, good parallels for the handwriting of P75 can be found in manuscripts produced in the fourth century* [p.406]... **In terms of codicology** (the format and construction of the codex), P75 fits comfortably in **a fourth-century context. Further, the other 'Bodmer papyri' with which it was discovered are... products of the fourth and fifth centuries** [p.407]... *evidence... point toward* **the fourth century as...** *more likely date for this codex.*"[24] To make a long story short, the two examples of early Greek manuscripts with the insertion of John 6:4, <u>did not happen until after Eusebius' Greek Bible - not before</u>! Researchers have been over-eager to date the P66 & P75 manuscripts centuries earlier in order to support their doctrinal agenda. The evidence does not support it.

Fifty years later a new '*official-best-most-authoritative version ever*' was made in Latin, the Bible of Jerome, replacing and attempting to erase the *Itala Bible*. Why was a new Latin version needed to replace the excellent translation of the *Itala*? The *Itala* was translated into Latin about 150 AD from the earliest Hebrew and Greek texts of the NT, many of them original manuscripts! The *Itala* should tell the tale of whether John 6:4 was in the earliest manuscripts or inserted by Eusebius. The *Itala* was the Bible of the Paulician refugees who settled in northern Italy. Its translation was called the *Waldensian Bible*.

---

[24] Hort cited in Nongbri, 2016:pp.406-407 & 436, Reconsidering... JBL, 135, #2.

Anyone who is interested enough to read the vast literature on this subject, will agree that **down through the centuries there were only two streams of manuscripts. The first stream which carried the Received Text in Hebrew and Greek, began with the apostolic churches**, and reappearing at intervals down the Christian Era among enlightened believers, was protected by the wisdom and scholarship of the pure church in her different phases; by such as <u>the church of Pella in Palestine</u> where Christians fled, when in 70 AD the Romans destroyed Jerusalem; by <u>the Syrian Church of Antioch</u> which produced eminent scholarship; by the <u>Italic Church in northern Italy</u>; and also at the same time by the <u>Gallic Church in southern France</u> and by the <u>Celtic Church in Great Britain</u>... [and] **by the <u>Waldensian, and the churches of the Reformation</u>**.[25]

In the Bibliothèque Nationale at Paris there is - what is said to be - the most ancient surviving manuscript of the Waldensian Gospel of John in Roumant. *"The Gospel of St. John contains proofs that its compilers... consulted the remains of the old "Versio Itala" and adopted the readings of that version whenever they saw reason to prefer them..."*[26] I have examined the Paris MS 8086 - **there is no John 6:4 *"passover... was nigh."* This is substantial evidence the *Old Itala* - the oldest compilation of the New Testament (*circa* 150 AD) - did not include John 6:4!**

"The reader... has a translation before him... prohibited in the 13th century... solely because it was in the vulgar tongue... to check the spirit of spiritual inquiry, which was spreading among the people."[27] **If there was no John 6:4, the ministry of the Messiah was 70 weeks - as prophesied in Daniel - not 3½ years! Neither was there a *'good Friday - Easter Sunday'* - sanctification of the *'Lord's Day'* by Yehovah! Yeshua rose at the end of the Sabbath. Constantine was not the return of the Messiah! Rome is not the capital of God's kingdom! The Pope is not God on earth!** Eusebius' doctrinal house of cards comes tumbling down into the dust - along with the rationale for forced conversion of Christians to the Roman Church - and the justification for executing those Christians who refuse! **A church in such gross error on these primary pillars of faith, and their awful consequences, has little credibility on other issues!**

[25] Ben Wilkinson, first ed. 1930, 2014:p.13, *Our Authorized Bible Vindicated*.
[26] William Gilley, 1848, Intro. xcix, *Roumant Version of John*. [27] *Ibid*, p. cv.

Chapter Four
The Underground Church

Let love never diminish. Abhor that which is evil.
Hold to that which is good.
Romans 12:9

The Messianic-Apostolic Church of Yeshua the Messiah did not disappear in the fifth century as church history tells us. It was not destroyed. It went underground. This underground church continued to move and expand and evangelize widely - constantly reaching out to the pagans of Europe and elsewhere. The major figures in this Neo-Messianic movement will be unknown to you for the most part. Their major roles in history have been minimized, demonized or erased - their writings have been destroyed. Their reputations have been blackened as have those of their followers of whom countless numbers were martyred. **As the power and extent of the Roman Church grew - their lust for domination grew along with it. The beliefs of other Christians did not matter. They were heretics. They must all bow to Rome!**

The Italick See was established in the north of Italy by those departing from Rome in the fourth century as Constantine was establishing his new church. The Italick See was never a part of the Roman Church. They did not split off from them. They existed before the Roman Church was established. They came to be know as *Valdenses*, people of the valleys. The Roman church launched crusade after crusade against them as Rome's military power grew. They were driven from the Piedmont plains further and further into the high valleys of the Alps. They had *The Received Text* of the Bible as their Scripture - called the *Itala* Bible - it was compiled two centuries before the Roman Church Bibles.

The Neo-Messianic movement of the Middle Ages went by many names but they were all one in the doctrine that mattered, restoring the Messianic-Apostolic Church of Yeshua the Messiah and practicing his Gospels as the early Messianics had done. Principal among these other groups were the Waldensians of northern Italy, the Cathars of southern France, the Jewish-Christian Conversos of Spain, and the Celtic Church of Saint Patrick in Ireland, Scotland, England, and elsewhere.

Vigilantius

Vigilantius (364-408 AD) was born in central Gaul [France]. His father owned a *'mansio'* - an inn and transit station for those Roman travelers going to Italy or Spain or vice versa. He grew up meeting educated and experienced travelers who knew much of the world. One of these was the well-known historian Sulpicius Severus who had a prominent estate nearby.

As a young man Vigilantius was employed as Sulpicius' estate manager. He was moved not only by Sulpicius' intellect and writings but also his efforts to feed and clothe the poor and heal the sick. It was probably Sulpicius who baptized Vigilantius as a Christian. Sulpicius became caught up in the Christian movements of asceticism and monasticism. He and Vigilantius visited Martin, bishop of Tours, who established the first monastery in Gaul. There, Sulpicius became a convert - and Vigilantius became a critic!

> The extreme austerities to which he [Martin] had subjected himself... produced a profound change in the life of both Sulpicius and Vigilantius, but in opposite directions... Vigilantius... could not remain blind to the fact that his patron was neither happier nor better for his visit to the bishop of Tours... the recollection of the ascetic prelate sleeping on the cold earth, with nothing but ashes strewed beneath him, and covered with sackcloth only - refusing a softer bed, or warmer clothing, even in severe illness - declaring that a Christian ought to die on ashes, feeding on the most unwholesome food, and denying himself every indulgence... exposing himself to the extremes of heat and cold, hunger and thirst.[1] [brackets mine]

Vigilantius became more skeptical traveling through Italy. Shrines were being raised - cathedrals even - **to the worship of saints, their images, plaster statues and *'relics'* of their lives. These were the idolatrous practices of paganism which were being incorporated into mainstream Christianity!** This clear and growing disregard of Scripture was abhorrent to Vigilantius.

---
[1] Wilkinson, 1944:pp.59-60, *Truth Triumphant: The Church in the Wilderness*.

The *Itala* and *Lucian's Greek Bible* were the Scriptures of both the Eastern and the Western churches excepting those of Rome, and Alexandria. The *Itala Bible* was the Bible that Vigilantius had grown up with. As Vigilantius sojourned, during his journey to the East, in northern Italy's Christian communities (in Piedmont & Lombardy) he learned of their history and their Gospels. The Gospels arrived early in Lombardy and this was the point from which they were disseminated into Western Europe.

> The Goths, Celts and Franks... united now by the invisible bonds of community... **prized their Latin Bible... called the *Itala***, *"because it was read publicly in all the churches of Italy, France, Spain, Africa, and Germany... on account of its being more ancient than any of the rest."** **To supplant this noble version, Jerome, at the request of the pope and with money furnished by him, brought out a new Latin Bible.**[2]

From Italy, in 396 AD, Vigilantius journeyed on to Jerusalem and to Bethlehem to meet Jerome, carrying a letter of introduction from Paulinus of Nola. Initially, he was welcomed by **Jerome, who, although a great lover of books - was a vicious hater of men** - the terror of his peers! Much of Jerome's writing was invective-filled take-downs of his opponents.

> [In] the cell of Jerome - here he [Vigilantius] found the ascetic clad in a vestment so coarse and sordid, that its very vileness bore the stamp of spiritual pride, and seemed to say, *'Stand off, my wearer is holier than thou!'* The face of the monk was pale and haggard. He had been slowly recovering from a severe illness, and was wasted to a shadow. Frequent tears had plowed his cheeks with deep furrows; his eyes were sunk in their sockets; all the bones of his face were sharp and projecting. Long fasting, habitual mortification, and the chagrin which perpetual disputation occasions, had given an air of gloominess to his countenance, which accorded but ill with his boast, that his cell to him was like an arbor in the Garden of Eden.[3]

Vigilantius had come to a crossroads, *"on the one hand there was Martin, bishop of tours, rushing from cave to cell in the excitement of supposed miracles, there was Sulpicius, turning from sound scholarship to fables and visions, and the gentle ..."*

---

[2] Wilkinson, 1944:p.65, *Truth Triumphant* - *citing William Gilly, 1844:p.116, from *Vigilantius and His Times*. [3] William Stephen Gilly, 1844: p.236.

"*...Paulinus of Nola groveling before the image of a favorite saint - the victim of delusions.*"[4] There were saner voices, contemporaries of Vigilantius - all speaking from northern Italy. **Helvidius, a pupil of Auxentias bishop of Milan (in Lombardy), had stood up to Jerome - challenging him on the corrupt Greek documents he was relying on as authoritative sources of his translation!**

Helvidius 340-390 AD

About 383, Helvidius wrote a treatise against the Roman Church's doctrine of the perpetual virginity of Mary. The Gospels speak of the Messiah having *'brothers and sisters'* clearly indicating his parents had marital relations. The debate was really about the unmarried state being considered a higher spiritual state than marriage. Many priests, denied marriage, had instead turned to scandalous sexual perversions. What little we know of his stand against the vices of the Roman Church comes through Jerome who wrote an *Epistle Against Helvidius*. All Helvidius' works have been lost or, more likely, destroyed!

Portrait done by his opponents "*Jovinian Judaizer & Traitor*"

Jovinian (340-405 AD), another scholar of high repute, wrote in 390 that the lives of married people were as acceptable in the sight of God as those who are celibate. Helvidius and Jovinian both believed the worship of images, saints and relics went against the Word of God. For saying this, Jerome condemned Jovinian in his *Epistola adversus Jovinianus*. Pope Siricus instituted public proceedings against him in Rome. Jovinian's writings have also been destroyed, leaving us with only the ravings of Jerome to judge him.

Vigilantius (370-406 AD) wrote his famous treatise against the vices of Rome, after his encounter with Jerome. "*The bishop of the diocese, Exsuperius of Toulouse, was strongly in favour of the views of Vigilantius, and they... spread widely.*"[5] **After sowing the seed of truth in the heartland of the Cathars - Vigilantius relocated to Lombardy!**

[4] Wilkinson, 1944:p.65, *Truth Triumphant*. [5] newadvent.org/fathers/3010.htm.

> **Toward the end of the fourth century... in Lombardy there were believers who opposed the worship of images....** Vigilantius, a well informed man... a native of Comminge, in Aquitaine... [and] a priest at Barcelona... During his travels in the east, he fell in with St. Jerome... [who] in vain attempted to convince Vigilantius, and to bring him over to his opinion respecting relics, saints, images and prayers addressed to them, tapers that were kept burning at the tombs, pilgrimages, fasts, the celibacy of priests, a solitary life, etc.
>
> **Vigilantius** remained immoveable. On his return, this opponent of the new doctrines **appears to have fixed himself in Lombardy**, where he found a refuge... in the region of the Cottian Alps.[6]

"*On his return...* [to] ***Lombardy***" - Vigilantius had sojourned there before and knew their Gospels and their doctrines. Jerome was well aware of this - judging by his own bitter statements. "*I saw a short time ago... that monster Vigilantius. I would fain have bound this madman by passages of holy writ... but he has departed... escaped; and from the space between the Alps... his cries have reached me. Oh infamous! He has found, even among the bishops, accomplices in his wickedness.*"[7]

So, it seems the dearly departed Vigilantius had partners in crime among the Waldensians. What was this monster's crime? Vigilantius was against celibacy of priests which had resulted in so much sexual vice - also the idolatrous worship of saints, their images, bones and relics along with pilgrimages to their holy shrines - all sanctified by the Church. Bountiful revenues, miraculous claims and ostentatious displays of faith so pleased Rome that it blessed and sanctified these practices.

Vigilantius and the Christians of Lombardy, like Helvidius and Jovanian before them, stood against all these acts of idolatry! In his Epistle(s) *Against Helvidius*, *Against Jovanian*, and *Against Vigilantius* - Jerome, that '*hater of men*' savaged those who opposed the Church of Rome. Nonetheless, that same '*lover of books*' praised the *Greek Bible of Lucian* and was the primary proponent of the *Hebrew Gospel of Matthew* as the first and "*authentic Gospel*" - the "*fountainhead!*" It was Jerome who translated Eusebius' Greek Bible into Latin.

---

[6] Antoine Monastier, 1859:p.10, *The History of the Vaudois Church.*
[7] *Hieronymous ad Riparium contra Vigilantium*, t.ii, p.158.

The prefaces to the *Hebrew Gospels* [HGC] were written (or translated from Hebrew) by St. Jerome late in the fourth century at the time he translated the *Hebrew Gospel* into Latin and Greek. There are three prefaces in Hebrew - before Matthew, Mark, & Luke. In the first line of the preface to Matthew, Jerome wrote, *"Saint Matthew, when the Gospel was first requested, he wrote this Gospel in **the holy tongue** [Hebrew] to leave this record of truth for his brothers"*[8] [translated by the author].

In the Hebrew preface to Luke in *The Hebrew Gospels from Catalonia* [HGC], Jerome wrote *"Those for whom the Gospel was already written in Judea and for Matthew in Lombardy.*"[9] This reference to **Lombardy** is also in the preface to Luke in the Peiresc Catalan manuscript of the Gospels which were translated from an extant Hebrew manuscript in the 14th century. The meaning is very clear, **The Hebrew Gospel - written for those in Judea - had made its way to Lombardy early on!** In that hot spot of early evangelism, the Gospel was translated into the vernacular. I was very puzzled about this citation of Lombardy when I first translated it, until I translated these Romance excerpts of the Waldensian Bible from Lombardy.

Various manuscripts of the Waldensian Gospels have survived - in those at Grenoble and Dublin, the first line of the preface to Matthew reads, *"**When Matthew had first preached the Gospel in Judea - they wanted it passed on to the people - so the Gospel was written first in Hebrew**"*[10] [translated by the author]. This first line of the preface to Matthew is mysteriously missing in all the Gospel manuscripts coming from Rome!

This beginning line of the preface to Matthew - which says the Gospel was first written in Hebrew - now stands as the pre-eminent marker of the Hebrew manuscript tradition! Evidence of a Hebrew manuscript tradition from exemplars of the Gospels known to have survived outside the grip of the Roman Church is **a major discovery!** One that will not be welcomed by Greek primacists. Nonetheless, Jerome himself validated the early arrival of the Hebrew Gospel of Matthew to Lombardy - where it was translated into the vernacular by the Waldensians. The Waldensian *"pastors were designated 'Barbas.' They were required to commit to memory the Gospel of St. Matthew..."*[10]

[8] *Hebrew Gospels from Catalonia* [Vat. Ebr. 100] p.74, Luke. [9]*Ibid*, Matt, p.2 .
[10] Alexis Muston, 1875, 2017:p.450, *Israel of the Alps*, vol. II. [10]*Ibid*, vol I, p.19.

In the Waldensian Gospel of John at the Biblotheque Nationale in Paris (MS 8086), it says in John 1:1, *"Lo filh era al comensament; el filh era am Dieu, e filh era Dieu. Aquest era al comensament am Dieu. Totas causas foron fachas per el; e nenguna causa non fou fach sens el; so che fou fach, era en lui vida: e la vida era lus dels homes."* Or in English, ***"In the beginning was the Son; and the Son was with God; and the Son was God.** This same one was in the beginning with God. Every thing was made by him; and no thing was made without him; so that which was made, was in him life - and that life was the light of men"* [translated by the author from Paris MS 8086].

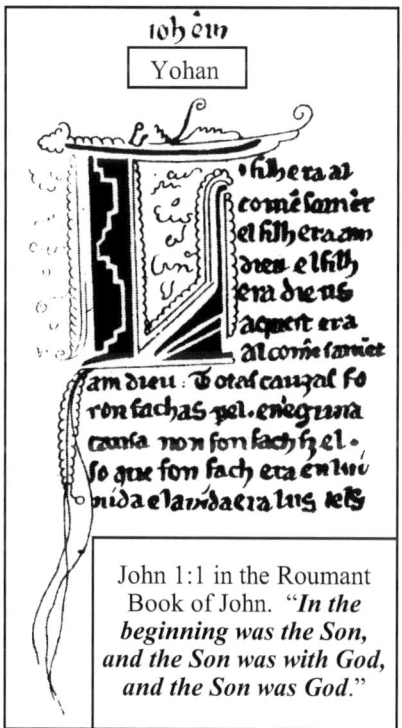

Yohan

John 1:1 in the Roumant Book of John. *"In the beginning was the Son, and the Son was with God, and the Son was God."*

"In the beginning was the Son" is another marker of the Hebrew manuscript tradition! That same passage from John 1:1 is in both the HGC and the Roumant Book of John, used by Waldensians, Cathars and Conversos. There are other markers, working from the annotated bibliography of Alexis Muston, in the Geneva MS #43 it refers to *Yeshu Xrist*."[11] Using a form of the name of Jesus in Hebrew, '*Yeshu, Yeshua,* or *Yeshuas*,' is yet another marker. **The Christians in Lombardy evidently had the Hebrew Gospel or one translated from it!**

The Waldensians, from '*Valdenses*' people of the valleys, in French '*Vaudois*,' had a translation of *The Hebrew Gospels* which had been compiled into an '*Old Italic*' (Old Latin) Bible, the *Itala*, predated the Vulgate. Prominent Protestant scholar, Reverend A. G. Ashdown said this about the Waldensian Bible, *"They had a version of the Bible in their local ancient Romance language.... derived from the Greek and Hebrew and not a translation of the Latin Vulgate."*[12]

[11]Alexis Muston, 1875:pp.450-456, *Israel of the Alps*, vol 2. [12]A. G. Ashdown, *The Evangelical Library Bulletin*, Spring 1986, #76, p.3.

It seems likely that the Old Latin was translated in the Syrian Antioch by missionaries going to the West. Existing manuscripts certainly show a strong Syrian and Aramaic tendency. This being the case, the Old Latin is associated with that city which is **the missionary center of the Book of Acts**, and had immediate concourse with those centers in Asia Minor which received the Epistles of Paul. History is so unanimous to **Antioch being the fountainhead of the Traditional Text [Received Text]... it has been called the** *"Antiochan Text."*

The 55 or 60 OL [Old Latin] manuscripts which remain for us today show varying amounts of corruption, and frequently disagree among themselves. As such they are but an imperfect reflection of the original OL [Old Latin] Text. The OL of North Africa show some of the strange cases of addition and subtraction associated with the so-called Western Text, while those of Europe are generally favorable to the Traditional Text.

It is the branch of the Old Latin [Bible] used in northern Italy that attracts our interest the most, and establishes one of the crucial chapters in Bible transmission history. This version, known as **the *Itala*, is associated with the Christians of the Vaudois, the valleys of northern Italy and southern France.** These noble believers withstood every attempt of Rome to *"bring them into the fold."* From the days of Pope Sylvester (early 300s) unto the massacre of 1655, they were slaughtered, their names blackened, their records destroyed; yet they remained true to the Scriptures. They are known by a number of names, but best as the Waldensians. Research into the text and history of the ***Waldensian Bible* has shown that it is a lineal descendant of the Old Latin *Itala*.** In other words, the *Itala* has come down to us in the ***Waldensian*** form, and firmly supports the Traditional Text [Received Text].[13]
[brackets mine]

The pattern we see in the Vaudois valleys of northern Italy and southern France is that the <u>same regions</u>, <u>same churches</u>, <u>same peoples</u>, and the <u>same issues</u> were consistently recorded over more than a millennium in opposition to the Church of Rome! The Roman Church argument about their beginnings has focused solely upon when they were first called Waldensians - a truly irrelevant debate! **The Vaudois sprang from the Apostolic Church and had rejected the idolatry of Rome since the fourth century. They had the true Word and they were willing to suffer and die for it!**

---

[13] Jack Moorman, 2005:pp.67-68, *Early Manuscripts and the Authorized Version*.

"You shall not make unto you any graven image, nor any likeness of any thing... You shall not bow down to them nor worship them" (Ex 20:4-6). This commandment seemed clear to Yeshua when his disciples were pointing out the wonders of the Temple in awe, *"Do you not see all these things... Truly I tell you, not one stone here will be left on another...."* (Matt 24:2). Herod had turned Israel into a nation that worshiped their Temple. Herod's Temple was truly a wonder of the ancient world but it was not sacred to Yehovah! Many Jews saw something to venerate - and failed to see it was just a building.

The Greco-Roman Church had long abandoned the Savior to embrace power. *"Professing themselves to be wise, they became fools, and changed the glory of the incorruptible God into an image made like to corruptible man"* (Rom 1:22). **The Holy Mother Church had become a god!** The Vaudois Christians of Lombardy understood this while the Church of Rome did not?

The Vaudois, and the Goths, had the *Itala* Bible in their own tongue! Anyone who could sound out the letters of their language could read it for themselves. Never underestimate the power of the Word! When Ulfias translated *Lucian's Greek Bible* into Gothic it swept throughout Europe like a tsunami - bringing millions of Goths to faith! **The Roman Church forbade the Bible in the vernacular - they even outlawed the reading of the Bible by laymen!** As a result, Christian faith was replaced once again by superstition and idolatry.

In the sixth century, *"Serenus, bishop of Marseilles, had succeeded in banishing images from his diocese,"*[14] for which he was chastised by Pope Gregory, *"We had been apprised that, animated by an inconsiderate zeal, you have broken in pieces the images of the saints, on the plea they ought not to be adored."*[15] Even in the eighth century *"the struggle of the faithful against these errors still continued."* Numerous northern bishops protested *"propagating the following errors: the celibacy of priests, the worship of relics, the adoration of images, the supremacy of the popes, masses for the dead, purgatory, etc."*[14] Rome was so habituated to these practices - and their revenues - that they continued the worship - or '*adoration*' - of saints, images and relics.

---

[14] Antoine Monastier, 1859: p.10, *The History of the Vaudois Church.*
[15] *Delectus Actorum*, t.i, p.443. [14] *Op. cit.*, in the work cited, Monastier, p.10.

Adoration of icons had started even in the fourth century, during the time of Jerome, and was opposed by Vigilantius. It had long been a major part of Roman Church practice. Over time, it was banned, then permitted, banned again, and finally at the Seventh Ecumenical Council, aka the Second Council held at Nicea in 787 AD, the adoration of images was unanimously approved by 350 bishops of both the Latin [Roman Catholic] and Greek [Eastern Orthodox] Churches.

> **As the sacred and life-giving cross is everywhere set up as a symbol, so also should the images** of Jesus Christ, the Virgin Mary, the holy angels, as well as those of the saints and other pious and holy men be embodied in the manufacture of sacred vessels, tapestries, vestments, etc., and exhibited on the walls of churches, in the homes, and in all conspicuous places, by the roadside and everywhere, to be revered by all... For the more they are contemplated, the more they move to fervent memory... **It is proper to accord them a fervent and reverent adoration.** [16]

Many Christians complained the Ten Commandments forbade idolatry of images - yet the Church had changed them! In response, the Roman Church claimed they did not '*change*' them, they only numbered them differently. The first and second were merged - actually the second "*You shalt not worship graven images*" was dropped as redundant - interpreted as the same as putting other gods before the Lord which was covered by the first. The last one was divided into two - since coveting a neighbor's ass - and a neighbor's wife's ass - were adjudged to be different. The Bible was not changed but the Catechism was. **All Roman Church materials now refer only to the '*new-official-best-most-authoritative*' Ten Commandments!**

There are a couple of problems. **One**, the Second Commandment is not redundant of the First - since it prohibits the worship of '*any image or any likeness of any thing*' not merely idols of gods. **The worship of '*images and things*' is exactly what the Second Nicene Council unanimously santified!** The opposition to worship of images, or '*iconoclasm*,' was declared a Jewish heresy and '*Judaizers*' were liable to extreme sanction. **Two, the cross was brought into the creed by Constantine.** It was never an icon of the Messianic-Apostolic Church. It is not mentioned in either the Greek or Hebrew Bibles, neither in the New Testament nor the Old. **Equating the human glorification of the cross as divine license for idolatry is gross error!**

---

[16] Public Declaration of the Second Nicene Council, published to all churches.

I know there are many readers who struggle to grasp an understanding of idolatry - especially as it relates to the cross. Independent of this book, I had prepared an article on the subject which I am now including with hope that it will help.

Crosstianity - A New Religion
Miles R. Jones - August 2021

It is *"a new religion that will bring you to your knees"* as the old song goes. I live in a community that has erected a seven-hundred-seventy-seven foot hollow cross on a hill overlooking the town. It is a beautiful place, a calm place, a spiritual place, with a gorgeous garden full of remarkable sculptures, a great fountain, scriptural verses inset into the walkways in three languages (English, Spanish & German), picnic tables among the shade trees, beautiful spiritual music playing, free religious literature, a truly great view of the countryside and, of course, a 777 foot cross. I go up there often enough. It is only a couple of miles from my home. The Messianic group of which I was a part even meets there for some of their Sabbath gatherings. Lots of people are getting saved there and it has become a powerful focal point of the faithful.

Most Christians are not aware that the cross was not put into the creed until the fourth century AD when Constantine, the Roman Emperor, created a new religion called Christianity. Constantine – at the crucial battle of Milvian Bridge outside Rome - saw a vision of a cross in the sky and heard the words *"Under this sign, Conquer!"* His soldiers quickly painted the cross on their shields and went on to conquer Rome. The rest is history, as they say, except for a few niggling details.

The pagan cross pre-dated Christianity and yes, it was used as a Roman standard in battle long before Milvian Bridge. The cross has a long pagan history. The vision was spin, invented a decade or so after the battle by Bishop Eusebius of Caesarea, to cement Constantine's appeal to Christians - already a significant part of the population of the Roman Empire. It worked, and **Constantine added the words *Cross* and *Crucifixion* into the Christian Creed. It may surprise the reader to know that the cross is never mentioned in the earliest Greek New Testament manuscripts.** It is a fourth-century Roman invention.

"The word 'cross' appears 28 times in the New Testament, and in all cases, it is translated from the Greek word 'stauros'. The original meaning of this word was not 'a cross' but 'an upright stake.' The words *cross, crucify,* and *crucifixion* were added into Scripture in the fourth century as part of the new religion along with a new Sabbath day (Sunday) and the new feast days of Easter and Xmas, Christmas. In Greek the X (chi) is the first letter in Christ. There are many religious symbols, icons and anagrams of the cross, representing Christ and Christianity.

The point is that there is a world of difference between praying AT the cross and praying TO the cross. Some may think this far too trivial a point, but it isn't really. Would it be better if we used a symbol from the Bible - such as the Menorah - designed by Yehovah himself? (Exodus 25:31-40) Would a 777 foot Menorah be better, more godly? Not really, not if you understand why the worship of images and idols is expressly forbidden. It is so much easier to worship the **SEEN** than the **UNSEEN** - to bow down to an image or icon in stone (or wood or metal or paint or plaster) rather than to stretch one's mind and spirit to walk in a covenant of absolute truth and love with the Creator. That is why the 2nd Commandment states, *"You shall not make unto you any graven image, nor any likeness of any thing... you shall not bow down yourself to them nor worship them!"* (Exodus 20:4-5).

Another icon meticulously designed by our Maker was the Temple. Devotion to it misled the Jewish people to become Temple worshippers. They subtly shifted their focus and allegiance from Yehovah to the Temple and its officials - high priests and such - known as the Sadducees - (Righteous Ones). The Messiah's *'Talmidim' - students*, who became His *Apostles* - were full of awe as they showed Yeshua the truly incredible Temple and surrounding complex that had been recently completed by Herod. Herod was known as the Great - because of his massive building projects. His majestic and beautiful gold-plated Temple gave this king spiritual legitimacy among the people - although he was one of the darkest, cruelest, most evil monarchs ever to ascend the throne. It was Herod Magnus (the Great) who ordered the slaying of all the infants of Bethlehem, and his son Herod Antipas who engineered the death of the Messiah.

Yeshua was not impressed with the Temple. *"See you not all of these things? Truly I say unto you there shall not be left here one stone upon another, that shall not be thrown down."* (Matthew 24:2). And so it happened, not 40 years later, the Romans burnt the Temple down, all the thin gold plate melted and ran between the stones, and literally every stone was thrown down from the others in order to scavenge the gold. Yeshua did not hesitate to condemn the idolatrous Temple worship in public either.

777-foot cross in Kerrville, Tx

"Tear down this Temple and in three days I will raise it up!" (John 2:19). This raised the ire of the Temple crowd. At His crucifixion they mocked him, *"You, who would destroy the Temple and rebuild it in three days, save yourself, and come down from the stake."* (Mark 15:29-30).

The Messiah did return from the grave in three days as He promised. He will also return among us again! **Will we recognize the Messiah when he returns?** I don't know that he will be doing the *robe-&-long-hair* thing anymore. **He may show up in a beat-up pickup wearing scuffed boots, faded jeans, and a T-shirt. I do not really know, but I do know that only seeing the surface of things is the problem, isn't it?**

I also know the good people of my community – I know their hearts and their devotion to the Word – so I am certain that many, I pray most of them will indeed recognize the Messiah and welcome Him. But what if the Messiah ignores the big, beautiful Cathedrals and Churches and Temples? After all, they have been built as appropriately grandiose places for Him to *"tabernacle among us,"* another phrase that does not appear in Scripture. What if Yeshua stands before our 777 foot cross and says, ***"This is not my symbol? Tear it down!"*** Do you think that might arouse some ire, perhaps even some violent passions? I suspect so. But then we would know, for sure, the difference between Crosstians - and followers of the Messiah, wouldn't we? [End]

Waldensian Rejection of Idolatry

The supremacy of Rome had by no means been established prior to 1000 AD. These disputes with the Vaudois churches over idolatry would eventually lead to the Reformation. Pope Zachary and "*Roman Catholic authors accused them of heresy.*"[17]

> We have ascertained, by the letter even of the pope, the existence, in the eighth century, of priests and Christians united in religious assemblies... not in subjection to the see of Rome... The prelates of the second council of Nicea having anathematized those who refused to worship images, Charlemagne observed,
>
> '*In so doing, they had anathematized and branded as heretics their own fathers, and as they had been consecrated by them - their consecration was null - therefore, they were not themselves true priests.*' [18]

Early in the seventh century, Claude was appointed bishop of Turin deep in the heart of Vaudois country in the Piedmont adjacent to Lombardy. "*I found the basilicks full of execrable impurities and images, contrary to the commands of the truth (of the gospel); and as I alone have overturned all these things that others adore, it is against me alone they are embittered.*"[19]

> We ought, then, carefully to bear this in mind, that all those who pay divine honors, not only to visible images, but to any creature, whether celestial or terrestrial, spiritual or corporeal, and who expect from it the salvation which comes from God alone, are of that class whom the apostle describes as **serving the creature more than the Creator...**
>
> There are many things that had a connection with Christ... **Let us adore asses since he entered Jerusalem mounted upon an ass... To serve God in this manner is to forsake Him.** [19]

Claude served northern Italy for seventeen years. He built upon the foundations set by Vigilantius, Serenus and "*the majority of bishops in the wide domain of Charlemagne.*" Claude - "*This bishop of Turin, a man of eloquence and austere manners, had a great number of partisans. **These persons, anathematized by the pope and persecuted by the lay princes, were chased from the open country and forced to take refuge in the mountains***."[20]

---

[17] Antoine Monastier, 1859:p.12, *The History of the Vaudois Church*.
[18] Dupin, *Nouvelle Bibliothèque*, t.v, p. 148. [19] *Op. cit.*, Monastier, pp.15 & 19.
[20] Costa de Beauregard, 1816, *Memoires Historiques*, t. ii, p.50.

In 945, Hatto was bishop of Vercelli in the Piedmont, he wrote in his epistles of believers who remained outside the church over doctrinal differences, *"Alas that these miserable offenders have separated themselves from our holy mother church and the clergy, by whose means alone you can attain salvation."*[21a] The doctrinal differences described in his letters were those of the Vaudois. Bishop Hatto's letter was an admission those believers in northern Italy had remained separate from the Roman Church.

In 1050, Pietro Damiano wrote to Adelaide (countess of Savoy and duchess of the Alpine regions of the Piedmont) complaining *"the clergy in the domains of this princess did not observe the ordinances of the church."*[21b] In 1108, Abbot Rodolph was quoted as *"speaking of a country which he was anxious to visit when he should cross the Alps, on his way to Rome: 'Moreover, he heard that the land to which he had intended to travel was a country polluted by an inveterate heresy respecting the body and blood of the Lord.'"*[21c] This refers to the Vaudois' rejection of transubstantiation - the doctrine that the wine and the host of communion actually became the blood and flesh of Christ when blessed. The Church paraded the host throughout the city before communion & required the faithful to bow before it!

In the tenth century, the count of Turin and the bishop of Asti joined forces to destroy the heretics in their district, *"pursuing them with fire and sword, committing them and their villages to the flames... These facts demonstrate the existence, in the tenth and eleventh centuries, of a church distinct from the Roman - in the north of Italy."*[21d] In 1120, Bruno d'Asti, bishop of Segni, wrote *"**from the time of St. Leo**... The [Roman] church was already so corrupted, that it was difficult to find an individual [clergy] not guilty of simony [trafficking in sacred objects] or who has not been ordained by simoniacs... We met with persons who... maintain the priesthood has failed in the church since that time"*[22] [brackets mine]. **"The Vaudois trace back their belief to Leo, an associate and contemporary of [pope] Sylvester, bishop of Rome in the time of emperor Constantine."**[21e] Despite these slaughters, the Vaudois remained strong in their Alpine valleys.

[21a] Antoine Monastier, 1859, p.26, *History of the Vaudois Church*, citing *Dacherii Spicilegium*, t.viii, p.110. [21b] *Ibid.*, p.26, citing *Opera Damiani*, p.556. [21c] *Ibid.*, Monastier, p.26, citing *Chronicle of St Thron*, by abbott Rodolph, 1108-1136.
[21d] *Ibid.*, p.28. [22] *Maxima Bibliotheca*, t. xx, col. 1734. [21e] *Op.cit.*, Monastier, p.28.

Missionary zeal was a defining trait of the Neo-Messianic movements of the Middle Ages. The Waldensians had sent out missionaries to all points of the compass.

> There can be no doubt that the evangelical truth which sought to manifest itself, was conveyed to different places, by persons who were not natives of the districts in which they propagated it... **We see by the writings of the Vaudois... that missionary work was held in honor among them... Italy is pointed out, on two occasions, as the native country of these abettors of heresy**... the heretics of Orleans had been won over to heresy by a woman from Italy, and the movement in Arras was owing to the teachings of persons devoted to the study of the Scriptures, who also came from Italy.[23]

These heretics to which we refer *"admit of... no veneration for the Savior's cross, the images of saints, churches and altars... They falsely pretend to follow the lives of the Apostles, saying that they may not lie, nor swear at all."*[23] These are the issues for which the Vaudois rejected the Church of Rome.

"The brethren in the valleys never lost the knowledge and consciousness of their origin and unbroken history... they could always assert... the uniformity of their faith, from father to son, through time immemorial, even from the very age of the Apostles."[24] Rorenco, in his 1630 history of the Waldenses, wrote, *"The Waldenses are so ancient as to afford no absolute certainty in regard to the precise time of their origin, but that at all events, in the ninth and tenth centuries they were even then not a new sect... Claude of Turin was to be reckoned among those fomenters of opinion which had preceded them."*[25] Other notable evangelists who sprang from within the brethren of the Vaudois were Pierre de Bruys and Henry the Italian.

Pierre came from Dauphiné adjoining the Vaudois valleys. About 1117, *"They began to disseminate their doctrines in La Septimanie, which... included Dauphiné and Provence. From Provence they passed into Languedoc and Gascogne from whence their so-called heresy penetrated Spain and England."*[23]

---

[23] A. Monastier,1859:p.35-38, *History of the Vaudois*. [24] Broadbent,1931:p.111, *The Pilgrim Church*. [25] Marco Rorenco, 1630, *History of the Waldenses*.

After great success in evangelizing together Pierre and Henry parted ways in order to spread the word farther. Pierre de Bruys, after 20 years of speaking out bravely - was seized and martyred - burned to death in 1126 at St. Gilles in Languedoc. Henry continued to Lausanne and Mans joined by other Italian brethren of the Vaudois. He obtained permission from Heribert, the departing bishop of Mans, to preach in the churches in his absence. **The populace were electrified by his preaching!** The clergy forbade the *"captivating orator"* to preach any further. There was a huge uproar! Despite this Henry was forced to leave. He proceeded to Poitiers, Périgueux, Bordeaux and Toulouse. Henry was arrested in Arles, condemned to death at a council in Rheims and thrown into prison where he died.

"The success of Pierre de Bruys and Henry was astonishing. The work in which they labored, seconded by brethren whose names have not come down to us, was rapidly consolidated and spread into many districts, in spite of the efforts of part of the clergy and the popes to destroy it."[26] **The pure Gospel had been revived among the stifled congregations of Catholicism, and the effect was like a spark among dry leaves!** The number of followers where they preached continued to swell, leaving the Roman Church in *"extreme desolation"* - many churches deserted - and its leaders bemoaning *"For a long time, in the neighborhood of Toulouse, there has arisen a damnable heresy... spreading like a cancer it has already infected Gascogne and many other provinces... especially in Burgundy and Flanders... the error has made such astonishing progress it gained over the greater part of the ecclesiastics and the nobility of... Languedoc."*[26]

To stop this Gospel tide building to a flood - the Roman Church called a series of *'emergency'* councils during the ensuing decades. They condemned the Neo-Messianic movement as *'heresy'* which did nothing to stop it. In 1208 the Crusade against the Cathars of Languedoc was launched. **The council of Toulouse decreed *"the Bible... was forbidden to the laity, and that... no part of it be translated into their own language."*[27] It was too late, the Word would not go back in the box! In 1210, the Roman Church took off the velvet gloves - implementing the Inquisition to root out those not killed in the Crusades!**

[26] Antoine Monastier, 1859:p.40-41, *A History of the Vaudois Church*.
[27] Eric Broadbent, 1931:p.109, *The Pilgrim Church*.

Peter Waldo - Poor Men of Lyons

An important player in this rising Gospel tide was Peter Waldo. He was a rich merchant and banker from Lyons. It is possible he took his name from his communion and connection with the Waldensians - *Pierre du Valdes*. He devoted himself to the study of Scripture and had begun to translate it into the Romance dialect by 1160. By 1173, taking his cues from Scripture he sold all his goods and distributed the money to the poor.

In 1179, in an apparent attempt to reconcile with the Roman Church, Waldo appealed to the third Lateran Council for recognition of his Scripture and permission to preach it. He was laughed at and scornfully ejected from the council with "*shouts of derision.*" By 1180 he devoted himself to traveling and preaching. By 1184, Waldo had been excommunicated and driven out of Lyons by Imperial edict. By 1177, followers of Waldo, called "*Poor Men of Lyons*" had spread the message as far as Frankfort and Nuremberg. Waldo traveled and preached until his death in Bohemia in 1217.

These Neo-Messianics were called by many names. In northern France and Germany "*Tisserands*" (weavers), in Bohemia the "*Bohemian Brethren,*" in Italy "*Valdenses,*" in France "*Vaudois,*" etc. Pope Gregory, in 1263, decreed "*We excommunicate and anathematize all heretics, Cathars, Patarenes, Poor Men of Lyons, Passagini, Josepini, Arnaldistae, Speronistae, and other, **by whatever names they may be known, having indeed different faces, but being united**...*"[55] David of Augsburg, an Inquisitor, conceded that formerly "***the sects were one sect.***" This "*united*" movement is never addressed in church chronicles.

> **Primitive churches were widespread in Europe** in the twelfth and thirteenth centuries... although many names were given to them, and there must have been a variety of views among so many, **yet they were essentially one**, and had constant communication and fellowship with one another.
>
> The doctrines and practices of these brethren, known as **Waldenses, and also by other names, were... an old tradition... close to that of apostolic days, and far removed from that which the dominant Churches had developed.**[28]

---

[28] Eric Broadbent, 1931:p.117, *The Pilgrim Church*.

The propaganda of the Roman Church was that all these congregations were recent, erroneous, heretical schisms of the *'Holy Mother Church'* of Rome. Waldensians were said to have originated with Peter Waldo in the late twelfth century no earlier than 1170. His followers were called *"Poor Men of Lyons"* or *"Leonists."* **Waldensians simply called themselves Christians!**

To Rome every other church was designated as a personality cult of heretics. Rather than be recognized as a widespread movement, they were dismissed as a plague of (heretical) pests! The *'plague of pests'* argument is so flimsy it only works if you demonize or destroy all those who disagree. Abbot Fleury wrote:

> These persons assemble on certain nights in a specified house… and recite the names of demons in the form of a litany - till, all at once, they see a demon descend in the shape of a small animal. Immediately all the lights are put out, which is the signal for general debauchery with the females present: one of the offspring of this intercourse, when eight days old, is brought into the midst of their assembly, thrown into a large fire, and burned to a cinder. They collect these ashes, and preserve them with as much veneration as Christians preserve the body of Jesus Christ… Such was the magical virtue of these ashes… they carried with them the powder of dead infants, and if they could make persons take any of it, they would directly become Manicheans [heretics] like themselves.[20] [brackets mine]

Fleury's accusations are ironic - the Roman Church was the only player in this story who burnt human beings to ashes! The propaganda against the Waldensians was so evil and exaggerated, when the Duke of Savoy went among his subjects to see if the stories were true, he exclaimed *"Is it possible that these are the children of heretics? What charming creatures they are! They are by far the prettiest children I ever saw."* The bishops had claimed they were born *"with black throats, rough teeth, and goat's feet."*[30]

So pervasive was the propagandizing of the Roman Church that the word *'Vaudois'* became synonymous with *sorcerer*. Centuries later in 1430, Joan of Arc was burned to death by the church - accused, and convicted, of being a *'Vaudoise.'*[29]

---

[29] Antoine Monastier, 1859:p.33 & 36, *The History of the Vaudois Church*.
[30] Alexis Muston, 1875, vol.1, p.36, *Israel of the Alps*.

La Nobla Leyzon - [Troubadour poem]

O Brethren, give ear to a noble lesson.
We ought always to watch and pray,
For we see the world nigh to a conclusion.
We ought to strive to do good works,
Seeing that the end of this world approaches.
**There are already 1100 years fully accomplished,
Since it was written thus, for we are in the last time**...

If there be anyone who loves and fears Jesus Christ,
Who will not curse, nor swear, nor lie'
Nor be unchaste, nor kill, nor take what is another's,
Nor take vengeance on his enemies,
They say he is a <u>Vaudès</u> and worthy of death!

This Troubadour poem states the Vaudès [Vaudois] existed 1100 years from the time of Christ. The claim of the Roman Church was, and remains, that the Waldenses were only followers of Peter Waldo, after whom they were named, who appeared on the scene about 1170 almost a century after the date of *La Nobla Leyzon*. An early historian of the Waldensians, Bernard de Fontcaud who died in 1193 (contemporary with Peter Waldo) *"makes no mention of Valdo in his work,"* entitled *Contra Valdenses et Arianos*. Another contemporary of Waldo, Eberhard de Bethune, also writes *"of the Vaudois without speaking of Valdo."* Either they knew nothing of Peter Waldo or did not associate him with the Vaudois, either way makes it clear *"that the Vaudois of whom he speaks are anterior to Valdo."*[31]

Since the time of Vigilantius (4th century), the same region, churches, and people - stood against Rome over the same issues. **"Vigilantius has been called 'The Forerunner of the Reformation'... the influence of his preaching and leadership among the Waldenses burned its way across the centuries until it united with the heroic reforms of Luther.** *As the Papacy promoted persecutions... against the Waldenses, it proclaimed the 'heresy' of these regions as being of the same brand as that of Vigilantius... later... attacks [were leveled] against Claude, bishop of Milan, and... his followers on the basis that he was infected with the 'poison' of Vigilantius."*[32] So, even the Pope acknowledged these Waldensian issues went back to Vigilantius.

[31] Alexis Muston, 1875, vol.1, p.18, *Israel of the Alps*. [32] Wilkinson, 1944, p.70.

Time after time, these Neo-Messianic reformers drew strength from *"the intimate connection"* such as that *"of Pierre de Bruys and Henry with the Christians of the valleys of the Piedmont... inheritors of the principles of Claude of Turin and the friends of Vigilantius."*[60] *"From the days of the Gallic reformer [Vigilantius]... churches of northern Italy and southern France bore an entirely different color from that* [of Rome]"[33] One reason was - **they had their own Bible in their own language!**

Northern Italy was a different communion than the Roman south, it was called the Italick Communion and its text the *Italick Bible*. The vast majority of Bible texts of the period worldwide were either the *Itala* (aka *Italick*), for Romance language speakers, or the *Textus Receptus* of Lucian, called the Antiochan, Traditional, or *Received Text*. Ulfias' *Gothic Bible* was translated from the Lucian text before the time of Eusebius. The Gauls, and other Celts, also used this *Textus Receptus,* transmitted and translated by the Galatians into their own Gallic (Celtic) language.

The Celtic Church

Saint Patrick converted Ireland with the Celtic Bible, *"It was the Celtic, or Galatian type of the New Testament which evangelized Great Britain... A large number of this Celtic community - colonists from Asia Minor - migrated to Ireland (Erin) and laid the foundation of the pre-Patrick church."*[34] Patrick was born in Britain about 389 AD, while it was still Roman territory. **Patrick's family were Jewish Christians. His ancestors had been brought there from Jerusalem centuries before.**

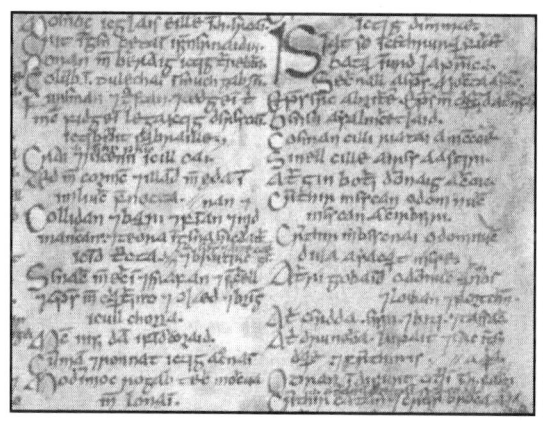

Book of Leinster, 1160 AD, page 353 (on left) ***"Patrick was truly of the Sons of Israel.*** When the Children of Israel were scattered by Titus and Vespasian in bondage throughout the four quarters of the world... then did Patrick's stock come to Britain."

---
[33] Antoine Monastier, 1859, p.52, *History of the Vaudois Church*.
[34] Benjamin Wilkinson, 1944, pp.70 & 75, *Truth Triumphant*.

Messianic believers in Jerusalem were warned by Yeshua in Luke 21:20 that *"when you shall see Jerusalem encompassed by armies, then know that the desolation thereof is nigh."* Jewish Christians fled to Pella, those left behind were enslaved and sent to Roman colonies - like Britain. The book of Leinster tells us Patrick's family were just such Messianics brought to Britain.

This is a stunning revelation! Patrick was a Messianic Christian and his Celtic Church was a Messianic Church! *"The Celtic Church was an outpost of first century Apostolic Christianity. Planted in 70 AD by Messianic Jews from Jerusalem. No wonder they did the same things the Apostles did. They had the same kind of Christianity the Apostles had. So the Celtic Church gives us the clearest picture, outside of the New Testament, of the early Apostolic Church!"* [35]

At the age of 16, Patrick was captured by raiders from Ireland and taken there as a slave. Patrick had turned away from his faith but now he returned to it with fervor. *"Constantly I used to pray in the daytime. Love of God and His fear increased more and more. My faith grew and my spirit was stirred up… Before the dawn I used to wake up to prayer."* [35]

Yehovah prophesied to Patrick and told him to return home. Patrick escaped, found passage on a ship, rejoined his family in Britain, and dedicated himself to the study of the Bible. When Patrick was ready, Yehovah sent him back to Ireland. *"It was not any grace in me, but God who conquered in me, so that I came to the heathen of Ireland to preach the Gospel… And if I should be found worthy, I am ready to give even my life for His name's sake unfalteringly and gladly, and there* (in Ireland) *I desire to spend it until I die. If our Lord should grant it to me."* [35]

Patrick preached the Bible… as the sole authority for founding the Irish Church… The training centers he founded, which later grew into colleges and large universities, were all Bible schools. Famous students of these schools - Columba, who brought Scotland to Christ; Aidan, who won pagan England to the gospel, and Columbanus with his successors, who brought Christianity to Germany, France, Switzerland, and Italy… [36]

---

[35] H.A. Ironside, 2017:p.16, *The Real Saint Patrick*, Crossreach Pub.. [35] *Ibid.*, p.8. [35] *Ibid.*, p.12. [36] Benjamin Wilkinson, 1944, p. 77, *Truth Triumphant*.

> Patrick was called the *'Great Reviver.'* "There is no saint for whom there are claimed so many resurrection miracles. There were as many as 39 of these... 33 in one report."[37]

> For the blind and the lame, the deaf and the dumb, the palsied, the lunatic, the leprous, the epileptic, all who labored under any disease, did he... restore unto entire health: and in these good deeds was he daily practiced. 33 dead men did this *'Great Reviver'* - raise from the dead.[37]

When Patrick arrived in Dublin, the son of King Alphimus had been found dead in his chamber. The tragedy doubled when it was discovered that his daughter had drowned that same morning as she went into the river to bathe. Word came to the king - of Patrick - whose work in miracles preceded him. Patrick raised both children from the dead! The whole of Alphimus' kingdom was baptized. **The Messianic Apostles had spread the Gospel through the known world with such miracles - it was the same here!** Within 30 years the whole of Ireland turned to God and His Son. During that time, Patrick inspired the building of 700 churches, ordained 5,000 priests, and consecrated 350 bishops.[37]

At the time, 99% of Europeans were illiterate, including most kings, and the vast majority of Catholic clergy. Among the Celtic Church, however, *"Every believer was taught to read and study Bible... people from Iona come and read the Bible in Hebrew, Greek, Gaelic and Latin."*[37] *"The... Latin version of Jerome was not publicly read in Patrick's day... The earlier Latin version of the Bible, **known as the Itala**, was publicly used... **It was 900 years before Jerome's Vulgate could make headway in the West against the Itala."*** [38] **The Word of Yehovah, Yeshua, and the light of the Holy Spirit, passed intact from each generation to the next, conquering the Celtic nations in their wake!**

Patrick and his followers came across a valley, in Ireland, filled with heavenly light and the voice of a multitude of angels. A follower of Patrick, named Comgall, in 555 AD, established an apostolic training center there in the *"Valley of Angels,"* called Bangor. **The Irish, and other Celts, dedicated themselves to perpetual praise of God - *'Laus Perennis.'***

---

[37] H.A. Ironside, 2017:p.10, *Real St. Patrick*, Crossreach Publications, US..
[37] *Ibid.*, Ironside, 2017:p.19&21. [38] William Betham, *Irish Antiquarian Researches*.

*"They followed the worship of the ancient Jewish temple, and maintained continual praise day and night... At any hour of the day or night there were at least 300 people lifting up continual praise... They released the power of God upon the land!... If you asked the Celts the secret of their spiritual power, they would tell you without hesitation it was 'Continual Praise!' They called it **Laus Perennis**."*[39]

Columba landed at Iona on Scottish soil in 563 AD. He traveled from Ireland across the sea in a tiny boat called a coracle along with 12 missionary companions. He established a monastery at Iona to train believers to go into the savage territory of the Picts to bring them to faith. *"Holy texts from around Europe were copied, poetry flourished... the monastery's intellectual horizons stretched right across Christendom. As a consequence **Iona** amassed one of the greatest libraries in Western Europe and **became a powerhouse of Dark Age learning**... The Book of Kells, now held in Trinity College Dublin, was crafted on Iona."*[40]

The last remnant of the early church was the Celtic Church in Scotland and Ireland! The Celtic Church was the last surviving outpost of miraculous Christianity. Men like Patrick, Columba, and many others continued to heal the sick, raise the dead, and perform miraculous signs and wonders![39]

Historians called Iona, *'the light of the Western world.'* **Iona was the light of God during the darkness of religious terror and tyranny of the Dark Ages!** Iona in Scotland - and other Celtic Bible centers - such as Armaugh and Bangor in Ireland, Lindisfarne and Whitby in England, were the light of God's truth. Elsewhere, the Bible was forbidden to be read by believers and it was a death sentence to translate it into the common tongue. Not in Iona, there the Gospel spread with a rapidity that is the trademark of *The Received Text* of the Word.

Adamnan, the successor to Columba at Iona, took in hand to write *The Life of St. Columba*. *"It was divided into three sections: 1) Divine Visitations (when the angels came down, times when the Shekinah Glory was visible!) 2) Prophetic Words, 3) Miracles that changed Scotland.* **On this island, the power of the early church was preserved for hundreds of years!**"[41]

[39] H.A. Ironside, 2017:p.18 & p.7, *The Real St. Patrick*, Crossreach Publications..
[40] bbc.co.uk/history/scotland/articles/iona. [41] Ironside, 2017:p.18 & p.7.

The living presence of God Almighty - the Shekinah Glory of Yehovah Himself - is the most powerful of spiritual visitations! The appearance of the Shekinah is spoken of in the Bible: at Sinai, in the first Temple, in the upper room at Pentecost (Shavuot) in Jerusalem. Also, historically, it appeared in Herrnhut in the Moravian Revival, the Welsh Revival, the Kentucky Revival. The Shekinah is barely mentioned in Catholic theology. One might assume it would draw attention to the fact there has been no known appearance of the Shekinah in the Roman Church. **The living presence of God has only descended upon Jews, Messianics, and Protestant reformers, heretics all!**

Brigid, patron saint of scholars. Women were educated and served equally with men in the Celtic Church.

The Celtic Church did not believe what Catholics believe! They didn't believe in purgatory, they didn't honor the Pope, they didn't pray to Mary. Their priests married and had children! They baptised believers in water by immersion... **They observed a 'Christian Passover,'** rather than a Roman Easter. They rested on the seventh day [Saturday], they even used the Hebrew time frame - They began their days in evening rather than morning.[72] **Above all else, they maintained 'Laus Perennis' - continual prayer and praise for several centuries!"**[42]

The Roman Church later appropriated the miraculous ministry of Patrick and his followers as their own. Patrick had no connection with Rome - although centuries later papal proponents labored mightily to create one. **Patrick stood in opposition to Rome!** Roman priests did not reach Ireland until 200 years later.

In 715, Rome and the nobility united, attacked Iona, expelled the Celtic clergy, and tore the heart out of the Celtic Church! The 'Laus Perrenis' of continual praise ceased and the Shekinah Glory of the living presence of God was seen no more. The daily presence of miracles came to an end!

---

[42] H.A. Ironside, 2017:p.14 & p.22, Crossreach Publications, US.

Chapter Five
The Age of Chivalry & Crusades

*Yet have I set my King upon my holy hill of Zion.
I will declare the decree: Yehovah has said unto me,*
"You are my Son, this day have I begotten you."
Psalm 2:6-7

The Roman Church controlled the narrative of history in the West, imbuing us with a romantic image of Medieval knights going forth to the Holy Land to save it from the infidel Muslims. In fact, the crusades were initiated to destroy the Roman Church's competitors including Messianics, Christians, Muslims, and Jews.

The historical narrative was perverted in other ways. Those who did not go along with the doctrinal dictates of the Church of Rome were declared '*heretic*,' slaughtered and slandered - blackening their memory in every manner conceivable even after death. Many, if not most of these heretics were those holding to the original Gospels and to restoring the Messianic-Apostolic Church of Yeshua the Messiah. They had *The Received Text* of the Bible which was compiled two centuries before the Roman versions. They considered many of the doctrines of Rome to be not only unscriptural but evil incarnate. They refused to comply with demands and threats that they bow to the authority of Rome. For this defiance - countless thousands were martyred during the Crusades and the Inquisitions over the centuries!

The influence of these Neo-Messianics created a unique and beautiful culture in the Middle Ages - often called Chivalry - bringing ideas and knowledge from the East. It raised women to equality with men. It promoted beauty, poetry and faithful romantic love as the primary rationale for relations between men and women. It preserved *The Received Text* of the Bible. **The Cathar Bible, and other Neo-Messianic Scriptures preserved the translation of *The Hebrew Gospels* via the *Itala*.**

Western civilization was permanently impacted by the effects of '*Courtly Love!*' It remains an ideal, a myth, an everlasting vision of Camelot and the quest for The Holy Grail. The bloom of that flower was trampled by the Crusades. The Cathars and other Neo-Messianic movements left a legacy - not only the dream of Camelot - but they sowed the seeds of the Reformation.

The Age of Chivalry

To understand the context of the times we must grasp the spiritual warfare between the *"sons of Zion and the Sons of Greece"* raging in the Middle Ages! The key to understanding the Age of Chivalry is in the hands of a 15-year-old maiden named Aliénor (*Eleanor*).

Eleanor was the daughter and heir of Duke (*William*) Guillaume X of Aquitaine. Eleanor of Aquitaine's grandfather was **Guillaume IX famed as the first of the troubadours**, *"medieval French poets who envisioned an ideal of courtly love, where a woman's love was envisioned to be a source of almost divine salvation and bliss, worthy of the patient work it took to court and win her affection."*[1]

Aquitaine comprised a third of France right in the center in between the power of Paris and the high civilization of the ancient Langueduc south. Aquitaine was the richest region of Europe - far richer than those of the kings of France or England.

---
[1] *Eleanor of Aquitaine: A Life from Beginning to End*, 2018, Hourly History.

The peoples of Europe had coalesced into nation-states but these countries were not yet a cohesive whole. The former tribal warlords were now the landed gentry, holding title, wealth and power greater than that of their kings. They operated most often as independent fiefdoms. Their noble families constantly intermarried in order to cement complex ever-changing alliances of power. The kings of France were often English and the kings of England often French, or at least half. Warfare among the power elite was constant and complicated.

The Roman Church also competed for power as the vestige of the Holy Roman Empire, claiming authority over all Christian nations in Europe. They had broken with the Greek Orthodox Church, now enthroned in Constantinople over the Byzantine Empire. The Nestorian Church, far to the East, though quite large in population and extent was of little notice or concern to the Europeans. The Arab Muslims had settled down seemingly immovable in Iberia. The Muslim Ottoman Turks were gaining strength in Anatolia [Turkey] gradually eating away at the territory of the Byzantines. **Although the Roman Church had developed a high culture and literature in Latin, their intellectual foundations were still based on Greek thought at its core.**

Duke Guillaume IX, Eleanor's troubadour grandfather, was often in defiance of the Medieval Roman Church. This may be a major reason why his son, Guillaume X set out on a pilgrimage to St. James of Compostela in order to rectify his family's opposition to the Church. It is unlikely that it worked since he died in Compostela on April 9, 1137 - leaving the 15-year-old Eleanor as the Duchess of Aquitaine - the wealthiest and most powerful woman in Europe! Louis VI, king of France (her legal guardian) immediately sent his 16-year-old son and heir Louis VII to marry her. On July 25, 1137 they were married and August 8th officially enthroned as Duke & Duchess of Aquitaine.

Already a whirlwind of change had seized the young Duchess when word came that Louis VI, the king of France, had died a week before on August 1, 1137. His son, Eleanor's new husband, Louis VII had already been crowned as co-ruler of France. **So, Eleanor of Aquitaine, a young teenager, instantly became queen of France. Quite the summer!**

It is said that Louis VII was so enamored of his beautiful young queen that some years later when he *'took the cross'* to lead the 2nd Crusade he could not stand to leave her. So, Eleanor took the cross as well, and joined him in leading the crusade.

A popular movement called *'The People's Crusade'* had been initiated by the preaching of Peter the Hermit. Hordes of peasants crossed Europe slaughtering Jews and sacking their communities - whipped up by the anti-Semitic rantings of Peter. *"A madness seized the cities of the Rhine... 'Let us be revenged for our Messiah upon the Jews.'"*[2] Once in Anatolia they were soundly defeated by the Turks.

Eleanor of Aquitaine
1122-1204
Teenage Queen of France

The Prince's Crusade, mostly a French affair called the First Crusade, was probably spurred by this popular uprising. Islamic expansion had taken the Holy Land and now was pushing deep into Anatolia. The First Crusade, called by Pope Urban II forty years earlier in 1095, caught the Muslims by surprise. The Crusade soon arrived in the Mid East - **retook parts of Anatolia and the Holy Land, establishing the Christian kingdom of Jerusalem which would stand for 150 years even though often threatened by Muslim armies**. The Holy Land was soon under siege when Turks took the key city of Edessa.

That was when Louis VII of France rallied his barons and rushed to the rescue of the Holy Land. Louis was trained as a priest not a soldier - only crowned heir after his older brother's death. Whether he acted out of piety, was carried away by the spirit of the times, or perhaps was showing off for his queen - we will never be certain. What is certain was the catastrophe of the Second Crusade. The Turks caught their train by surprise in the mountains and cut them in two. Although the king and queen escaped, many others were killed. Under constant attack, Louis retreated to the sea where he and Eleanor took ship to Antioch.

[2] Hugh Schoenfield, 1936, reprint 2009:p.103, *History of Jewish Christianity*.

Louis abandoned many of his troops on the shore unable to find or pay for enough ships to carry them. Generally the barons paid for their own troops, equipment and expenses in the field. Perhaps this was Louis' rationale for leaving them. Whatever the reason - it was a disaster! *"These soldiers met an unhappy end, facing deprivation and illness before finally falling prey to Turkish attacks."*[3] Eleanor was alternately blamed for the disaster or heralded as an amazon warrior, riding a horse, armed like a man leading a troop of women-at-arms. **What was far more likely is that the young Eleanor played no part in the defeat but was profoundly disgusted at the needless death and destruction caused by her husband's incompetence.**

They arrived in Antioch which was ruled by Eleanor's uncle, Raymond. Raymond wanted Louis to take his remaining troops to help defend Aleppo. Louis wanted to make pilgrimage to Jerusalem. Eleanor wanted an annulment of their marriage. She refused to go to Jerusalem. After visiting some holy sites and a few more unsuccessful military engagements, Louis and Eleanor went back to France ...in separate ships. Louis arrived in Italy without problem. Eleanor's ship became entangled in a sea battle between Normans and Byzantines and was captured by the latter. Norman ships soon seized the Byzantine vessel and freed the captive queen of France.

Eleanor had given birth to a daughter, Marie, before leaving on the crusade. Soon after returning to France she gave birth to a second daughter, Alix. Her failure to give birth to sons finally convinced Louis to bow to her desire to annul the marriage and it was done by the same archbishop who had married them 15 years before. The reason given was *consanguinity*, they were too closely related - being cousins.

Eleanor was now free to go back to Poitiers, the capitol of Aquitaine. Twice on her journey other nobles attempted to abduct her into a forced marriage. However, they were second sons. Eleanor knew she could do better. Within two months she married Henry II of England, the Duke of Normandy. Henry was a Plantagenet, a direct descendent of William the Conqueror. Eleanor had probably fallen for Henry when he had visited the court of France in 1151, after her return from the crusades. Their marriage clearly seemed to be prearranged.

[3] *Eleanor of Aquitaine: A Life...*, 2018, page 146, Hourly History.

Henry and Eleanor were married in Poitiers on May 18, 1152. While Henry went off to make war, Eleanor stayed home in Poitiers - soon giving birth to a son, William. Louis rapidly regretted letting the rich prize of Aquitaine slip out of his hands. The marriage agreement between Eleanor and Louis deliberately left Aquitaine in her hands, not his. Now that Eleanor had a son by Henry - Louis' hopes of inheriting or controlling Aquitaine through their daughter Marie evaporated.

Along with allies, Louis moved to invade Normandy. Henry beat them back then rushed back to England to join in the civil war against their king, his cousin Stephen. Stephen offered a truce whereby Henry would support him in exchange for designating Henry as his heir - and Henry agreed. The next year Stephen died leaving Henry as king of England. **Eleanor was now queen of England!** Another whirlwind had engulfed the young queen, barely thirty and in the full bloom of her beauty. She eventually gave birth to five sons by Henry and three daughters plus her two by Louis made five daughters. **Three of her sons became kings and two of her daughters became queens.**

Eleanor ruled England during long periods while Henry was fighting on the continent. Twice the queen ordered armies into the field to put down rebellion in the king's absence. Nonetheless, Eleanor returned to Aquitaine for much of her time. It was there she initiated, with the help of her daughter Marie, the famous Court of Love. *"Knights, troubadours and poets came to do homage to Eleanor... and witness the miracle that had been wrought at her court."*[4] That miracle was *Chivalry*!

> The very embodiment of courtly poise and authority, Eleanor listened as two knights – one young and of bad character, the other older but of good – petitioned for her decision on a matter of great importance. Both men desired the love of the same woman. The younger argued that if the object of their affections chose him, then he might be inspired to be a better man... The queen, however, was not convinced... it was not a wise decision for the young woman to love someone with so bad a reputation, especially when one more deserving also vied for her affections... so saying, she pronounced for the older, settling yet another matter brought before the renowned Courts of Love.[4]

---

[4]Willow Winsham, 2017, *Sex & Citadel: Eleanor of Aquitaine & Courtly Love*.

When I first saw the painting *The Accolade* by Edmund Leighton many years ago, I immediately grasped a sense of it. People watching soldiers go off to war are often astonished at their youth, still children it seems. In this portrait the teenage queen knights a boy probably no older than her - sending him out to lay his life on the line to protect her realm, her subjects and her honor. Any modern man would have to wonder whether the new knight was in love with the queen. Any man of the Age of Chivalry would have no doubt that the brave young knight was head over heels in love with his beautiful queen. **That was Chivalry!**

The Accolade by Edmund Leighton - 1901

In the language of the south of France, Occitan, it was called '*Paratge*' meaning literally that all men of Chivalry were peers. "*Paratge denoted a whole world view… a philosophy, as alien to the modern mind as it was to the French crusaders.*"[5] It meant something more than courage in battle, respect to women, civility, gentility, and honor - even more than our word *Chivalry*. It meant a search for beauty and harmony in love, art, music and most especially in the spiritual realm. "*While stories of Arthur and his gallant knights flourished throughout Christendom, Eleanor and her ladies were living the reality – Poitiers little short of a real life Camelot!*"[6] **It was here a knight learned to be true to his beloved, his queen, no matter her rank… to be brave and devout to his mission of the Holy Grail… not to find a treasure but to drink from the chalice as had the Messiah and to know the good, the truth, the light… it was nothing short of a new, gnostic, religion - <u>that of the Underground Church</u>!**

[5] Languedoc-france.info/190403_paratge.htm.   [6] W. Winsham, 2017, *op. cit.*

The Underground Church Spreads Through Europe 1000-1300 AD

Cathars and Chivalry

"*Catharism... was by origin an Italian, Mediterranean and Balkan heresy, and came to the 'pays d'oc' by means of a journey from east to west.*"[7] The '*pay d'oc*' was Occitania, now known as Languedoc on the Mediterranean coast of southern France, and the '*langue d'oc*' was Occitan, closely related to its sister tongues Catalan [in Spain] and Provencal [France & Italy].

> During the eleventh century a Gnostic religion that had survived orthodox persecution for many centuries in the Byzantine Empire and on the Balkan Peninsula – the Bogomil religion – found its way to the Languedoc region of Southern France and to areas of Northern Italy. There it took root and flourished over the next three centuries as the Cathar religion - the tradition of the '*Good*' and '*True Christians*,' the *Bons Hommes*... simply called themselves '*Good Christians*.' During these same centuries in the area around the southern Pyrenees a form of heterodox mysticism took hold... that had historical and archetypal roots in the Gnosis and Gnosticism of late antiquity. **At precisely this time, and in the same area of southern France, there came the first flowering of the Troubadour traditions** and of the Jewish Gnosticism of Kabbalah. To the south in Spain, the mystical tradition that gave root to a Gnostic school in Islam took form.[8]

---
[7] Emmanuel Ladurie, 1978:p.287, *Montaillou: Portrait of a Medieval Village*.
[8] Gnostic Society, *Cathar Texts & Rituals*, gnosis.org/library/cathtx.htm

In many ways, chivalric ideals were married to Cathar beliefs. Rapidly spread by the troubadours from Spain - the culture of southern France, and soon all of Europe, became enraptured by a new *'way of life'* and thought - totally different from their feudal norm. Into a rigid caste system of class, wealth, privilege and power, was introduced the equality of all who practiced the *'way.'* Troubadours were equal whether peasant or prince. A warrior who fought with chivalry and courage might be knighted on the spot by another knight. All aspired to knighthood.

Troubadours were rock stars. Kings were inspired to become troubadours and they welcomed poor traveling troubadours as brothers. Cathar preachers, called *parfaits* (perfect ones), practiced the poverty, celibacy and equality only given lip service by the Roman Church, whose *"prelates lived and behaved like nobles, to whom they were generally related by ties of kinship, deriving large revenues from their ecclesiastical domains."*[9]

Cathars included women equally with men as believers (*credentes*) and teachers (*parfaits*). This was in an era where women were otherwise treated as chattel! Most marriages were arranged. Love was not a consideration. But there were women troubadours who were treated equal to their male counterparts. **Knights, Cathars and troubadours were all elevating women far above their previous status! The equality of women was a central practice of the Neo-Messianic Cathar faith.**

It was a gnostic faith. Gnosticism, **from the word *gnosis* - to know -** was integral to the grail quest. The ultimate objective of this chivalric ideal was a mystical journey to a higher level of spirituality - **a hidden knowledge that could not be put into words.** *"The institution of knighthood and the military profession were sanctified by the concept of religious chivalry."*[9]

The gnostic elements of the gospels are unmistakable - such as when Yeshua returned from the dead and took his disciples up on the mountain in Galilee to reveal *"the mystery of the kingdom of God"* before ascending into heaven (Mk 4:11, Matt 28:16, Acts 1:3). As Paul said, *"**For now we see through a glass, darkly; but then face to face: now I know in part but then shall I know even as also I am known**"* (Ist Corinthians 13:12).

---

[9] Roger Boase, 1978:p.47, *The Troubadour Revival*. [9] *Ibid.*, Roger Boase, p.19.

Catharism was introduced into Languedoc by members of the nobility. Troubadours played a central role in the spread of the ideas of Catharism and Chivalry. *"Many of the wandering troubadours were men of great piety."*[10] Change came from the primitive Christianity of the east through the Balkans into Italy - and from the Islamic west through Spain funneling ancient Greek, Hebrew and Arabic classics into France and Europe, including *The Hebrew Gospels*. France was caught in a pincer between these galvanizing influences flowing from both ends of the Mediterranean. It was called the Dark Ages because the Church forbade these ideas. Sometimes, however, ideas will not be denied!

It was through the sect of the Paulicians in the Balkans that *"the old Jewish Christians had found a voice with which they might still speak through the mouths of men of another race."*[11] Church history claims the Messianic Church disappeared in the fifth century but it had only gone underground, fleeing the fury of Roman persecution and sowing primitive churches among the peoples in the Balkans and elsewhere outside the Roman grip. There they converted new Messianics who were not Jewish.

These Neo-Messianics carried on the beliefs of the primitive church - and the Jewish Christian blood joined with theirs. *"Out of the Paulicians came the Thonrakes, Josephinists, Bogomils, Cathars, Albigensians, and Waldenses, and all their off-shoots,* **changing their names** *in their manifold manifestation,* **but scarcely their basic doctrines***, as the stream of missionaries made their way through Bulgaria, Bosnia and Hungary, along the Carpathians to the Alps and Pyrenees."*[11]

The mandate to restore the Messianic Church, its beliefs and the practices of Yeshua and his Apostles never waivered. **"We may fairly regard these groups as part of one movement, a protesting movement, preserving alive the elemental spirit of Jewish Christianity."**[11]

That leaves us with some critical questions. How could a religion that exalted celibacy be tied to a movement of amorous love? How could a religion that was pacifist have coexisted, even interacted with a militant Chivalry?

---

[10] William Stephen Gilly, 1848:p.124, *The Roumant Version of Gospel of John*.
[11] Hugh Schoenfield, 1936, reprint 2009, p.125, *History of Jewish Christianity*.

This movement of amorous Courtly Love did not originate with the Cathars. It began in the East and was passed to the West through stories such as that of Scheherazade. Long before '*A Thousand and One Arabian Nights*' became a Disney classic - it was very explicitly pornographic! The stories picked up power and poetry in Sepharad. "*Many of the early troubadours were... Catalan or Aragonese by birth.*"[12]

There was a sudden shift in attitudes towards warfare, towards marriage and towards conventions governing the expression of emotion. The romantic ideal, now largely taken for granted, that marriage should be based on love and free choice became widespread, and gentleness became the mark of a '*gentleman.*'[12]

A constant need for Spanish warriors to fight the Moors in the centuries-long struggle led to a massive influx of men entering the ranks of knighthood. The resulting imbalance of men to women in the Spanish nobility became a prime influence causing noble women to be highly valued and put upon a pedestal. It was hardly the whole reason. The spirit of the age had carried away the mind of man - Chivalry came to be thought of as the reason the Golden Age had blossomed and the lack of Courtly Love the reason for the breakdown of that glorious social order.

Hundreds of troubadours set out from Catalonia to southern France and the rest of Europe to gift them the '*Gay Science of the Troubadours!*' The knights of the round table of King Arthur have been thought to be the impetus for the Age of Chivalry. The Welsh historian Nennius (*circa* 800-830) was the first to mention the mythic king fighting against the Saxon invaders in the 6th century. "*Arthur's fame spread beyond Wales and the Celtic world, particularly after the Norman conquest of 1066 connected England to northern France.*"[13] It was Geoffrey of Monmouth who first elaborated the story into a gallant tale of magic.[14] However, it was the French who appropriated the myth in the service of love - rewriting the history of Britain to dress it in the garments of Chivalry. **So, Arabic stories of love and lust were married to a Welsh myth of gallantry, given voice by Sephardic troubadours, and exalted in the French Courts of Love!**

[12] Roger Boase, 1978:p.7, *The Troubadour Revival*. [13] history.com/Arthur/2017.
[14] Geoffrey of Monmouth, 1136, *History of the Kings of Britain*.

Although the Neo-Messianic religious movements roiling Europe at the same time did not originate Courtly Love they did help to shape it. In Spain, *"much of the messianic zeal that one finds in these love poems cannot really be understood except within the context... of the influx of 'conversos' into Christian society."*[15] Although the original movement was about physical passion it changed as it filtered through society at all levels.

> It is a custom in Spain amongst men of quality,
> even if they are not in love or have passed middle age,
> that they should, whilst attending the court,
> feign love by serving and favoring a particular lady,
> and that they should spend as much as befits their rank on
> festivities and other things organized by way of pastimes
> and amorous intrigues, without being troubled by Cupid.[16]

By the time of the Troubadour Revival in the Late Middle ages this had gradually become the norm. Troubadours had become professionals for hire. They would write poetry extolling the virtues of their patronesses - whom they would never touch. Or they would provide the tongue-tied with words for those ladies they admired from afar. **Although the sexual mores of the era were very loose - the celibacy of Cathar *parfaits* had brought a sense of balance into the cultural equation for which they were greatly admired. Cathar teachers did not solicit money, eat meat, or touch women** - a stark contrast to the pervasive perception of Roman priests as gluttonous, greedy, and lustful.

Neither did the idea of militant Chivalry begin with the Neo-Messianic Movement but *"by the belief, Islamic in origin, that those who die fighting unbelievers will be awarded eternal delights in Paradise."*[17] From the mind of Hassan Ben Sabah, and his assassins - to the popes - who guaranteed entry into heaven for all crusaders! During the persecution of the Cathars not a single one of their *parfaits* picked up arms **but many other Cathars did fight, helping to imbue Chivalry with the new idea of using might in the service of truth. 'Might for Right' rather than 'Might makes Right' became a chivalric ideal!** By contrast, slaughter had become Rome's final answer to silencing opposition.

---

[15] Roger Boase, 1978:p.117, *The Troubadour Revival*.
[16] Fernandez de Oviedo y Valdes, 1878, *Batallas y Quincuagenas*.
[17] Americo Castro, 1971, *The Spaniards: An Introduction to their History*.

Crusade against the Cathars

Cathars grew in influence in Languedoc throughout the twelfth century. Catholic chroniclers record that Cathars had become the majority religion in many places, and that Catholic churches were abandoned and in ruin. Of the Catholic clergy that remained some, perhaps most, were themselves Cathar believers. The Papacy responded initially by instigating preaching campaigns and engaging in public debates, both of which proved humiliating failures for the crack teams of theologians sent by the Pope.[18]

In 1208 Pope Innocent III joined with northern French nobles to extinguish the Cathars of southern France, also called Albigensians. The nobles of the south geared up to resist the invaders even though many were Catholic. **The crusaders were led by the papal legate Arnaud Armaury**. They arrived at the threshold of Cather territory at Beziers, a town of about 20,000 inhabitants. Several hundred Cathars lived in Beziers but the citizens of the town refused to give them up. **When his commanders asked Amaury what to do he gave his infamous command, "Kill them all! God will know his own!" All the inhabitants of Beziers were slaughtered down to the last man, woman and child!**

Troubadour Song of the Cathar Wars

The Cardinal from Rome proclaiming
That death and slaughter must lead the way,
And in and around Toulouse
No man shall remain alive,
Nor noble Lady, girl or pregnant woman,
Nor any created thing, no sucking infant,
But all must die in the burning flame.

Catholic history has tried to spin the slaughter, claiming the defenders opened up the gate to jeer at the crusaders - *vilaines* (untrained irregulars) responded by rushing in - and massacred them all! It is argued that no senior churchman would have given such an appalling order. The massacres continued - giving the lie to claims it was not planned to terrorize other cities like Carcassone, Montreal and Fanjeaux by what happened at Beziers.

[18] *"Cathar Beliefs in the Languedoc,"* www.cathar.info/cathar_wars.htm/

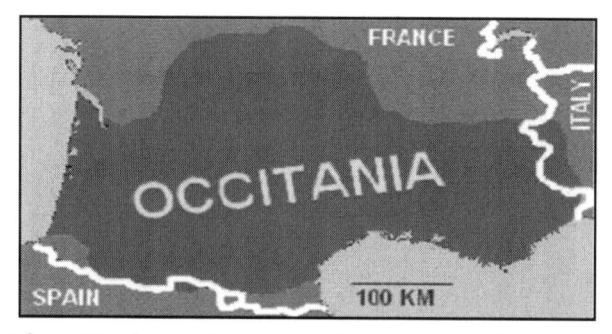

After Beziers, the crusaders marched to Carcassone, besieged it and cut off their water supply. The city surrendered two weeks later on August 15, 1209. The entire population was dispossessed and forced to leave the city naked. Simon of Montfort took command at this point. As a result of these defeats, many cities of the south surrendered to the French invaders including Albi, Castelnaudary, Castres, Fanjeaux, Limoux, Lombers and Montreal. Other cities fell after a short siege such as Lastours, Bram and Minerve. **In the conquered towns, Cathars were given the chance to convert to Catholicism. Most Cathars refused, thousands were slaughtered or burned alive!**

Raymond of Toulouse became the leader of the Occitan forces consisting of both Cathars and Catholics. The war seesawed back and forth during the next thirty years. The population of Occitan did not consider themselves French. There were uprisings against the French invaders who took many of their cities. Raymond fought off a siege of Toulouse and recaptured thirty towns and cities of the south. King Peter II of Aragon in Spain allied with them. At the battle of Muret in 1213 it was the French crusaders who were outnumbered. Simon of Montfort outflanked the Cathar coalition and killed King Peter. Cathar lines broke resulting in horrendous slaughter. The Cathars were vanquished!

After the defeat, Raymond fled to England. Simon of Monfort was made the Count of Toulouse for his victories. The Pope gained immense territories and in 1214 the French king Phillip II now took command to take some of the spoils. It was not until 1244 that the Cathars retreated to Mont Segúr, their final stronghold. After a long siege they were defeated. 200 Cathars were burned alive! Occitania had been crushed by the Pope, but Catharism lived on, covertly in the city, overtly in the country.

"In our Occitania, every city, every castle was a nest of poetry. The troubadours sang of the Spring, sang of the happiness of living, sang of beauty."
Troubadour Poem

To the people of Occitania, their defeat by the French Catholic crusaders was the death of Chivalry (*'Paratge'*). The conquest was not enough to eliminate Catharism which was deeply rooted. Once the armies had done their bloody work, the first of the Inquisitions was established to deal with the still-strong faith of the Cathars in the mountains, countryside and hiding in the cities. Simon of Montfort was buried in Toulouse in a grand tomb with a flowery epitaph proclaiming his exalted saintly status in heaven. As always, troubadours sang of his *'splendor!'*

At Minerve on 22 July 2010, the inhabitants of the town installed a memorial to their slaughtered ancestors which says, in Occitan: *"Minerve remembers PARATGE!"*

> The epitaph says, for those who can read it,
>   That he is a saint and martyr who shall breathe again
>   And shall in wondrous joy inherit and flourish
>   And wear a crown and sit on a heavenly throne.
> And I have heard it said that this must be so -
>   If by killing men and spilling blood,
>   By wasting souls, and preaching murder,
>   By following evil counsel, and raising fires,
>   By ruining noblemen and besmirching **Paratge**,
>   By pillaging the country, and by exalting pride,
>   By stoking up wickedness and stifling good,
>   **By massacring women and their infants,**
> **A man can win Jesus in this world,**
> **Then Simon surely wears a crown,**
> **resplendent in heaven.**[19]

The Roman Church was no longer seeking salvation - only destruction of their competitors whether Christian, Muslim or Jew! Simon of Montfort had won his spurs in the Fourth Crusade which, directed by a Catholic Cardinal, sacked the city of Constantinople, the center of Greek Christianity, accompanied by stupendous slaughter of its Christian inhabitants!

[19] www.languedoc-france.info/190403_paratge.htm.

The Roman Church chronicles depict *'heretics'* as guilty of every conceivable demonic and degenerate perversion imaginable. These exaggerated claims are so extreme and so pervasive - that as a researcher I am forced to discount all of it unless proven by other evidence. I do not count confession under torture, or threat of torture, as evidence. **I am amazed the successors of the torturers do not recognize these *'confessions'* are an indictment of the accusers, not the accused!**

One unique example was *The Fournier Register*. Jacques Fournier was appointed (from 1318-1325 AD) Bishop of Pamiers in Ariège, over Montaillou a village tucked away in the Pyrenees Mountains right on the border between Occitan France and Catalonia, in Spain. The countryside was still a stronghold of Catharism a century after the crusade crushed the Cathar presence in the cities. Fournier was zealous and ambitious. Fournier *"had distinguished himself by his inquisitorial pursuit of heretics."* He made an amazingly detailed record of everyone questioned.*

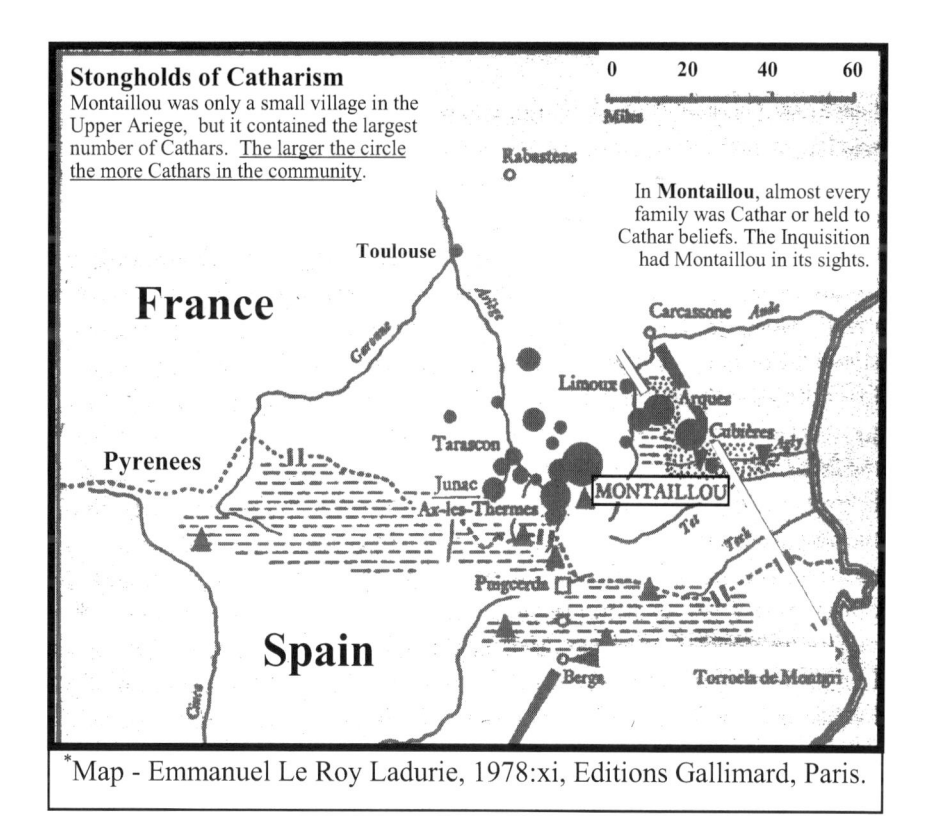

Stongholds of Catharism
Montaillou was only a small village in the Upper Ariege, but it contained the largest number of Cathars. The larger the circle the more Cathars in the community.

In **Montaillou**, almost every family was Cathar or held to Cathar beliefs. The Inquisition had Montaillou in its sights.

*Map - Emmanuel Le Roy Ladurie, 1978:xi, Editions Gallimard, Paris.

Fournier had an effective means of questioning, he just let people talk and took exact notes of everything they said. In his three volumes of testimony we have the most extensive and unique look at Catharism in existence. It is like a reality show of a Medieval village with no secrets left uncovered! It belies the presentation of Cathars as monsters in church history.

> Pierre and Guillaume Authié... were clerks... [notaries]; they had wives and children; they were rich. One day, Pierre, in his house, was reading a certain passage in a book [the Cathar Bible]. He told his brother Guillaume... to read the passage. After a moment, Pierre asked Guillaume, *'How does it strike you, brother?'* And Guillaume answered, *'It seems to me that we have lost our souls!'* And Pierre concluded, *'Let us go, brother; let us go in search of our souls' salvation.'* **So they got rid of all their possessions and went to Lombardy, where they became good Christians** [Cathars]. There they received the power of saving the souls of others; and returned to Ax-les-Thermes.[20]
>
> (From *The Fournier Register* of the Inquisition) [brackets mine]

Lombardy was the location of the Waldensian *'School of Martyrs.'* The Cathar Bible is mentioned various times in *The Fournier Register*. Although most peasants were not literate, the *'goodmen'* - Cathar *parfaits* - typically were. *"Nevertheless, books remained rare and precious. The respect felt for them by the illiterate people of the village paralleled their touching reverence for learning and for people who were educated. Guillamette Maury of Montaillou, exiled in Catalonia, was overcome with admiration... for the Cathar Bible itself... And* [considered that] *a goodman without his books was a soldier without his sword"*[21] [brackets mine].

"Other parfaits... had access to what Jacques Authié **called the double scripture: the bad scripture which emanated from the Roman Church, and the good scripture, the scripture which saved, known to the goodmen and proceeding from the Son of God**.*"*[22] This makes it clear the Cathar Gospel was not the same as that of the Latin Church. The Roman Church claims itself as the original church and its gospel as the original gospel. By this logic, all other churches and gospels must be erroneous perversions of the Roman Catholic original - clearly not the case!

---

[20]*Fournier Register*, vol. ii, page 403. [21]vol.ii, p.63. [22]vol.iii, p.236. [23]vol.ii, p.504.

This claim by the Roman Church is both self-serving and untrue. We have devoted much research and discourse in this book to tracing the path of the original Messianic Church and the original *Hebrew Gospels*. The Neo-Messianic Churches were described as a *"dissenting movement,"* and considered to be *"the single most important element in the Christian Middle Ages."*[24]

In the case of the Waldensians in Lyons and the Cathars in Southern France, one of the defining characteristics of this dissent was their activity devoted to the translation of the Bible into the vernacular.[25]

We must include the Jewish-Christian Conversos of Catalan in this group since they translated *The Hebrew Gospels* into Catalan. There was a strong interactive influence back and forth across the border, *"there was a sort of continuum between Occitania and Catalonia. No problem of comprehension was involved for them in going from Tarascon and Ax-les-Thermes to Puigcerda and San Mateo. Linguistically speaking, the Pyrenees scarely existed."*[26a] Once the Roman Church monopoly of the Gospels was breeched, a new fire of faith was lit in the hearts of the people! Some of *"the more cultivated laymen [were] able to read a text... [when] written in the vulgar tongue... Occitan."*[26b]

Guillaume brought me the book... It was a *'Gospel'* in a mix of Latin and Romance, which contained many things I had heard the heretic Pierre Authié say.[26c]

Translation of the Gospels into the native languages which the people could access directly themselves, by reading or being read to, sparked an intense desire for a return to the purity and power of the original Messianic-Apostolic Church - a desire which would lead inevitably to the Reformation! The people of the region cared deeply for their salvation but considered the Roman priests so degenerate no rituals they performed were valid. *"It is no good confessing to the priests. They keep whores, and all they want to do is eat us up, as the wolf destroys the sheep... **the goodmen follow the path of God, they alone can save souls.... As for the priests, they can not absolve a man of his sins. Only the goodmen can do this***."[26d]

---

[24] Jeffrey Russell, 1965, *Dissent & Reform in the Middle Ages*, Univ.Cal. Press.
[25] Jarette K. Allen, 2011, *La Bible en Occitan.* [26a] Ladurie,1978:p.286, *Montaillou*.
[26b] *Ibid*, p.239. [26c] *Ibid*, p.237. [26d] *Ibid*, p.298.

The Underground Gospels

The *Romance* language was the successor to Latin, different enough to no longer be considered Latin, but uniform enough to still be considered the common tongue of the Mediterranean. The reality was the Romance language differed slightly from each neighboring area to the next where it came to be called Roumant, Limosin, Provençal, Occitan, Catalan, Castilian etc. In time they developed into separate languages (Italian, French, Spanish, Portuguese). There is still much study to be done of the Gospels of the Underground Church in the manuscripts of these ancient dialects. **These were pre-existing Gospels surviving from the time of the Messianic-Apostolic Church** - dismissed as nothing more than errant copies of the Latin Vulgate!

> The *Vision of Isaiah*... is an apocalyptic book of great antiquity and unquestioned authenticity, probably dating to before the second century; it manifests early Gnostic Christian influence. It was known to early Christian writers; Jerome and Epiphanius both quote sections of the text. The *Vision of Isaiah* was possessed by the Bogomils in the twelfth century and had reached the Languedoc in a Latin translation by the early thirteenth century. Cathar possession and use of the ***Vision of Isaiah* is very well attested and witnesses both their access to transmissions of early Christian writings from the East**, and their identification with traditions of Christianity that had preserved and honored these writings. [27]

Two books of Cathar ritual survived, written in Latin and Occitan. *"Without doubt, the Cathars had a stronger claim than the Roman Church to represent the teachings and practices of the Early Christian Church. Its tradition represented ancient practices abandoned or amended by the [Greek] Orthodox Church and then further amended by the Roman Church...* **Cathars represented the last witness to the earliest Christian Church!** *Cathars... were aware of... the route by which their tradition came to western Europe."*[28] Cathar rituals were closer to the early Gospels. *"It was the Gnostics who kept these ceremonies in their pure form... Rome began to enrich their services with pomp and splendor, till they lost their old simplicity."*[29]

---

[27] Lance Owens, 2018, http://gnosis.org/library/Cathar-Vision-Isaiah.htm
[28] *"Cathar Legacy,"* www.cathar.info/cathar_legacy.htm.   [29] Sir Steven Runciman, 1994:p.173, *The Medieval Manichee*, Cambridge University.

When Pierre Maury of Montaillou asked who were these *'goodmen,'* he was told *"The goodmen alone follow the path of truth and justice which was followed by the Apostles."*[30]

They do not take other people's possessions. Even if they find gold or silver on their path, they do not "lift" it and put it in their pockets - they follow the faith of the Apostles - a man is better saved in the faith of the heretics than in any other faith there is.[30]

Tithes to the Roman Church had turned into mandatory taxes! The new bishop, Jacques Fournier, was busily imposing new and profoundly hated taxes such as *'carnelage'* - giving one out of ten of the newborn lambs to the Church, or a tithe on beets, turnips and grain crops not taxed or collected up to that time. The nobility were exempt from these church taxes which further aggravated the animus of the populace. For non-payment of tithes one could be excommunicated and forbidden to attend the village church built by their own hands and with their materials and funds. In 1308 the entire population of Montaillou, from 12 years old on up, were arrested by the Inquisition for non-payment of tithes.

Once the Inquisition had you - they typically took your land and possessions. Guilluame Fort, of Montaillou was burned at the stake during this event along with four Waldensian heretics from the town of Pamiers. Most were released later but it provoked a mass migration of residents into nearby Catalonia. Many, if not most, were ruined by the Inquisition. The Church seized their lands and the local priest, Pierre Clergue, and his brother Bernard Clergue the *'bayle,'* local agent of the court, were allowed to use and profit from the seized lands until resold. **Heresy was a very profitable business for the Roman Church!**

They called Pierre Clergue, *"the little bishop"* of Montaillou. Once a Cathar sympathizer, he was now a priest and agent of the Inquisition. Quite the lothario, the priest was known to blackmail women, *"either you sleep with me or I'll see that you are denounced to the Inquisition in Carcassonne."*[31] When Mengarde Maurs confronted him, he arranged for the authorities to have *"her tongue cut out for speaking ill of the priest."*[32]

---

[30] Emmanuel Le Roy Ladurie, 1978:p.309, Editions Gallimard, Paris.
[31] *Fournier Register*, v.i: p.279. [32] Ladurie, p.41.

Apostolic Succession

To Gnostic believers, keeping track of their predecessors was paramount. It was through the laying on of hands the power and the *"knowledge of the good"*[33] was passed from one generation to the next. Other than their claim to succession, we have little early record of it. Before one dismisses this claim it would be wise to remember the power, knowledge and authority passed via the genealogy of the Old Testament, and the New (in Matthew chapter 1 and Luke chapter 3), up to the anointing of Yeshua Ha Mashiach and in turn his Apostles. In this book we have followed Yeshua's family and descendants as well as the survival of the Messianic-Apostolic Church. **That lineage still lived!**

On page one - of chapter one - of Volume One we began with the theme that, *"The 'sons of Zion' received a mysterious power as a result of the covenant at Har Yehovah."* To be more precise the covenant and its powerful blessing began at human creation. It was blunted by disobedience - renewed with Abraham - the covenant was carved onto the tablets at Sinai - the hereditary blessing split into a priestly line with Moses & Aaron - later a royal line under David - produced many miracles - was sometimes thwarted by evil ones in the line of blood - the power of the blessing was seemingly lost but the line was re-established by the archangel Gabriel in the births of the *'goelim'* (redeemers) Yohanon and Yeshua - passed to his successors who led the Messianic Church (James, Simeon, Jude etc.) and to the Apostles who were charged with carrying it to the nations. The power of this blessing of the covenant with Yehovah came with secret knowledge of the *"mystery of the kingdom of heaven"* (Mark 4:11), a very gnostic concept.

The entire Bible consists of the narratives and miracles that arose as this power passed through the persons of the lineage of blood and belief. This was the plot, the storyline, the main idea, the entire theme of the entire Bible, including the New Testament! Then... it disappears? That the Gnostics recorded in memory the continuing passage of that blessing from generation to generation - exactly as it was done in Scripture - is just not that hard to believe. I am glad someone did! The Roman Church later claimed this power as their exclusive franchise.

---

[33] *'Knowledge of the good'* is often cited in Cathar testimonies of the Inquisition.

"The Cathars themselves claimed a continual chain of descent, each Parfait having joined the inner circle of the Elect by being given the *Consolamentum* by an existing Parfait. Therefore, there existed a continuous chain of succession from any Parfait all the way back to the original biblical Pentecost. If this looks suspiciously like the doctrine of Apostolic Succession claimed by Catholic and other mainstream bishops, **it is worth bearing in mind the mainstream Church is known to have copied the idea from a Gnostic sect in the fourth century, then fabricated lines of apostolic succession for missing centuries!**"[34]

As related by the Roman Church:

"The identity of the oral tradition with the original revelation is guaranteed by the unbroken succession of bishops in the great sees going back lineally to the apostles. . . . supplied by the Holy Spirit, for the message committed was to the Church, and the Church is the home of the Spirit. **Indeed, the Church's bishops are . . . Spirit-endowed men who have been vouchsafed *'an infallible charism of truth.'*** "

"The apostles had committed it orally to the Church, where it had been handed down from generation to generation. . . Unlike the alleged secret tradition of the Gnostics, it was entirely public and open, having been entrusted by the apostles to their successors, and by these in turn to those who followed them, and was visible in the Church for all who cared to look for it." [35]

The Roman Church, in defense of their claim to Apostolic Succession, acknowledged that the Gnostic Church did, indeed, have this tradition of a continual succession of descent from the original Apostles to their ongoing practitioners.

Historically, we know the Gnostic Church was older than the Roman Church. It existed from the time of the Nazarenes and Ebionites. The Roman Church claim is that this *"Spirit-endowed... original revelation... committed orally... and handed down... **was entirely public and open.**"* **That is not possible given the Roman Church prohibition against laymen reading the Bible - and the prohibition against publishing Scripture in the vernacular!** So, if laymen could not read it, only the Roman Church prelates possessed this *"secret"* oral knowledge! **This all certainly looks like an appropriation of the Gnostic claim!**

[34] *Cathar Legacy*, www.cathar.info/cathar_legacy.htm,*"Do Cathars Still Exist?"*
[35] J.N.D. Kelly, 2001, page 37, *Early Christian Doctrines*, Continuum Publisher.

Two points stand out in this debate over Apostolic Succession. **One**, the Gospel had been spread throughout the known world by the Messianic Apostles while the Roman Church was still in its infancy. The Roman Church was not the source of this *"original revelation,"* nor were they the sole recipients, nor were they given some kind of special anointment by Yehovah, Yeshua or Cephas (Peter) to lead Christendom. All churches have originally sprung from apostolic succession.

Two, Scripture shows us Yehovah had often dealt with a corruption in the lineage of this blessing. He withholds the power of the blessing from those who are evil. **The Roman Church, and all of Christianity, are a spiritual battleground! The Church has done enormous good... but at times and places, its leaders have fallen into evil. If we are blind to evil then we do not have eyes to see!** Whether Catholic, Protestant or Gnostic - you shall know them by their fruits!

"The Church was fatter than it looked; its gizzard was bigger than its heart. Instead of adopting Gospel poverty, it devoured the money of the faithful. One means of doing this was through indulgences."[36a] The sale of indulgences, even to pre-pardon sin was to become a major focal point of the Reformation. Crusaders were promised forgiveness for slaughter, looting and pillage. Pedophiles were granted a pre-pardon for impending rape and sexual abuse of boys and girls they had their eye upon. Sexual perversion within the hierarchy of the Church - from priests to popes - was pervasive. *"Priests were still allowed at this period to live with their housekeepers, concubines (or focarias). Permission to do so was granted by the bishop in return for a financial consideration."*[36b] Assassins were forgiven for murder - all before the act - for a price, of course.

Prelates of the Church lived in opulence. Those who disagreed with the doctrines and practices of the Church faced being imprisoned, burned alive, or slain by the sword. Cathedrals were built upon revenue from the sale of indulgences. Indulgences were sold wholesale to friars who wandered the countryside reselling them for a markup.

The Roman Church was now selling salvation!

[36a] Emmanuel Ladurie, 1978:p.334, Editions Gallimard, Paris. [36b] *Ibid*, p.168.

Peter was never the Roman Pope!

It may surprise the reader to know the Catholic claim to Apostolic Succession has even less historical documentation than the Gnostic claim! It is claimed by the Roman Church, that Peter was the first Pope of Rome. **But there is no record that Peter ever set foot in Rome!** Scripture certainly does not support that claim. Peter's last Epistle was written from Babylon. Some spin this by claiming Babylon was a code word for Rome. However, Paul was the Apostle chosen by Yeshua to testify in Rome, the obvious choice - a Roman citizen - who spoke Greek and Latin. Church lore claim Peter and Paul died in the persecution by Nero. Paul says he was abandoned by all in Rome, except Luke. Paul does not mention Peter, unthinkable really if Peter were there. Luke does not mention that Peter was in Rome anywhere in Acts.

My editor, Rae Lloyd-Jones, provided me with such meticulous documentation on the whereabouts of Peter throughout his ministry - that I became convinced she should be writing this book instead of me. In any case, following up on this issue - I discovered that **Catholic sources concede the fact there is no proof Peter was ever in Rome**, but hasten to add it does not matter. Below is a quotation from www.catholic.com:

> A key premise of [opponents] argument is the assertion that Peter was never in Rome. It follows that if Peter were never in Rome, he could not have been Rome's first bishop and so could not have had any successors in that office. How can Catholics talk about the divine origin of the papacy... when their claim about Peter's whereabouts is wrong?...
>
> the question, of whether Peter went to Rome and died there, is inconsequential... one of his successors could have been the first holder of that office to settle in Rome.[37]

I couldn't have said it up better myself. Note, neither is there any documentation of a successor to Peter becoming bishop of Rome. It is hard to have a debate when your opponents concede the argument from the get-go. So much for the Roman Church bishops inheriting *"an infallible charisma of truth"* via Apostolic Succession starting with St. Peter. The divine appointment of Peter as the first pope is always cited as Rome's ultimate authority - for killing fellow Christians - among other evils.

---

[37] https//www.catholic.com/tract/was-peter-in-rome.

The Cathar Legacy

The first Inquisition was instituted by the Roman Church to root out and destroy the remaining Cathars after their military defeat. The Inquisition became a license to imprison, dispossess and destroy anyone. It corrupted all who held that power. It was a means of taking believers' money and property, or their lives if they objected. The Cathars had always known that their faith came with a very real danger of death.

> Historically, Western Christians have always abandoned their faith *en masse* whenever they have been put under pressure to do so. From early Christians during the reign of Diocletian to priests during the French Revolution, believers have preferred to abandon their faith rather than lose their lives. Throughout the Middles Ages the masses were fed fanciful tales of heroic martyrdom, but no amount of propaganda could conceal the fact that even Christian armies (including monks and priests) would generally recant under pressure. Anyone who had already been on crusade to the Holy Land would have firsthand knowledge of colleagues who had converted to Islam when captured and pressed by their Moslem captors.
> **Western Christendom was therefore surprised to find that Cathar Parfaits consistently opted to be burned alive rather than renounce their faith when faced with greater pressure than Catholics faced at Moslem hands.** [38]

The prior of the Abbey of Steinfeld wrote to the Pope that when Cathars were *"thrown into the fire and burned... What is more marvelous, they bore the agony of the fire not only with patience but even with joy! At this point, Holy Father, were I with you, I should like you to explain whence comes to those limbs of the devil - constancy such as is hardly to be found even in men most devoted to the faith of Christ."*[39]

After the capture of Mont Segúr in 1244, twenty-five Cathars took the *Consolamentum,* became parfaits and were burned alive with 200 other parfaits to sanctify the true Messianic-Apostolic faith. **Not since the Messiah and his Apostles had such steadfastness of faith been demonstrated by Christians under duress!** Inquisitor Bishop Fournier of Ariège - was rewarded for crushing the Cathars - becoming Pope Benedict XII.

---

[38] www.cathar.info/cathar_legacy.htm. [39] From *Letter 472* of Saint Bernard, cited in Wakefield & Evans, 1991:p.129, *Heresies of the High Middle Ages*.

Cathars had done a far better job preparing their *parfaits* to teach Scripture. **"The best Catholic preachers consistently lost in open debate with Cathar Parfaits. Such embarrassment led the Roman Church to prohibit the circulation of the Old Testament among laymen. For ordinary people to read a Bible, or even to possess one, would soon become a capital offence, and many proto-Protestants would be burned alive for it."**[40]

The Second Lateran Council in 1139 had prohibited priests from marrying. Previous bishops had built huge ecclesiastical domains - and their families - after the bishop's death, vied for ownership of lands and properties with the Church. Sadly, it was more of a property decision. After denying them marriage rites, priests - *en masse* - engaged in illicit sex outside of marriage. The Roman Church was eventually forced to incorporate popular practices and beliefs of the Cathars - in this case, celibacy of priests - although with mixed results. Roman priests had a long way to go to clean up their reputation.

> The priests steal all men's possessions - as soon as they have baptized children, they start to slip away, carrying the oil lamps and the candles. To say Mass, to do anything at all, they want money. They do not live as they ought - that is why they have lost the power to absolve sins - both their own and others.'[41]

Although we refer to them as Cathars or Albigensians, they only referred to themselves as "*Good Christians*." Cathar strength was in their sincere desire for Salvation and the dramatic contrast between the corrupt Roman Church and her priests, and the Messianic desire to return to the purity of the original church.

Priests, such as Pierre Clergue, were often lustful and manipulative. Andreas Capellanus, a priest who became immersed in the Court of Love at Poitiers, wrote a fascinating book, *The Art of Courtly Love*. In it he justified priestly lust by asserting "*hardly anyone ever lives without carnal sin, and since the* **life of the clergy is, because of the continual idleness and the great abundance of food**, *naturally more liable to temptations of the body than that of any other men... let him apply himself to love's service.*"[42] In reference to peasant women, "***do not hesitate to take what you seek and to embrace them by force****... use a little compulsion as a convenient cure for their shyness.*"[42]

[40] The Cathar Legacy.com/Identity & Nature of God. [41] Ladurie,1978:p.336, *Montaillou*. [42] Andreas Capellanus, 1150, 1960:pp.142-150, *Art of Courtly Love*.

Cathars had a totally different moral focus on Courtly Love. In a tavern in Foix, near Montaillou, the Cathar patrons, *"discussing the burning at the stake of a Waldensian, commented 'He commended his soul to God and to the Blessed Mary... he adored them both in courtly fashion so he is not a heretic.'"*[43] True love without lust was the Courtly Love of the Cathars. *"****Troubadours****... the more religious cultivators of the 'Gai Saber,' few as they were...* **preserved Provence, Langueduc and Lombardy from overwhelming licentiousness.**"[44]

In attempting to present itself in the same light as the popular Parfaits, the papacy created new preaching orders like the Dominicans and Franciscans. The Dominicans in particular are a very obvious attempt to copy the Parfaits. When they were set up they travelled around the Languedoc countryside in pairs, walking, dressing simply in sandals and plain habits, avoiding the ostentation of other churchmen, and preaching poverty. In this they were consciously and explicitly emulating Parfaits. **You can see them today, still wearing their black robes, almost identical to the habit of the people they were responsible for exterminating.** Again, the first nunnery, set up by Dominic Guzmán (Saint Dominic), was a copy of a convent for Cathar Parfaites. To emulate Cathar asceticism, celibacy was imposed on the Roman Catholic clergy after centuries of lip service.[45]

Dominicans later became the chief enforcers of the Inquisition - fervent in torturing and burning Christians! *"Popular protest against tithes and indulgences was not the only thing which linked the conquered Cathars of 1320 to the victorious Reformers of 1520-1580, whether German Lutherans or the Huguenots of Languedoc. Both movements were concerned with the Pauline theme of justification by faith. '****Baptism of water profits nothing... water has no virtue to save the soul. It is only faith which saves the soul****'"*[46] - Cathar Pierre Maury of Montaillou.

"Fundamental themes of the distant Reformation were already familiar in the mountains of Occitania in the 14th century!" [46]

---

[43] Ladurie,1978:p.307, *Montaillou*, citing *Fournier Register*, volume i, p.174.
[44] Gilly, 1848:p.133, *Roumant Book of John*. [45]*Cathar Legacy*.com/Identity & Nature of God. [46]Ladurie, 1978:pp.335-6, citing *Fournier Register*, v.iii,p.202.

Differences of Doctrine

"*Adoptionism*" was the belief that Yeshua became divine at baptism when the Holy Spirit descended into him like a dove. This has extensive repercussions to Christology - the theology that explains the son of God - and especially to the doctrine of the Trinity. Note that to the Jews - for Yeshua to be a '*son of God*' was scriptural. Being Yehovah's '*anointed one*,' a Messiah, was also scriptural. **However, being a divine '*god*' himself - went against the foundation of Judaism - which was monotheism**. Adoptionists believed Yeshua kept himself sinless so that at his baptism he was '*begotten*' by Yehovah and anointed, giving him divine power which he did not have before!

Since the beginning there were two different groups of Jewish Christians - Nazarenes and Ebionites. The Nazarenes were followers of Yeshua of Nazareth, most from Galilee in the North. "*It is clear that there was nothing in the extant fragments from the Gospel of the Nazarenes which was heretical in nature... Nazarenes affirmed Jesus' resurrection from the dead... [and] point to an understanding of the dual nature of Jesus, possibly including his own awareness of his divinity and humanity.*"[47a]

The Ebionites also believed Yeshua was the son of God, their Messiah and Savior. They were, in the beginning, followers of Yohanon Ben Zachariah - John the Baptist - who preached and baptized in Judea in the South. "*Fragments from the Gospel of the Ebionites demonstrate that their beliefs and Christology are distinct from those of the Nazarenes... They demonstrate that the Ebionites rejected the virgin birth. They suggest an adoptionist or Gnostic view of Jesus' divine sonship and relationship to the Holy Spirit.*"[47b] The Ebionites were Adoptionists.

The Ebionites created their own Gospel, the *Gospel of the Ebionites*, which deleted the divine birth narratives of Yeshua and Yohanon. Gods begetting more gods was part and parcel of pagan religion - Judaism was unique because there was only one God - Yehovah! Ebionites did believe Yeshua was the son of Yehovah - anointed by the Spirit of God entering into him at his baptism while a voice from heaven declared, **"*This is my son in whom I am well pleased. This day have I begotten you*.*"***[48]

[47a] Kenneth Howard, 1993:p.71, *Jewish Christianity*... [47b] *Ibid*. [48] Luke 3:22, *Beza Codex* among many others, as cited in Ehrman, 2003: p.223, *Lost Christianities*.

It is easy to feel superior to the primitive Ebionites who seem to have gotten the basics so very wrong. **The problem with this theological elitism is that Luke 3:22 *"Today I have begotten you." - "is found in virtually all our oldest witnesses."*** [49] It was omitted to match the doctrine of the predominant Greco-Roman church. *"This is one proto-orthodox alteration that proved remarkably successful... it is the altered form of the text that is found in the majority of surviving manuscripts and reproduced in most of our English translations."* [50] This is not the only example that we will find of changes to the New Testament made in order to support church doctrine.

The offending verse is from the prophecy in Psalms 2:6-7, *"Yet have I set my King upon my holy hill of Zion. I will declare the decree: Yehovah has said unto me, **'You are my Son, this day have I begotten you!'*"** I have no intention of trying to convert the reader to the doctrine of Adoptionism. Logically, there are only two stances one can take. Either one doctrine has gotten it all right - and everyone else is wrong - or all doctrines are fallible, none can claim perfect understanding of God and His Son! I subscribe to the latter belief.

The facts are that all the earliest manuscripts of the Gospel of Luke contain the adoptionist formula, *"Today I have begotten you"* in Luke 3:22. During the doctrinal war waged by Rome any belief disputing Roman dogma was a death sentence! **The offending verse, Luke 3:22, was scrubbed from Scripture!**

The Hebrew Gospels of Catalonia [HGC] do not contain the adoptionist formula. The HGC reflects the Nazarene doctrine which is basically orthodox. Nonetheless, Messianic scribes were caught between these two traditions, the Hebrew and the Greco-Roman. Torn between the surviving *Hebrew Gospels* and the predominant doctrinal tradition of the *Latin Vulgate* - sometimes they would convey the Hebraic tradition - and other times insert the Latin version into the copied text. **Without a doubt, *The Hebrew Gospels of Catalonia* are the child of two parents - *The Hebrew Gospels* and the *Latin Vulgate*. The confluence of the Neo-Messianic tradition and the Greco-Roman tradition were to clash violently during the Middle Ages!**

---

[49] Bart Ehrman, 2003: p.223, *Lost Christianities.* [50] *Ibid.*, Luke 3:22 is in the *Beza Codex,* for one prominent example, and most all other early manuscripts.

Chapter Six
Messianic Church in Sepharad

*The exiles of Israel shall return to the land of Canaan...
the exiles of Jerusalem who are in Sepharad
shall repossess the cities of the Negev.*
Obadiah 1:20

The Messianics in Sepharad were Hebrews! The largest population of Jews and Messianics lived in Spain - **a vibrant community of half a million Jews during the Middle Ages!** More than half of these Sephardim became *Conversos*, Jewish converts to Christianity. Since the time of the Apostles there had been a strong and growing Messianic Church in Spain. They had *The Hebrew Gospels* - which Messianic disciples carried everywhere they evangelized. The early church fathers commented on the widespread dispersal of *The Hebrew Gospel* into Syria, Alexandria, Yemen, Anatolia, India and Sepharad [Spain]. The Arabs referred to these early Christians in Spain as *"Nazarenes."*[1]

The Messianic Movement in Spain had their own churches, bishops, yeshivas, Hebrew Bibles and *Hebrew Gospels*! Conversos who came to believe in their Hebrew Messiah wanted the sacred Word in the sacred tongue - Hebrew. *The Hebrew Gospels* had already been translated into Catalan for those Messianics who no longer knew Hebrew. We have that manuscript as well - the *Pieresc Bible* - from it the *Gospels* were re-translated into Hebrew, circa 1480, for use in the Messianic Church. **The Spanish Inquisition was begun in 1478 for the primary purpose of crushing the resurgent Messianic Church!**

In 1492, King Ferdinand and Queen Isabella completed the Reconquista by reconquering Granada - the last stronghold of Islam left in Spain. In the same year they proclaimed an edict expelling all Jews and seizing their assets. Jews had until July 31, 1492 to convert or exit Spain, leaving all their land and possessions behind. **The stated purpose was to end Judaizing of Conversos!** Many Jews converted, others emigrated. In the same month Columbus sailed for the New World, so many Jews were leaving the ports, that Columbus' voyage was delayed until August 3, 1492. Columbus took with him many Jews fleeing the expulsion and Messianics fleeing the Inquisition.

---

[1] Dario Fernandez-Morera, 2016:p.206, *The Myth of the Andalusian Paradise*.

The first Islamic conquerors had come in 711 AD followed by other waves of Moorish warriors - the Almoravids in 1086 and the Almohads in 1147 - each more fundamentalist than the ones who came before. Islamic tolerance of the Jews was often more the exception than the rule. In 1066, the Muslim population of Grenada rioted *"in a pogrom that destroyed the city's Sephardic community. Muslim sources tell of other anti-Jewish Muslim riots in 'taifa'* [Moorish] *kingdoms, including in Cordoba again in 1135."*[2] Now Jews fled into the Christian provinces for protection. The Christian kings of Castile, Navarre, and Aragon defeated the Almohads at the Battle of Las Navas in 1212 AD.

> The splendor of the Jewish culture of medieval Spain (*"Sepharad,"* in Hebrew), would be hard to exaggerate. In a symbiotic relationship with Muslim and then Christian rulers, Jews enjoyed **from the eighth through tenth centuries (in [Muslim] Al-Andalus) and from the eleventh through the fourteenth centuries (in Christian Spain)** as much stability and legal protection as they had ever had. They prospered economically and demographically, and made up a larger proportion of the population than in any other European country... Jews considered Spain a historically Jewish country, and their new homeland. **Jewish intellectual life and the Hebrew language were reborn in Spain.** There was the greatest flowering of Hebrew poetry since Biblical times.[3] [brackets mine]

The Golden Age was now coming to its long and painful ending. That intellectual flowering - catalyzed by the *Convivencia* between Christians, Moslems and Jews - by 1391, had been replaced by ethnic cleansing. The glorious outpouring of books of knowledge to the rest of Europe from the Greeks, Persians, Arabs, Nestorians, and Hebrews - had now been superseded. *"In Spain, as elsewhere, the Hebrew libraries were frequently condemned to public flames by ecclesiastical edict."*[4] **This tragedy was obscured in history by the more hideous one of the Roman Church burning fellow Christians - Messianics who held to the commandments of Yehovah and Yeshua!** The Golden Age was ever a fragile flower, seasonal in its nature, punctuated by warfare, persecution, and pogroms. Now it was over, a victim of Gentile Christian rage against all things Hebrew!

---

[2] Dario Fernandez-Morera, 2016:p.182, *The Myth of the Andalusian Paradise*.
[3] Fernandez-Morera, 2016:p.187-8. [4] James Finn, 1841, 2012:p.238, *Sephardim*.

By 1390-91, Christian tolerance towards the Jews had dissolved into class envy. As converts, Messianics were now permitted to hold professions of importance in the state. Due to their superior education, many Messianics rose rapidly to positions of influence. **Messianics had education, numbers, wealth, position, power, and protectors among the Spanish nobility.** To counter this, the Church turned to demagoguery, whipping the Spanish people into a violent frenzy. Fernan Martinez, archdeacon of Ecija, *"preached openly in the streets of Seville"* - the destruction of the Jews! The multitudes were enraged:

> Rabid fury was wreaked... Synagogues and dwellings were pillaged or burned, and half their tenants massacred. From Seville the storm passed on to Cordova, where the same horrors were repeated. On that identical day of the next year, all this was repeated in Toledo, Logroño, Valencia, and Barcelona. Numberless Jews were put to the knife... farms and rural homes were burned... [many] accepted baptism (11,000 in Valencia alone), rather than incur the loss of life and goods**...** Neither priest, bishop, nor archbishop protested against the butchery, although more than 3,000 fell in the first onslaught... **Should some stranger from a far-off land... find**... whole families of corpses, with gasping gashes on their bodies, and limbs stiffened in every convulsive posture - **would he suppose all this had been done in the name of God?** [5] [brackets mine]

Over time the Jews would be blamed for plagues, murders, witchcraft, poisoning of wells, and the sacrifice of Christian children in order to mix their blood into their matza bread for Passover! *"Thus were the faithful people taught to shudder at Jewish society, as involving every thing that is loathsome and inhuman. No deeds could be more inconsistent with* [Jews] *their religious feelings and practices...* **The early Christians were accused of similar atrocities...** *The heathen public believed the Christians kill children at their eucharistical assemblies, when every person present dipped his bread in the blood."*[6] There were more pogroms over the next century. Still, *"conversions continued voluntarily after the cessation of the pogroms of 1391.... As many as 50,000 more Jews joined the Christian fold by 1415."*[7]

---

[5] James Finn, 1841, 2012:pp.283-285, Sephardim.   [6] *Ibid.*, Finn, pp. 344-345.
[7] Jane Gerber, 1992:p.117, The Jews of Spain, The Free Press, New York.

Conversos, Jewish converts to Christianity in Spain were called Marranos. I refer to them as Messianics. **The great myth about the Messianic Movement in Spain was that all Conversos were Crypto-Jews!** There were horrible incidents of forced conversion - but voluntary conversions were more the norm for most Jews becoming Christians. Forced conversion was an absolute evil that was nonetheless practiced by all parties at times: the Jews during the Maccabean Wars, Muslims during the Crusades, and Christians during the Inquisition. **Forgotten, in this maelstrom of religious conflict, were the sincere Jewish converts to their Messiah. It is to these true Messianics, and their descendants, whom this book is dedicated. It was these true Messianics who, under constant threat of death, preserved** *The Hebrew Gospels*!

> The difference between the converts of 1391 and those of 1412-1415 was, nevertheless, decisive. While the former were a product of an external cause (fear of being murdered by a riotous mob), the latter were a product of both external and internal causes… The influx of the new converts into the Marrano camp had a disastrous moral effect upon the Jewish elements within it. **The very fact that most of Spain's Jews were now in the Christian orbit, and that the voluntary converts now constituted the majority of the Marranos, made… further resistance, appear more futile than ever before.**[8]

Sephardim Conversos	Christ Believers	Christ Unbelievers
sons of Zion: Hebrew Tradition	*Messianics*	Crypto-Jews
sons of Greece: Western Tradition	New Christians	Secularists

The heretofore unrecognized *Messianics* are the focus of this book! Secularists might equally be described as '*assimilationists.*' They simply wished to leave the bloody business of religion - and assimilate into the Western world they lived in. They wanted to be '*sons of Greece.*'

---

[8] Benzion Netanyahu, 1999:pp.120-121, *The Marranos of Spain*, Cornell U. Press.

"The Spanish Inquisition was created in 1478 because of a heresy which Church authorities called 'judaizing.' Judaizers were Christians who allegedly continued to practice Jewish ceremonies and espouse Jewish beliefs."[9] The Spanish Inquisition's reign of terror lasted until 1834, a total of 356 years, more than three and a half centuries! Long after the Protestant Reformation, long after the Catholic Counter-Reformation, long after the Enlightenment had dawned upon the religious battlegrounds of Europe - **the Spanish Inquisition continued, periodically, its ghastly goal of exterminating any Christians tainted by Judaism - stamping out any hint of the Hebraic roots of Christianity!** The last execution, of a heretic schoolmaster, was in 1826.

> **The New Christians, many of whom were sincere enough believers in Christ, yet could not altogether forsake their own people nor the customs that time had hallowed.** What was there wrong in their standpoint? We may ask today. Yet we know that even now with all the liberality of faith that has come with more enlightened days, the Jewish Christian who wished to retain his national and ancestral practices, while utterly loyal to his Savior, is looked upon askance, and the genuineness of his Christian convictions is doubted. But in the darker days, **the mere fact of Jewish origin was, in itself, often sufficient to call down the jealous vengeance of an apostate Church. God save us from trial by clergy!** [10]

Most historians have accepted the Roman Church narrative that all Marranos were Crypto-Jews who rejected Christ and practiced Judaism in secret. Benzion Netanyahu is one prominent scholar who disagrees, *"The overwhelming majority of the Marranos, at the time of the establishment of the Inquisition were not Jews, but 'detached from Judaism,' or rather to put it more clearly, Christians; in seeking to identify the whole Marrano group with a secret Jewish heresy, the Spanish Inquisition was operating... a fiction."*[11] The Church and the Spanish kings wanted to destroy, or drive out, the Jews and confiscate their wealth. **The Inquisition, Netanyahu concluded, had another agenda. They wanted to destroy the Jewish Christians - called Marranos!** After all, the Spanish Inquisition had no authority over Jews who had not converted to Christianity.

---

[9] Lu Ann Homza, 2006:p.xv, *The Spanish Inquisition: Anthology of Sources.*
[10] Hugh Schonfield, 1936, 2009, p.134, *The History of Jewish Christianity.*
[11] Benzion Netanyahu, 1999:p.3, *The Marranos of Spain*, Cornell Univ. Press.

Many Jews converted voluntarily, others were forced. The first group were sincere Christians. The second, compelled to convert, were called *Anusim*, *'forced ones,'* in Hebrew. Lost in the slander was the reality that most of their descendants became sincere Christians. The second generation Christians were also of two types. One assimilated to the Roman Church, scrubbing all traces of Judaism from their lives. *"In the decade preceding the Inquisition, the overwhelming majority of the Marranos were Christianized... They had no desire or intention to return to Judaism, and consequently did not practice Judaism secretly."*[12]

The other group embraced Messianism, which had existed in Spain since the first century. Toledo was the center of the first century Church in Sepharad, begun among the Jews as a Messianic Assembly, later joined by Gentiles. The Sephardic Jews were famous for their Old Testament Hebrew Bibles, the Hebrew *Tanakh*. These Messianics were well aware their Savior - Yeshua Ha Mashiach - was a Hebrew, and his story took place in Hebrew and was written in Hebrew. They wanted Scripture in Hebrew!

The Hebrew Gospels still existed among them! Many Conversos resolved that if they were going to be Christians, they were going to embrace their Hebrew Messiah - not a Greek one! Their Scripture would be in the sacred tongue - Hebrew - the *Tanakh* and *The Hebrew Gospels*. They would celebrate Passover - and worship on the true Sabbath. **Their religion would be that of the Messianic, not the Roman, Church!**

Replacement Theology proclaimed Gentile Christians were now the chosen people. The truth is - Messianic Jewish believers were the real heirs - the rightfully chosen people. For Supersessionism to prevail - the Messianics had to be destroyed!

The aim of the Inquisition...was <u>not</u> to eradicate a Jewish heresy from the midst of the Marrano group, <u>but to eradicate the Marrano group from the midst of the Spanish people</u>...

It's purpose was to degrade, impoverish and ruin the influence of the Marranos in all spheres of life, to terrorize and demoralize them individually and collectively - **In brief, to destroy them psychologically and physically so as to make it impossible for them to rise again as a factor of any consequence in Spain.**[13]

---

[12] Benzion Netanyahu, 1999:p.142, *The Marranos of Spain*.   [13] *Ibid.*, p. 4.

Reason for the Expulsion of the Jews

Over time, a new religion, neither wholly Jewish nor wholly Catholic, evolved among the secret Jews... fasting, abbreviated prayers... shortened festivals that could be covertly observed at home, and a special set of rituals... **converts would remain courageously loyal to this new faith** even *in extremis*, as is evident from literally tens of thousands of Inquisition dossiers. **The echoes of this fortitude would reach across the Atlantic into the New World.**[14]

That *"new"* religion was, in truth, the original religion of Messianism - a Hebrew faith started by the Hebrew Messiah which used Hebrew prayers, observed Hebrew feast days, held to the Hebrew Sabbath - and believed Yeshua Ha Mashiach was their Savior! Crypto-Judaism was different. Converts who rejected Christ in secret, seldom lasted beyond the first generation. By the second generation, the saving grace of the Messiah became predominant. Those who scrubbed their faith of Judaic practices became *"New Christians."* Those who turned to their Hebrew Messiah became *"Messianics,"* and kept their Sabbaths.

When Ferdinand and Isabel united the thrones of Castille and Leon, the Roman Church convinced them to end the conflict between *"New"* and *"Old"* Christians by initiating the Spanish Inquisition (in 1478). *"The Inquisition focused on Christian conversos accused of Judaizing."*[15] *"Any manifestation of Judaism would earn the death penalty for heresy."*[16] Because of the virulent anti-Semitism preached, *Old Christians* would not congregate with *New Christians*. *"Kings of the fifteenth century were able to do little to keep anti-converso hostilities in check."*[14]

Only 14 years after the Inquisition began, the Roman Church prelates returned to Ferdinand and Isabel to demand the expulsion of all the Jews - for the supposed sin of re-Judaizing Conversos. **The Spanish Inquisition in 1478, and the Expulsion of the Jews from Spain in 1492, were initiated for the same reason, *Judaizing*, the ultimate sin!** *"In our land there is no inconsiderable number of judaizing and wicked Christians who have deviated from our... faith"* - a clear reference by Ferdinand and Isabel - to the Messianic Jewish Christians!

---

[14] Jane Gerber, 1992:pp.143-44, *The Jews of Spain*, Simon & Schuster, N.Y.
[15] Davila, Diaz, & Hart, *Fractured Faiths*, 2016:p.18. [14]Jane Gerber, 1992:p.124.
[16] Cullen Murphy, 2012:p.73, *God's Jury*, Houghton Mifflin Harcourt, N.Y.

Anti-Messianic Pogroms and Laws

The anti-Semitism preached by Roman priests, built upon class envy and blood libel, had morphed into anti-Converso hatred. Both Jews and Conversos were subject by law to attend sermons haranguing the perfidy of the Jews, dehumanizing and insulting them in every way possible. Many Conversos returned to Judaism as a result of this demoralizing animosity. ***"The conviction began to spread that Jewish ancestry or 'race,' not professed religious belief, defined who was a Jew.*** *Therefore, as conversos continued to rise to prominence in every walk of life, calls for restrictions and discrimination against them mounted... The hostility toward Jewish converts climaxed in Toledo in 1449 in a pogrom aimed exclusively at the conversos."*[17] First of many.

> **We declare the so-called '*conversos*,'** offspring of perverse Jewish ancestors, must be held by law to be infamous and ignominious, **unfit, and unworthy to hold any public office** or any benefice within the city of Toledo, or land within its jurisdiction, or to be commissioners for oaths or notaries, **or to have any authority over the true Christians of the Holy Catholic Church**.[18]

These '*purity of blood*' laws systematically stripped Messianics of their positions and professions. ***"The conversos were now isolated as a new class, neither Jewish nor Christian, that was unassimilable and could not be redeemed.*** *Paradoxically, the restrictive laws became increasingly complex as the actual Jewishness of the conversos became more remote, even mythical."*[19] The blood laws were to last for centuries.

> **Spaniards have succeeded in creating a nation of madmen!**
> We still distinguish between New Christians and Old Christians... We search for Jewish blood which hardly exists, almost one hundred years after the expulsion of the Jews. With such an attitude, it can only bring dishonor on us.[20]

Persecution did not stop there. *"The officers of the Inquisition seemed to harbor a special animus toward converts who held positions of influence as courtiers and financial agents of the crown, although converts from all strata were victimized."*[21]

---

[17] Jane Gerber, 1992:p.127, *The Jews of Spain*. [18] A. Sicroff, 1960, *Les Controverses des statuts de pureté de sang en Espagne*. [19] Jane Gerber, 1992:p.127. [20] Cecil Roth, 1932, 1964, *The Spanish Inquisition*. [21] Gerber, 1992:p.130.

Disputations to Convert the Jews

The Barcelona Disputation of 1263 was convened by James I of Aragon. James had a sincere desire to convert the Jews, but also employed many Jews in high positions who ran his affairs efficiently. He was inclined to be fair and appreciative. The Dominican Friar Pablo Christiani, a converted Jew, had convinced the king that he could prove Jesus was the Messiah from the writings of the Talmud. James asked Moshe Ben Nachman, aka Nahmanides, a prominent Jewish scholar to argue the other side. Nahmanides agreed, on the provision that both were given absolute freedom to speak their arguments without retribution. The king agreed. The debate took place in the palace of the king, before the royal court and many Christian dignitaries.

Although Christiani was knowledgeable on the Talmud, he was not the equal of Nahmanides in either knowledge or skill at debate. Once Friar Pablo Christiani had brought forth his evidence, Nahmanides replied:

> It is well known that the incident of Jesus took place during the period of the Second Temple. He was born and killed prior to the destruction of the Temple, while the sages of the Talmud, like R. Akiba and his associates... Those who compiled the Mishnah, Rabbis and R. Nathan, lived many years after the destruction. All the more so R. Ashi who compiled the Talmud, who lived about four hundred years after the destruction. If these sages believed that Jesus was the messiah and that his faith and religion were true... Why did they not convert and turn to the faith of Jesus, as Friar Paul [Pablo Christiani] did? ... If these sages believed in Jesus and in his faith, how is it that they did not do as Friar Paul, who understands their teachings better than they do? [22]

The Dominicans asked that the debate be discontinued! James I awarded Nahmanides the prize of 300 gold coins. The following Shabbat the king addressed the Jewish congregation in the Major Synagogue of Barcelona. He later said of Nahmanides that never before had he heard *"an unjust cause so nobly defended."*[23] **In 1265, Nahmanides was arrested by the Dominicans for *'blasphemy.'* The king, true to his word, protected Nahmanides. Once freed, Nahmanides fled, never to return.**

---

[22] Report of Moses Nahmanides, *The Disputation of Barcelona*, archived 2006, medspains.stanford.edu. [23] Slater, et. al., 1999, *Great Moments in Jewish History*.

The second disputation took place at Pamplona in 1375, between Cardinal Pedro de Luna and Shem Tov ibn Shaprut. The young Jewish scholar Shem Tov was compelled to debate the Cardinal on original sin and redemption. In the presence of bishops and learned theologians, Shem Tov bested the Christian Cardinal Pedro de Luna, who would later become Pope Benedict XIII. The future pope had learned his lesson - never again would there be a fair debate between Christian and Jew.

Shem Tov was also forced to flee - due to the war between the English and Castilians. He went to Aragon, where, in 1380, he completed his classic work the *Evan Bohan* (*Touch Stone*). The *Evan Bohan*, consists of 14 chapters (or '*gates*'), much of it in the form of a dialog. '*Gate*' Twelve was the Hebrew Matthew, recopied from *The Hebrew Gospels*, in order to add polemical arguments for any Jew forced to debate his beliefs. Shem Tov wrote of the books of the Gospel and his intention of doing the same argumentation to the other Hebrew Gospels. *"Here is completed the Gospel of Matthew, which will be followed by the Gospel of Mark."*[24] Shem Tov never completed that project, but he revised his *Evan Bohan* various times. It has been reproduced by hand in dozens of versions which have been found throughout Europe, often confused with other versions of *Hebrew Matthew*:

> In 1879 the German orientalist **Adolf Herbst published two other Jewish Hebrew translations of Matthew**, also used by Italian and Spanish Jews to combat attempts at conversion... However **these two manuscripts have no direct connection to [Shem Tov] Ibn Shaprut**. They are a Spanish manuscript published and edited by Sebastian **Münster** (and now lost) and a related (surviving) Italian Jewish manuscript purchased by Bishop Jean **du Tillet** and published by Jean Mercier (1555)**.**[25]

The Munster and du Tillet manuscripts are often attributed to Shem Tov as '*proof*' that his *Hebrew Matthew* is merely a translation from the Latin! The other critique of Shem Tov's *Hebrew Matthew* is that the Hebrew word used '*to copy*' can also mean '*to translate.*' The claim is that Shem Tov was a translation not a copy of a surviving *Hebrew Gospel*. The same has been said about *The Hebrew Gospels from Catalonia*.

---

[24]George Howard, 1995, *Hebrew Gospel of Matthew*, Mercer University Press, Macon, GA. [25]Julius Fürst, Bibl. Jud. iii. 259 et seq. (where Shem Tov Ibn Shaprut is confounded with Shem-Ṭob ben Isaac of Tortosa).

The Hebrew word [עתק] Shem Tov used 'to transcribe' or 'to copy' the books of the gospel, can also mean 'translate.' Most words have numerous meanings. This is not generally a problem since the context of the communication will make clear their meaning. In Shem Tov's introduction, he says, "*I abjure by God every 'copyist,' that he not 'copy' the books of the gospel unless [he write] in every place the objections that I have written...*" Shem Tov addressed this caution to other Jews, after warning that propagating the gospels in Hebrew is forbidden to Jews, so make sure to include his explanation for doing so. This can only mean 'copying' the Hebrew text, not translating it.

In commenting on Matthew 21:9, Shem Tov criticizes the original Hebrew text of Matthew, "*reading* אתיג *instead of the Masoretic Text of Zech (9:9) which reads* המיר... *The conclusion is inescapable: this section of Matthew was not translated into Hebrew by Shem Tov.*"[26] **If Shem Tov is questioning the choice of Hebrew words in the Hebrew text of Matthew - because it differs from the Hebrew Tanakh - then he did not translate it into Hebrew! He is criticizing the Hebrew text he is copying.**

Another crucial aspect of Shem Tov's Hebrew Matthew is perinamosia, a uniquely Hebrew type of internal rhyme within a sentence. This is often called Hebrew word puns but that is a misnomer, because it is not intended to be funny. It is intended to be beautiful, just like rhymed poetry, and most of all, memorable. Shem Tov's Hebrew Matthew has perinamosia on practically every page which is expected in Hebrew prose. George Howard lists dozens of examples. The classic example is, "*You shall call his name Yeshua, because he will 'yoshia' (save) his people.*" Here is another, "*You are an 'even' (stone) and upon you I will 'eveneh' (build) my church.*"[27] From the same root, '*Yeshua/yoshia*' and '*even/eveneh*' have an echo, a similar sound and sense. This word play - replete in Hebrew Matthew but often lost in translation - is further evidence the original was Hebrew.

> The text is written in a kind of Hebrew one would expect for a document composed in the first century but preserved in late rabbinic manuscripts. **It is basically composed in biblical Hebrew with a healthy mixture of Mishnaic Hebrew and later rabbinic vocabulary and idiom.**[28]

---

[26]George Howard, 1995:p.178-9, *Hebrew Gospel*. [27]*Ibid*, p.197. [28] Ibid, p.223-4.

The Tortosa Disputation 1413-14

"In terms of scale and splendor, the greatest of the disputations was that of Tortosa."[29] It was also the revenge of Pope Benedict XIII, the former Cardinal Pedro de Luna, for his embarrassing defeat in debate with the young Jewish scholar, Shem Tov Ibn Shaprut. *"Benedict summoned representatives of all the [Jewish] communities of Aragon and Catalonia, and aimed at nothing less than the complete conversion of the Jews of these areas."*[29] The champion of the Christian side was Hieronymus de Santa Fe, a converted Jew, formerly Joshua Halorki. **Conversos were always the debaters chosen for the Christian side because no Gentile Christian had sufficient knowledge of Hebrew Scripture to contest with an educated Jew!**

From the first, every advantage was taken by the Christians. Fairness was never part of the agenda. *"The Tortosa Disputation was held* [under] *conditions of terror... The Jewish delegates were in constant fear for their lives."*[30] In 1391, a wholesale massacre of Jews had taken place throughout the country. Many Jewish communities had been destroyed. Many of the most prominent Jewish scholars and leaders had been killed.

Now a new rabble rouser priest named Vincent Ferrer, who was later canonized as a saint, traveled the country accompanied by terrifying bands of flagellants! He had whipped up such anti-Semitic fervor that he had forced the implementation of anti-Jewish laws stripping Jews of any rights and forcing many into beggary. The aim was to force the Jews into conversion, while their Jewish leaders were compelled to be at the debate, *"Vincent Ferrer was making a tour of the towns from which the rabbis summoned to the disputation had been drawn... always accompanied by mob risings against the Jews.*

It was in this atmosphere of fear for themselves, their families and their communities that the rabbis took part in the Tortosa Disputation."[31] Rabbi Halevi spoke for the Jewish delegation, *"We are away from our homes; huge damage is resulting in our communities from our absence; we do not know the fate of our wives and children; we have inadequate maintenance here and even lack food, and are put to extraordinary expenses."*[31]

---

[29]Hyam Maccoby, 1982, 1993:p.82, *Judaism on Trial*. [30]*Ibid*, p.83. [31] Ibid, p.84.

Pope Benedict deliberately prolonged the dispute to wear down the Jewish rabbis. Whenever he wished, Benedict *"gave orders that the whole disputation was to start again from the beginning."*[32] The proceeding went on for 69 sessions, one every week or two for more than 21 months, almost two years. The rabbis were not allowed to leave, nor to participate in a fair debate. At one point, Hieronymus cited incorrectly a passage from Raymund Marti's *Pugio Fidei*. Rabbi Halevi had a copy of the actual text to prove him wrong - then Hieronymus snatched it out of his hands and pretended to read the alleged passage from it! By this point, the debate had descended into farce. The Jewish rabbis finally resorted to silence to end the confrontation, *"the weary defense of people baited beyond endurance."*[32]

> The silence of the Jewish scholars was, of course, taken by the Christians as complete defeat. The Pope and the King of Aragon issued a joint declaration and ordinances condemning the Talmud and ordering its censorship, **at the same time bringing in new laws to reduce all Jews to pariah status.** All over the kingdom - Jews were mercilessly harassed and many communities totally destroyed...
>
> The rest of their time in Spain, until their final cruel expulsion in 1492, was a story of mounting tragedy.[32]

The first new law was - *"All Jewish books are to be burned!"*[33]

The Conclusions of Greek Thought

The majority of Jews had now become Christians, many by the heinous use of force, but most converted of their own free will. *"What was the reason for that plague of conversion that attacked Spanish Jewry in such an unprecedented manner?"*[32] According to the Jewish sages of the era, *"Faith in Judaism had been shattered before it was abandoned; and what had shattered that faith... was not Christianity, but the thorough-going, long lasting and corruptive influence of secular [Greek] philosophy."*[32] *"There is no doubt that this - philosophy and the heresies that grew from it - was the cause of our community's destruction."*[34]

The Sephardim had *"denied their traditional teachings while reading into them the conclusions of Greek thought".*[35]

---

[32] Netanyahu, 1999:pp.96-97, *The Marranos of Spain*. [33] Finn, 1841:p.363.
[34] Shem Tov ben Shem Tov, 1556:p.4a, *Sepher ha-Emunot*. [35] Netanyahu, p.99.

There arose today slaves who broke away, who turn into heresy the words of a living God… **The arguments of the Greek, have darkened the eyes of Israel at this time!** [36]

This opinion, though unanimous among the remaining Jews at the time, was mostly wrong. A large segment of the Sephardic Conversos did not reject their Hebrew roots. They embraced their Hebrew Messiah, Yeshua, along with the *Tanakh* and *The Hebrew Gospels*, the feast days, and the true Sabbath.

The rise of new polemical literature, however, reveals a situation fundamentally altered. It shows that the polemicists now recognized the emergence of **a new type of convert, one who took to Christendom not by force of circumstances, or for reasons other than religious, but because of his belief in the teachings of Christianity, in their historic truth and religious promise. The neophytes referred to were socially not of Jewish, but of Marrano origin.** [37]

One of the new polemicists was Profiat Duran. Just as the Christians had attempted to prove the Talmud prophesized and sanctified the Messiah, known to them as Jesus Christ, "*so Duran tried to show that the early Christian writings, and primarily Jesus' sayings, contained an admission of the righteousness of Judaism.*"[38] It was an attempt to call back Jewish Conversos (Marranos) to their Hebrew roots. Instead, it enticed many Marrano Conversos to the new faith - the Messianic faith - that had never lost the righteousness of its Hebrew roots.

The Jews, their religious culture and high intellectual civilization, would eventually rebound after their diaspora from Spain. The Messianics would carry their faith to the New World. These Messianics, rather than the orthodox Jews, were the real threat to the governing power of the Church. The Spanish throne may have lusted after their wealth, but **the Roman Church wanted them, and their Messianic faith, destroyed forever!** The Inquisition was their weapon to achieve that agenda. **Even history was rewritten so that the resurgent Messianic Church and *The Hebrew Gospels* of Spain never existed!**

---

[36]Netanyahu, 1999:p.102, *The Marranos of Spain*. [37]Ibid, p.84-85. [38]Ibid, p.85.

The Spanish Inquisition 1478-1834

> The figures indicate clearly who bore the brunt of the Inquisition. **99.3% of those tried by the Barcelona tribunal between 1488 and 1505, were conversos of Jewish origin. The tribunal, in other words, was not concerned with heresy in general. It was concerned with only one form of religious deviance: the apparently secret practice of Jewish rites**... [Conversos were] faced by the activity of the inquisitors, who now identified as heresy what many converso Christians had accepted as normal practice within their framework of belief.[39] [brackets mine]

This agenda was no mystery - but must be stated - since so many aspects of the Spanish Inquisition are typically confused and often contradictory, as well as reflecting deceitfully contrived spin. From the start, *"The Spanish Inquisition was founded to investigate, punish, and reconcile conversos who continued to practice Judaism."*[40] It was also evident in Ferdinand and Isabella's expulsion order to the Jews, blaming *"**judaizing and wicked Christians** who have deviated from our Holy Catholic Faith."*[41]

> The Spanish Inquisition endured for 350 years. Its first *auto-da-fé* ['*act of faith*' - burning of heretics] was held in Seville, February 6, 1481. The event was a shadow of what such occasions became a century or two later, when hundred of penitents would be led in procession through crowded streets, their sentences pronounced and carried out before an audience of magnates, prelates, and many thousands of onlookers. The king himself might attend. **The choreography of the ritual was meant to invoke the Day of Judgment, when all who have ever lived must face the final justice of God!**[42] [brackets mine]

The huge pyres blazing with the crackle and smell of burning flesh, the cries of the victims in their death throes, the assembly of the royalty of Church and State, the crowds cheering and jeering at their agony - **all designed to present the jaws of hell opening to swallow all Messianics who dared to oppose the authority, power, and dogma of the Roman Church, condemning Messianics to perpetual agony for eternity!**

---

[39]Henry Kamen, 1997:p.57, *The Spanish Inquisition: An Historical Revision*.
[40]Lu Ann Homza, 2006:p.13, *The Spanish Inquisition: An Anthology of Sources*.
[41]Cullen Murphy, 2012:p.73, *God's Jury: Inquisition*.   [42] *Ibid*, Murphy, p.66.

Flight of the Messianics

The first auto-da-fé of the Spanish Inquisition was celebrated on 6 February, 1481, when six people were burnt at the stake... **Conversos, [although] no more than a handful of people had been executed... did not trust the motives or the mercy of the inquisitors...** Over the next few months throughout Andalusia, according to the chronicler Hernando del Pulgar, **thousands of households took flight, women and children included**: *'The absence of these people depopulated a large part of the country, the queen was informed that commerce was declining... she said that the essential thing was to cleanse the country of the sin of heresy.'*[43] [brackets mine]

Historians, then and now, have had various confusing and conflicting opinions - who were these Converso victims of the Inquisition? *"The most plausible view of the matter is probably that held by very many at the time, namely* **that all were practicing Christians, but that some were sympathetic to Judaism**.*"*[44] The Conversos had remained separate from Old Christians - considered upstarts who vaulted to the top of the ladder once converted. After all, Jews could read the classics of medicine, mathematics and science in Hebrew and Arabic. Christians could not.

A factor that undoubtedly contributed to tension, over and above anti-converso feeling, was the conversos' own sense of a separate identity... **proud to be both Christian and of Jewish descent... They were... clearly, a *nation*...** complaints of the Old Christians [were] that the conversos acted *'as a nation apart'*... a people of totally opposed ideas... the converso attitude was the claim they were *better* than Old Christians, because **together with Christian faith they combined direct descent from the lineage of Christ.'** In Aragon **they called themselves proudly *'Christians of Israel.'***[45]

*"The idea of **a converso 'nation'**... rooted itself irrevocably in the mind of Jewish Christians."*[45] **Gerber called it *"a new religion, neither wholly Jewish nor wholly Catholic... converts would remain courageously loyal to this new faith even 'in extremis!'"***[46] Netanyahu called them *"a new type of convert, one who took to Christendom... because of his belief in the teachings of Christiantty."*[47] **The Messianic Nation had truly been born - or perhaps *'reborn'* from the first century - but the Roman Church was soon systematically tearing it apart!**

[43] Henry Kamen, 1997:p.47, *The Spanish Inquisition*. [44] *Ibid*, p.41. [45] *Ibid*, p.42. [46] Jane Gerber, 1992:pp.143-144. [47] Benzion Netanyahu, 1999:p.84.

Signs of a Judaizer

> **If they celebrate the Sabbath**, wear a clean shirt or better garments, spread a clean tablecloth, **light no fire**, eat the food which has been cooked overnight in the oven... **or perform no work on that day**; if they **take neither meat nor drink on the Day of Atonement**, go barefoot, or **ask forgiveness of another on that day**; **if they celebrate the Passover with unleavened bread**, or eat bitter herbs; if on the Feast of Tabernacles they use green branches or send fruit as gifts to friends; if they marry according to Jewish customs or **take Jewish names**; **if they circumcise their boys**... if they wash their hands before praying, **bless a cup of wine before meals and pass it round among the people at table**; if they pronounce blessings while slaughtering poultry... soak the flesh in water before cooking, and cleanse it from blood; if they eat no pork... if, they **give Old Testament names to their children**, or **bless the children by the laying on of hands**... if they wash a corpse with warm water; if they recite the Psalms without adding: "Glory be to the Father, the Son, and the Holy Ghost."[48]

If any superficial element of Judaism was observed - then the accused was a Judaizer - a simple accusation was equivalent to a guilty verdict. Any Jewish custom, no matter how harmless or traditional - was a certain confirmation of Judaizing.

A Converso's belief in the Messiah, whether called Yeshua or Jesus Christ, was immaterial before the court - proven false by any Judaic practice, observing Passover or the Sabbath. A Converso's imitation of his Savior by doing as his Hebrew Messiah, Yeshua, had done was, in fact, proof of his guilt! **One of the most "*dangerous practices was the presence of a Hebrew Bible in the house!*"**[49]

> "*Even… Jewish works in translation would have exposed the owner to persecution; indeed, in the whole vast Inquisitional literature, there is barely a mention of the seizure of Judaistic writings after the sixteenth century.*" The "*voluminous ancient sacred literature…*"[50] **of the Hebrews was destroyed by fire**, replaced by the Roman version of the Bible.

---

[48] Llorente, "*Histoire de l'Inquisition,*" i.153, iv., "Boletin Acad. Hist." xxii.
[49] James Reston, 2005:p.210, *Dogs of God.* [50] Cecil Roth, 1966:p.175-176, *A History of the Marranos*, Harper, NY.

The Missing Messianic Factor

"The differing opinions among scholars in our day are testimony to the highly confusing nature of converso culture."[51] In actual fact, the beliefs and behaviors of the Conversos are not so confusing. **Historians have simply refused to accept the existence of the Messianic Movement!** Nonetheless, history is a science, a social science, and it does yield to logic. Let us look at things logically. The people of the book, Christians and Jews, hold the Old Testament in common. The absolute difference between Jews and Christians is belief in the Hebrew Messiah - Yeshua - better known to Gentiles as Jesus Christ. Jews who embraced Christ as their Savior followed in the footsteps of their Hebrew Messiah. Belief in Christ, or Yeshua, is one of two major factors.

The second factor is whether the Conversos held to their Hebrew tradition or chose to assimilate to the Western [Greco-Roman] tradition. **Those Jewish-Christian believers in the Messiah who held to the Hebrew Sabbaths as Yeshua had done, were true Messianics, the missing factor in the equation!** Others were New Christians who jettisoned their Hebrew culture. Yet others, *"Easy-going Jews who converted for convenience became, naturally, easy-going Christians."*[51] Jews, who converted out of convenience - not out of belief in either faith - would be secular assimilationists. And those Jews who converted by force, without any belief in the Messiah, were the much-ballyhooed Crypto-Jews. These are the two major factors with four logical outcomes:

Sephardim Conversos	Christ Believers	Christ Unbelievers
sons of Zion: Hebrew Tradition	***Messianics***	**Crypto-Jews**
sons of Greece: Western Tradition	**New Christians**	**Secular Assimilationists**

[51] Kamen, 1997:p.41, *The Spanish Inquisition*. [51] *Ibid*, Kamen, p.37.

Kamen opined, "*We may conclude that there was not, in the late 1470s, any proven or significant Judaizing movement among the conversos... there was no systematic 'converso religion' in the 1480s to justify the creation of an Inquisition. Much of the evidence for judaizing was thin, if not false.*"[52] Kamen's condemnation of the Spanish Inquisition as operating on a '*fiction*' is welcome - especially when countering the solidarity of historians that all Conversos were Crypto-Jews, "*which appear to justify the establishment of the Inquisition.*"[52]

To be sure, there is no possible Christian justification for the Inquisition, unless you drop the *Christ* out of Christian! However, Kamen's conclusion is skewed as well! It does not take into account the Messianic Factor. The *Hebrew Gospels from Catalonia* come from the late 1470s, and constitute irrefutable evidence of a '*judaizing*' Messianic Movement with enormous appeal during those cataclysmic times to great masses of Jews - who were, "*motivated by a fervent conviction the messianic era was near.*"[53]

"*A new catalogue of the Hebrew manuscripts in the Vatican Library published in 2008... adds that it* [*The Hebrew Gospels from Catalonia* aka Vat. Ebr. 100] *can possibly be **dated to 1479***"[57] [brackets mine]. If this is true then it scuttles Kamen's conclusion, "*there was not, in the late 1470s, any proven or significant Judaizing movement among the conversos... there was no systematic 'converso religion.'* "[54]

The Hebrew Gospels [HGC] were written by Messianics - Jewish Christians who wrote in Hebrew using Jewish conventions - such as always substituting '*Hashem*' or '*Adonai*' for the name of God. This was not written for Jews, who rejected the New Testament - nor for Old Christians, who rejected Hebrew Scripture. It was not written as a polemic since there are no arguments against Christianity. As the primary scholar translating *The Hebrew Gospels from Catalonia*, I can say without reservation, the Messiah and his Word are both treated with profound reverence. **It's undeniable!** ***The Hebrew Gospels* were resurrected by and for Messianic believers - as the foundation of their movement - a '*systematic Converso religion.*'** The Messianic Church had been reborn!

---

[52] Henry Kamen, 1997:pp.40-41, *The Spanish Inquisition.* [53] Jane Gerber, 1992:p.119, *The Jews of Spain.* [54] Harvey Hames, 2012:p.286, *A 15th Century Hebrew Version of the Gospels*, citing Ben Richler, 2008:p.67.

Henry Kamen cites deep confusion and conflict among prominent historians, *"Yitzhak Baer states uncompromisingly that 'the conversos and Jews were one people, united by destiny.' 'Every converso,' writes another historian, 'did his best to fulfil Mosaic precepts, and one should regard as sincere the aim they all set themselves: to live as Jews.'"*[55] **Yet on the same page Kamen questions -** *"The ambiguous religion of conversos raised a crucial question. Were the conversos Jews?"*[55]

"Among the Jews there appear to have been no doubts about the Christianity of the conversos... The most convincing testimony of all can be found after the founding of the Inquisition. The failure of Jews, in those years, to make any significant move to help conversos, shows that they were conscious of the gap between them."[56] As long as they were thought to be forced, the Jewish community embraced the Conversos as their own.

"In Mallorca, a rabbi commented that the conversos here were virtually practicing Jews, from the Christian point of view. Enjoying official tolerance, they remained as Christians. And it was their voluntary Christianity which marked them out in Jewish eyes as renegades, meshumadim."[57] If the Conversos were indeed *"virtually practicing Jews,"* why were they derided as *'meshumadim,'* renegades? Early on, the rabbis had determined that *anusim* - forced converts - were still their brothers in the faith. *"In... Aragon, royal decrees made it plain the forced conversions were unacceptable. Jews could... return to their own religion."*[55]

None of this makes sense without the Messianic Factor! Many Conversos practiced the Mosaic precepts although they were committed Jewish Christian believers in the Messiah. They were practitioners of what must have seemed to outsiders as that *"ambiguous religion of conversos."* Although continuing Hebrew practices, they were still committed Christians. Once it became evident the Conversos and their descendants were not returning to Judaism - Jewish attitudes changed into bitter opposition. Many New Christians led the persecution of Jews - and many Jews informed on Conversos during the Inquisition.

---

[55]Henry Kamen, 1997:p.37, *The Spanish Inquisition*, citing Yitzhak Baer, 1966: vol 2, p.424, *A History of the Jews in Christian Spain*, and Haim Beinart, 1981:p.242, *Conversos on Trial*. [56]Kamen, p.38. [57]*Ibid*, p.37. [58]*Ibid*, p.10.

Pulgar reports that within the same converso household some members might be sincere Christians and others active Jews... many *'lived neither in one law nor the other,'* retaining key Jewish customs while practicing formal Christianity. **None of this altered the essentially Christian culture of most conversos. The syncretic nature of much of their religious practice left their faith unaffected.**[59]

The narrative that all Conversos were Crypto-Jews is patently ridiculous, defying not only logic and the surviving evidence but also the saving grace of the Messiah. **The existence of the Messianic Church and** *The Hebrew Gospels* **in Spain during the Middle Ages can no longer be doubted!** But their existence has been assaulted with severe criticism and deceitful slander. **The first words** of *The Hebrew Gospels from Catalonia* (HGC) are **"With the help of heaven, I begin this,"** in Aramaic using Hebrew letters:

בסד אתחיל דא

Pinchas Lapide, who reviewed *The Hebrew Gospels* in his book *Hebrew in the Church*, wrote this about it. *"The Hebrew manuscript Vat. Ebr. 100 of the Vatican Library... was in all probability made under duress by a Jewish scholar...* **The first words, preceding even the introduction, are bs"r 'thyl, which can be translated as 'I am beginning under duress.'**"[60] In discussion with Nehemia Gordon about this issue, he agreed to research it and sent me the following comment:

> בסד Bet Samech Dalet is a ubiquitous acronym, which stands for
> בסיעתא דשמיא Aramaic for *'with the help of heaven.'*
> Orthodox Jews write this in the upper right corner
> of every piece of paper they write on, whether it's
> a page in their diary or their shopping list.
>
> It's almost unbelievable that someone as knowledgeable
> as Lapide would misread this as בצער אתחיל
> *'I begin in distress'* and then mistranslate
> his misreading as *'I begin under duress!'*[61]

Lapide offered a few more, equally spurious, criticisms but he is so biased, so far off base, there is no point in examining them.

[59] Kamen, 1997:p.38. [60] Pinchas Lapide, 1984:p.48, *Hebrew in the Church*, Eerdmans, Grand Rapids, 1976 in German as *Hebräisch in den Kirchen*.
[61] Personal email communication with Nehemia Gordon, 2018.

Converso separateness had a certain logic. The large number of converts after 1391 could not be fitted into existing social structures. In Barcelona and Valencia in the 1390s they were given their own churches, in each case a former synagogue. They also set up their own Converso confraternities.[62]

This happened across Spain. One of these co-religious organizations was the *yeshiva*, religious school. Cecil Roth points out a new discretion was required in light of the Inquisition: *"For this purpose,* **the ancient Jewish rite of Bar Mitzvah, at the end of the 13th year,** *when a boy entered upon his full religious responsibilities... became transformed into initiation to the secret rites and mysteries of Marranism."*[62] Antonio Castello was *"martyred at Lisbon in 1647... for instructing children in Jewish practices at the age of 13...* **the religion into which a child was thus initiated was... far removed from integral Judaism.**"[63]

The Bar Mitzvah was first ritualized in the Middle Ages in France and Spain.[64] **To the Messianic Church it was the sacred continuation of the Bar Mitzvah of Yeshua in Luke 2:46 when, at the age of twelve, he went to Jerusalem** for Passover and *"after three days they found him in the Temple, sitting in the midst of the rabbis, both hearing them, and asking them questions. And all that heard him were astonished..."*

In the early stage of the Messianic Movement, Messianic yeshivas existed, as did Messianic Churches often within former synagogues, they had Converso priests and Converso bishops some of whom were former rabbis. The Messianic Church also had Hebrew Bibles, and *The Hebrew Gospels*!

Why is there any question of a resurgent Messianic Church in Medieval Spain which sincerely believed in the Hebrew Messiah and imitated his Hebrew practices? By now it should be clear - **the Roman Church wished to erase the Messianic Church along with** *The Hebrew Gospels!* The Church spun the narrative that Marranos were merely an heretical sect of crypto-Jews, not Christians at all! That was their *modus operandi* for all believers who did not bow to Roman authority and doctrine! All were heretics, not Christians! **Your faith meant nothing - your life meant nothing - nor the lives of your family - if you followed the Hebrew Messiah!**

[62]Henry Kamen, 1997:p.42, *The Spanish Inquisition*. [63]Cecil Roth, 1966:p.174, *History of the Marranos*. [64]Michael Hilton, 2014, *Bar Mitzvah: A History*.

Part 4

The New World

*The Gospel of the kingdom shall be preached
in all the world for a witness unto all nations;
And then the end shall come.*

Matthew 24:14

Chapter Seven
The Hammer of the Inquisition

The time is coming when anyone who kills you will think they are offering a service to God.
John 16:2

The purpose of the Spanish Inquisition was to utterly destroy the Messianic Movement in Spain! The procedures of the Inquisition were the weapons to carry out that destruction. They do not reflect any attempt at truth or justice but rather a rigged game with evil, malicious, and murderous intent. Conversos accused of heresy were imprisoned without knowing for what crime. They could not defend themselves against unnamed informants. The Inquisitors did not convict the accused on the evidence but instead depended on confessions obtained by torture.

Victims, unable to defend themselves against anonymous witnesses and unknown accusations, were tortured until they confessed to *something!* The *'legal'* representation they were permitted, only after confession, was a sham. Their *'lawyer'* had only the Inquisition's case against them and routinely recommended they confess and plead to be reconciled with the Church. They remained imprisoned and the judgement of the Inquisition Tribunal was not known to the accused until the very day of the *'auto-da-fé.'* *"Innocence became a near impossibility for anyone accused. The best one could hope for was to be 'reconciled' to the Church and merely lose land and property, or to be jailed indefinitely in an ecclesiastical prison."*[1]

Many thousands of Conversos were burnt at the stake. Others died from the effects of torture. Many more were reconciled with the Church! Nonetheless, their property was seized, their families reduced to beggary, their reputation and their family's would be blackened for generations to come - always in danger of the Inquisition renewing charges against them or their descendants. Countless more Conversos died in prison, or from anti-Converso violence and pogroms. Many more died of deprivation after their family's property was seized - reducing them to starvation. Many fled in order to survive - often suffering robbery, rape, murder, and famine. **The Inquisition was the hammer that drove Messianic immigration to the New World!**

---

[1] James Reston, 2005:p.109, *Dogs of God.*

The Inquisition was a tragic story of villains and victims, of heroes and martyrs! It was played out on a world scene replete with momentous events and historic social change. The Renaissance was made possible by the Golden Age of Spain. The influx from the East of lost knowledge of the Greeks and Hebrews came to Europe via Messianic and Jewish scribes. That ended with the onslaught of pogroms leading up to the Inquisition. Once the Muslims were vanquished, the Jews were also expelled from Spain. The horror of the Spanish Inquisition was launched - to last 356 years - and destined to destroy mighty Spain itself and its empire! Columbus, a Messianic himself, opened up the New World in 1492. Emigrant Jews - fleeing the expulsion, and Messianics - fleeing the Inquisition, settled there in droves. **The horrors of the Spanish Inquisition planted the seed of Reformation deep within the consciousness of Europe!**

Purpose of the Inquisition

The first Inquisition, called the Medieval Inquisition, was initiated in 1231 by Pope Gregory IX to deal with the Cathars. In 1252 a papal bull was decreed by Pope Innocent IV *"which justified and encouraged the use of torture!"*[2] This should be a crystal-clear indicator that **the Inquisition**, whenever and wherever it was used, **was not about salvation, or justice, or even evidence - it was about destroying the competitors to the Roman Church** - and terrorizing all to bow to Rome's authority.

"In 1478, Ferdinand the Fifth of Aragon, the husband of the celebrated Isabella... obtained a bull, or papal decree, from Pope Sixtus introducing the Inquisition into Castile."[3] **The purpose of the Spanish Inquisition was to utterly destroy the Messianic Church** and brand a wound so deep into the collective consciousness of the Messianic Movement - that they would never again raise their heads to challenge the supremacy of the Roman Church! It is quite apparent that King Ferdinand was *"hankering after the great wealth possessed by the Jews."*[3] Isabella the Pious, at first protective of the Jews, was finally brought around by her confessor Tomas de Torquemada. He became the first Grand Inquisitor and unleashed a cruel reign of terror!

---

[2] Cullen Murphy, 2012:p.9, *God's Jury*, Houghton Mifflin, New York, N.Y.
[3] Janet Gordon, 1896:p.4, *The Spanish Inquisition*, Nimmo, Hay & Mitchell Publishers, Edinburgh, Scotland.

One can still find websites and individuals who justify or dismiss the Inquisition. The ultimate defense - in the final analysis - is that the victims were, after all, *"heretics!"* *"History does not justify the hypothesis that the medieval heretics were prodigies of virtue, deserving our sympathy."** These apologists downplay the effects of the Inquisition and ignore it as much as possible - as was done with the rejection and destruction of the original Messianic-Apostolic Church. This original apostasy barely merits a footnote in church history - if it is acknowledged at all! May the reader not be so pliant as to forget.

> The Inquisition, only recently abolished in Spain... was a mighty engine of oppression, it brooded like an incubus over the land, repressing all progress and freedom of thought, and menacing prince and peasant alike with its pitiless invisible arm. Sitting in secrecy, its judges exercised in effect an irresponsible despotism, unchecked save by the feeble remonstrance of consciences seared by the perpetual commission of cruelties which seem almost incredible. Its arrests were made secretly, and a midnight; and its conduct to the prisoners in its power was systematically pitiless and unjust. Under a pretended mask of law and justice it falsified facts, and kept back or concealed circumstances which might have proved the innocence of its wretched victims, so that it was almost impossible to obtain an acquittal, particularly if the suspected person were rich; wealth being found, under the jurisdiction of this tribunal, which had no revenues except what it drew from the confiscation of heretics, to be a frequent provocative to the imputation of that crime...
>
> An impenetrable curtain of the deepest gloom veiled from the eyes of the public the dread inner world in which the inquisitors perpetrated their deeds of cruelty and injustice. One after another, the busy merchant, the eloquent preacher, the enlightened savant, the noble[man]... liberalized by travels in distant hands, were seen to disappear, to reappear again upon some morning of doom, in the dread *sanbenito*, at the fatal place of burning - shrinking from the light of day, haggard, enfeebled, with limbs distorted by the rack and pulley, the trembling, shuddering actors in the ghastly *auto-da-fe!* Verily there is no sadder, more shameful chapter of human suffering and wrong, than may be read in the record of **what men have done, ostensibly for conscience sake, and to do God service - as if the merciful Creator and Preserver of universal nature had been some Moloch - insatiably thirsting for human blood!** [4]

**The Catholic Encyclopedia,* 1907, entry on *"Inquisition."* [4]Janet Gordon, 1896:pp.2-3, *The Spanish Inquisition*, Nimmo, Hay & Mitchell, Edinburgh.

The first Inquisitors

"The Monks from whom the first inquisitors were chosen, were members of the recently established and fanatical order of the Dominicans."[5] Dominic Guzman (1170-1221 AD) was an ascetic Monk who established the Dominican order. Dominic sold all his earthly goods, including his precious manuscripts, and gave all his money away to the poor. According to Jean Guirand, his biographer, *"Dominic abstained from meat, 'observed stated fasts and periods of silence, selected the worst accommodations and the meanest clothes, and never allowed himself the luxury of a bed."*[6] Even as he was dying he instructed his fellow priests to lay him upon sackcloth stretched out on the floor.

In 1204 Dominic traveled through the south of France where he *"met with Cistercian monks who had been sent by Pope Innocent III to preach against the Cathars* [without success]. *Dominic attributed the Cistercians' lack of success to their extravagance and pomp compared to the asceticism of the Cathars."*[7] Dominic had no involvement with the Inquisition of the Cathars - that was still 20 years in the future. It is impossible to imagine that the gentle, giving Saint Dominic would countenance the torture of the faithful for lack of doctrinal purity. So the deviation of his order into serving as **torturers of the Inquisition**, a century later, can only be seen as a travesty of his life's mission! In any case, **it earned the Dominicans the everlasting shame of the sobriquet - "*Domini Canes*" the '*Dogs of God!*'**[8]

Procedure of the Inquisition

The Inquisitor would go into a community and *"preach a sermon, urging heretics to abjure their beliefs, and would declare a period of grace during which they could repent with relative ease. At the same time he would commence to hear accusations against specific individuals. When the period of grace expired, he would set about conducting trials."*[9]

---

[5] Janet Gordon, 1896:p.3, *The Spanish Inquisition*, Nimmo, Hay & Mitchell Publishers, Edinburgh, Scotland. [6] Jean Guirand, 1913:pp.116 & 156, *Saint Dominic*, Duckworth Publishing, Britain. [7] Walter F. Hooks, 1846:p.467, *An Ecclesiastical Biography: A Brief History of the Church in Every Age*, Rivington Press, Oxford. [8] James Reston, 2005, *Dogs of God*, Anchor Books, N.Y.
[9] Cullen Murphy, 2012:p.35, *God's Jury*, Houghton Mifflin, New York.

"The period of grace was a trap... Its lenient terms coupled with its 'sell-by' date, encouraged people to come forward quickly and own up to something - anything - if only to put the matter behind them. It also encouraged them to turn in their neighbors - an inducement [that] feeds on tainted motives. **In a sense the period of grace ended up 'creating' heresy.**"[10]

The accused were arrested and imprisoned. They were not told who informed upon them nor the charges against them. According to the rules set by Rome, they could only be tortured once. However, the Inquisition was not of a mind to be restrained by such rules. False witnesses were common. Informants were enticed by offering a share of the confiscated property of the accused. Such informants were still assumed to be truthful. Enormous pressure was put upon penitents to give up their neighbors. Possible charges of heresy or other means were used to extract accusations. For example, **a notary at Jaén,** *"locked a young girl of fifteen in a room, stripped her naked, and whipped her until she agreed to testify against her mother!"*[11]

Torture was not supposed to draw blood (which it did frequently), or cause grave injury (which it did frequently), nor lead to death (which happened often enough). A physician was supposed to be present to prevent such things. I know of no reports where a physician was actually present either during torture or to give treatment afterwards when a victim most typically died. The *'torture once rule'* was often interpreted as once for each charge, or if the torture was not done *"correctly"* then it could be reapplied. The Priest-Inquisitors worked in pairs - just in case the accused died due to an excess of zeal - *"As for clerics participating in torture - surely it would be permissible if inquisitors absolved one another (as they came to do)."*[12]

Imprisonment of the accused may last years until the next auto-da-fe. Only on the day of execution were they to know their charges and judgement. Many died in prison awaiting final judgement. The Inquisition kept extensive records on all those accused. Yet when the Roman Catholic Church finally did an assessment of how many died in the Inquisition, those dying in the prisons were not included as victims of the Inquisition.

[11] Henry Kamen, 1998:p.74, *The Spanish Inquisition*, Yale University Press.
[12] Cullen Murphy, 2012:p.56, *God's Jury*, Houghton Mifflin, New York.

Three Levels of Prisons

*"The prisons of the Inquisition, these were of three kinds, and were called, according to their varying degrees of rigour, the **public**, the **intermediate**, and the **secret** prisons. The first, which were airy and well-lighted apartments, were reserved for prisoners not suspected of heresy, but of other crimes... which the Inquisition... acquired the privilege of punishing."*[13] It should go without saying that these were for the nobility, the wealthy and influential. Since an accusation of heresy was virtually a guilty sentence in itself, they were charged with other crimes - which they may well have committed. Yet being made prisoners of the Inquisition was clearly to terrorize them. The threat of an accusation of heresy, real imprisonment, torture and death - was omnipresent - without needing acknowledgement. This manipulation made the prisoners compliant to the desires of both the throne and the Inquisition. The ***public*** prisons were clearly to leverage something from the accused - cooperation, money, information or simply an unmistakable threat of what awaited further defiance!

"The second series of cells, also well-lighted, and tolerably comfortable, were used for those servants of the Inquisition who, although guiltless of the taint of heresy, had committed some breach of their contract."[13] As strange as this may sound to the reader - this gives me some redemptive hope about the priests of the Apostate Roman Church. Remember the Inquisition only had authority over fellow Christians. **Apparently, so many priests balked at the bidding of the Inquisition to imprison, torture and burn alive their fellow believers that a whole prison system was needed to coerce them into the grisly tasks they were ordered to perform!** Unfortunately, no *mea culpa* writing of any of these imprisoned priests, forced into evil, has ever survived. It would tell us so much. One can only imagine that some, perhaps many, priests were martyred in secret.

"The third, which consisted of damp, foul, underground vaults, were for those unhappy individuals who, suspected of heresy or heretical leanings, formed the natural prey of this tribunal."[13]
These secret prisons were the heart of darkness!

---
[13] Janet Gordon, 1896:p.7. *The Spanish Inquisition*, Nimmo. Hay & Mitchell Publishers, Edinburgh, Scotland.

"The wretched occupants of these foul, unwholesome dungeons were often chained to the wall, where they passed away the slow days in bleak, blank isolation, with no light except such faint glimmers of heaven's sunshine as could struggle through a slit in the thick walls, and fall upon them where they sat in utter solitude, which was unbroken, save when an inquisitor came...

Until then, the accused would in all probability have been ignorant of the crime laid to his charge... His visitor then proceeded to examine him rigorously as to his parentage and genealogy; and if he was so unhappy as to have... Jewish blood in his veins, as a great proportion of Spaniards had, or to have an ancestor suspected, or accused of heretical leanings, the fact was put down, to be afterwards used against him, apparently on the supposition that a corrupt fountain cannot send forth anything but impure waters."[14]

The writing was on the wall - the Inquisition was targeting Messianics - within two years the first *auto-da-fe* would be held, burning believers alive for their lack of Roman faith. Few were deceived. **"Conversos... did not trust the motives nor the mercy of the inquisitors... Over the next few months... thousands of households took flight, women and children included**: *'The absence of these people depopulated a large part of the country.'*"[15] Those who stayed - hoping to weather the storm - turned to the Word of God, *The Hebrew Gospels!* It was at this perilous moment that the Gospels in Hebrew were restored. Whatever manuscripts were out there had gone underground with the brutal onslaught of the Inquisition. *The Hebrew Gospels* were retranslated back into Hebrew from the *Catalan Gospels* which had originally come from the extant *Hebrew Gospels*.

The Hebrew Gospels from Catalonia (HGC)

Very few scholars have bothered with *The Hebrew Gospels from Catalonia*. A Hebrew manuscript of the Gospels comes with the stated assumption that it is a translation from the Latin or Greek, thus proclaiming it of no possible importance. We will examine their authenticity in detail once more when we discuss the discovery of *The Cochin Hebrew Gospels* in a later chapter.[16] See the Appendix for a brief proof of their first century origin.

---

[14] Janet Gordon, 1896:pp.3-4, *The Spanish Inquisition*, Nimmo, Hay & Mitchell Pub., Edinburgh, Scotland. [15] Henry Kamen, 1998:p.47, *The Spanish Inquisition*, Yale U. Press. [16] Also in Jones, 2019, *Sons of Zion vs Sons of Greece*.

Analysis of The Hebrew Gospels

The Hebrew Gospels from Catalonia were first mentioned in the literature by Humbertus Cassuto, who first cataloged the Hebrew archives of the Vatican in 1956. Before that mention, the record is silent for almost 500 years upon this manuscript. It is very significant that the existence of *The Hebrew Gospels* was discovered only after World War II. The Holocaust dramatically changed Vatican attitudes towards all things Hebraic, causing them to tone down the anti-Semitic bias and adopt a scholarly appreciation for these ancient biblical manuscripts. Cassuto's brief mention of *The Hebrew Gospels* noted "*that **the version of the Gospels contained in this manuscript differs essentially from those we have known to this day**... it has been made from a Catalan version.*"[17]

The first researcher to take more than a superficial look at Vat. Ebr. 100, *The Hebrew Gospels from Catalonia,* was Mathias Delcor in 1981.[18] Delcor translated chapter 10 of Matthew and compared it with the Shem Tov. Delcor had the knowledge of the ancient tongues of Provençal and Catalan necessary for this study. It is not Delcor's skills which concern me but his presumptions. Greco-Roman primacy of the New Testament demands we begin with these presumptions; **1) All original manuscripts of the Gospels were in Greek, therefore - This manuscript is a translation originally from Greek (or Latin). 2) Since these were done by Jews - there was some sinister motivation in this manuscript to attack the faith of Christians.**

> I have chosen to translate from Hebrew - chapter 10 of Matthew... My choice has been motivated... by the fact it announces the persecutions [the Apostles] suffered by their co-religionists, the Jews, in the synagogues.
>
> **A Jewish translator would no doubt have a certain attitude in regard to the texts relating these things, which reveals at the same time his mentality.**[19]

Delcor did his research and published it in 1981. It seems the anti-Semitic bias, so typical of the Middle Ages, was still alive and well in the 20th century.

---

[17] Humbertus Cassuto, 1956:pp.144-145, *Codices Vaticani Hebraici* 1-115, Bybliotheca Vaticana. [18] Matias Delcor, 1981:p.202, "Un manuscript hébraïque inédit des quatre évangiles conservé a la Bibliothéque Vaticane" (Vat. Ebr. 100), *Anuario de Filología,* volume 7, pp.201-219.   [19] *Ibid.,* Delcor, 1981:p.202.

It is not a question of whether or not there are anti-Christian propaganda documents in Hebrew. They exist. I am simply highlighting the bias of starting with that presumption. All efforts are devoted to finding sinister intent - and no effort to the possibility **there is none to be found!**

> **It is known that for a long time the translation of the Bible into the Catalan language was prohibited.** In 1235, the Archbishop of Taragon forbid the possession of a book of the New Testament or the Old Testament because of the danger of disseminating Albigensianism. In fact, during the 13th century, in the south of Langueduc... **a translation of the New Testament had been made after a Latin text used in the country by heretic Cathars.**[20]

We have already examined the evidence of the authenticity of the Cathar Bible - that it pre-dated the Latin Vulgate. **Yet here we see it presumed to be a translation from a Latin text**. Delcor is using this as a set-up to his conclusion: *"We see then that by the 15th century... The Gospel in a Catalan translation had already been common. It was, therefore, possible an educated Jew could have procured a copy and translated it."*[21]

Delcor is insinuating, if not declaring outright, that *The Hebrew Gospels from Catalonia,* although translated from Catalan, were originally first translated from Latin - and **not only that but they are of heretical origin!** One can certainly try to argue the text is from Latin, or Greek. However, to begin with that assumption is to never explore the possibility of a Hebraic origin.

Delcor falls right into this trap of faulty premises when he concludes his comparison of Vat. Ebr. 100 - **chapter 10** of Matthew, with the translation of Hebrew Matthew **chapter 10** in the Shem Tov. *"**The comparison** between [Shem Tov Ibn] Shaprut and our manuscript... **obliges us to conclude negatively. We are really in the presence of a version totally different** than that of the celebrated Spanish Rabbi."*[22] If Delcor had looked past his presumptions he might have concluded differently. On the following page are some of the results of my comparison of the entire book of Matthew in *The Hebrew Gospels from Catalonia* and the entire *Shem Tov Hebrew Matthew.*

---

[20]Matias Delcor, 1981:pp.218-219, "Un manuscript hébraïque inédit des quatre évangiles conservé a la Bibliothéque Vaticane" (Vat. Ebr. 100), *Anuario de Filología,* volume 7, pp.201-219.   [21] *Ibid,* p.219.   [22] *Ibid,* p.216.

I did the initial translation of **all** the chapters of Matthew in *The Hebrew Gospels from Catalonia* [HGC]. Then I compared them to George Howard's translation of **all** the chapters of the Shem Tov Manuscript [STM] of *Hebrew Matthew*. [23] **There are many matching verses found in no other versions of Matthew - only in *The Hebrew Gospels* [HGC] and the *Shem Tov* Manuscript [STM].** Here are two examples, for more - review the complete analysis in chap. two, pp.48-51 of this book.

In Matthew 5:35 of the [New] King James Version [KJV], which is basically a straight translation from the Latin Vulgate, it says *"Jerusalem...city of the Great King"* while both the HGC and STM say *"city of God."* We have support for our Hebrew Gospel version since **there is a *scholia* (note) in the margin of the *Codex Sinaiticus* of the Greek *Septuagint* at Matt 5:35 which says** *"In the Hebrew Gospel it says city of God."* There are many other examples of very unique matching verses.

Another unique example is Matthew 28:9, when Yeshua was resurrected and met the two Marys on the road. In the KJV it says *"Jesus met them saying, All Hail."* In the HGC, Yeshua says *"[May] God save you."* - in the STM it says essentially the same *"[May] God deliver you."* Note this is the way believers were commanded to address each other - **using the name of God! *"All Hail!"* is not a Hebrew greeting!** It is the Roman military salute in which the greeter slams his fist on his breastplate and thrusts it into the air. Adolf Hitler later adopted the Roman military salute as the official Nazi salute. **Thanks to *The Hebrew Gospels* we can assure you that Yeshua did not greet his followers with the Nazi salute!** We can also conclude the HGC and the STM came from a common Hebrew source text.

Why does this matter? Some would think it a trivial point. Not so. **We have authenticated a first century source of *The Hebrew Gospels from Catalonia*!** (See the Appendix) **If the Shem Tov Hebrew Matthew comes from the same common Hebrew source text as *The Hebrew Gospels*, then the *Shem Tov* has come from a first century source as well!** *"In my judgement, Shem Tov the polemist did not prepare this text by translating it from the Latin Vulgate, the Byzantine Greek, or any other known version of the Gospel of Matthew. He received it from previous generations of Jewish scribes..."*[23]

---

[23] George Howard, 1995:p.1, *Hebrew Gospel of Matthew*, Mercer Univ. Press.

Delio Proverbio did an important study of the provenance of Vat. Ebr. 100 [HGC]. It was obtained by the Vatican Library from the collection of bibliophile banker Ulrich Fugger. *"Indeed, the current Vat. Heb. 100 was located in Augsburg, ancestral city of the Fuggers, until 1567."* [24] This manuscript of *The Hebrew Gospels* became part of the Vatican collection in 1623.

Another manuscript was bound on top of the *"Hebrew version of the four Gospels: the Hebrew version of* **Sindbad** *al-hakim,* or *"History of the Seven Viziers, the well-known fairytale collection... which the Arab tradition has preserved... incorporated into the* **Thousand and One Nights**.*"*[24] **These tales of Sinbad** (aka **Sindebar**) were some of the stories in the *Thousand and One Nights* (of Scheherazade). We have already discussed their importance in transmitting and preserving knowledge of ancient Greek, Persian, Arabic and Hebrew culture from the Orient. It is noteworthy *Scheherazade* makes a reappearance here - bound on top of *The Hebrew Gospels!* There is no doubt this was done to hide *The Hebrew Gospels*. Binding beneath another text was a well-known medieval method for preserving endangered manuscripts.

Harvey Hames did some of the more extensive investigation into *The Hebrew Gospels from Catalonia*.[25] He mentions that the prefaces to Matthew, Mark, and Luke come from Jerome in the fourth century. *"It is not a literal translation, but a paraphrase with some additional comments."* Jerome often spoke of his translation of *The Hebrew Gospel* into Latin and Greek. He added these prefaces in Hebrew at that time. Therefore, they would not be a translation from the Greek. As Hames confirms, *"For instance,* **the introduction to Matthew states it** [the Gospel] **was written in Hebrew for the Jewish followers of Jesus...** *The Hebrew translation does not contain the preface to John which might suggest the translator used a* [earlier] *manuscript that became the basis for the Pieresc manuscript of the Gospels."*[25] (brackets mine)

---

[24] Delio Vania Proverbio, 2000, *"Vangeli Ebraico"* [Hebrew Gospels] in - *I Vangeli di Popoli: La Parola e l'immagine del Cristo nella culture e nella storia*, ed. Francesco d'Aiuto - Giovanni Morello - Ambrogio Piazonni, Vatican City: Biblioteca Apostolica Vaticana, pp.372-374.

[25] Harvey Hames, 2012:p.291, *Translated from Catalan: A 15th Century Hebrew Version of the Gospels*, In *Knowledge and Vernacular Languages in the Age of LLull...*, Publicacions de l'Abadia de Montserrat, Barcelona.

In his preface, Jerome clearly stated that Matthew was first written in Hebrew. You will not find that statement in any Greek or Latin preface to the Gospels! Hames surmised that *The Hebrew Gospels from Catalonia* [HGC] were perhaps not copied directly from the Pieresc but from a common ancestor in Catalan at that time. It is likely that common ancestor was the extant *Hebrew Gospels*!

"This possibility should also be considered regarding the chapter divisions in Matthew. In the Hebrew version [of Matthew from the HGC], *there are 54 chapters,"*[26] rather than the 28 chapters of Matthew in modern versions, including the Pieresc. This *"perhaps reflects an older Catalan manuscript."*[26] Or, as I have suggested, an older *Hebrew* manuscript.

So, where did these 54 chapter divisions in the HGC Gospel of Matthew come from? The earliest comment on *The Hebrew Gospel* was from Papias (60-130 AD), *"Matthew collected the 'oracles'* [sayings of the Messiah] *in the Hebrew language."* In the Shem Tov *Hebrew Matthew* there are 114 chapters - twice as many as the 54 of Matthew in the HGC.

In the Shem Tov, each time Yeshua speaks, a new chapter is begun even if it has only a few lines. **Each saying of Yeshua is set apart! The 54 chapters in the HGC *Matthew* follow the same pattern** even though there are half as many. When Yeshua speaks, a new chapter begins - setting apart each saying of the Messiah - as Papias noted in the first century.

Hames cites the Hebrew preface to Matthew, *"Jesus Christ, about whom they speak was a human."* Then he comments, *"This could be seen as a polemical statement whereby Christ's divinity is denied by the translator, thereby perhaps giving an indication about the identity of the author and the reason for translation."*[27] Two points here; 1) nowhere in the HGC does it use *Jesus Christ* but always *Yeshuas Mashiach*. 2) **it seems obligatory for researchers to find something anti-Christian in *The Hebrew Gospels*!** Hames does note, *"However this is not in keeping with the rest of the work where the translator makes no conscious effort to polemicise against Christian doctrine."*[28]

---

[26] Harvey Hames, 2012:p.291, *Translated from Catalan: A 15th Century Hebrew Version of the Gospels*. [27] Ibid., Hames, p.292. [28] Ibid., p.292-293.

Hames goes on to say *"But what of the Gospel texts themselves? Can it be established that the Hebrew version was translated from the Catalan? What is fascinating is that **in the Hebrew translation, the first four verses of Luke are missing and the translation starts from the fifth verse - and the same happens in the Pieresc manuscript as well.*"[29]

The Hebrew Gospels' book of Luke **begins** with the fifth verse, "*In the days when Herod was king of Judea.*" And so **begins** the Pieresc manuscript of the Gospel of Luke as well. It was Epiphanius (315-403 AD), one of the early Messianic (Jewish-Christian) believers and bishop of Salamis, who wrote. "*They call it The Hebrew Gospel... the **beginning** of their Gospel has this... In the days when Herod was king of Judea.*"[30]

But what of the first four verses? Why are they not in the Hebrew version? **The first four verses of the Greek canon of Luke say it has been copied from the written witness of the Hebrew Apostles**. This is all solid evidence of the authenticity of *The Hebrew Gospels*. This *'prologue'* of Luke is never quoted from the pulpit. Silence is a most effective argument - as few will question this prologue - unless its precise meaning is pointed out.

> [1]For as much as many have taken in hand to set forth in order those things which are most surely believed among us.
>
> [2]Even as they delivered them unto us, whom from the beginning were eyewitnesses and ministers of the word.
>
> [3]I resolved also, having traced all things from the start with accuracy, to write them unto you in order...
>
> Prologue to Luke 1:1-3

The wording "*taken in hand to set forth in order those things*" makes explicit reference to the writing of the gospel narrative by others **before** the author of Luke. "*Even as they delivered them unto us*" means the author had the narratives of those others who "*from the beginning were eyewitness and ministers of the word.*" This refers to the original Hebrew Apostles of Yeshua the Messiah. **Since Greek Luke is a copy as stated in Luke 1:1-4 - and Hebrew Luke does not include the proclamation that it a copy - then logically Hebrew Luke is the original!** [31]

---

[29] Harvey Hames, 2012:p.293, *Translated from Catalan: A 15th Century Hebrew Version of the Gospels.* [30] James Edwards, 2009:pp.68 & 117, *The Hebrew Gospels.* [31] Miles Jones, 2019:p.174, *Sons of Zion versus Sons of Greece.* **The first 4 verses are also missing in the Hebrew Luke of Vat. Ebr. 530!**

Pere Casanellas wrote the latest article (in 2014) on the study of Vat. Ebr. 100 (along with Harvey Hames). Casanellas, like Hames and Delcor before him, is a superb and highly skilled researcher. Perhaps that is why I find the same presumptions on parade to be so disappointing.

> **There are small but significant hints that the translator was a Jew writing for a Jewish audience**, in order to provide them with knowledge of these core Christian texts (**possibly to help them undermine Christian polemicists**). However, the possibility also exists that this translation was carried out by a converso for **others who**, in the aftermath of 1391 & the Tortosa disputation, **had converted or were considering conversion, in order to inform them about their new faith**.[32]

The Hebrew Gospels from Catalonia are a translation from the Catalan. The real question, which is never addressed, is whether the Pieresc Catalan text itself - or its predecessor - came from the extant *Hebrew Gospels* of the era. In personal correspondence with Pere Casanellas, I got the following clarification, "*The Hebrew version was done from the same Catalan text that the Pieresc manuscript copied... **the whole manuscript Pieresc seems copied from the Vulgate**... I do not think probable that the Pieresc Gospels have been copied from the Hebrew or that have any influence of a Hebrew text of the Gospels. This deserves to be studied...*"[33]

Casanellas says there are "s*mall*" hints that the author is a Jew? **Of course the author is a Jew! He is writing for a Messianic Jewish-Christian audience! Who else would be rewriting this Hebrew Gospel and for what other audience?** He uses exclusively Jewish conventions in his writing, substitutes for the name of God, as well as a host of other conventions gained only from a Hebrew religious education. Only a rare few Gentile scholars over the millennia were competent enough to translate into Hebrew! There is also the astounding statement that the translator was **either** a manipulator of the Word in order to undermine Christian beliefs - **or** a convert trying to bring others into the faith! **So, was he a devil or an angel? You cannot take both sides of the argument!**

---

[32] Pere Casanellas & Harvey Hames, 2014, "*A Textual and Contextual Analysis of The Hebrew Gospels translated from Catalan.*" In Melilah: Manchester Journal of Jewish Studies, 2014, Volume 11, pp. 68-81.

[33] Personal correspondence w' Pere Casanellas, Aug 19, 2014, CBCat, Barcelona.

Regarding the analysis of the text for its Catalan predecessor, Casanellas and Hames are on firm ground. First, *"Proper names, especially names of persons, are in general clearly transcribed from Catalan... names usually appear in their Italian form in the headings of chapters, which must have been added by the copyist who Italianized the translation."*[34] In other words, this text may have been recopied by Italian scribes after it left Catalonia. This is a possibility first advocated by Proverbio.[35] Readers who have read my chapter in *Sons of Zion* about the Acculturation Principle[36] will recognize this as normal - from a text originating in Catalonia that ended up in the Vatican Library in Italy. It will likely take on elements of each culture as it is recopied.

"Several other Catalan words are found transcribed in the translation and are not translated into Hebrew:" Evangeli (Gospel), *evangelistes* (Gospels), *vibres* (vipers), *sendat* (fine silk fabric), *en (la) popa* (in the stern). One particular verb used often is the Catalan word *escandalitzar* (to offend or scandalize) which is used some 32 times in the Hebrew text.[37] In Chapter Two of this text, I give some other examples, including *San* (Saint), *peseta* (weight of silver - coin), and *diumenge* (Sunday).

A critical word in the HGC is *Scenopegia,* in John 7:2, which is the Greek word for the Feast of Tabernacles (*Sukkot* in Hebrew). This is an indicator that the *Gospel of John* in the HGC was an early translation from a Greek text into Hebrew as mentioned by Epiphanius (315-403 AD) in the fourth century, **"the Hebrew base-text of Matthew could be found in the Jewish treasuries in Tiberius, along with <u>Hebrew translations of the Gospel of John</u> and the Book of Acts."**[38] If the Hebrew translators had known the word *Scenopegia* meant Sukkot they would have translated it as such. So it is likely that the original source manuscript for the *Gospel of John* in the HGC was Greek.

---

[34] Pere Casanellas & Harvey Hames, 2014:p.70, *"A Textual and Contextual Analysis of The Hebrew Gospels translated from Catalan."*

[35] Delio Proverbio, 2000, *"Vangeli Ebraico"* in *I Vangeli di Popoli,* pp.372-374.

[36] "The Acculturation Principle - Any text transported, translated, copied and recopied into another language and culture will tend to take on elements of that culture. Distance from origin across time, place and culture tends to determine the degree of differentiation." Jones, *Sons of Zion,* 2019, p.233.

[37] *Op. cit.*, in the work already cited, Casanellas & Hames, 2014:pp.71-72.

[38] Epiphanius, *Panarion,* 30.3.8-9.

Casanellas and Hames soon return to the well-worn theme of the '*Jew-trying-to-undermine-Christian-doctrine.*' "*Interestingly, the term used for crucifixion and the cross is 'shti-va-erev,' i.e. 'the cross.' 'Shti-va-erev' is a term adopted by the Jews in the Middle Ages to disguise the fact that they were speaking about the cross or the crucifixion and it is used widely in anti-Christian polemical works.*"[39]

It seems evident these researchers do not know that the word "*cross*" does not appear anywhere in the Greek text of the New Testament. In the Greek text, Yeshua was crucified on a "*stauros*" - a '*stake.*' The "*cross*" was not put into the Christian creed until Constantine. **So "*cross*" & "*crucifixion*" are a fourth-century Roman invention! The meaning of "*shti-va-erev*" in Hebrew is "*crosswise.*" So what is the outrage here?**

"*Some omissions* [from the Vulgate] *that are found in the Hebrew translation are found also in Pieresc… It is worth stressing that the Hebrew translation follows the order of the words in the Pieresc and the modes and tenses of the verbs…* **The additions to the text of the Vulgate that we find in the Hebrew translation are also to be found in the Pieresc manuscript.**"[40] Examples are Matthew 9:36-37 and 27:28. Readers would do well to examine this research for themselves, it is available online.[41]

"*It should be noted, however, that the Hebrew translation often differs from the Pieresc manuscript, implying that the translation was carried out using an older manuscript than Pieresc which contained a lot of variants from the Pieresc manuscript.*"[42]

So despite the opinion given earlier, *The Hebrew Gospels from Catalonia* are not a straight translation from the *Vulgate* in every chapter and verse. They surmise the HGC was copied from an even older version. Could this have been a version like the extant *Hebrew Gospels* - which would explain the many similarities we have illustrated? The flailing about from one side of the argument to the other means they cannot justify their position.

---

[39] Pere Casanellas & Harvey Hames, 2014:p.78, "*A Textual and Contextual Analysis of The Hebrew Gospels translated from Catalan.*" In Melilah: Manchester Journal of Jewish Studies, 2014, Volume 11, pp. 68-81.

[40] *Ibid.*, in the same place, Casanellas & Hames, 2014:p.75.

[41] The Melilah article is at, http://www.melilahjournal.org/p/2014.html.

[42] *Op. cit.*, in the work cited, Casanellas & Hames, 2014:p. 74.

Casanellas and Hames state that the *"details of the Hebrew text show that it was not translated from the Latin text of the Vulgate."* This is surely a major reason they believe *"the Catalan translation found in the Pieresc MS was the basis for **the Hebrew... [which] translation was carried out using an older MS than the Pieresc.**"*[43] In other words, the Pieresc manuscript was copied from an older text and it was that text which was translated into Hebrew. It was also that predecessor text that may have come from the known *Hebrew Gospels* of the 14th century in Spain, or heavily influenced by the Hebrew. **Casanellas is of the opinion the predecessor text was copied from the Latin Vulgate - which contradicts the statement above!** One day we will find that text and know the full story.

Messianic and Jewish scribes of the era were often acknowledged to have relied heavily upon Hebrew sources in their translations of Scripture.[44] They were also famous for their Hebrew Bibles. The copyist of a Hebrew text of Scripture might add something from the Latin Vulgate into the text thinking it had been left out by mistake, or vice-versa. This is what I have called a *'mixing of the streams.'* More often than not - a new manuscript was the result of comparing various versions - sometimes from different sources.

The two competing sources were the text of the *Vulgate* and the text of the *Itala*. The *Itala* had strong Hebraic roots while the *Vulgate* had Roman origins. **There is no doubt in my mind that *The Hebrew Gospels from Catalonia* are a child of two parents, the Hebrew and the Roman!**

It may be difficult to impossible to figure out at this late date exactly how those Hebrew elements of the Gospels survived in texts that had been translated from one language to another. But one thing is very clear - survive they did! **There are unmistakable elements of the first century *Hebrew Gospel* in the surviving texts we have of it - such as *The Hebrew Gospels from Catalonia, Shem Tov Hebrew Matthew,* the Vat. Ebr. 530, and *the five manuscripts of The Cochin Gospels*!**

---

[43] Pere Casanellas & Harvey Hames, 2014:p.72 & 74, *"A Textual and Contextual Analysis of The Hebrew Gospels translated from Catalan."* In Melilah: Manchester Journal of Jewish Studies, 2014, Volume 11, pp. 68-81.

[44] Ryan Szpiech, 2007, *"Bibles from Catalan,"* The Medieval Review. Indiana University.

The Hebrew Gospels had to disappear!

With the onslaught of the Inquisition, *The Hebrew Gospels* had to disappear! Otherwise, *The Hebrew Gospels* would have been destroyed. What better place to hide than within a text of *The Catalan Gospels*. It is a likely rationale for much of the textual confusion we have been discussing in these pages. After all, **One of the most *"dangerous practices was the presence of a Hebrew Bible in the house!"*[45]** No longer were the Christians eager to learn and convey the wisdom of the East and the accumulated knowledge of the Hebrews. **The *"voluminous ancient sacred literature..."*[46] of the Hebrews was destroyed by fire!** The only Scripture allowed was the Roman Bible!

Threshold of Evidence

Even though the Messianics with their Hebrew Shabbats, Hebrew feast days, and *Hebrew Gospels* were easy targets of the Inquisition - the threshold of evidence was so low that anyone of Jewish blood was in danger. It might be a seemingly harmless comment made 20 years ago, the fact that no smoke was coming from one's chimney on the Sabbath, or the report of an informer that could never be identified or examined by the accused. Many believers went to the stake on fabricated evidence.

"In 1484 Inés de Belmonte admitted that she had habitually observed Saturday as a day of rest, she was condemned as a heretic."[47] Juan de Chinchilla, in 1483, had many colleagues who testified he was a practicing Catholic. *"The only witnesses against him spoke of things they had seen... twenty years before. On their evidence he was burnt at the stake."*[48] Upon such slender presumptions thousands were condemned and destroyed.

Mary of Bourgogne from Saragossa was a widow who had married a wealthy Jewish man. One of her servants was seized and tortured until he falsely implicated Mary. The servant was put to death - then Mary was imprisoned. *"She was eighty-five when the inquisitors first got her in their clutches."*[49]

---

[45] James Reston, 2005:p.210, *Dogs of God*.
[46] Cecil Roth, 1966:p.175-176, *A History of the Marranos*, Harper, NY.
[47] Henry Kamen, 1997:p.39, *The Spanish Inquisition: A Historical Revision*, Yale University Press, New Haven and London. [48] *Ibid.*, Kamen, p.62.
[49] Janet Gordon, 1896:pp.248-251, *The Spanish Inquisition*, Nimmo, Hay & Mitchell Publishers, Edinburgh, Scotland.

Although Mary of Bourgogne's *"life had been blameless and exemplary,"*[50] after five years in prison she was tortured - dying in agony - unable to even drag herself to the water she desperately needed for her parched throat! The Inquisitors declared her guilty, seized her property, and burned her bones in effigy at the auto-da-fe in 1559. Many wealthy widows suffered this fate.

"The officers of the Inquisition seemed to harbor a special animus toward converts who held positions of influence as courtiers and financial agents of the crown..."[51] However, because of their usefulness to the Crown, these wealthy and influential men were sometimes untouchable. **"Everyone knew that the Marranos' wealth was... a factor attracting punishment by the Inquisition."**[52] Marrano was Spanish for *pig*, and the common saying was '*you have to break the pig to get into his bank.*'

Once these powerful men had passed on, their widows and their fortunes became easy marks for the Inquisition. It is a fact cited by various researchers that more women were victims of the Inquisition than men. Lu Ann Homza gives various case histories.[53] Not only were they the most targeted but *"women comprised the vast majority of* [those] *who maintained their Judaism to the end and thus died the deaths of true martyrs."*[54]

Most all of these widows were Messianics refusing to renounce their Hebrew Messiah. The labeling of all these martyrs as Crypto-Jews is demeaning! *"There was never any doubt as to whom the Inquisition was directed against. Of 1,199 people tried in Catalonia between 1488 and 1505 - most in their absence since they had fled -* **all but eight were conversos**.*"*[55]

The Inquisitional powers had been granted to the throne of Spain by Pope Sixtus, however it soon became evident that greed was a stronger motivation than piety. At the highest levels of the Church in Spain - and the Crown - that greed was evident!

---

[50] Janet Gordon, 1896:pp.248-251, *The Spanish Inquisition*, Nimmo, Hay & Mitchell Publishers, Edinburgh, Scotland.

[51] Jane Gerber, 1992:p.130, *The Jews of Spain: A History of the Sephardic Experience*. The Free Press, N.Y.

[52] Benzion Netanyahu, 1999:p.162, *The Marranos of Spain*, Cornell Univ. Press.

[53] Lu Ann Homza, 2006:13, *The Spanish Inquisition*, Hackett Pub., Cambridge.

[54] Cecil Roth, 1966:p.175, *A History of the Marranos*, Harper, N.Y.

[55] Henry Kamen, 1997:p.53, *The Spanish Inquisition*, Yale Press, New Haven.

The Inquisition in Aragon was carried out *"with the quiet help of Cardinal Rodrigo Borgia, the powerful Spanish cardinal, who, like Ferdinand, salivated at the prospect of seizing the property of wealthy Aragonese coversos."*[56] **Rome had lost control of the process - leading Pope Sixtus IV to issue a declaration condemning the Inquisition that he had authorized!**

April 18, 1482 - Pope Sixtus IV issued this Papal Bull in protest:

> In Aragon, Valencia, Mallorca and Catalonia the Inquisition has for some time been **moved not by zeal for the faith** and the salvation of souls, **but by lust for wealth**, and that **many true and faithful Christians**, on the testimony of enemies, rivals, slaves and other lower and even less proper persons, **have without any legitimate proof been thrust into secular prisons, tortured and condemned** as relapsed heretics, deprived of their goods and property and handed over to the secular arm **to be executed**, to the peril of souls, setting a pernicious example, and causing disgust to many.[57]

Worship of a Foreign God

Solomon ben Verga, a Jewish rabbi of the era, portrayed the perspective of Ferdinand in this way, ***"If you will denounce [your] God, be baptized and bow in worship to my God***, *then the fat of the land you will eat with me. But if you refuse and rebel, I will exile you far away to some other land. After three months, there will not be a crumb left of anything that is called Jacob!"* [56b]

To the Jews, and Messianics, worship of a foreign god was a capital sin. Christians had appropriated the mantle of the chosen people, changed the sacred name of God and His Son to Greek, and proclaimed this new god demanded a doctrine of anti-Semitism that demonized all things Hebrew - including the Sacred Name Yehovah, the Hebrew Messiah, Torah, Sabbath day, Feast Days of Yehovah, and *The Hebrew Gospels*! **This new Christian god was a Hebrew-hating god!** *"The suffering of the Jews in which divine justice delights..."*[58] All Messianics were required to condemn and hate anything remotely Hebrew. **Many Messianics refused to bow - dying by torture or burning - without saying a word!**

[56] James Reston, 2005:p.106, *Dogs of God*, Anchor Books, NY. [56b] *ibid*.p.262.
[57] Henry Charles Lea, 1908:p.587, *A History of the Inquisition in Spain*, vol.1.
[58] Frederick Rolfe citing Mirandola, 1901:p.103, *Chronicles of the house of Borgia*, Sagwan Press, openlibrary.org.

*"**Many instances are recorded, in which every variety of anguish that human ingenuity could devise, failed to wring from the sufferer one incriminating word, either against himself or others!**"*[59] Although many of the Inquisition's victims were completely broken - many Messianics had a faith as strong as that of the original followers of the Hebrew Messiah! These *"converts would remain courageously loyal to this new faith even in extremis, as is evident from literally tens of thousands of Inquisition dossiers."*[60] *"The polemicists now recognized the emergence of a new type of convert, one who took to Christendom not by force of circumstances, or for reasons other than religious, but because of his belief in the teachings of Christianity, in their historic truth and religious promise."*[61] Contrary to many historians' views, these Conversos held firmly to belief in the Hebrew Messiah and *The Hebrew Gospels*. To call them crypto-Jews is wrong.

The Boast of the Inquisition

*"A Franciscan Inquisitor once confided to King Phillip IV of France... **that if Saints Peter and Paul had appeared before his tribunal, he had no doubt that the techniques he employed would be able to secure their convictions!**"*[62]

Anyone who questions the difference between the archetypes of the Hebrew Messiah and the Greek Christ should consider this - our Messiah and his Apostles would be guilty of all these charges of *'judaizing.'* The Roman Church Inquisitors would take the Messiah into their dark dungeon, torture him, replace his crown of thorns with a *'coroza'* dunce cap for those condemned, mock and ridicule him in public, tie him to the stake, and burn him alive to the cheering of crowds - in a spectacle as ghastly as that of his original Roman executors!

The *'auto-da-fe,'* act of faith, was designed to present to the public the Day of Judgement - a vision of the jaws of hell opening to swallow heretics for an eternity of torture in the fire! It was intended to terrorize the populace into unquestioning obedience to the power of the Roman Church - **but most especially to destroy the Messianic Church and *The Hebrew Gospels!***

---

[59] Janet Gordon, 1896:p.11, *The Spanish Inquisition*, Nimmo, Hay & Mitchell Publishers, Edinburgh, Scotland. [60] Jane Gerber, 1992:pp.143-44, *The Jews of Spain*, Simon & Schuster, N.Y. [61] Benzion Netanyahu, 1999:p.84, *The Marranos of Spain*, Cornell University Press, London. [62] Cullen Murphy, 2012::p.23, *God's Jury*; Houghton, Mifflin, Harcourt; Boston & New York.

It was intended to burn the message so deeply into the collective subconscious of all Messianic believers - that if they wanted to survive they must reject and revile all things Hebrew! That would include the Hebrew Torah, *The Hebrew Gospels*, the Hebrew Sabbath, the Hebrew Feast Days, the Hebrew Messiah Yeshua and Yehovah the Hebrew God! **All in the name of Christ - the Greek Christ! The Hebrew Messiah who sacrificed his life that the Hebrew people be saved - is now held up as their Greco-Roman judge and condemner!** As I have said, *"the Romans changed the Church much more than the Church changed the Romans."* **The Holy Mother Church had become their god!** *"It is better for an innocent man to be condemned than for the Inquisition* [of the Church] *to suffer disgrace."*[63]

What did the Church gain? They forced the conversion of hundreds of thousands of Conversos to the Roman faith through terror, torture and burning at the stake. They took the possessions of the Conversos for their own greed. **What did they lose?** The Spanish dramatically weakened their nation, and lost their empire prematurely, as we shall see in the following chapters. **The Roman Church lost her credibility as the scion of Christ!** When the unholy alliance of church and state finally weakened centuries later, removing the boot from the neck of the people - they rebelled - rejecting both church and state.

Take a modern-day European secularist and scratch the surface of their unbelief and out will ooze the still unhealed putrescence of the Inquisition! The Roman Church gained hundreds of thousands of converts in the short term - and lost hundreds of millions in the long term. *"Early modern Europeans inherited a fully-fledged apparatus of persecution and an intellectual tradition that justified killing in the name of God."*[64] We will continue to see its effects far into the future, *"the campaign against English Catholics and dissenters from the established church, or the campaigns against doctrinal foes by Calvin in Geneva and Zwingli in Zurich... Sometimes the visionary dimension is secular..."* What can one say to the bloody guillotine of the godless state of revolutionary France, or the Holocaust of the Nazis, or the millions slaughtered to implement Communism? They simply did what the Roman Church preached and practiced!

---

[63] Quoted by the Papal Envoy to Spain in 1565, from Cullen Murphy,2012:p.65, *God's Jury*; Houghton Mifflin Harcourt; Boston. [64] Ibid., Murphy, page 188.

Can the Church now say God disapproves the killing of those with doctrinal differences? It cannot - at least not until it repents of the original apostasy - the condemnation of the Messianic-Apostolic Church and the long and bloody quest to destroy it as a competitor! The Crusades against competitors and the Inquisitions against the Messianic and Neo-Messianic Church over the centuries were simply a continuation of that original apostasy. In accordance with principles established by the Greco-Roman Church itself, adopted in turn by all their offspring churches, even atheists can claim they are *"justified by a vision of the one true path,"*[65] as they destroy all who think differently, whether they be numbered in the hundreds or the hundreds of millions. If the principle is correct then the scope of its reach is like-wise justified. *"Might makes Right"* - the Hellenic will to power through violence seems to have won. The Greco-Roman *"sons of Greece"* seem to be triumphant!

However, appearances can be deceiving - **there has always been a remnant of true believers - followers of the Messiah who walked the earth - the Hebrew Messiah!** These Messianic followers carefully preserved *The Received Text* of the Scriptures, including *The Hebrew Gospels*. The torch was passed from the early Jewish Christians to Gentile believers - who were still dedicated to restoring the Messianic Church of the first century. **These new Messianic congregants, mostly Gentile now, we refer to as <u>Neo-Messianic</u>.** These Messianics and Neo-Messianics were never a part of the Apostate Church. During the Medieval period, the hammer of the Inquisition forced many of this remnant to emigrate to the New World as well as to many and varied parts of the Old World. **There, they would breathe new life into the Old World.** *The Received Text* **of Scripture they had guarded through endless persecution was to spark the Reformation!**

---

[65] Cullen Murphy,2012:p.188, *God's Jury*; Houghton Mifflin Harcourt; Boston.

Chapter Eight
Columbus & the New World

*If they have persecuted me they will persecute you…
because they know not Him who sent me.*
John 15:20-21

Our story now splits into two parts, East and West, the Old World and the New World. Both stories speak of unsung momentous Messianic accomplishments.

Columbus was a Messianic! He went to great lengths to cover his true identity. His voyage was financed, not by Isabella's crown jewels - as has been popularized in legend - but by Messianics. They were fleeing Spain and needed safe haven at any price! Columbus left Spain during the final expulsion of the Jews in 1492. His ships' manifests show a number of Hebrew names, some were known to be Conversos, many others were hiding their Hebrew blood. He left with a ship carrying Jews fleeing the Expulsion and Messianics fleeing the Inquisition. He left with a Greek map pointing to the Indies by going West, not East. He took a Hebrew translator - fully expecting to encounter the lost tribes of Israel at their destination. **This is the untold story of Columbus and his voyage of discovery to the New World!**

Columbus was the son of a Portuguese prince, the Duke of Beja, and a Jewish noblewoman who was a Converso. He was the illegitimate son of the Duke but nonetheless was raised in his household. He was a cousin to King John of Portugal. Columbus gained his superb navigation skills at the school of Prince Henry the Navigator which his father Duke Beja had attended. It is only by virtue of these advanced skills that Columbus succeeded in finding the Americas and returning alive. It was a far more perilous voyage than most of us are aware.

Columbus changed his name to hide the fact that he was a second-generation Messianic. Even a partial portion of Hebrew blood was enough for the Inquisition to arrest you, convict you, and execute you. The Inquisition preyed upon the wealthy and influential. Not only did he change his name but he disguised his past, claiming to come from Genoa in Italy. Columbus left a colony of 39 people in the New World on his first voyage - many of them Messianics. **How do we know these things?   ...Read on!**

Columbus was Messianic!

"Columbus came from the kingdom of Aragon and his native language was Catalan... Christopher Columbus' origins were not obscure by chance, but rather the result of the famous explorer's having purposely hid the fact that he was a 'converso' - a Jewish convert to Christianity!"[1] So, he was Catalan - or maybe not - the truth is that Columbus was one of the most secretive personalities of history. Washington Irving, who was paid by the **Italian Consulate** to write Columbus' official English biography, dutifully reported that he was born in Genoa, Italy. Irving also covered detailed evidence that he was of Portuguese nobility and like his father, the Duke of Beja, had studied at the school of the famous Henry the Navigator in Portugal. **Columbus himself destroyed the records of his family history!** Was he trying to hide he was the bastard son of a Portuguese Prince and a Jewish noblewoman? Or was it that being a Converso of Jewish blood, even second or third generation, could expose him to the Inquisition? On his deathbed, his sons Diego and Hernan begged him to reveal to them their true ancestral roots - but Columbus took his secret to the grave... or so he thought. His sons recited a Hebrew Kaddish prayer at his death.

Columbus could not speak Italian nor did he ever go to Italy in all his travels to the courts of Europe. There is no known relative nor descendent of Columbus from Italy. Columbus could speak and write well in Portuguese and in Hebrew. One cannot escape certain conclusions springing from these facts. How did Columbus gain entry to rub shoulders with royalty all over Europe? One simple answer is that he was one of them. Illegitimacy did not necessarily prevent a scion of noble blood from assuming the title to which he was due by parentage. In 1978, Patrochilio Riviero and Mascarenas Barrero, two prominent Portuguese researchers, declared Columbus to be the son of Duke Beja, a price of Portugal, which would make Columbus the cousin of the king of Portugal, King John the Second.[2] He was the son of Prince Don Fernando - the Duke of Beja - and Lady Isabel Gonzalves Zarco, a noblewoman and a Jewess, the daughter of the famous Jewish-Portuguese navigator Joao Gonzalves Zarco. **His name was Salvador Fernando Zarco which he changed to Cristobal Colon - aka - Christopher Columbus.**

[1] *Columbus was Catalan - Possibly Jewish*, December 4, 2018, Jerusalem Post citing Estelle Irizarry, Professor at Georgetown University. [2] Paul Perry, 2018, *Secrets & Mysteries of Christopher Columbus,* a Dave Horner film.

Columbus was born in Cuba, Portugal - in the Duchy of Beja. One of the first of the islands that Columbus encountered - he named Cuba. Not only that but more than forty place names designated by Columbus himself on the island of Cuba, were place names from around Cuba, Portugal. **More than forty place names in Cuba with the exact same names of places in the Duchy of Beja, Portugal!**[3] Keep in mind that these are Portuguese names - not Spanish or Italian names.

When Columbus was first presented to the King and Queen of Spain, he wore the triple pomegranates from the coat of arms of the Duke of Beja. Columbus was raised in the household of the Duke of Beja - as his son - otherwise he would not have been permitted to wear the colors of Beja. A false link to nobility would be easily uncovered and would have ruined Columbus' chances of royal support. It was rumored that Columbus was an agent of the Portuguese king, John the Second, who was his cousin. When Columbus returned from his discovery of the New World, he landed first in Lisbon, Portugal - where he spent several days with the Portuguese king before returning to Spain.

It was the wife of the Duke of Beja who ended up helping negotiate a treaty between Spain and Portugal that divided up the uncharted territory of South America between them. Strange as it might seem that the Duchess would adopt a bastard son - these things happened more often than one might suspect. So many children died young - having a surviving son could make all the difference between keeping your ancestral title and lands - or having to relinquish them to the crown because you have no heir.

In that treaty of Tordesillas, in 1494, King John the Second of Portugal demanded the boundary of demarcation be moved 370 leagues West, more than 1000 miles. How might the Duchess of Beja and King John have known how to swing such a negotiation? **The very existence of Brazil was not even known at the time... except to Columbus!** This was a master stroke for Portugal, aided and abetted by their native son! Within the Archives of the Indies in Seville, a safe conduct pass was found, signed by King John of Portugal. It was brought to Spain by Columbus when he first arrived. Long thought lost, it declared Columbus to be a friend - and agent - of the crown of Portugal.

---

[3] Paul Perry, 2018, *Secrets... of Christopher Columbus,* documentary film.

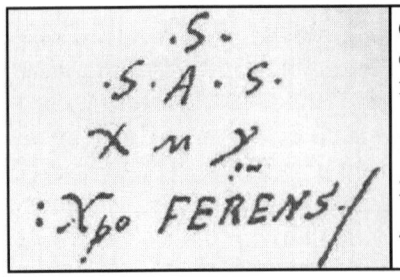

·S· ·S·A·S· X ʍ y :X͟ᵨₒ FEREN͟S/	Columbus signature is a fascinating cipher, or cryptogram. It is in Greek followed by Latin - read in two ways: 1) Salvador Fernando Zarco, or 2) Christopher Colon [4] Decrypted by Mascarenhas Barreto.

1) The Greek letters XRTO are the Templar acronym for Savior - *Salvador*. Feren is short for Fernando, his father's name. The final S is a backward Z for Zarco, so it reads Salvador Fernando Zarco, his true name.
2) To read it the other way, note the '*colon*' at the first, like in English, followed by Xo...fer, the X for '*Christ*' plus '*o...fer*' - Colon, Christopher.

The Duke of Beja was a Knight Templar who had gained his seafaring skills under "*The great Prince Henry the Navigator [who] had died in 1460. But his crusading spirit lived on, vibrantly, inspiring Portuguese navigators to press on further and further south to the magical passage around Africa to the spice kingdoms of India and Goa. That spirit trumpeted their motto: 'Crusade, Knowledge, Power.' Of these, 'Crusade' was the first and most important commandment! The cult of Prince Henry the Navigator was the seagoing arm of the Templars... Christianizing infidels was the highest Christian calling!*"[5] The red cross so prominent on the caravels of Prince Henry, and Columbus, was the Templar Cross. Columbus had been sent to the school of Prince Henry to get his credentials as a Navigator in the tradition of his father Count Beja, and grandfather Joao Gonzalves Zarco.

Of course there were other motivations for these mariners, **"*The search for the gold of Black Africa and the muscle of black slaves was always subsumed in the higher and more noble -sounding goal of Christianizing the infidel.*"**[6] The skill and daring-do of these mariners and the commerce which followed them had made Portugal the most affluent country in Europe - and Lisbon the busiest port. Now, finding a sea route to the spices of India, avoiding the lengthy and expensive camel caravans crossing the desert sands to the Mediterranean, was their Holy Grail.

[4] Mascarenhas Barreto, 1988, English version 1992, The *Portuguese Columbus: Secret Agent of John II*, McMillan Press, N.Y. [5] James Reston, 2005:pp.115-6, *Dogs of God: Columbus and the Inquisition...*, Anchor Books, N.Y.
[6] *Ibid*, in the same place, Reston, p.116.

"*The lure of spices was more for their use as a food preserver than for their lively taste. To find a way to obtain spices for a reasonable price became a national goal.*"[7] Think of salt - one of those spices in short supply - once it became readily available - the population of Europe tripled! Producers could preserve meats and other foods giving time to get them to market. But for Columbus, his correspondence reveals another motivation, more important than spice, slaves, treasure, or the Roman Church.

Messianic Zeal

Simon Wiesenthal, the famous Nazi hunter, wrote a book called *Sails of Hope*,[8] in which he researched and made the case that **Columbus was motivated by a deep Messianic zeal to find safe refuge for the many thousands of Jews fleeing the Expulsion, and the many thousands of Messianics fleeing the Inquisition**. One very real reason to believe this evidence is that it was - by far - the overriding concern of practically all Jews and Messianics at that moment in time. It certainly was the principal motive for Columbus' supporters who financed his voyage. Columbus gained an audience with King John of Portugal who was galvanized by Columbus' proposed voyage! But his junta of navigators did not want to change their focus from reaching the tip of south Africa which promised a sea route to the Orient.

King John and Columbus both knew the highly speculative and financially risky voyage could be better financed in Spain. Spain was expelling all their Jews - and their Conversos were fleeing the Inquisition in frightening numbers. Neither were allowed to take their money or possessions with them. **There was a mountain of money - in Spain - to finance a voyage to find a safe haven for the Jews and Messianics!** King John gave Columbus a safe-conduct pass - basically a letter of introduction to the Spanish court - where Columbus "*quickly established himself among the most prominent Converso figures at court.*"[9] As planned, "***The voyage of Columbus was** not funded by the royal house of Ferdinand and Isabella. It was rather **financed by prominent business men who were Messianic Jews**... Their names were **Louis Santangel** and **Gabriel Sanchez**.*"[10]

---

[7] James Reston, 2005:p.117, *Dogs of God: Columbus and the Inquisition…*, Anchor Books, N.Y. [8] Simon Wiesenthal, 1973, *Sails of Hope: Secret Mission of Christopher Columbus*, McMillan Press, N.Y. [9] Jane Gerber, 1992:p.xvii, *The Jews of Spain*, Free Press, NY & London. [10] Jerusalem Post, Dec 4, 2018, citing Estelle Irizarry, History Professor at Georgetown University.

The Financing of Columbus' Voyage

Ferdinand and Isabella were indeed intrigued with Columbus' proposal to reach the Orient by going west rather than east. Queen Isabella had granted Columbus a retainer and asked him to remain patient. They were in the midst of a war to expel the Muslims from Grenada, their last stronghold in Iberia. When that was over they could talk about Columbus' plan.

Granada fell January 2, 1492. Within two weeks Columbus was summoned before the Crown. He had been given a stipend for new clothes and a mule to ride. Columbus had honed his presentation to a fine polish but after giving it to the two sovereigns there was an uncomfortable silence. Finally, Ferdinand spoke. The war against Granada had depleted Spain's treasury to the point that no expensive enterprise of this nature could be contemplated at that time. Columbus left them angry and disgusted. He spoke to his Converso supporter, Luis Santangel - the royal treasurer - outside in the corridor and informed him he would be leaving for France, and then to England, to procure the funds he needed for his voyage.

Santangel immediately gained an audience with the Queen. He was eloquent in reinforcing the great promise of the proposed voyage and then, alluding to Columbus' determination to seek funds from Spain's opponents, he concluded, *"It would be a great damage to Her Crown and a grave reproach to Her Highness if any other prince should undertake what Columbus offered Her Highness."*[11] **The final point was Santangel's offer to obtain the financing himself. Columbus' voyage was approved!**

Columbus had demanded hereditary rights to the lands he discovered and claimed for Spain. Within weeks, the Crown had issued the expulsion order for all Jews to convert to Christianity or leave Spain. The Jews had four months before the deadline. Columbus *"lived in a largely Jewish and New Christian world of navigators, cartographers, astronomers, and mathematicians... Iberian Jews and conversos assisted Columbus in developing his Enterprise of the Indies."*[12] The Conversos trusted Columbus - not the Crown - financing would not be forthcoming if his rights were not granted. King Ferdinand blinked first, giving Columbus hereditary rights to any lands discovered.

---

[11] Kirsten Downey, 2015:p.242, *Isabella: The Warrior Queen*, Amazon Books.
[12] Edward Kritzler, 2008:p.16-17, *Jewish Pirates of the Caribbean*, Doubleday.

Was safe haven for Jews and Messianics Columbus' primary motivation? That depends upon whether he was a Converso - or not! *"Columbus sometimes dated his correspondence by Jewish reckoning from the date of the destruction of the Second Temple... rather than by the birth of Christ....* [not to mention] *the strange cipher used in all of his letters to his son except the only one Diego was told to show to the Queen... the Hebrew abbreviation for 'beEzrat haShem' ('with the help of God') that is commonly found in Jewish correspondence."*[13] There are various other decisive indicators, *"His staunchest supporters... were Jewish -* **he seemed to prefer the company of conversos...** [though he had] *to be careful of scurrilous rumor and ambitious Inquisitors. Most definitely!"*[14] *"It is clear that* **he had an unusually strong interest in Jewish matters***, which would be understandable and indeed* **common among conversos but definitely atypical for a Spanish Old Christian.***"*[13] Although the financing of Santangel and Sanchez was critical - if Columbus was faking - **he ran the risk of burning at the stake for judaizing!**

> Six identifiable *conversos* were aboard the three vessels that left for the New World on the night of the expulsion of the Jews. Others might have been present as well, but it was typical for *conversos* to hide as much of their Jewish background as possible in order to evade the scrutiny of the Inquisition... Perhaps Santangel [& Sanchez, whose son was on the voyage]... **shared the dream of many contemporaries that Columbus might find a kingdom of the Lost Tribes, a possible asylum for Jews far from the reaches of the Inquisition.**[15]
> [brackets mine]

Columbus married well, *"In 1478 he made a decent marriage, Filipa Perestrello e Moniz may have been no beauty, but she belonged to a prominent family in the second rank of Portuguese society... close to the royal families of Portugal... Filipa's maternal grandfather had fought alongside Prince Henry in the great Portuguese victory at Ceuta... in 1415. Her father, Bartholomew Perestrello, had been an important explorer... Italian blood ran thick. Her father's family had roots* [in]*... Genoa,"*[16] **His wife's family history provided Columbus with a perfect cover for his Genoa 'origin!'**

---

[13] Jane Gerber, 1992:p.xix, *The Jews of Spain*, Free Press, NY & London.
[14] James Reston, 2005:p,130 footnote, *Dogs of God: Columbus & the Inquisition*, Anchor Books, NY. [15]*Op. cit.* Gerber, p.xx. [16]James Reston, 2005:p.123-4.

In Columbus' journal, he makes it clear where his motivations lie. *"I could feel His hand upon me. It was the Lord who put into my mind the fact that I could sail from here to the Indies... No one should fear to undertake any task in the name of our Savior, if it is just and if the intention is purely for His holy service."*[17] Columbus wrote a book entitled the *Book of Prophecies*, which examined in great detail the biblical prophecies concerning far distant lands, undiscovered tribes, migration of peoples - focusing on the Covenant given to Abraham, Moses and Joshua about the Promised Land. Yehovah had promised to bless them - as a nation - if they would enter the Promised Land and make of it a nation of God.[18]

The earliest English colonists, *"The Pilgrims and Puritans actually referred to themselves as God's New Israel. But **it was not that they thought they, and the Christian Church, had 'replaced' Israel... They saw themselves as being called into a direct continuation of the covenant relationship between God and Abraham.**"*[19] As Yehovah had said to Abraham, *"Go... into the land that I will show you. And I will make of you a great nation, and I will bless you"* (Gen 12:1-2). *"And I will establish my covenant between me and you and your descendants after you"* (Gen 17:7). From the evidence, it seems that this was in Columbus' mind from the beginning. In any case, historians claim that *"American government owes its inception to the covenants of the first churches on her shores."*[20]

> On the morning of August 3, 1492... the Santa Maria had cast off her lines, set sail, and was gliding down the river with the ebbing tide. As Columbus' ships reached the place... just before emptying into the ocean, a last shipload of Jews was also waiting for the tide. They too were leaving now, bound for the Mediterranean and the lands of Islam... None of that shipload of forlorn exiles could have dreamed that **the other three ships on the river were leading the way to a land that would one day provide a welcome haven to their people.**[21]

---

[17] Columbus' journal of the voyage was lost but was rewritten by Bartolome de Las Cases who accompanied Columbus on his third voyage. Translated by Cecil Jane, 1930:pp.146-7, *The Voyage of Christopher Columbus*, Argonaut Press.
[18] August J. Kling, translator, in *The Presbyterian Layman* magazine, Oct 1971.
[19] Edward Kritzler, 2008:p.16-17, *Jewish Pirates of the Caribbean*, Doubleday.
[20] *Ibid.*, p.22. [21] *Ibid.*, pp.37-38.

The Voyage to the New World

There are only three ways in which sailing ships can move, other than being towed by rowers - always a last resort. **The Captain must be a virtuoso of the winds, the tides, and the currents!** He must know the harbors and the reefs and safe passages of any coastline that he sails. Now a new mastery has been added. He must be able to navigate across the vast stretches of ocean without any landmarks. The sun, moon, and stars, his compass, and astrolabe are his only guides. **Columbus was just such a virtuoso!** This is potent evidence that Columbus did indeed study at Henry's school of navigation. **He was on the cutting edge of seamanship!** These were uncommon skills and Columbus would need every bit of his formidable talents to accomplish his mission, and to survive it!

Prince Henry had dramatically advanced the science of navigation. One could approximate their distance from the equator, that is their latitude, by the distance of the sun and stars above the horizon at certain times of the day and night. Now, one could compute their approximate longitude by sighting the North star through view ports in the astrolabe. It was not a precision instrument yet - but it helped! The astrolabe had made its way to Europe from Muslim Spain. By the 12th century there were a handful of expert treatises on the astrolabe in use. *"The oldest surviving, moderately sophisticated scientific work in the English language is a Treatise On The Astrolabe, written by the English poet and philosopher Geoffrey Chaucer* (1343-1400)."[22]

Columbus sailed southwest by south to the Canary Islands, seemingly out of the way. He had a plan that demonstrated his advanced knowledge of the seas. The prevailing winds in the northern ocean were called the *Westerlies*, from the west, but as one went south the prevailing winds were coming from the northeast, called the *Trade* winds. From the Canaries he could catch the Trade winds to take him West then sail north to catch the Westerlies for the return voyage. It was genius! No one had ever thought of this before for a good reason. **Neither Columbus, nor any man of his crew, had ever been more than 300 miles from the mainland!** They sailed from the Canaries on Sept 8, 1492, and a month later, by virtue of the powerful Trade winds, they were more than 2000 miles from Europe!

[22] James Morrison, 2007, *The Astrolabe*, Classical Science Press.

Mutiny Onboard

October 9, 1492, Columbus' two other captains, the Pinzon brothers, Martin and Vicente, demanded an emergency meeting. Columbus was not pleased. It would require all ships to stop by steering into the wind so the captains could row over to the Santa Maria. **The captains were delivering an ultimatum!** If Columbus did not turn back soon the sailors would mutiny, take over the ships, and turn back themselves. Columbus was faced with giving up his dream. He was angry and frustrated, but he too was aware of the sullen defiance of the crew as the Trade winds pushed them faster and faster, further and further, from their homes and the hope of ever getting back alive. Their minds were full of sailors' nightmares of the sea. What was out there? Was there an edge that one went over like a waterfall with no end? Were there monsters further out in the ocean than anyone had ever been? They knew of whales that could easily overturn their small caravels - what other frightening dangers awaited?

Columbus negotiated three days more to sight land or he would turn back. He felt he had no choice. The danger of mutiny was too real to ignore. He offered a 10,000 maravedis reward for the first man to spy land, almost $7000! The next morning Columbus recorded in his journal that they had made an unbelievable 59 leagues (about 180 miles) during the past 24 hours! The crew grew ever more alarmed by the speed of the ships widening the chasm between them and the safety of land! The nerves of the men were at a snapping point. That day debris from land was sighted, a branch with blossoms.

The tension broke! The men jockeyed to take turns aloft as lookouts. That night they sighted a tiny light far in the distance! Not all the men were convinced that land was near. **On the third and final day, at 2 am, the excited call was heard coming from the Pinta,** *"Tierra!"* **(***'Land!'***)** In the moonlight one could see a white cliff ahead on the horizon. Columbus slowed to avoid the ever present reefs near shore. The hours dragged as they approached the unknown coastline cautiously. They reached the island just as the sunrise broke over the horizon.

**"A new day was dawning, and with it,
a new era for humankind!"**[23]

[23] Peter Marshall & David Manuel, 1977:p.42, *The Light and The Glory*, Revell Publishing, Grand Rapids, MI.

That Thy Holy Name May be Proclaimed

Columbus was the first to set foot on the New World, on the island which he named San Salvador for the Holy Savior. They planted an eight-foot oak cross on the shore. Columbus prayed, ending with this sentiment: *"You have created the heaven and the earth, and the sea; blessed and glorified be Thy Name, and praised be Thy Majesty, which has deigned to use us, Thy humble servants, **that Thy Holy Name may be proclaimed in this second part of the earth!**"*[23] Columbus was a Messianic who knew Hebrew and the Scriptures. He knew the Sacred Name of Yehovah, and one must presume **he did what he said, declaring the Sacred Hebrew Name of Yehovah on the New World as he took those first steps!** In a letter to Queen Isabella, Columbus declared, *"I believe that earthly paradise lies here which no one can enter except by God's leave."*[24]

On San Salvador, Columbus encountered the native Indians who were eager to trade or simply give of what they had in a gesture of friendship. Columbus described them as beautiful and friendly people in a paradise of exotic fruits, plants and animals.

> They ate food that no white man had ever tasted before - sweet juice-giving fruit, & corn, and a pulpy bread made from cassavas. Most of all... they could now drink pure spring water.
>
> The scents of the rain forest were intoxicating, and large birds with plumage of bright reds & yellows & greens filled the air.[25]

It seemed so much like paradise that Columbus himself said he never wanted to leave. **Ah, but what is paradise without gold, silver, and precious stones? These are the things that make sovereigns swoon!** The discovery of gold was quickly realized - to the everlasting sorrow of the inhabitants. To please these new arrivals the natives led them onward in their quest. Columbus sailed completely around the island of Cuba only 90 miles from the mainland of Florida. The natives led him to Hispaniola, now the island of Haiti and the Dominican Republic, where natives wore ample gold jewelry and masks. Columbus traded with them in exchange for a chest full of gold.

---

[23] Bjorn Landstrom, 1966:pp.66-75, *Columbus*, MacMillan Pub., New York.
[24] J.M. Cohen, ed., 1969:pp.220-221, *Four Voyages of Christopher Columbus*, Penguin Books, U.K. [25] Peter Marshall & David Manuel, 1977:p. 45, *The Light and The Glory*, Revell Publishing, Grand Rapids, MI.

When it came time to return, 39 crew members volunteered to occupy the first colony in the New World, there on Hispaniola. The Santa Maria had run aground and had to be abandoned. Columbus returned on the Nina.

Upon the return, the ships encountered a storm worst than any they had ever experienced. The storm separated the ships. It blew viciously for a week, taking the Nina and dropping her in the Azores. The first crewmen ashore were arrested by Portuguese authorities. Columbus managed to secure their release. Getting under sail again the Nina endured yet another week-long storm as violent as the first. This second tempest drove them for another week ripping their sails to shreds. Driven by the immense storm the Nina found itself tossed onto the Portuguese coast, just north of the Lisbon River. **It was here Columbus had his finest hour - displaying the most incredible courage and skill!**

> The little vessel with no canvas… was blown ever closer to its doom. The storm was peaking in intensity. In minutes they would be dashed to pieces on the rocky coast. With huge waves breaking on the shore there was no way any of them would survive. **One slim chance remained… if they could make it to the river's mouth!**
>
> But that would mean they would have to take the wind almost broadside - a dangerous maneuver even under the best of conditions. **To attempt it in this monstrous sea without sails was suicide!** The Admiral gauged their drift and ordered the helm over accordingly... Carefully noting their speed through the water and the action of the waves at the river's mouth, he called out constant corrections to the helmsman at the tiller as he compensated for the ship's yaw. **He had to shout to make himself heard above the din of the storm - he was at once calm and exhilarated - challenged at the very limit of his God-given abilities…**
>
> **It would all be decided in the next minute!**
>
> *"Lean her to starboard! More! That's it - hold her there - now steady, steady as she goes. Now! Hard a-larboard! Hold her, hold her!"* The whole ship groaned and heeled over so far that the sea began to come over her gunwales. The men screamed! It looked as if she were about to go all the way over. But she held and then slowly straightened as a giant wave lifted her and fairly hurled her into the river's mouth! [26]

---

[26] Peter Marshall & David Manuel, 1977:pp.53-4, *The Light and The Glory*, Revell Publishing, Grand Rapids, MI.

After a three day visit with King John of Portugal, Columbus had restored his canvas and set sail for Spain. There he was showered with money and honors beyond anything one might imagine. He entered the court and told his narrative of the paradise across the seas… then he brought his Indians in with their feathers, paint, piercings and spears - brightly colored parrots on their shoulder. Finally, at the climax, Columbus opened the chest of gold before the two sovereigns. Ferdinand and Isabella fell to their knees before Columbus, and the court, and thanked God!

It must have seemed God had rewarded them amply for their bloody crusade against the Moors and the brutal Inquisition against the Messianics. And so it has been narrated in church history - but the truth is a more complicated story. Columbus returned on his second voyage the following year to find his colony wiped out. The Indians he had taken to Spain, who could now translate the natives' reports, told the story:

> No sooner had the Nina departed the year before, than the Spaniards who were left behind had started indulging their lust with Indian women. Nor were they satisfied with one each but took as many as they could get. No longer did they barter for gold. They simply seized it, doing violence to any Indian who protested. Quarrelling among themselves and killing one another, they [the crew] had split into factions, and were thus easily ambushed and overrun. [27]

There were factions among the colonists, about 10-15% were Messianics. Some of the crew tried to stop the killing, restore order and decency. **It was a harbinger of things to come!**

This is the true story of the Spanish conquest - although the Portuguese would show themselves to be even worse. Where did this behavior - of rape, robbery and murder - come from? Were these not Christian soldiers dedicated to bringing the Savior to the infidels? **In all truth, they were a perfect reflection of the Roman Church! The blessings of salvation were now being dispensed by the sword!** Was this not exactly what was happening in every city of Spain, and soon to be in Portugal? Fellow Christian believers were tortured, women and possessions taken at will. After all, they were heretics, and like the infidels, their lives were forfeit. All protest was met with slaughter.

---

[27] Peter Marshall & David Manuel, 1977:p.60, *The Light and The Glory*, Revell Publishing, Grand Rapids, MI.

Upon Columbus' return from his third voyage he was arrested! The crown had figured out that he had served as an agent of King John of Portugal. Rather than treason, he was accused of mismanaging the island domains of which he was Viceroy. During this time Columbus put together *The Book of Prophecies* with the help of his religious counselor, the very learned monk Gaspar Gorricio. *The Book of Prophecies* was "*a well-constructed piece of propaganda designed to defend himself against the charges made against him and, above all, to justify his own actions... It's purpose was to locate within the historical schema of the salvation of the human race, the discovery of the Indies, presented as the first step toward the liberation of Jerusalem and the Holy Land from Muslim domination, and to assign a prominent role in these events to Christopher Columbus.*"[28] It also attempted to prove, in the process, "*that universal domination must be granted to the crown of Spain.*"[29]

This "*form of messianic political propaganda in favor of the crown*"[30] was characteristic of the times. Columbus was released even before *The Book of Prophecies* could be published. He was too big a jewel in the crown of the Spanish monarchs to tarnish, much less destroy, but his financing was cut. By his fourth - and last voyage - Columbus was stranded in Jamaica - his third-rate ships no longer seaworthy enough for the return.

Columbus had sailed to Panama and bartered with the Indians there for several dozen gold medallions. His younger brother Bartholomew and his son Fernando were with him on this voyage. He made it as far as Santa Gloria Bay in Jamaica before he had to beach his two ships. They were springing so many leaks they would not make the journey across the Atlantic. "*His worm-eaten caravels, described by his son as, 'more full of holes than a bee's honeycomb,' barely made Jamaica.*"[31]

Columbus was at the lowest point of his entire life. His older seamen mutinied, led by the captain of the second ship, Francisco Poras. Poras rallied the men to mutiny and escape, convinced that Columbus had stranded them in Jamaica rather than going on to the colony at Hispaniola. Columbus let them go.

---

[28] *The Book of Prophecies edited by Christopher Columbus*, published in 2004, pp.1&5, as part of *Repertorium Columbianum*, Roberto Rusconi, editor, Wipf & Stock Publishers, Eugene, Or. [29] *Ibid.*, p.8. [30] *Ibid.*, p.33. [31]Edward Kritzler, 2008:p.18, *Jewish Pirates of the Caribbean*, Doubleday, N.Y.

The rebel-leader seized the dozen canoes Columbus had bartered from the Indians. Forcing the natives to row, the rebels made three attempts to overcome the fierce currents of the 108-mile wide channel to Hispaniola. On their final try, they gave up, though only after throwing eighteen Indian paddlers overboard, and chopping off the hands of those who clung to the side. Five months later, after a two-week march across the island, marked by rape and pillage, they were encamped in an Indian village a half mile from Santa Gloria, intending to seize the admiral's ships...[32]

Columbus was in complete despair when he learned the mutineers were preparing for battle against him. His younger brother Bartholomew convinced him to let him lead a counter attack. Columbus had about fifty teenage loyalists remaining.

They were sons of the Messianic families who financed the voyage. Not only did they have a fiscal interest in the outcome, but *"their families, being wealthy conversos, were targeted by the Inquisition... to keep their sons safe, Columbus' backers persuaded him to take them along."*[33] They surely knew, or suspected the secret, that Columbus was one of them - a Converso!

Bartholomew armed the teenagers and they advanced on the older seamen. The mutineers laughed at the approach of the teenage Conversos. However, their arrogance was misplaced. **Bartholomew and his teenage Conversos slew the first six rebels who attacked them and Bartholomew soon has Poras at sword-point. The other mutineers surrendered and were disarmed. Poras was put in irons in the hold of the ship.**

Columbus' next problem was the natives. After their brutal treatment by Poras' mutineers, they refused to provide any more food to Columbus and his crew. Columbus had Zacuto's Almanac which calculated a full lunar eclipse was due February 20, 1504. Columbus bet on the accuracy of Zacuto and set up a 'feast and palaver' for the Indian chief Huero and his tribe on the evening of the lunar eclipse. ***"Attend tonight the rising of the moon. She will rise inflamed with wrath, signifying the punishment God will visit upon you."***[34]

---

[32] Edward Kritzler, 2008:p.20, *Jewish Pirates of the Caribbean*, Doubleday, NY.
[33] *Ibid.*, Kritzler, p.22. [34] *Ibid.*, Kritzler, p.23.

"*When the eclipse began shortly after sunset, Columbus retreated to his cabin. 'The Indians grew so frightened,' wrote Fernando, 'that with great howling and lamentation they came running in all directions to the ships, laden with provisions, and praying for the Admiral to intercede with his God that He might not vent His wrath upon them.' When the moon was in full shadow, Columbus emerged. He had pleaded with his God, he told them, who agreed to forgive them as long as the Indians kept the Christians supplied. As proof, 'they would soon see the moon's anger and inflammation pass away.'*"[35]

When **Columbus** was at his lowest point, stranded on Jamaica for almost a year, he **wrote a letter to Queen Isabella that is absolutely chilling in the power of its prophetic voice:**

> We have been confined 10 months, lodged on the decks of our ships. My men have mutinied. My brother, my son, and those that are faithful are sick, starving and dying. Governor Ovando of Santo Domingo has sent to see if I am dead rather than to carry me back alive. I conclude your officers intend my life should terminate here.
>
> Should I die in Jamaica and my proprietary rights withdrawn, **ingratitude will bring down the wrath of Heaven, so that the wealth that I have discovered shall be the means of stirring up all mankind to revenge, and the Spanish nation shall suffer hereafter!** [36]

It was from the very shore Columbus was standing upon that the '*wrath of Heaven*' would indeed be brought down upon the Spanish nation! Jamaica would become the base of the fleets of the dreaded Buccaneers, financed and led by Messianic privateers, merchants and ship-owners - **that would bring the Spanish Empire to its knees!**

No doubt Columbus believed he would meet his end on that island. It is hard to imagine him saying such bitter but honest words to the Queen unless he thought they were his last. It was indeed for the best that Isabella never received the letter since he had no way to send it. The rescue ships did arrive and Columbus returned to Spain where he died not long afterwards, in 1506.

---

[35] *The Life of Admiral Christopher Columbus by His Son Fernando*, (1540, 1992:pp.264-65, Rutgers U. Press, New Brunswick, N.J, cited in Kritzler p.23.
[35] Edward Kritzler, 2008:p.19, *Jewish Pirates of the Caribbean*, Doubleday, NY.

Only Columbus' legend remains - and the truth - as we can piece it together. Columbus' survival due to his teenage Converso fighting force is only one of the many untold stories in the Messianic saga of the New World. Hopefully, this work will crack open the door to truth and more of those stories will be told. Even with the sketchy information we have, it is clear the Messianics were not the brutalizing force that the Old Christian Spaniards were. Columbus always traded for gold. He never seized it, nor raped and pillaged the natives. Columbus' attitude is spelled out in the archives obtained by Washington Irving:

> I would not rob nor outrage the country since reason requires that it should be settled,
> **and then the gold may be procured without violence.**[37]

The greed for gold, and the brutal oppression of native peoples, such as the burgeoning and lucrative African slave trade, were hidden beneath the pious facade of *"christianizing the infidels..."* *"It was seen as an act of charity, guided by the will of God, even as the Africans violently resisted the brutality of their purported saviors."*[38] The Church profited from it, as they did from the brutal oppression of their own Messianic congregants. The Spanish Inquisition followed closely upon the discovery and conquest of the Americas. The Inquisition was world-wide and continued to pursue, imprison and execute Messianics from Mexico to India.

Columbus, and his heirs, over the course of the next century, forbade the Inquisition in any lands under their authority!

---

[37] Washington Irving, *Life and Voyages of Christopher Columbus*, vol.2, p.614.
[38] Peter Marshall & David Manuel, 1977, *The Light and The Glory*, Revell, Grand Rapids, MI.

Chapter Nine
Messianic Diaspora & the Renaissance

*You meant it for evil, but Yehovah used it for good,
so it would come to pass that many are saved!*
Genesis 50:20

The New World was colonized in large numbers by Jews and Messianics, about 10-15% - consisting of those fleeing the Expulsion and the Inquisition. The Messianics of Spain and Portugal were severely persecuted - many fled to other lands in Africa, Asia, Europe and the Americas taking their skills and knowledge with them. **These Messianics and Neo-Messianics, along with their Jewish brothers, were to transform the world as we know it!** The international banking system, the modernization of technology, and the Renaissance were all, to a significant degree, due to their accomplishments.

The European Renaissance, during the 14th-17th centuries, was the most incredible blossoming of art, science, and philosophy the world had ever seen! It began in Florence, Italy, but **the origins of the Renaissance are to be found in the Golden Age of Spain.** The new wealth pouring forth from the New World to the Old World, lent itself to patronage of the arts and sciences - uplifting and transforming them in myriad ways.

We are going to take a thin slice of history to illustrate the influence of the Messianic community in the Renaissance. During the Golden Age of Spain (10th-13th centuries) the forgotten knowledge of the Greeks came flooding back into Europe, augmented by the genius of the East. *"Jacob ibn Tarik... is said about the year 820, to have carried astronomical books from Ceylon to Baghdad, and Joseph of Spain to have introduced to the Western World, from India, the so-called Arabic numerals. While Baghdad was the centre of the West Asiatic learning,* **Moslem Spain became the home of civilization in Europe.***"*[1]

It was this Golden Age, first in Spain, that spread to Italy then throughout Europe in the Renaissance. The anti-Semitic pogroms against both Jews and Conversos culminated in the Inquisition against Messianics and the Expulsion of the Jews. That persecution killed the Golden Age and led to the Diaspora of Jews and Messianics from Spain.

---
[1] Elkan Adler, 1987:pp. x, *Jewish Travellers in The Middle Ages*, Dover, N.Y.

Origins of the Renaissance

The advances in astronomy and navigation, such as the astrolabe, allowed the Portuguese navigators to find the route around the Cape of Good Hope into the Indian Ocean and onward to the spice cities of India then to the silk road of China and other very lucrative trading destinations. These new advances also permitted Columbus to plant Spain's flag in the New World. The result was a massive increase in world trade and wealth.

Much of this new wealth and priceless knowledge flowed through the Iberian Peninsula of Portugal and Spain. *"The Caliphs of Cordova were great patrons of learning and... one bookish Caliph after the other sent Jewish bibliophiles throughout the East searching for books for the splendid libraries that grew up in Cordova, Toledo, and elsewhere."*[2] *'Jewish'* bibliophiles always included a large number of Conversos among them, since the communities of Jews and Conversos were quite often intertwined. Books from the East translated by Messianic and Jewish scribes during Spain's Golden Age provided dark-age Europe with the seeds of renewal.

The Iberian gateway of knowledge from the East, gold and silver from the West, and precious trading goods from all over - set the stage for the Renaissance. Only a few decades after Columbus, the richest vein of silver ore ever discovered was found in Potosi, Peru, high in the Andes. It was of amazing purity (50%) unheard of in the mining of silver. The vein went to a depth of 300 feet making Potosi the richest boomtown in the world! The galleons of Spain were soon glutted with silver but that is only the beginning of the tale.

Slaves were in high demand to do the work of mining and agriculture in the New World, especially in malaria-ridden areas. Only African slaves would do - as certain West African tribes had a genetic immunity to malaria.[3] Galleons from Spain would load up with black slaves in Africa, bought from slavers at a fraction of what they would sell them for in the New World. There they sell their slaves and load up with silver in Peru, cheap at the source, and continue onto the newly discovered sea route to China - the richest trading country in the world at the time.

---

[2] Elkan Nathan Adler, 1987:pp. xi, *Jewish Travellers in The Middle Ages*, Dover Publications, N.Y. [3] Charles Mann, 2011, chapter 11, *1493:Uncovering the New World...* Random House Audio Books, N.Y.

Due to total mismanagement of their coinage, the Chinese currency collapsed in the mid 1500s.[4] **The Chinese had no viable means of exchange!** Silver was used but it was so rare and expensive it could not meet the need. Then Spanish galleons appeared in China chock full of scarce pure silver money! The traders exchanged silver for huge amounts of silk and porcelain, cheap in China - precious in Europe, before returning, having profited shamelessly on each leg of their journey. Some 1/3 to 1/2 of New World silver was going to China - who had an endless demand for silver only matched by their huge stocks of priceless goods to trade. As a result of this brand new world-wide trade, Europe was awash in wealth like never before! The avalanche of new scientific and cultural knowledge was also key; new books from the East, new art from China, new music from Arabia, new food crops from the Americas, new animals, new ideas, new opportunities!

Out of all this opulence of both wealth and knowledge flowing into Europe - the Renaissance was born! Messianics, and Jews, were at the forefront of all these events! *"After the expulsion of the Jews from Spain in 1492, there was... considerable immigration... of the so-called* **Marranos** [Messianics]... *persons who... embrace Christianity but retained their Jewish loyalties... rendering Italian Jewry the more capable of participating in Renaissance intellectual life...* **They [Messianics] were prominent and active out of proportion to their numbers***."* [5]

The story begins with Columbus and the Age of Discovery, when secret Jews sailed with the explorers, marched with the conquistadors, and were among the first settlers in every New World colony. This early history is largely unknown because few - then or since - realized that these pioneers were Jewish. Forbidden entry into the New World because of their religion, Iberian Jews posed as New Christians from Portugal, the one settler group that was not required to prove their Catholic ancestry. **Most Portuguese operating in the Spanish Empire were New Christians, called conversos, and many maintained their allegiance to their ancestral faith.**[6]

---

[4] Charles Mann, 2011, chapter 11, *1493:Uncovering the New World...* Random House Audio Books, N.Y.   [5] Cecil Roth, 1959:p.7, *Jews in the Renaissance*.
[6] Edward Kritzler, 2008:p.viii, *Jewish Pirates of the Caribbean*, Doubleday Publishers, N.Y.

A mercantile people, Jews in the New World went about their business as traders and shipowners, thus becoming the first merchant class in the Spanish Empire. As long as they pretended to be Christian and delivered the goods, no one questioned their religiosity too closely. They set up the first sugar factories, pioneered grain, coffee, and tea cultivation, and traded sugar, tobacco, gold, and silver with covert Jews on the Iberian Peninsula… **In Mexico and Peru… Jewish merchants controlled the silver trade!** [7]

Expelled from Spain, hundreds of thousands of Jews fled to anywhere they could find a safe haven, and joined hundreds of thousands of Messianics fleeing the Inquisition. Safe haven was only to be found in the New World, the Muslim lands (now controlled by the Ottoman Turks), Holland and Italy.

In Italy, Pope Sixtus IV had granted the Spanish monarchs a papal bull authorizing - and giving them control of - the Spanish Inquisition. Things got out of control very quickly, as reflected in the pope's denunciation of the Spanish Inquisition[8] - which he was later pressured to retract. To compensate, the pope permitted safe haven for escaping Jews and Messianics in Italy.

After the expulsion from Spain at the end of the 15th century, **some of the most cultured of the exiles settled [in Italy]…** the nerve center of Italian Jewry was Rome, under the eye and generally the protection of the Popes… leaders of Italian humanism - collectors of manuscripts, patrons of the arts, devotees of music, students of the humanities, enthusiasts for classical antiquity. Scholars and artists from all parts of Italy flocked to enjoy their enlightened patronage; and Jews too were able to take advantage of this benign atmosphere…[9] [brackets mine]

Hence, in all these cities [of Italy] there were relatively large Jewish colonies… They were reinforced later in the 16th century, by **numerous Marrano refugees from Portugal**.[10]

Florence… Jews were thus to be found in that lovely city **in its finest hour**… [and] **they both participated in and reflected its eager intellectual life**.[11] [brackets mine]

---

[7] Edward Kritzler, 2008:p.ix, *Jewish Pirates of the Caribbean*, Doubleday, N.Y.
[8] Henry Charles Lea, 1908:p.587, *A History of the Inquisition in Spain*, vol.1.
[9] Cecil Roth, 1959:p.8, *The Jews in the Renaissance*, Jewish Publication Society, Philadelphia. [10] *Ibid.*, in the same place, p.10. [11] *Ibid.*, p.11.

> Spain [was] puffed up with conquests… but these triumphs, and the masses of transatlantic gold, could never replace their Moorish agriculturists, or their Jewish merchants; they could not supply a population to the vacated fields and cities…[12]

Barcelona is a good example but far from the only city that suffered deprivation at the flight of the Jews and Messianics: *"Barcelona suddenly was stagnant. For the Jews of Barcelona had provided the intellectual energy and the financial backbone of the city, and they had left 'en masse'… The Jewish quarter had graced the city with its finest schools, its best doctors, its poets & philosophers, and in the blink of an eye, they were all gone!"*[13]

The disappearance of the Messianic population was just as sudden and severe, and began even earlier than the Expulsion of Jews in 1492. The Inquisition began its bloody work in 1478, but even this was preceded by pogroms against the Messianics. The Conversos, due to their Hebrew education, had shot to the top of the food chain once converted to Christianity. Their conversion opened the door to service in the royal court as doctors, financiers, and diplomats. Professions previously forbidden were now wide open to them. Trades that had been closed to them were now permissible. Conversos had, or could get, the money to set-up and engage in such trading right away. Particularly lucrative was banking. Various cities had given licenses to Jews to provide loans to the common man who had no such access to such financing before. The Jews and Messianics had long been bankrolling the royals and the landed gentry. Now such banking was above board and acceptable. **The result was vicious class envy by the commoners who perceived Conversos as becoming rich overnight while their lot remained as dismal as ever!**

When bigoted priests whipped up the outrage of the common people into a mob, anti-Converso rioting occurred in 1449, 1467, 1473. *"Marrano communities were severely hit, and actually destroyed, after the great outbursts of 1473, which particularly ravaged the Marrano communities in Cordova and Jaen."*[14]

---

[12] James Finn, 1841:p.410, *Sephardim*, Rivington Press, London, U.K.
[13] James Reston, 2005:p.293, *Dogs of God*, Anchor Books, N.Y.
[14] Benzion Netanyahu, 1999:p.145, *Marranos of Spain*, Cornell Univ. Press.

Once the Inquisition began - it depopulated Spain - region by region. The Messianics fled by the thousands. Of those who remained, tens of thousands were burned at the stake within the first two decades, others were dispossessed of their lands, homes and valuables. Even when released with a penance, it was not uncommon to be forbidden to work in one's previous profession. Families were deprived of their breadwinners and thrown into the streets to starve, which many did. It was a horrible fate that befell *"the Marrano cities, especially in Andalusia, that were abandoned as a result of the Inquisition's persecutions."*[15]

The Inquisition was purging Spain of its Messianics!

> The smoke of the [auto da fe] are rising toward the sky in all the kingdoms of Spain and the islands of the Sea. A third of them [Messianics] has been consumed, a third runs here and there to hide, and the rest of them live in great fear and extraordinary weakness... [brackets mine]

Arama sees in the claims of the Inquisition no substance, but a sheer expression of hostility. It is a kind of obsession with the Christians to hate the Marranos.

...<u>Merely a part of the divine scheme to subject the Marranos to such punishment!</u>[16]

The Roman Church and the Spanish Crown held onto the evil power of the Inquisition for 356 years. First, the evil drained them of their finest minds and most productive citizens, then it took their population, their wealth, their colonies, their Empire, and even their monarchy. **Messianics who could leave - left!**

> *"Speedily, after the expatriation of the Jews, and during the hottest reign of the Inquisition, the vaunted royal descent, in both Spain and Portugal, became extinct: and in the former of these a succession of mad or idiotic sovereigns has tended greatly to make monarchy itself a laughing stock."*[17]

> The colonies one by one have vanished... population of the [Iberian] Peninsula, in the nineth century was forty millions, is now reduced to between ten and eleven millions; that of Toledo is dwindled from two hundred thousand to twenty thousand... the realm is bankrupt, without a navy... naked to her enemies.[18]

---

[15] Benzion Netanyahu, 1999:p.145, *Marranos of Spain*, Cornell Univ. Press.
[16] *Ibid.,* Netanyahu, 1999:p.154-5, citing Arama. [17] James Finn, 1841:p.411, *Sephardim*, Rivington, London. [18] James Finn made these comments in 1841, only seven years after the final end of the Spanish Inquisition in 1834.

Where did all these Jewish and Messianic emigrants go? A major destination of choice was Italy. *"Not only were the Jews welcomed in the Venetian states, and so powerfully sheltered in Florence that it was said, 'a man might as well strike the grand duke as a Jew:' but pope Clement VII invited even the Jews who had been forcibly baptized to come and live as they pleased in his dominion."*[19] There, the Renaissance came about as a result of this internationalism - bringing together new ideas and technologies - many of them carried to Italy by Messianic, and Jewish, emigrants from Spain, and elsewhere. *"At this time the world was full of Jewish refugees, forced to remove from one country to another - bringing with them new currents, ideas, and conceptions;* **the great historic role of the Jewish people during the past two thousand years***."*[20]

We must focus on finance as a chief factor of economic prosperity, artistic and scientific advancement. Although **Jews, and Messianics, were forbidden to take any money out of Spain** - out of necessity they had set up what would become an international banking system. It allowed them to deposit money in one country and draw it out in another, also to receive loans practically anywhere in the world based on their credit-worthiness. *"The end of July [1492] saw multitudes of noble-minded Israelites forsake their homes, their fathers' graves, and all their old associations of infancy and ancestry, to wander they knew not whither, a dignified triumph of passive courage...* **notwithstanding all their losses in the breaking up of their property - <u>they carried off thirty million ducats!</u>***"*[21]

"There was also a kind of underground railroad clandestinely maintained by Sephardic refugees for the crypto-Jews left behind in Iberia... and [an] evident desire to retain their ties with Marranos there... [so they] could also help them... in removing their assets abroad in preparation for flight."[22] **The flight of the Jews and Messianics represented an enormous transfer of wealth and technology to the countries who gave them refuge!** *"The Jews were the carriers of Europe's latest technological secrets, whether in medicine, artisanry, or trade. Many of them had studied in the advanced universities..."*[23] [brackets mine]

---

[19] James Finn, 1841:p.428, *Sephardim*, Rivington Co., London.   [20] Cecil Roth, 1959:p.18, *Jews in the Renaissance*, Jewish Publication Society, Philadelphia.
[21] James Finn, *ibid.*, p.401.   [22] Jane Gerber, 1992:p.163, *Jews of Spain*, Free Press, NY.   [23] Jane Gerber, *ibid.*, p.164.

Inheriting the Golden Age

Morviedro, near Valencia in Spain, illustrates the key mechanism of the Golden Age, as detailed in Mark Meyerson's book *A Jewish Renaissance in Fifteenth Century Spain*.[24] The town of Morviedro was quite possibly the oldest Jewish colony in Sepharad, and originally one of Solomon's trading outposts during the time of the first temple in the 7th century BC. This is ascertained by a Hebrew inscription in their cemetery which reads, *"This is the tomb of Adoniram, The servant of king Solomon; Who came to collect the tribute, And died..."* In 1st Kings 4:6 where the officers of Solomon are recorded, it states *"Adoniram the son of Abda was over the tribute."*[25]

The Golden Age of Sepharad had been ended by the atrocities of the Inquisition - established in 1478 to extinguish the Messianic Church - and by the Expulsion of the Jews in 1492. Morviedro had avoided the ravages of the Church and Crown due to their special circumstance - resulting in a Renaissance of their community just as horrors were coming to pass in other parts of Spain. They were a town outside of Valencia, which had expelled their Jews to Morviedro. The other inhabitants of the town were quite aware that the Jewish and Messianic presence was the fountain of their prosperity. There was no marching of blood-thirsty mobs against Morviedro. The Valencians had no Jews to be whipped into a frenzy about, and the prosperous Gentile citizens of Morviedro were gratified by their partnership with the Jews.

Those Jews who converted, of which there were many, typically moved into Valencia. They maintained a fruitful collaboration with their Jewish relatives in Morviedro. They often joined them for Passover and *"occasional synagogue attendance was not an unusual phenomenon for either New or Old Christians."*[26] **There is a principle to be recognized here!**

The Golden Age was the catalyst for the Renaissance - both came about in those times and places when Jews, Messianics, and Christians were collaborating in relative harmony. Muslims also played their part, as they had much to add. When that harmony was destroyed by the Inquisition, Expulsion, and later the Counter-Reformation - the golden years came to a halt!

---

[24] Mark Meyerson, 2004, *A Jewish Renaissance in 15th century Spain*, Princeton Press. [25] Cited in Chapter One of this volume, *"The New Jerusalem"* pp.11-13.
[26] Theodor Dunkelgrün, 2020:p.103, *Bastards and Believers*, Univ. Penn. Press.

The refugees who came to Italy from Spain after 1492, and the cultured Marranos from Portugal who followed them, gave... a new stimulus to the vernacular literary interests of Italian Jews. **Indeed, in the 14th century the Jews of Aragon and Castile had taken a direct part in the Spanish literary revival, their share in which cannot be overlooked**... the earliest known specimens of Castilian and Spanish poetry are the snatches and refrains preserved in Hebrew characters in the poems of the great Hebrew singer Jehudah Halevi, and dating back to the early years of the 12th century. The family of Abrabanel brought something of this spirit with them when they settled in Italy... **the most memorable 16th century contribution by a Jew to Italian literature... [was] Abrabanel's philosophical classic, "The Dialogues of Love."** [27]

In every area of endeavor, Jews and Messianics were prominent players! The majority of Jewish refugees, as well as many Messianics, fled to the lands of Islam in Africa, the Mideast, and Turkey. *"To the horror of some European observers, refugees were able to bring their knowledge of how to make gunpowder and munitions to the arsenals of Istanbul, Fez. Marrakech, and Cairo."*[28] One can hardly blame the Sephardic refugees. *"The unforgettable cruelties they had endured had not ended with the extinction of Judaism in Iberia. Periodic eruptions of Inquisitorial zeal sent shockwaves throughout the Sephardic diaspora as boatloads of emigrés brought harrowing stories of new persecutions. Special memorial services would be held in the new Sephardic communities for victims of the latest 'auto-da-fe.'"*[29]

In the East the refugees' knowledge of languages, the cultures of Europe, and their *"deep and abiding resentment toward Spain"* made them ideal, and trusted, diplomats capable of accomplishing *"delicate feats of diplomacy at the highest level of government."* [30] *"It is testimony to their resilience as well as their talents that only one generation after the expulsion,* **a Golden Age of Jewish culture emerged in Turkey.** *Scarcely had the first exiles settled down when a remarkable burst of creativity manifested itself early in the 16th century...* **Dozens of major intellectual figures began writing... and publishing in the emerging Hebrew presses - thus spreading their influence.**"[31]

[27] Cecil Roth, 1959:p.108-9, *The Jews in the Renaissance*, Jewish Publication Society of America, Philadelphia, PA. [28] Jane Gerber, 1992:p.164-5, *The Jews of Spain*, Free Press, N.Y. [29] *Ibid.*, p.164. [30] Ibid., p.163. [31] *Ibid.*, p.169.

As far as Sephardic enterprises were concerned:

> Perhaps their greatest cultural innovation was the art of Hebrew printing. Soon after printing was introduced in Rome in 1470, the open-minded Jews of Iberia took to this new technique with delight. By the 1480s, Hebrew printing presses functioned in Spain at Guadalajara and Hijar, in Portugal at Lisbon, Leira, and Faro. **At the time of the expulsion, printers carried their type with them into exile, <u>setting up presses in Italy</u>**, in Fez and in Turkey... in Istanbul... in Salonika... in Smyrna... in Egypt...
>
> > a voluminous literature flooded from the presses...
> > testifying to the enormous productivity...
> > of the first generations of resettlement. [32]

"Iberian Hebrew presses were the result of a Jewish-Christian partnership."[33] This was the accepted pattern of many, if not most, Hebrew enterprises. Conversos had direct access to professions and licensing of businesses that Jews often did not. Conversos had influence among Christian society and its leadership that Jews did not have. Conversos were usually more trusted, because of their conversion to Christianity, than were Jews. Banking was another major enterprise in which Jews and Messianics cooperated and excelled.

> From the second half of the 13th century on, it became usual for the Italian communes, first in central Italy and then in the north, to invite Jews... to open '*loan banks*'... and in due course the admission of the '*loan bankers*' inevitably led in every (or almost every) case to the admission of Jews without restriction of occupation, and thus to the formation of a normal community. This then is the background in general terms in **the establishment of the Jewish colonies in northern Italy in which the Renaissance was principally enacted.**[34]

Although the Italian Renaissance is the focus of this chapter, it needs to be noted this was a pattern that occurred elsewhere, *"In Holland, the Jews... had their numbers rapidly increased from the* [Iberian] *Peninsula... freedom from Spain and its Inquisition afforded them a wide expansion of commerce and they greatly served the prosperity of Amsterdam, Rotterdam, and Antwerp."*[35]

---

[32] Jane Gerber, 1992:p.158, *The Jews of Spain*, The Free Press, N.Y.
[33] Theodor Dunkelgrün, 2020:p.105, *Bastards and Believers*, U. of Penn. Press.
[34] Cecil Roth, 1959:pp.6-7, *The Jews in the Renaissance*, Jewish Pub. Society.
[35] James Finn, 1841:p.434, *Sephardim*, Rivington Press, London.

One last thing must be mentioned before we leave this all-too-brief summary of the origins of the Renaissance. Hebrew education went wherever the Jews and Messianics went - and took root there. *"New schools of higher Jewish learning soon dotted the Ottoman map. The most famous, the Yeshiva in Salonika known simply as the Talmud Torah, was founded in 1520 by Sephardic exiles and would function for four centuries... the school was noted for a cosmopolitan **student body drawn from all over the** [Ottoman] **Empire and Italy**, and for a broad curriculum that included Talmudic and Hebraic studies, Greek and Latin, medicine, astronomy, and the natural sciences."*[36]

> The educational system among the Jews of Renaissance Italy was readjusted... with the new conceptions that had come to prevail in the outside world. The old Talmudic disciplines were by no means neglected. But these were supplemented by studies in accordance with the Renaissance attitudes... [37]

The Great Hellenistic-Jewish Conflict

That age-old conflict was reframed in terms of whether or not the Messianics were *judaizing* the Christians. *"The great Hellenistic-Jewish conflict over the spiritual mastery of the ancient world... has nothing to do with what happened in Spain thirteen centuries later!"*[38] **Actually it does** - but not in terms of *judaizing*. It is the **Renewed Covenant** that is the fault line between Messianic and Greek Christianity. **A war of ideas was still raging between the *"sons of Zion and the sons of Greece!"***

Jeremiah 31:32-33 states, *"Behold the days are coming, declares Yehovah, when I will make a **renewed covenant** with the house of Israel and with the house of Judah. It will not be like the covenant I made with their fathers."* **In Hebrew, it says a *Brit Hadashah*, a Renewed Covenant**. The word *hadashah* can mean either *new* or *renewed*. Why *renewed*? *"This is the covenant I will make... I will put my Torah in their minds and inscribe it in their hearts. And I will be their God and they will be my people."*

**The Torah is not rejected, nor are the Jewish people!
It is a continuation with changes - a renewal - not a rejection!**

---

[36] Jane Gerber, 1992:p.169, *The Jews of Spain*, The Free Press, N.Y.
[37] Cecil Roth, 1959:pp.33-34, *The Jews in the Renaissance*, Jewish Pub. Society.
[38] Benzion Netanyahu, 1999:278, *Marranos of Spain*, Cornell Press, Ithaca, NY.

In Spain we have the resurgence of the Messianic Church, the original Church of the Hebrew Messiah - Yeshua - complete with *The Hebrew Gospels*. To these believers belongs the true mantle of the chosen people. **Yehovah's chosen are those who embrace both His son, the Hebrew Messiah, and His Torah!** The later ***Greek New Testament*** anointed God's son as the head of a Hebrew-hating church, rejected the Messianic Church and sought to destroy it. You do not have to be a theologian to see this is evil. **It is a continuation of the original apostasy to destroy the rightful heirs - declaring them all crypto-Jews so as to say that the Messianics, and their Church, never existed!**

The Myth of Messianics as Crypto-Jews

We see in historians' constant references to c*rypto-Jews* - a complete failure to recognize the Messianic factor - there were Conversos who held to a sincere faith in both their Hebrew Messiah and their Hebrew Scripture, the Torah and *The Hebrew Gospels*. Rarely do we see an historian come close to this realization. Here is one who did:

> Conversion is seen here as a fundamentally positive phenomenon - that is, **not as an apostasy from Judaism but as an affirmative embrace of Christianity**... God did not reject Jews and Judaism by sending the Messiah to Gentiles, God confirmed the value of Judaism by having his son be born a Jew... Conversion was, for those conversos, a cause of pride and power.[39]

Rather than constant negative assessments of Messianics as faking their faith, Stuczynski (cited above), and a precious few others, are beginning to see sincere Conversos, as they saw themselves, **becoming whole - in their Messianic identity - for the first time in their lives!** Jews had never known the Bible as a complete whole, its ancient prophecies of the Messiah incomplete without the New Testament realization of them. Both were puzzle pieces joined together now - the glorious big picture at last!

Christians, indoctrinated into the insanity of rejecting Yehovah's Torah as *'judaizing'* - the ultimate evil - could not see the big picture either! **Rejecting the Torah of the Covenant (Old Testament) was as inconceivable to Messianics as renouncing their Hebrew Messiah!**

---

[39] Citing Claude Stuczynski in Theodor Dunkelgrun, 2020:p.18, *Bastards and Believers*, University of Pennsylvania Press, Philadelphia.

A covenant with Yehovah is a binding contract. The Old Covenant and the Renewed Covenant have been changed to the Old Testament and the New Testament. The new churches could not give the Word the stamp of a contract since they were intent upon changing it to suit their doctrine. Take for example, the Ten Commandments, if you were a heretic or infidel, you could be deceived (Thou shalt not lie), dispossessed (Thou shalt not steal), or killed (Thou shalt not kill) with impunity. New rules for a new church seeking power.

Much has been made of the words of Paul that the Old Covenant gives way to the New. There are differing interpretations of Paul's words. Regardless, I must ask the reader to prayerfully consider these questions because they have eternal consequences. Does Paul's word have the authority to overrule the Word of Yehovah? Does Constantine's word have the authority to overrule the Word of Yehovah? Does the pope's word have the authority to overrule the Word of Yehovah? Does your opinion have authority to overrule the Word of Yehovah?

The Messianics held to the Word of Yehovah. Both Christians and Jews see Messianics as flawed and fractured. This is a reflection of Jews rejecting their Hebrew Messiah - and Christians rejecting the divine law of Torah. **It is historians, both Christians and Jews, who are flawed and fractured, unable to see the whole - seeing their small sliver of the picture as sacrosanct - while all else is adjudged, or prejudged, as false.**

The Messianics, according to Alonso Palencia, *"decided to leave those inhumane lands"* [Spain & Portugal] *"but not Christendom."*[40] References to crypto-Jews or covert Jews or Conversos returning to Judaism must be interpreted in this light. **Messianics became believers in the Son of God but never left Judaism!** Observing the Sabbath, celebrating the Feast Days of Yehovah or studying Torah in Hebrew - **are all part of their worship of the Hebrew Messiah!** Crypto-Jews were but a fraction of the picture - not the whole picture. Neo-Messianic believers were like unto the Messianic believers of the first century.

These Neo-Messianics brought to Spain, then to all of Europe, <u>a Golden Age!</u>

---

[40] Benzion Netanyahu, 1999:p.251, citing Alonso de Palencia in *Crónica de Enrique IV*, vol. III, p.133.

Chapter Ten
Hebrew Pirates of the High Seas

For your sake we are killed all the day long, we are accounted as sheep for the slaughter. **Nay, in all these things we are more than conquerors through him that loved us!** Romans 8:36-37

During the Middle Ages, the Apostate Church had become an overt spiritual battleground between good and evil - spilling massive amounts of Messianic blood during the Spanish Inquisition! Nonetheless, it propelled Messianics to do things they would never have done while settled comfortably in their beloved Sepharad. *"In the Age of Discovery, known conversos were involved in nearly every venture as explorers, pilots and conquistadors, or behind the scenes as financiers, shipowners and administrators!"* **The Messianic diaspora took them to all corners of the newly discovered world where they became the masters of international trade and banking!** However, now the Spanish too were losing blood, treasure and territory. It was the first world war - fought in every corner of the globe!

To wreak their revenge upon Spain - Messianics became pirates of the High Seas! From the Mediterranean to the Gulf of Mexico to the Indian Ocean and the China Seas, Messianic and Jewish trading vessels plied their trade, and Hebrew-owned corsairs with Hebrew names and swashbuckling Hebrew buccaneers took away the gold and silver of the Spanish in amounts so overwhelming they eventually shut down the Spanish Empire! The Hebrews allied with Britain and Holland to attack the Spanish from English Jamaica, gaining rights to live and worship in their nations and colonies. Later, these Hebrew privateers became the first navy of the American colonists fighting for freedom from British rule. In 1812, Messianic privateers were the key to victory against the British at New Orleans.

In India the Saint Thomas Christians had thrived for 1500 years. In 1498, then Portuguese gun ships landed followed by the Jesuits and the Inquisition. In an astonishing display of cruelty, the Portuguese Inquisition at Goa commits atrocities that manage to dwarf those of the Spanish Inquisition! They crushed the St. Thomas Church making them bow to the Roman faith. The Apostate Church was purely about power, not salvation!

[1] Edward Kritzler, 2008:p.46, *Jewish Pirates of the Caribbean*, Doubleday, N.Y.

In events that can only be explained by the power of Yehovah, the Hebrews turned the disastrous twin evils of the Expulsion and the Inquisition into a worldwide triumph! *"**Conversos in the New World dominated commerce!** In the sixteenth century, when the known world doubled in size and international trade became big business, **they established a trade network that spanned the globe!**"*[2]

> Dealing with the People of the Book was very attractive. **Their innovative letters of exchange and credit made capital portable**. For instance, a shipping merchant trading in pirate waters doubled his risks if he returned with gold. On the other hand, if he could leave the gold and return with a draft on a Jewish banking house, he was safe... In a world trade network at the onset of international trade, Jewish merchants were the world's most coveted capitalists.[2]

At the time, almost every major sea power had a policy of licensing pirates to take enemy ships and share the proceeds with them. They called these licenses, *letters of marque*, and they are enshrined in the U.S. Constitution (Article 1, Section 8). So these privateers were not outlaws, simply extensions of the power of the warring nations of the day. Hebrew merchants excelled at privateering - especially against Spain - with whom they had a deep-seated desire for vengeance! Their trade network *"doubled as a worldwide intelligence network... In coded correspondence with fellow merchants in other colonies, they were able to ascertain what ship was sailing when: its cargo, route, and destination and what its captain may have secreted in his cabin. Thus informed,* **Jewish merchants** *were the brains behind the brawn - financing, advising, and sometimes* **leading the Caribbean's emerging fighting force: a ragtag crew of misfits of every nation...** <u>**the dreaded buccaneers of the Spanish Main!**</u>*"*[3]

Hebrews and Messianics were the foremost mapmakers of the Age of Discovery. It was the Hebrews who *"perfected the nautical instruments and astronomical tables the early explorers sailed with... Jewish pilots, adept at reading maps and using navigational instruments, were recruited... Had they not been, many an explorer would have been lost in the vast oceans."*[4] The early explorers, Vasco de Gama, Pedro Cabral, and Amerigo Vespucci, were all guided by **a Converso pilot, Gaspar de Gama.**

---

[2] Edward Kritzler, 2008:p.4-5, *Jewish Pirates of the Caribbean*, Doubleday, NY. [3] Ibid., p.6. [4] Ibid., p.30.

Vasco de Gama, who credited his *"Hebrew tutor for teaching him navigation, mathematics, and astronomy,"*[5] was commissioned in 1494 by King Manuel of Portugal to find the eastern route around Africa to India. De Gama had been attacked by local pirates all along the east African coastline so when he neared the subcontinent of India he was wary. At an island off the coast of Calcutta, a richly dressed man approached the ship, hailing it in Spanish and asking to speak to the Captain. He said that he was a New Christian, named Moncaide. Once de Gama's sailors seized him and his men - he quickly divulged that, because of his extensive seafaring knowledge and experience, he had been put in command of the navy of Rajah Samorin, ruler of Calcutta. He agreed to call off the ships sent to attack them, pilot de Gama's ships into Calcutta, and present him to Samorin.

Having aided the foreigners, Samorin's naval commander Moncaide the Converso was no longer trusted, and so he accepted de Gama's offer to return to Portugal with him. In Lisbon, he asked to be rebaptized in his new host country and took the name Gaspar de Gama after his captain. He spoke at length with King Manuel about the many places he had been. The King referred to his new Messianic advisor as '*Gaspar, the Jewish pilot.*'

King Manuel commissioned Pedro Cabral to explore this new route to the Indies, as long as he took Gaspar the pilot with him. In addition he sent Mestre João, his brilliant Converso physician, on the voyage to chart the expedition since he was expert at calibrating the new improved astrolabe. Rounding the Cape Verde Islands off of the coast of Africa, they were blown off course by major storm winds and currents, taking them further and further west toward the still uncharted New World. They ended up landing off the coast of Brazil - which they claimed for Portugal. Cabral conferred with Gaspar and Mestre João. They agreed the landfall was not a large island - but a new continent!

The South American continent had been discovered by Pedro Cabral and his two Messianic advisors, Gaspar the pilot and Mestre João, his navigator! Cabral headed back across the Atlantic around Africa and on to India where he landed at Calcutta. On the way back, Cabral stopped in the Atlantic again to provision at Cape Verde on the west coast of Africa.

[5] Edward Kritzler, 2008:p31, *Jewish Pirates of the Caribbean*, Doubleday, N.Y.

Another Portuguese fleet had stopped there for provision as well, sent to map the western route to the Indies across the Atlantic that had been discovered by Columbus. Their advisor was Amerigo Vespucci, an experienced seaman and navigator. Amerigo wrote that Gaspar the pilot was *"the most informed man among Cabral's followers... a trustworthy man who speaks many languages and knows many towns and provinces from Portugal to the Indian Ocean, from Cairo to the island of Sumatra."*[6]

Thanks to Gaspar's detailed guidance, Amerigo Vespucci was able to take command of the Portuguese fleet, and successfully explore the northern coast of South America, which Cabral had just discovered by accident. In Vespucci's account of these adventures, he proclaimed that in trying to reach Asia he had discovered a *'New World!'* The popularity of Amerigo Vespucci's account of his discoveries led a mapmaker named Martin Waldseemüller to call it *"the land of Amerigo!"* The name took, and Columbus' New World became known as **_America!_ The incredible experience and expertise of a single Messianic, Gaspar the pilot, had played a critical role in exploring and mapping both the eastern and the western routes to Asia, and opening wide the door to the New World!**

Vespucci reported to King Manuel that a certain tree, *brazilwood*, which produced a valuable red dye, was found in abundance in South America. The king contracted with a prominent Messianic shipping merchant Fernando de Noronha. Noronha brought other influential Conversos into the deal - **the first capitalist venture in the New World was Messianic!** Although these men were expecting profit, *"their interest in the far-off land was to find a refuge to live free from persecution."*[7] In 1503, they sent a fleet of five ships accompanied by Amerigo Vespucci. Vespucci later left them to go find the southern passage to India around South America. *"Conversos...established logging camps along six hundred miles of coastal land now known by the name if its valuable tree, **Brazil**. By 1505, the dyewood business was netting the partners fifty thousand ducats a year. Next to gold, brazilwood was then the most valuable product to come out of the New World."*[7] Christian-Converso partnership was more the norm than the exception. Magellan also had a Converso partner and financier, Juan de Aranda.

---

[6] Samuel Tolkowsky, 1964:p.123,*They took to the Sea: A Historical Survey of Jewish Maritime Activities*, German edition. [7] Edward Kritzler, 2008:p38, *Jewish Pirates of the Caribbean*, Doubleday, N.Y.

Spanish Messianics (New Christians) needed a license to emigrate to the New World. The New World was forbidden to Spanish Conversos. The Spanish Crown was becoming painfully aware of the brain drain they had created by the twin demons of Expulsion and Inquisition. Spain did not want to lose any more of their indispensable Messianic merchants and professionals. The situation was vastly different in Portugal where the king recognized Portugal's small population and vast Empire were at odds. Portuguese Conversos did not need a license to emigrate, even those who had fled there from Spain were encouraged, even recruited, to go to the New World. The bishop of Cuba once remarked that *"practically every ship arriving is filled with Hebrews and New Christians."*[8] Although the Spanish colonies did require a license to migrate - it was not required for ship crew and personal servants. **Many ships were owned by Conversos, so refugees signed on as sailors then jumped ship in America.** Messianics who did obtain a license to migrate to the New World - left with a plentiful staff of Conversos posing as servants.

"Conversos with the aptitude and capital to develop colonial trade, comfortable in an Hispanic society, yet seeking to put distance between themselves and the homeland of the Inquisition, made their way to the New World."[9] *"Since Spain forbade their conversos to migrate, a self-proclaimed Portuguese national operating in the Spanish realm was likely to be a converso."*[10] Spanish refugees would, universally, claim to be Portuguese - so much so that the label *Portuguese* - in the New World, became a synonym for *Converso*. One Inquisition report stated, *"Potosi is filled with Portuguese, all* [of them] *of the Hebrew nation... the export of silver is almost exclusively in the hands of crypto-Jews!"*[11] **Whether called New Christians, Conversos, Portuguese, or crypto-Jews - all were Messianics!**

The Spanish were riding high! *"In their own generation, they had defeated the Moors, kicked out the Jews, enslaved the Indians, and conquered more territory than Rome had in five centuries. In forty-two years, their country had swelled from an alliance of Christians fighting over a few thousand square miles to a world empire governing millions. In the process, Spain had become the richest most powerful nation in the world!"*[12] Even headier things were still to come!

---

[8] Seymour Liebman, 1970:p.46, *The Jews in New Spain*, Univ. of Miami Press.
[9] Edward Kritzler, 2008:p47, *Jewish Pirates of the Caribbean*, Doubleday, N.Y.
[10] *Ibid.*, Kritzler, 2008:p.40. [11] *Ibid.*, Kritzler, p.149. [12] *Ibid.*, p.51.

| Maximilian I Holy Roman Emperor | Mary Duchess of Burgundy | Ferdinand II King of Aragon | Isabella I Queen of Castille |

| Phillip I Archduke of Austria | Joanna Queen of Spain |

| Charles V Holy Roman Emperor |

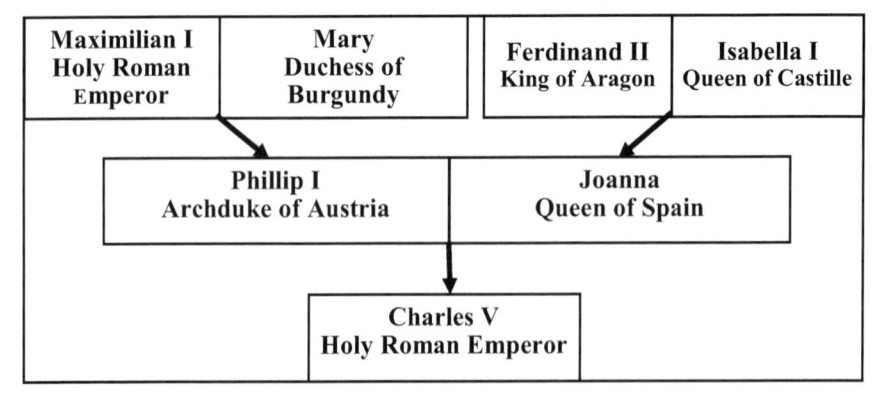

A New Era of Imperialism

Ferdinand of Aragon and Isabella of Castille had united Spain, merging the various regional kingdoms that had preceded them. Isabella died in 1504. Ferdinand died in 1516. They had five children. The two eldest, including their only son John, did not live to adulthood. The thrones of Aragon and Castille, and therefore all of Spain and her colonies, passed to their surviving eldest daughter Joanna.

Joanna was wed in 1496, at 16 years old, to Philip the Fair, Archduke of Austria of the Habsburg line with extensive lands in Germany, Austria and Italy. His father was Maximilian I, the Holy Roman Emperor. At the death of his mother, Mary of Burgundy - the richest woman in Europe - Philip inherited both the Burgundy lands and money. These were Burgundy in France and the Netherlands (aka Holland, Belgium and Luxemburg) which became the Spanish Netherlands when Philip, by marriage to Joanna, became King of Castile in 1506. He died a few months later - leaving Joanna pregnant with their son Charles.

Charles won the inheritance lottery! Charles V, the son of Phillip & Joanna, was born on February 24, 1500 - at the beginning of the new Age of Colonization. Charles became Duke of Burgundy and Lord of the Netherlands in 1506, King of Spain in 1516, including their vast colonies in the New World, and King of Naples, Sicily & Sardinia (Spanish domains at the time). **He became the Holy Roman Emperor** and Archduke of Austria in 1519, at the death of his grandfather Maximilian. As Lord of the Habsburgs his domains stretched from Germany to northern Italy, plus a few odds and ends I have not mentioned.

All without spilling a drop of blood!

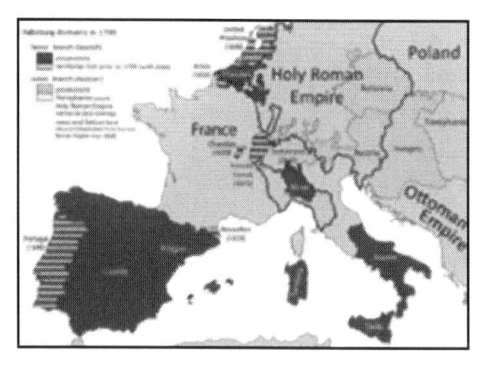

The Habsburg dominions, also called the Habsburg Empire, in the centuries following Charles V - The Holy Roman Emperor (1519-1555)

The Holy Roman Empire began with the Frankish king Charlemagne in 800, later referred to as the *First Reich. Reich* means *empire* in German. It was revived in 962 by King Otto of Germany, later called the *Second Reich*. In the 13th century it began to be called The Holy Roman Empire. In 1312, at the council of Cologne, it became The Holy Roman Empire of the German Nation - reflecting its German roots. After Charles V, the Habsburgs were a major power in Europe for five centuries. The empire slowly shrank to the point that it was finally dissolved by Napoleon in 1806. **Nazi Germany resurrected the mystique of the Holy Roman Empire, calling itself the** *Third Reich*.

Charles Dances a Jig!

In July 1534, Emperor Charles V awaited his treasure ships. They were overdue. Expected in May, they did not come. June passed with no ships. Finally in July, Charles' Spanish galleons arrived and unloaded 21 million pesos worth of silver![13] Charles "*danced a wild jig around with his son Philip and dwarf jester Perico* [who said] '***Your Father is Lord of Half the World, soon you will be Lord of All!***'"[14] Charles, it is said, laughed with no end. "*In Charles' lifetime, his subjects explored and settled a world three times as big as the one into which he had been born!*"[15] Despite successes beyond the wildest dreams a king could have, Charles was discovering what the Romans had learned. An expanding empire has two problems. It is expensive to take and to hold, and if it does not produce enough revenue it costs money. As it gets larger, it quickly becomes ungovernable. The patchwork quilt of Charles' widespread empire caused him to spend most of his reign traveling, warring, and administering.

[13] 535,500 kilograms - about 1.2 million pounds of silver! [14] Will Bradford, ed., 1850:pp.367 & 439, *Correspondences... of Charles V*, Bently Publishers, London. [15] Edward Kritzler, 2008:p56, *Jewish Pirates of the Caribbean*.

Charles had plenty of enemies. England and France were always nibbling away at his empire. The Reformation was transforming the Habsburg subjects into Lutherans who had become a force that could not be ignored. The Roman Church involved Charles in two wars to put the Protestants back into their place. Charles could no longer indulge the Church. He needed the northern (Protestant) princes to hold off Suleiman at Vienna.

These were the Ottoman Turks under Sultan Suleiman whose armies had overrun Persia, and now were moving into Europe, taking control of Hungary by 1526 and assaulting the gates of Vienna, Austria in 1529. Having captured Constantinople in 1453, their goal in this new century was to control the Mediterranean Sea. Suleiman, however, did not have a navy. Suleiman made the pirate Barbarossa the admiral of his fleet. **While Barbarossa was busy on land building the navy - on the sea the fleet was led by his brave Captain - Sinan the Jew.**

Spain had now expelled both the Moors and the Jews from their homeland committing insufferable cruelties in the process. At the conquest of Granada in 1492 the Muslims had been promised they could live forever in peace and observe their religion. It was Charles, in 1532, who ordered them to convert or flee. *"The Moors who had crossed over to North Africa* [called the Barbary Coast] *after their defeat at Granada - were joined by a second wave in 1532... Made furious by their forced exile they made up the bulk of Barbarossa's crews."*[16] The Jews were also furious! *"The displaced citizens of Judea took to the sea, becoming the region's major shipowners, merchants, and traders...* **Sephardic merchants financed the Moors' devastating raids on the coastal towns of Spain and Italy and shared the booty... Together, the two exiled immigrant groups forged a formidable force!***"*[16]

"In 1522, three treasure-laden ships dispatched to [Charles] *from Mexico City by Cortés had been captured and diverted to France by an Italian pirate... the discoverer of New York harbor - Verrazano. The Aztec plunder the Italian delivered to the royal court in Paris included a half ton of gold, 682 pounds of pearls, jewel boxes encrusted with topaz, mirrors of polished obsidian, an emerald as large as a man's fist...* **and of even greater value, the sea charts of the captured Spanish pilots!***"*[17] All the major powers now want in on the treasures of the New World!

---

[16] Edward Kritzler, 2008:p58, *Jewish Pirates...*   [17] *Ibid.*, Kritzler, 2008:p54.

Barbary Pirates - the Terror of the Seas!

"The Barbarossa brothers were already experienced pirates in the Mediterranean when Spain completed its conquest of Granada in 1492, defeating the last vestige of Islamic rule in the Iberian Peninsula, and Muslim immigrants from the region took refuge in North Africa"[18] They had been privateers under the Ottomans for a period but now were working with the North Africans. Spain and Portugal were seeking to expand their territory along the North African coast. In 1516 the Barbarossa brothers, Khidr and Aruj, led a force that captured Algiers in the western Mediterranean. This brought them to the attention of the Ottomans who sought to bring them in as allies. Aruj was made Governor of the Regency of Algiers, and Khidr was made governor of the Western Sea, basically the Pirate Admiral of Algiers.

In 1518 Aruj was killed fighting the Spanish. In 1520, Suleiman (known as *the Magnificent*) became Sultan of the Ottoman Empire. After Barbarossa's fleet captured Tunis in 1531, Suleiman made him *Kapudan Pasha* - Grand Admiral of the Ottoman Empire. Barbarossa had a fearsome and well-earned reputation. *"The Barbary Pirates (known as corsairs) sacked and burned villages and carried off men, women, and children. If not ransomed, the males were stripped, chained naked to the oars, and forced to row until they died of fatigue. The women were sent to harems, and the children were raised as Muslims."*[19]

Sinan the Famous Jewish Pirate

Sinan, the trusted war captain of Barbarossa, was a refugee from Spain. It was he who led the Ottoman fleet into battle. Although Admiral Barbarossa got the credit, it was Sinan who did the fighting. *"On August 20, 1534, Sinan... led a hundred ships into the harbor and occupied the North African city of Tunis - hitherto a possession of Spain - in the name of Suleiman... Now with the crescent flag flying over Tunis - he held dominion over the entire Mediterranean, No longer could Charles' ships venture safely beyond home waters -* **instead the Mediterranean had become an alien sea dominated by Muslim corsairs and Jewish merchants.**"[20] Charles fought back and retook Tunis in 1535 - **but in 1538 - Sinan** *"the Jewish corsair destroyed most of Spain's naval fleet off the port of Preveza in Greece!"*[21]

---

[18]John Rafferty, *Suleiman the Magnificent*, Encyclopedia Brittanica Online.
[19]Kritzler, 2008:p58-9, *Jewish Pirates of the Caribbean.* [20]*Ibid*, p.60. [21]*Ibid*,p.68.

Hebrew Pirates

Samuel Palache was born in 1558 in the Jewish Ghetto in Fez, Morocco. His father descended from a six-century line of rabbis, and was head of the Jewish Yeshivah. Samuel and his younger brother, Joseph, were conversant in a number of languages. They spoke Spanish at home but also Portuguese and Arabic, and had learned Hebrew (& Chaldean) at Yeshivah. The Jews of Fez thrived in the professions the Arabs disdained.

> Like the Catholic clergy, the mullahs castigated financiers as parasitic usurers and forbade their followers from engaging in such matters. The vagaries of finance were thus left to the Jews, who minted coins, collected taxes, loaned capital, and backed proven ventures like the marauding voyages of the corsairs.[22]

Raised on the stories of Sinan the pirate, the Palache brothers were also educated assiduously in Torah. Brought up on this strange mix of Judaism and piracy, it is not surprising they soon took to the seas to battle the Spanish. **The brothers quickly gained a *"reputation as merchant pirates... after a successful cruise, the brothers would brazenly enter Spanish ports pretending to be innocent traders and boldly seek out buyers for their repackaged booty*."**[23] This audacious behavior brought them to the attention of the Sultan of Morocco who engaged them as trade ambassadors. Apparently, getting over on the Spanish was exactly the kind of trade he wanted. To go into Iberia, they needed an entry permit obtained from Melilla, the Spanish outpost in Morocco. There they convinced the Duke they had valuable information to trade, not merely goods. Their diplomatic trip to Madrid was a bust as word of their derring-do preceded them. In 1603, Samuel moved to the Netherlands where, by 1608, as an international diplomat, he ended up advising Prince Maurice.

> In 1579, when the rest of Europe was still a dangerous place for Jews, Prince Maurice's father lit a lamp of political and religious liberty when he unilaterally declared his nation's independence from Spain. Assembling the six other leaders of the northern provinces, they agreed in the Union of Utrecht to support his war effort and affirm. **'*freedom of conscience*' as a founding principle of the United Netherlands**.[24]

---

[22]Kritzler, 2008:p.77, *Jewish Pirates of the Caribbean*. [23]*Ibid*, p.78. [24]*Ibid*,p.81.

Half the merchant ships in Europe had been built in The Netherlands. They were a major sea power, well able to fend off the Spanish. In 1580, Spain annexed Portugal. Soon thousands of Conversos were burning in the Portuguese Inquisition. A new wave of Converso emigration flowed out of Portugal. Palache petitioned the city fathers of Amsterdam to allow the refugees to settle there, promising they would "*develop the city into a flourishing commercial center by means of their wealth*" and worldwide trade network. The Dutch agreed to admit the Conversos, provided "*they are sincere Christians!*"

> So it was that the first conversos who followed Samuel to Holland found that it was one thing for a nation to declare religious toleration and another for that nation to practice it… They had to Judaize in secret…
>
> [However] When the émigrés left the peninsula, they took with them investment capital from conversos who stayed behind. Each community served as the other's agent. Thus the riches of the New World, via Lisbon and Seville, followed them to Amsterdam.[25]

"*Holland was already a flourishing mercantile state… Most trade, however, was in bulky products of relatively low value - grain, timber, iron and salt. This changed with the influx to Amsterdam of Jewish merchants, who specialized in the far more lucrative commodities of sugar, spices… and tobacco.*"[26] Messianic merchants had connections with other Conversos all over the New World and beyond. **They turned Amsterdam into "*Europe's richest trade mart, a supermarket to the world!*"**[27]

Samuel had proposed to Prince Maurice that Holland ally themselves with Morocco who, like them, despised the Spanish enough to overlook their religious differences. The compact was made in 1611, with Samuel negotiating the deal. In fact, Samuel was authorized by Sultan Sidan to sign the treaty in his name. Palache was granted a monopoly of trade between Morocco and the Netherlands. He exchanged precious gems from north Africa for Dutch arms. In addition, **the Dutch supplied ships for a Moroccan pirate navy to attack the Spanish, led by Samuel Palache, its new Converso admiral!** As another perk, Holland permitted the first synagogue to open in Amsterdam in 1612, '*Rabbi*' Samuel Palache was elected its first president.

[25]Kritzler, 2008:p.85, *Jewish Pirates of the Caribbean.* [26]*Ibid*, p.99. [27]*Ibid*,p.100.

Samuel continued to fight the Spanish until well into his 60s - even convincing Spain to pay him 200 escudos a month to provide inside information on the secret dealings of Holland and Morocco with the English. I am frankly stunned that the lifelong enemy of the Spanish - could be so persuasive as to pull off such a scam! Samuel Palache died in 1615 and was buried in Amsterdam with unprecedented honors. *"Six mounted horses dressing in black pulled the hearse. Prince Maurice and the city magistrates marched behind the bier, honoring the man and the community he led... 1,200 men, women and children of the nascent Jewish community also turned out... among the marchers were* **Samuel's brother Joseph**, *who would succeed him as the Sultan's agent, and* **Joseph's five sons, who continued their uncle's work ... Before the century was out, they would succeed in winning their peoples' rights in a hostile world!"**[28] That epic battle for freedom and human rights was fought and won in the New World.

Holy Terror Descends on the Colonies

The Inquisition did not have mercy. Even Conversos who repented were required to donate one fifth of their property to the Roman Church. Those who did not repent lost everything. Their families were reduced to beggary. *"The long-established secret Jewish communities in Peru and Mexico came to a flaming end... the dungeon, the rack, and the stake - marked a decade-long [1638-1650] succession of autos-da-fé that decimated the [Messianic] community in both countries."*[29] [brackets mine] Now the same scene was occurring in both the New World and the Old. **No one escaped the clutches of the Holy Terror!**

> January 16, 1605, freezing winds blowing off the Atlantic did not deter the citizens of Lisbon crowding the roadside to jeer the prisoners on their way to the plaza to be tried at the auto-da-fé. The victims, barefoot and naked to the waist, were whipped along the icy cobblestone streets by white-hooded guards of the Holy Brotherhood. On horseback, heading the procession, were the *familiars* (officials) of the Holy Office, wearing black tunics silhouetted with a white cross. Behind them, the 155 half-naked penitents stumbled along, six abreast, their backs lashed raw by the guards' studded whips. The Judaizers carried unlit candles to signify that the light of the True Faith had not yet illuminated their souls… Prisoners not admitting their guilt were tortured until they did, and those who remained unrepentant were liable to be burned.[30]

[28]Edward Kritzler, 2008:p.93-94, *Jewish Pirates...* [29]*Ibid.*,p.8. [30]*Ibid.*,p.93.

But things had changed - a full century of Messianic wealth and influence in the New World was coming into play. *"**The week before** [**the Lisbon auto-da-fé in 1605**], **King John had agreed to a bribe of two million ducats to forgive their offenses**. On the day of the auto-da-fé, a 'General Pardon for Crimes of Judaism' was to take effect. Portugal's other two tribunals in Oporto and Coimbra freed their 255 prisoners at first light, but Lisbon's Inquisitor, incensed at the pardon, held off until his Judaizers had experienced the parade of shame and been sentenced before setting them free. He then waited another month to inform and release those who had not confessed* [and were sentenced to death by burning alive]."[31] [brackets mine]

Meanwhile, on the other side of the world. Messianics of the colonies were recognizing that - to Emperor Charles - *"They were his essential heretics, efficient pawns in his global chess game, to be moved about and sacrificed at will."*[32] **Messianics were content with the status quo in the Americas, but - once Spain brought the Inquisition to the colonies - it altered Messianic goals, which coalesced into** *"nothing less than to bring down the Spanish Empire!"*

"For most of the first century after the discovery - the fanaticism that characterized the Holy Office did not carry over to the New World."[33] The Hebrews were needed to do the hard work of empire-building. Eventually, as the investment and industry of the Messianics took root and expanded - producing massive wealth for Converso traders - the Inquisition moved in to take it from them. The Spanish Empire had *"knowingly licensed New Christians... no one questioned their faith... [but] once they had established the lucrative commercial routes that directed all trade through Seville and Lisbon, they were expendable!"*[34]

"New Christians comprised about 65-75% of the total Portuguese mercantile community while hardly totaling more than 10% of the population."[35] Spain was not any different. In the New World, that proportion was repeated, if not increased. But now, Old Christians wanted to gain control of the lucrative trade. **The means to that end was the Inquisition!**

---

[31]Edward Kritzler, 2008:p.94, citing H.P. Salomon, 1982:pp.43-46, *Portrait of a New Christian*, Centro Cultural Portugués. Paris.   [32]*Ibid.*, Kritzler, 2008:p56.
[33] *Ibid.*, Edward Kritzler. p.57.   [34] *Ibid*, p.73.   [35] Daniel Swetschinski, "...*The Adventure of Caribbean Jewish Settlement*," Am. Jewish Historical Society (Dec 1982), volume 2, pp.216-217, In Kritzler p.285n.

The Converso Hernando Alonsa had marched with Cortés in his capture of Mexico. Alonso received a tract of land north of Mexico City and provided beef and pork for the colony, becoming the richest farmer in the Americas. Six years after his service to the Crown, he was denounced to the Inquisition and burnt alive on October 27, 1528, the first person to be executed in the New World. However, it was still rare. The Crown still needed its Conversos. But *"in the last decade of the sixteenth century... the Holy Terror descended on the New World!"*[36]

The Cohen Henriques Brothers

Two Converso victims of the 1605 Lisbon auto-da-fé, who were pardoned and released, were Joseph Diaz Soeiro, who was tortured three times during the Inquisition, and Antonio Vaez Henriques. They soon made their way to Amsterdam and changed their names, now Joseph ben Israel and Antonio Cohen Henriques. Joseph's son Menasseh, and Antonio's sons Moses and Abraham attended Yeshivah together. Like their fathers, they spoke Spanish, Portuguese, Hebrew and Dutch. Menasseh ben Israel became a prominent scholar, prosperous enough to be painted by Rembrandt. Moses and Abraham preferred the swashbuckling stories of Rabbi Palache.

"Hispanic nobility had considered the mercantile profession beneath them... **For centuries, Iberia's Jews had been the peninsula's merchant class...** *Palache had opened up North African trade as a gateway to the Ottoman Empire, and early émigrés had capital and access to trading partners in the New World."*[37]

These teenaged Dutch-born Messianics were the first to breathe free air. **They** *"invaded the New World, and in an* **unremitting struggle lasting decades, took on and defeated those who would deny Jewish rights!"**[38] Moses *"embarked on a spectacular piracy career that would span half a century. Abraham followed him to the New World where he became a powerful international merchant."*[39] **Free-born Conversos turned to the opponents of Spain - England and Holland - in setting up a privateer fleet to challenge the Spanish Empire.**

[36] Edward Kritzler, 2008:p.73, *Jewish Pirates of the Caribbean*, Doubleday.
[37] *Ibid.*, Kritzler, p.98.   [38] *Ibid*,p.102.   [39] *Ibid*,p.111.

Jamaica Becomes a Haven for Conversos

The colony of Jamaica had been a persistent thorn in the side of Charles. It was constantly losing money. Half the colony had died off and the survivors wanted out. He sent more Jewish colonists but to no avail. *"Jamaica was a losing proposition... The answer he settled on was to deed Jamaica to the Columbus' kin. Since the summer of 1536, Charles had been negotiating with Diego Colon's widow, Maria de Toledo, to settle a lawsuit she brought to recover Columbus' rights of discovery."*[40] However, she rejected Charles' offer because it did not give her power over the church in Jamaica. Charles eventually gave in. *"In February 1537, Charles formally ceded Jamaica to the Columbus family...* **For the next century, the family kept Jamaica - alone in the Spanish Empire - out of bounds to the Inquisition!***"*[41] As a result, Conversos flocked to the haven of Jamaica. Before long, half of the population of Jamaica were Hebrew, including two Messianic governors. The tiny island that Charles did not want was eventually to bring down his empire.

> This will be a loss to the Crown because Jamaica... provides all the neighboring countries as well as the Main, and New Spain, and is the centre of them all. If times should change... whoever is Lord of Jamaica will be Lord of those places on account of its situation...
> **His Majesty should on no account part with it!**[42]

But first, there was darkness before the dawn. The Inquisition did finally arrive in Jamaica. In 1622, the Church had *"transferred local authority over the* [Jamaican] *Church to the archdiocese of Santo Domingo."*[43] Now the Old Christian landowners *"patiently awaited the opportunity to charge that the island was riddled with heresy."*[43] It had been *"reported to the king that Jamaica was a rogue island, existing solely on 'illicit trade.'"*[44] **Messianics'** ***"horizons were rapidly narrowing: in Spain and Portugal, Inquisition burnings were on the increase and the great autos-da-fé in Mexico and Peru had left the remnant of Jews in Spanish lands looking to move on!"***[45]

Problem was - there was nowhere to move on to!

---

[40] Edward Kritzler, 2008:pp.65-6, *Jewish Pirates of the Caribbean*, Doubleday.
[41] *Ibid.*, pp.66-7. [42]Frank Cundall & Joseph Pietersz, 1919:p.13, citing Pedro Manzuelo, Royal Treasurer of Jamaica in *Jamaica Under the Spaniards*, Archives of Seville, Jamaica. [43]Kritzler, *op. cit,*, p.159 [44]*Ibid*, p160. [45]*Ibid*, p196.

Saint Thomas Christians

Eusebius spoke of the regions where the Apostles evangelized. *"'The inhabited world' was divided into zones of influence among the Apostles -* ***Thomas in the region of the Parthians,*** *[**Persia**], John in Asia, Peter in Pontus... Andrew in Scythia."*[46] The literature of the region presents much mention of Thomas' establishment of churches throughout Persia and into India. Thomas landed in India at Kerala Province on the southwest coast of the subcontinent. Thomas was martyred in 72 AD.

> **He arrived at Cranganor, a town situated a little to the north of Cochin**, and where the most powerful among the princes who ruled in Malabar then resided. Having here wrought many miracles, and established a church, he journeyed southward...
>
> [He] extended the knowledge of the faith so widely as to excite the envy and hatred of the Brahmins. Two of them watching an opportunity, stirred up the people against him; they fell on him and stoned him. One of the Brahmins remarking some signs of life in the holy apostle, pierced him with a lance, and thus completed his martyrdom.[47]

The Saint Thomas Christians had lived in peace for a millennium and a half before the Portuguese, led by Vasco de Gama, arrived in 1498. *"It was a dark night for the St. Thomas Christians when the Jesuits, supported by the guns of Portugal, arrived in India. It was the lot of Portugal to erect an astonishing empire in the East... Seven areas* [were] *seized by the Portuguese men-of-war and completely claimed by the crown as imperial domain."*[48] The west coast of India centered on Goa, where Cochin and the St. Thomas Christians were located. The Jesuits came with the conquerors in order to convert the St. Thomas Christians to Catholicism. *"One expedition followed another, until the Portuguese supremacy was established.* **As the result of several wars, Goa, at the wide mount of the Mandavi River, was seized, strongly fortified, and made the capitol of the new empire**.*"*[49] Warehouses were soon bursting with the merchandise to be exchanged between East and West. Palacial mansions and estates of the Portuguese lined the river.

---

[46]Eusebius, 4th century AD, *History of the Church: Volume III*. [47]John Mason Neale, 1850:p.145, *A History of th Holy Eastern Church*, vol 1, London.
[48]Ben Wilkinson, 1944:p.305, *Truth Triumphant*, Hartland, Va. [49]*Ibid.*, p.307.

> **The Jesuits**… It was the unhappy lot of India to experience the crushing weight of these haughty monks. These men were skilled in sublimated treachery and trained for years in the art of rapid debate in which they could trap an opponent by the cunning use of ambiguous terms, consequently, the simple, trusting St. Thomas Christians were no match for them...
> **Jesuits were past masters of the ways of deception.**[50]

The Inquisition was established at Goa in the year 1560. *"The Portuguese Inquisition in Goa, became the most severe and cruel of all the Portuguese territories. The Inquisitors in Goa became the most fanatic and violent of the Portuguese Catholic Church."*[51] Those who would not renounce their faith and bow to the doctrine and authority of the Roman Church were burned.

> Those condemned to the flames would be chained to a high stake many feet above the pile of faggots. Then two Jesuits would wail out an exhortation to repent. **When finally the nod of the Inquisitor was given, blazing torches on long poles were dashed into the faces of the agonizing martyrs -** and this continued until their faces were burned to cinder. The flames were then applied below, and as the roaring fire mounted higher and higher, it consumed the sufferers who died for their faith.[52]

Many were condemned to death as *Judaizers* because they observed the Sabbath on Saturday, the seventh day. A papal prelate, Alexis de Menezes, was appointed to be the archbishop of Goa. He arrived in 1599 to enormous pomp and circumstance. The leader of the St. Thomas Christians, Mar Abraham, had just died and while they awaited a new leader from the seat of the Assyrian Church in Babylon, archdeacon George was in charge. Menezes immediately focused all the heat he could bring to bear on the unprepared leader to subscribe to the doctrines of Rome. *"The patriarch at Babylon* [ordained and sent] *a new head to the church in India, Ahatalla. He was seized when he landed at Mailapore near Madras, shipped to Goa, and burned at the stake!"*[53] Menezes then summoned the confused and terrified archdeacon George before him.

---

[50]Benjamin Wilkinson, 1944:p.307, *Truth Triumphant*, Hartland Pub., Va.
[51]Jai Sharma, 2015, *Portuguese Inquisition - A Brief History*, Indiafacts.org.in.
[52]Wilkinson, *op.cit., in the work cited,* 1944:p.310. [53]*Ibid., in same place*, p.321.

The Synod of Diamper 1599

Archbishop Menezes had arrived less than two weeks before the Synod was held in Diamper, about 14 miles east of Cochin. Accompanied by some terrified and subservient officials from the Assyrian Church, Menezes, *"the agent of Rome who succeeded in crushing the Assyrian Church...* **was** *a man of invincible tenacity and consummate craft"*[54] who would stop at nothing to force the St. Thomas Christians to bow to Rome. The St. Thomas Christians, like the Reformers, held to *The Received Text;* the Bible of the Greek Church, the Church of the East, and the churches of the West through the centuries. It was now ripped from their hands!

The doctrines to be agreed to were basically those of the Council of Trent (1563 AD).

1) *The Vulgate* **was the true Bible not** *The Received Text*
2) **Roman Church Tradition was of equal authority with the Sacred Scriptures.**
3) **The priests only, and not the laity, were capable of rightly interpreting the Scriptures.**[55]

"The war galleys of the Portuguese lay in the harbor... To the scandal of Christianity, [Menezes] *forced the evangelical shepherd to surrender the rights of the people.* **Quailing before the Jesuit archbishop, Archdeacon George signed... away their 1500 year old heritage!**"[56] *"In addition to eliminating the Syrian Bible, it was demanded that all Syrian books be delivered up, altered, or destroyed, that every trace relating to the patriarch of Babylon or to the doctrines of the St. Thomas Christians was to be condemned; and that all St. Thomas Christians were to be subject to the Inquisition at Goa."*[57] **The writings of the St. Thomas Christians were destroyed** *"to obliterate all the cultural ties which bound her to the past. Manuals of church activities were torn to pieces, records of districts and documents relating the manifold contacts of this wonderful people were burned.* **What a wealth of evangelical literature was ruined in a moment!**"[58]

Who can tell how much of the literature destroyed went back even to apostolic days, and would have thrown great light upon the work of the apostle Thomas and upon the early years of the Church of the East![58]

---

[54]Benjamin Wilkinson, 1944:p.312, *Truth Triumphant*, Hartland Publishing.,Va.
[55] *Ibid.*, p.308. [56] *Ibid.*, p.314. [57] *Ibid.*, p.316. [58] *Ibid.*, p.319.

The Spanish Armada

Although the Portuguese Inquisition at Goa lasted for centuries, its power waxed and waned along with the power of the Portuguese in the region. That power was diminishing. In 1580 Spain had annexed Portugal into an *Iberian* union. Phillip II, now king, in an excess of hubris decided to invade England and reinstate Catholicism, in short, seeking to make Spain the supreme superpower of Europe. The execution of the Catholic Mary Queen of Scots in 1587 by Elizabeth I of England was a decisive factor. Mary was Spain's ally. Perhaps the last straw was a bold attack by Sir Francis Drake who caught 20 Spanish warships in Cadiz harbor later that year and destroyed them.

In 1588, Phillip launched '*la felicissima armada*' of 150 ships, the largest ever seen in Europe. Phillip considered his glorious Armada to be invincible. Jewish and Messianic spies in Portugal warned England of the Armada well in advance, including the date it left port for the attack. The Armada, led by the Duke of Medina Sidonia, sailed up the English Channel seeking deep harbor with the loyalist army of their ally the Duke of Parma in the Spanish Netherlands. Admiral Charles Howard, with Sir Francis Drake as second in command, led the English fleet - about half the size of the Spanish Armada. After skirmishing all the way up the Channel, the Spanish anchored off Calais.

The next morning the English engaged the Armada at the battle of Gravelines. Although they were outnumbered they did have advantages. The English ships were longer, faster and more maneuverable. Their gunships were lower - giving them more stability and the ability to carry more guns. Their guns were longer range and more accurate than those of the Spanish. The English had sent in fireships drifting on the prevailing tide among the anchored fleet. They destroyed only a couple of warships but left the Spanish galleons scattered and disorganized. The battle was intense - but the English firepower proved superior.

Within the Armada itself, however, all hope was gone. Huddled together by the wind and the deadly English fire, their sails torn, their masts shot away, the crowded galleons had become mere slaughterhouses...

the seamen were cowed by the terrible butchery.[59]

---

[59] John Green, 1890, *A Short History of the English People*, Macmillan, London.

The Spanish Armada 1588

The English lost a few hundred seamen - the Spanish and Portuguese lost 15,000 along with 51 warships! The Spanish Armada was ordered to sail north. The Duke of Parma's men could not be taken aboard without harbor. The harbors of the Netherlands were held by the rebels of the independent Dutch Republic. The Armada was caught in the open sea during a fierce four-day storm - many more warships were lost. Only 65 ships returned to Lisbon harbor. The gunship diplomacy of the Spanish, and Portuguese, was weakened for years to come.

The Uprising of the St. Thomas Christians

"The victory of the English over Spain [and Portugal] paved the way for the Jesuit defeat on the Malabar coast."[60] Although it took many decades, the St. Thomas Christians finally reacted to the horror of the burning alive of the new head of the church, Ahatalla, the travesty of the staged Synod of Diamper, and the martyring of their brethren.

"A cry of horror ran through the Malabar churches. At the summons of protest they came from town and village. Before a huge cross at a place near Cochin they assembled by the thousands to take their stand against the Papacy... They took their oath renouncing the Papacy... nearly 400,000 Christians lost to their church... This happened in 1653, and the incident is known as Coonan Cross."[61] Today, the church in India remains divided between the Assyrian Church and the Roman Catholic.

---

[60]Ben Wilkinson, 1944:p.320, *Truth Triumphant*, Hartland Pub. [61]*Ibid.*,p.321.

New Holland in Brazil

The Dutch had allied with the English during the assault of the Spanish Armada, whose goal was not only to invade England but also to end the newly gained Dutch independence (in 1579). *"Dutch privateers, know as Sea Beggars, defeated Spanish attempts to crush their rebellion and funded the war with plunder."*[62] The Dutch decided to throw their hat in the ring in pursuit of New World riches. In 1623 the Dutch West Indies Company was formed (modeled after the Dutch East Indies Co.). Sugar exports were booming as were profits, and unlike gold and silver, sugar was renewable. **Prince Maurice of Holland had "decided to fight Spain by targeting her colonies...** *its initial mission was to conquer the sugar colony* [of Brazil] *and then seize the silver mountain of Potosi, which for half a century had financed Spain's armies and funded her empire."*[63]

In May of 1624, the Dutch invaded Bahia, Brazil, with 3,300 men, a number of whom were Jews and Messianics. **"Prince Maurice agreed to a policy of religious freedom in the conquered territory**, *and that the Jewish soldiers could form their own company."*[64] Vice Admiral Piet Heyn captured the two main forts adjacent to the port and the defenders fled. It was the first settlement in the New World openly granting religious freedom to Jews and Conversos. It was a short-lived victory. *"On March 29, 1625, a combined armada of fifty-two Spanish and Portuguese warships landed 12,566 men on the coast of Bahia... On May 1, 1525 the Dutch surrendered."*[65] The Spanish demanded they hand over the Hebrews participating in the invasion. The Dutch refused, insisting they be treated as Hollanders.

"The Dutch occupied Bahia for a year. The ambitious plan had failed. Disheartened, the army limped home to a near bankrupt country, made poor by the cost of the invasion and occupation."[66] Yet all was not lost. Admiral Heyn had allied himself with a trusted advisor in Moses Cohen Henriques, the Dutch-born Hebrew raised on the stories of Samuel Palache, his mentor. Moses had followed his brother Abraham to the New World and become a successful privateer. Moses convinced the Dutch West Indies Co., *"**it made more sense to attack at sea the Spanish fleet that carried the ore to Seville rather than to mount a land invasion to capture the silver mountain** [of Potosi]."*[67]

[62]Edward Kritzler, 2008:p.80, *Jewish Pirates of the Caribbean.* [63]*Ibid.*,p.112. [64]*Ibid.*,p.119. [65]*Ibid.*,p.120-21. [66]*Ibid.*,p.122. [67]*Ibid.*,p.125.

"*Moses... had proven himself in the Bahia invasion, and so was invited by Heyn to sail with him... The treasure fleet's departure... was a closely guarded secret - one that young Moses Cohen Henriques somehow became privy to... In any event, Moses was able to alert the Company of the fleet's intended sailing date. This allowed sufficient time to man and outfit twenty-five sailing vessels to sail to Cuba and await the fleet's arrival.*"[68]

Spain's treasure fleet usually consisted of **two** heavily armed armadas of twenty to thirty ships. The ships would bring with them "*the treasures of the Orient; the silks, jade, rugs, ivory, porcelain, and spices that had been carried by the Manilla galleons to Acapulco, then by mule to Vera Cruz.*"[69] In 1628, the Dutch intercepted the first fleet of sixteen vessels, catching them by surprise and forcing the surrender of one galleon, causing nine cargo ships to be talked into surrendering. Two other cargo ships were caught at sea and surrendered. The last four galleons were trapped at Matanzas Bay in Cuba. After a few volleys of cannon they surrendered as well. The treasure was taken, along with the four galleons, while the other ships were burned. The second heavily-armed fleet arrived in Cuba too late to avert the disaster!

The booty from the Spanish treasure fleet was 177,000 pounds of silver equivalent to 48 million dollars in today's currency, plus gold and copious valuable trade goods! "*In the course of two centuries, fifty attempts were made to capture the treasure galleons. Only theirs succeeded!*"[69] **One must credit the worldwide intelligence network of Jews and Messianics, brilliantly utilized by Moses Cohen Henriques, for the Dutch fleet's spectacular success!**

In 1630, the Dutch tried again - landing 7,000 soldiers at Recife in Brazil's Pernambuco Province. Moses Henriques was on the ground in Recife plotting with the Conversos to support the invasion. He then went back to Amsterdam to join the invasion fleet. He knew Pernambuco very well and the Dutch listened to his advice. "*After the conquest, Moses settled in Recife and pursued a successful career as a licensed pirate. With his share of the booty, estimated at one ton of silver, he bought ships, munitions, and an empty island off Recife to serve as his base... For the period 1623-1636... Dutch privateers captured 547 Iberian ships, an average of nearly one a week.*"[70] Moses was later to advise "*Jamaica's famed buccaneer Henry Morgan.*"[71]

[68] Edward Kritzler, 2008:p.126. [69] *Ibid.*, p.127. [70] *Ibid.*, p.130. [71] *Ibid.*, p.128.

Puritans in England and America

One result of the Reformation in England was the desire for self-rule rather than investing all power in the king. This put King Charles I of England in opposition to the Parliament. In 1642 a series of civil wars broke out - eventually won in 1651 at the Battle of Worcester by General Oliver Cromwell, the leader of the Parliamentary army. In 1653, Oliver Cromwell was designated Lord Protector of England. He was later offered the crown by Parliament but he refused it.

Cromwell was a Puritan. The Puritans were a powerful movement in England that felt the Reformation had not gone far enough. *"They believed the Church of England was too similar to the Roman Catholic Church and should eliminate ceremonies and practices not rooted in the Bible. Puritans felt they had a direct covenant with God to enact these reforms."*[72] This did not go over well with the Church nor the Crown. They were, however, strong supporters of Parliament and **Puritan support eventually led to the rise of Cromwell and the triumph of Parliamentary self-rule over the monarchy in England!** Initially, however, the Puritans were mightily oppressed - causing certain groups to immigrate to New England in the early 1600s. These groups were separatist Puritans and were called Pilgrims. They considered themselves separate from the Church of England. The first group of Pilgrims landed at Plymouth Rock in 1608. A second group of Pilgrims landed at Massachusetts Bay Colony in 1618.

These separatist Pilgrims held to the belief in the seventh-day (Saturday) Sabbath. Like other Puritans they also rejected the Catholic holidays as pagan and they were not observed.

> The early Puritans didn't like Easter any more than they liked Christmas. **They banned Christmas** in 1659, fining anyone five shillings for celebrating the holiday.
> **They ignored Easter**, Whitsunday and other holidays.
> **May Day celebrations, which included the hated Maypole, were punished severely.**[73]

---

[72] The Puritans, 2021, History.com editors.
[73] Newenglandhistoricalsociety.com/puritan-easter-devils-holiday.

"Puritanism gave Americans a sense of history as a progressive drama under the direction of God, in which they played a role akin to, if not prophetically aligned with, that of the Old Testament Jews as a new chosen people."[74]

Puritan beliefs came to define Americans as self-reliant, staunchly moral, and supporters of local covenant self-rule. **The Puritans endowed America with constitutional self-rule under God, an idea that transformed the world!** The basic beliefs of the early Puritans *"recur in the related religious communities of Quakers, Baptists, Presbyterians, Methodists and a whole range of evangelical Protestants."*[74] **Were the Puritans Neo-Messianic? In many ways they most definitely were!**

The Messianic doctrines had been weakened over the centuries. For example, the Puritans used the Geneva Bible which predominated in America throughout the 16th and 17th centuries. *"The Geneva Bible (1560) translates the Tetragrammaton as **Jehovah** in Exodus 6:3, Psalm 83:18, and two other times."*[75] The rest of the time, *The Geneva Bible* adopts the convention *LORD* for Yehovah, thus limiting use of the sacred name which occurs thousands of times. While all Puritans condemned the pagan holidays, only the separatist Pilgrims observed the Saturday Sabbath. They valued education at a time most Catholic and Church of England ministers were still illiterate. Puritans were required to study the Old Testament as well as the New. Nonetheless, they did not return to the feast days of Yehovah in Scripture. The Messianic influence was strong - predominate in some times and places - but not others. They were fervent believers but - like the Zealots of yore - that did not always work out well. *"**Their efforts to transform the nation contributed both to civil war in England and to the founding of colonies in America as working models of the Puritan way of life.**"*[77] In England, at one point, Puritans dominated the government under Cromwell.

---

[74] The Puritans, 2021, History.com editors. [75] en.wikipedia.org/wiki/Jehovah.
[77] www.britannica.com/topic/Puritanism.

It was Yeshua who taught us the difference between the letter of the law and the spirit of the law. Puritans were definitely the inheritors of the Messianic banner when it came to welcoming *"the personality of the Holy Spirit into a spiritual influence."*[78]

> In Britain, the publication of the Authorized Version of the Bible [*The Received Text*] became the inspiration of Puritanism. and biblical speech and nomenclature so permeated the national life that it seemed as if the true People of the Book were the inhabitants of the islands [of Britain].[78] [brackets mine]

"The tide which had carried Christianity steadily away from the Jewish apostolic faith was now at its turn, and thousands not of the Hebrew race began to turn their eyes Zionwards, literally and spiritually!"[78] Still, there was plenty of resistance.

Britain had originally been Sabbath-keeping in its Celtic Church practice. Among many of the Reformation Churches there were smaller groups who held to the seventh-day Sabbath. There were Seventh-day Sabbatarians among the Puritans in both England and Holland, Seventh-day Baptists, Anabaptists and other small churches who kept the Sabbath. During the Reformation there was much discussion and conflict over the Sabbath day. In general, mainstream Protestants held to the Catholic Sunday, and there was much oppression against those who would not comply.

> The Lutheran princes and prelates practiced upon the [Sabbatarian] Anabaptists all the cruelties to which they themselves had been subjected by the Roman hierarchs. The names of Luther, Calvin, and Zwingli have been marked in this manner with an indelible stain. The conscientious Sabbatarians neither expected nor found sympathy in the bosoms of these men.[79]

---

[78] Hugh Schonfield, 1936, 2009:p.145, *The History of Jewish Christianity*, Duckworth Publishing, London, U.K. [79]Tamar Davis, 1851, *The General History of the Sabbatarian Churches*, Lindsay & Blakiston, Philadelphia.

Cromwell's *'Grand Western Design'*

Cromwell wanted into the game of riches in the New World. He formulated *"what he called his Grand Western Design, an ambitious plan to carve out a Protestant empire in the Spanish New World!"*[80a] Part of this grand plan was the return of Jews (& Messianics) to England. Cromwell believed this to be a harbinger of the return of the Messiah. It is also true **Cromwell, like Charles of Spain and virtually every other monarch, had come to recognize the Messianics -** *"this exiled entrepreneurial class, as unparalleled creators of wealth - the merchants, traders, accountants, insurers, and commodity buyers, conversos all, who with their foreign agents dominated empire commerce!"*[80b]

The second element of the *grand design* was to seize a base in the Caribbean. In August of 1654, Cromwell summoned the Spanish ambassador and threw down the gauntlet - bluntly stating that *"friendship with Spain could continue only if Englishmen were granted freedom of trade and religion in the New World."*[80c] *"Impossible!"* replied the Spaniard. Cromwell had already begun strategic planning for seizing a major piece of the New World, its trade, and its riches. Cromwell was advised by the Messianic *"leader of London's covert Jews, Antonio Carvajal, whose knowledge of Caribbean affairs was unmatched* [and who] *counseled Cromwell to follow up on Captain Jackson's raid."*[80d] **In 1643, "Captain William Jackson**, *a privateer in the tradition of Sir Francis Drake,* **sacked Jamaica** *and went home convinced England could count on the Jews there to assist an invasion."*[80e]

"Carvajal owned ships that plied the seven seas. He had agents in most major ports, and the political intelligence he gathered made him one of Cromwell's most trusted advisors."[81] He had arrived in London with exuberant flair, appearing at the gates of London riding a beautiful white Arabian stallion, with a string of mules carrying gold bullion! He had just departed the Canary Islands - one step ahead of the Inquisition! Carvajal soon became the leader of London's covert Converso community. *"Carvajal imported silver bars from converso merchants in Seville... Peru and New Spain. From the time the ore left the mines and was melted into bars, his own were embossed with a particular stamp...* **Carvajal hoped to persuade England's new ruler to allow Jews legally back into England**.*"*[82]

[80a] Edward Kritzler, 2008:p.182, *Jewish Pirates...* [80b] *Ibid.*, p.169. [80c] *Ibid.*, p.183. [80d] *Ibid.*,p.184. [80e] *Ibid.*, p.173-74. [81] Kritzler, p.184. [82] Kritzler, p.183.

The invasion fleet departed in 1654, commanded by Admiral William Penn, whose son would be the future founder of Pennsylvania. After a disastrous and humiliating attempt to invade Hispaniola **they finally arrived in Jamaica, which - as advised - surrendered gladly!** After an initial salvo of the port, the defenders fled. *"The next morning, two Jamaican officers rode up under a flag of truce... The officers, Francisco Carvajal and Duarte Acosta, were secret Jews!* [These] *officers signed the peace treaty, and reportedly drafted it as well."*[83] Half of the Jamaican army were Conversos so there was no resistance.

> Cromwell honored the one man who had correctly advised him on the invasion plan. Summoning Antonio Carvajal and his two sons to his office. Cromwell awarded them English citizenship, making them the nation's first legal Jews in 365 years… **Cromwell's actions sent a message to Jews... that they might henceforth look to him as their defender.**[84]

"Cromwell knew that once he withdrew his army and navy, the colony would require a defensive force that could protect the colony, wage war on the Spanish, and at the same time feed itself. [He] *knew precisely where to find such a force."*[85] They called themselves the Brethren of the Coast. Large herds of cattle had escaped to roam free in Hispaniola and they multiplied - growing fat on the grass of the lush tropical island. A group of outlaws made their living by poaching the wild cattle and cooking them on a greenwood grill known as a '*boucan.*' Some 600 boucaniers set up a base on nearby Tortuga in the fortified port of Cayano. The Spanish authorities, attempting to rid themselves of these '*boucaniers,*' slaughtered the wild cattle. The boucaniers now needed a new means of survival. When one of their own, *"Pierre le Grand and a small crew went out in a canoe and returned with a treasure galleon, **the sea was theirs!**" "**The day of the boucanier was over - the day of the buccaneer had begun!**"*[86]

"So began the golden age of piracy!"[87]

"In 1657 [Cromwell] *instructed Jamaica's commander... to extend a formal invitation to the buccaneers of Tortuga to call Jamaica home."*[88] There they partnered with the Conversos who financed them, supplied intelligence, and often led them at sea.

---

[83] Kritzler, 2008:p.190, *Jewish Pirates*, Doubleday, NY. [84] *Ibid.*, p.193-94.
[85] *Ibid.*, p.202. [86] *Ibid.*, p.205. [87] *Ibid.*, p.206. [88] *Ibid.*, p.222.

Although there were already pirates galore waiting for the occasional unguarded Spanish trading vessel - content with the crumbs that fell from the Spanish empire - **now there was all-out war!** If the history of war tells us anything - it is the difference between a rabble and a focused, skilled and well-led force with a magnificent objective - united against a hated foe! Pirates flocked to Jamaica as did Jews and Messianics.

> Iberian Jews, welcomed by Cromwell… now arrived in Jamaica from all over the New World and abroad. Here they could throw off their converso cloaks and live free and prosper. Together with brethren from Holland and England, the Jewish community included shipowners from Mexico and Brazil, traders from Peru and Columbia, and ship captains and pilots from Nevis and Barbados. **Joining with Jamaica's Portugals, their combined knowledge of New World trade (both legal and illegal) was unsurpassed.**[89]

There was plenty of swashbuckling to go around! In 1666, the Converso Captain Balthasar the Portuguese, despite being dramatically outgunned, captured a rich galleon off the coast of Cuba carrying 70,000 silver pieces of eight!* Unfortunately, Balthasar was intercepted and captured by three Spanish men-of-war who took him to the port of Campeche in Mexico. *"Knowing he was to be hanged the following day, Balthasar, unable to swim, fashioned a crude pair of water wings from two empty wine jars, killed his guard and slipped overboard."*[90] The search for him yielded nothing as he hid in a hollow tree in a Mangrove swamp for three days.

Balthasar then made a crude raft *"and floated downriver to a secluded harbor frequented by buccaneers. There he met up with a Jamaican pirate crew 'who were great comrades of his own.'"*[90] Balthasar convinced twenty men to join him in retaking his ship. In a small boat they entered the harbor undetected and convinced the remaining guards aboard the ship they were traders from the mainland - one might imagine with rum to sell. The guards realized their mistake too late and the pirates recaptured the ship. **Balthasar sailed out of the harbor scot-free - once again master of his prize ship full of silver - from the very spot he was condemned to hang only days before!**

[89]Edward Kritzler, 2008:p.224, *Jewish Pirates*, Doublday, NY.   [90] *Ibid.*, p.232.
* *Piece of eight* is a silver dollar coin worth eight Spanish reales.

The Golden Age of the Buccaneers

At first, each buccaneer crew was a force unto itself, electing (and disposing) captains at will to cruise the sea for merchant ships and stray galleons. This changed in 1659, when Jamaica's naval commander, Commodore Christopher Mings, called them all together. Only a strong leader could unite men so fiercely individualistic, and Mings, who rose through the ranks from cabin boy, was a tough old sea dog who fit the bill.

Rather than run down ships at sea, he proposed that they unite under his command and attack Spanish towns. On their first venture, **Mings and his men plundered three towns... and returned with a haul valued at 1.5 million pieces of eight!** [91]

"News of Ming's exploit brought other buccaneers, merchants, tavern owners, prostitutes, and assorted and sordid pleasure-seekers to the port... [which grew] *to the largest, most opulent town in the English Americas."*[92] ***"Mings triumph paved the way for the golden age of piracy under the command of one of his young captains, known to history - as the Buccaneer Admiral - Sir Henry Morgan."***[92]

In 1664, the English appointed Thomas Modyford as the new Jamaican governor with strict instructions to recall the buccaneers. However, the ship Modyford's eldest son was sailing on to Jamaica was taken by Spaniards and his son tortured before being murdered. Modyford and Morgan, although different in so many ways, were perfect partners to run the pirate capitol of Jamaica. Modyford wrote his superior in England, *"I cannot but presume to say we should in any measure be restrained while the Spaniards are at liberty to act as they please upon us!"*[93] Now with Governor Modyford running interference:

From 1666 to 1670, the buccaneers and their leader Henry Morgan invaded the fabled cities of the Spanish Main and held its citizens for ransom. Using the same Inquisition tortures (and at times the same apparatus), they forced the Spaniards to surrender their wealth.

"In five years of non-stop plundering, Morgan... backed by Port Royal's Jewish merchants, attacked and plundered 18 cities... 35 villages and unnumbered ships."[94]

---

[91]Kritzler, 2008:p.222, *Jewish Pirates....* [92]*Ibid.*, p.223. [93]H.R. Allen,1976:p.75, *Buccaneer Admiral Sir Henry Morgan*, Barker, London. [94]Kritzler, p.235.

Morgan's climactic exploit was the sacking of Panama City. Panama City was safely tucked into the Pacific side of the South American continent. *"Separated from the buccaneers by a twenty-five-mile-wide isthmus of almost impassable mountains, rivers, and jungle, its citizens believed they were secure."*[95] As Morgan described it - **"The famous ancient City of Panama is the greatest Mart for Silver & Gold in the World.** *For it receives the Goods that come from old Spain in the King's great Fleet, and delivers to the Fleet all the Silver and Gold that comes from the Mines of Peru and Potosi!"*[96]

In February of 1670, Captain Henry Morgan and his tough buccaneers - who had just cut their way through the dense jungles, scaled the rugged mountains, and forded the raging rivers - sacked and burned the untouchable treasure trove of the Pacific! **The haul of gold, silver and goods was immeasurable!**

The deprivations of the pirates visited upon the Spanish were awful! They slaughtered, raped, tortured and burned the cities and towns of the hated Spaniards! The war first waged upon the Messianics came full circle in its violence and destruction - but upon the Spanish this time! **The Spanish reaped what they had sown!** From Port Royal in Jamaica, the Messianic *"merchants and ship owners... used the buccaneers to wage a successful surrogate war on the lands of the Inquisition that effectively ended Spain's hegemony in the New World, and in the process they reaped the rewards both legal and financial."*[97]

"**Within 15 years, pirate raids on the Spanish Main, organized and financed by the [Messianic] merchants of Port Royal [Jamaica] broke the back of the Spanish Empire!**"

"**In Henry Morgan, the Jews had found their Joshua.**"[98]

In 1670, England and Spain signed the *"**Treaty for Composing Differences, Restraining the Depredations & Establishing Peace in America.**"* The war between Spain and England was over and Spain recognized England's territories in America. The buccaneers were disbanded. Charles II of England had continued the policies of Cromwell. Jews and Messianics were now citizens, permitted to live and worship their conscience in England and all her colonies. The Dutch had also granted the Conversos citizenship, as did the new nations of the Americas.

[95] Kritzler, 2008:p.239-40, *Jewish Pirates*. [96] Phillip Lindsay, 1951:p.151, *The Great Buccaneer*, William Funk, N.Y. [97] Kritzler, p.255. [98] *Ibid.*, p.10.

The Inquisition did reach the future territories of The United States. In the 1590s, victims of the Inquisition were burned in Santa Fe or taken to Mexico City. These included the colonial governor of New Mexico, Don Luis de Carvajal. The massive Inquisition records, in Spain, discovered Converso blood in his family which was enough to bring him down. He died in prison in 1591, members of his family were burned at the stake. "In *1601 forty-five more conversos were executed. Between 1574 to 1603 there were 115 people accused of Judaizing.*"[99]

The Inquisition also came briefly to New Orleans. Originally founded as a French colony on the delta of the Mississippi River in 1718, it was taken over by Spain in 1762. In 1801, it was ceded back to the French due to the conquests of Napoleon. He promptly sold the entire vast Louisiana Territory (which included the entire Mississippi basin up to the Canadian border) to the United States for 15 million dollars! **New Orleans had become a haven for pirates and a lawless, raucous place, known as "*The Wickedest City in the World!*"**

On December 6, 1788 a Capuchin monk, Antonio de Sedella "*had been instructed to establish a tribunal of the Holy Office in New Orleans and discharge his functions with the utmost zeal!*"[100] Sedella arrived in New Orleans on a secret mission to prepare the Inquisition. In Spring of 1789, Sedella wrote a letter to Governor Miró of New Orleans, informing him of his appointment as Inquisitor. "*He wrote further that he would soon require soldiers to assist him in apprehending and punishing heretics, as his preliminary preparations had been completed.*"[100]

"*Strange things* [later] *came to light. There were found secret rooms, iron instruments of torture, and other indications of a private court... old newspaper files tell of the discovery of an underground passage which led from the back of the Cathedral... in the direction of the Capuchin monastery.*"[100] "*Governor Miró received Sedella's communication late in the afternoon - that same night the priest was roused from slumber to find a squad of soldiers at his door. The soldiers placed the priest under arrest and took him aboard a ship which... the next day... sailed for Cadiz.*"[100] **There was no further attempt to impose the Inquisition upon the fiercely independent citizens of New Orleans!**

---

[99] Roger Martinez-Davila, Josef Diaz, et al., 2016. *Fractured Faiths*, Frescobooks, N.M. [100] Herbert Asbury, 1973:p.40, *The French Quarter: An Informed History of the New Orleans Underworld*, Alfred Knopf, Ga.

"In the American Revolution, a dozen prominent Jews sided with the rebels as privateers. Celebrated as founders of early Jewish congregations, these men owned and operated more than a few of the pirate ships that captured or destroyed over six hundred British ships and took cargos and prizes with an estimated value of $18 million in today's dollars."[101] Jews, and Messianics, formed a large part of the American Navy during the Revolution. For this reason, *letters of marque* are enshrined in the U.S. Constitution, article one, section eight, clause eleven.

Americans fought the British again in 1812 and came close to losing when the British invaded and burned Washington. During some of the darkest days of the conflict, the British invaded New Orleans with the intention of controlling navigation on the entire Mississippi basin - about 1/3 of the current continental U.S., which would have been disastrous to the U.S. In 1814, Colonel Andrew Jackson was sent to mount a defense. Having only a few federal troops, he quickly allied himself with the local forces including those of the Messianic pirate Jean Lafitte. Lafitte kept British troops from debarking at the port, instead they had to land at the mouth of the Mississippi and cross through the swamplands to get to the city. They arrived January 8, 1815. The defenders, a multicolored assortment of militia, frontiersmen, Black freemen, Indians and pirates had built ramparts at Chalmette, just south of New Orleans. No one has described the battle better than Johnny Horton did in his classic folk song:

Battle of New Orleans

In 1814 we took a little trip,
 Along with Colonel Jackson down the mighty Mississip.'
We took a little bacon and we took a little beans,
And we caught the bloody British in a town near New Orleans.

chorus: We fired our guns and the British kept a'coming,
 But there wasn't nigh as many as there was a while ago,
 We fired once more and they began a'running,
 On down the Mississippi to the Gulf of Mexico.

We looked down the river and we see'd the British come,
And there musta been a hundred of 'em beating on the drum,
They stepped so high and they made their bugles ring...
We stood behind our cotton bales and didn't say a thing.[*]

---

[101] Kritzler, 2008:p.253, *Jewish Pirates*, Doubleday, NY.
[*] Available on Youtube.com, Johnny Horton, *Battle of New Orleans*.

<u>chorus</u>: We fired our guns and the British kept a'coming,
But there wasn't nigh as many as there was a while ago,
We fired once more and they began a'running,
On down the Mississippi to the Gulf of Mexico.

Ole Hickory said we could take 'em by surprise,
If we didn't fire our muskets 'til we looked 'em in the eyes.
So we held our fire 'til we seen their faces swell,
Then we opened up our squirrel guns and really gave 'em... Well,

chorus...

They ran thru the briars and they ran thru the brambles,
And they ran thru places where a rabbit couldn't go,
And they ran so fast that the hounds couldn't catch 'em...
On down the Mississippi to the Gulf of Mexico.[*]

Despite the exaggerated rhetoric - the battle was a close call! Jackson gave the command, *"Don't fire until you see the whites of their eyes!"* The British General Pakenham had more than 10,000 troops, he lost 2036 of them. The Americans had 4732 defenders, they lost only 71 men. Never underestimate the shooting skills of a frontiersman who can't eat - if he can't shoot!

The British disputed the legality of the Louisiana Purchase. If they had captured New Orleans and controlled the Mississippi Basin they would hold the center third of the continent. They would not have given it back after the cessation of hostilities. The British General Sir Edward Pakenham was a brave leader and a fine tactician. He rode into battle along with his troops and had his horse shot out from under him. He mounted another and led on. Soon after - he was killed by the accurate and constant fire from the American lines.

Nonetheless, Pakenham had already set his excellent battle plan in motion. He had sent a detachment upriver to land behind American lines and capture their artillery batteries. They did so and succeeded! They sent word to Pakenham to send 2000 troops and the way was open to New Orleans. **Jackson would be caught in a pincer between a large army and a smaller one in his rear that would turn his own gun batteries against him!**

---

[*] Available on Youtube.com, Johnny Horton, *Battle of New Orleans*.

On the main battlefield, Pakenham had ordered the 93rd Northumberland brigade to test the left flank of the American line bordering on the Mississippi. They advanced to their position with orders to attack if they sensed any weakness - but their commander was killed in the advance. Having no orders either to attack or retreat they held their position like a stone wall - when one soldier was killed the soldier behind him filled in his place in the wall. They stood and fired back while being raked by cannon firing grapeshot and the constant barrage of American sharpshooters. The carnage was incredible! But the British soldiers held their position until orders came forward to withdraw. They formed up and marched in perfect disciplined order to the rear. The Americans ceased fire, refusing to shoot these brave soldiers in the back, and applauded them as they marched away.

When word came that the detachment had captured the American batteries, General Pakenham lay dead on the battlefield. His second-in-command, Major General Samuel Gibbs, had also been killed in the conflict. Command now fell to General John Keane who had been badly wounded. Witnessing the bloodshed of thousands of British dead and wounded littering the battlefield, General Keane ordered the forward detachment to withdraw, snatching defeat from the jaws of a likely victory.

Jackson had won! And Jean Lafitte was thereafter hailed as *"the Pirate who saved America"* for the critical contribution of his artillery on land and his ships at sea. **Lafitte was a Messianic** who had been raised by his grandmother. She gave him a Hebrew Bible he carried with him always. He wrote in his journal:

"I owe all ingenuity to the great intuition of my Jewish-Spanish grandmother, who was a witness at the time of the Inquisition… My grandfather was a freethinking Jew.. but this did not prevent him from dying of starvation in prison for refusing to divulge... details which the Inquisition demanded from all Jews... [This] inspired in me a hatred of the Spanish crown and all [their] persecutions - not only against Jews!"[102] [brackets mine]

The American nation survived due to the help of Messianics!

[102] Kritzler, 2008:pp.253-254, *Jewish Pirates*, Doubleday, NY.

The seventeenth century commenced with Jews outlawed in most of Europe and the New World - it ended with their freedom. The participants in their liberation struggle are known. They were the children of refugees from the Inquisition who in the early 1600s, after having led underground lives in Spain and Portugal, settled in Amsterdam. Accepted by the Dutch as a valued merchant class, they raised their children in the free air of Holland, where a select group of them, following the example of their warrior rabbi, took it upon themselves to change things.

Over the course of a half century of leadership (1623-75), they invaded the New World, battled the Inquisition, and orchestrated their people's freedom! [103]

The Inquisition gradually changed from a torrent of misery to a trickle, then eventually sputtered to a stop. *"In 1559, a Roman mob sacked the original headquarters of the Inquisition... They set free more than seventy prisoners and then put the place to the torch!"*[104] **Simon Bolivar, *the great liberator*, was financed and aided in his struggle with Spain by the Conversos of Curaçao.** He marched through South America in the early 1800s liberating the colonies one by one. As he did so their new constitutions granted religious freedom - and the fires of the Inquisition were put out one by one! Spain grew weak. Hispanic nobility disdained the **mercantile** profession - grown lazy and arrogant from the **riches** of the New World. Once deprived of **both** - Spain rapidly declined into a third-world country.

"It is estimated that conversos numbered around ten thousand in the mid-seventeenth century, or 5 percent of the 200,000 settlers in the New World, up to 15% on the islands"[105] [50% in Jamaica]. Messianics were an underground community. Like others, Messianics inhabited a moral continuum from faith, courage, and heroic self-sacrifice to ungodly depravity. Messianics were soldiers, sailors, sinners, saints, traders, traitors, heroes, spies and fakes. **But more than any other group, Messianics forged a New World - not simply of territory - but of human rights and opportunities that still lead the entire world in lifting the masses of all colors, races, and religions out of poverty, oppression and ignorance!** Knowing the suffering humans have endured throughout history - I call the modern era a *'golden age'* for billions of people!

[103] Kritzler, 2008:pp.10-11, *Jewish Pirates*, Doubleday, NY. [104] Cullen Murphy, 2012:p.106, *God's Jury*, Houghton Mifflin Harcourt, N.Y. [105] Kritzler, p.254.

Chapter Eleven
Reformation & *The Received Text*

Behind the Reformation, as behind almost every spiritual movement of note, one finds the personality of a Jewish Christian.[1] (Hugh Schonfield)

    The specific Jewish-Christian whom Schonfield was referring to was Nicholas of Lyra (1270-1349 AD). Lyra's Messianic writings had a profound influence on Martin Luther - providing the theology to initiate the Reformation. Luther spoke out bravely about the excesses of the Roman Church and the need for reform. More than that was needed, however. It was the recovery of *The Received Text* of the Bible from the Neo-Messianic Waldensians in the West and the Greek Church in the East that triggered the revolution. Once *The Received Text* of the Bible was published in European languages - within 30 years two thirds of Europe became Protestant! In 1806, *The Cochin Hebrew Gospels* were discovered by Claudius Buchanan in India.

    The wars were far from over - the casualties of religious wars over the next few decades were in the millions. Nor did burning at the stake cease. At first, the reformers themselves burnt dissidents (heretics) at the stake. Protestant congregations were averse to this, since stopping religious bloodshed was, to many Protestant minds, the point of Reformation.

    However, the witch-burning hysteria of the years from 1450-1750 resulted in as many as 80,000 executions, most by Protestants. Clearly, something was missing from the Reformation that this blood spilled over spiritual beliefs continued unabated. It negates claims of superior morality by the Protestant movement. **There were voices raised that the Reformation did not go far enough - that it was arrested in mid-stride!**

    Anti-Semitism was one of the holdovers that refused to die. Martin Luther, conciliatory toward the Hebrews at first, turned into a rabid anti-Semite when he could make no inroads among the Jews. Witch burnings, a mostly Protestant phenomenon, took the lives of more victims than the Inquisition. The new hysteria spread to the New World. At Salem, the witch trials and executions would destroy the reputation of Puritans for-

---

[1] Hugh Schonfield, 1936, 2009:p.124, *Jewish Christianity*, Duckworth, London.

Origins of the Reformation

October 31, 1517, Martin Luther nailed his *95 Theses** against the selling of indulgences to the door of Wittenburg Cathedral. This is considered the start of the Reformation. However, every historian recognizes there were potent movements in Europe - to return to the Messianic-Apostolic roots of the faith - long before the one that could not be stopped. We have written at length about the Waldensians of northern Italy, Cathars of southern France, and Conversos of Spain and Portugal, as well as the Celtic Church of Ireland, Scotland, and England. The Celtic Church also spread to the continent, particularly in Germany, Switzerland and surrounding regions of central Europe.

In tracing the survival of the true gospel and the true Church, one finds points of light breaking through the most ancient texts - often obscure and long-ignored texts. Here there may be an event, there another, and with enough work the points of light are connected into a clear mosaic of the entire story! It is a prodigious experience to see the light breaking through the surviving pages of these ancient texts. It is the heart of our story.

"In the seventh century, the Irish Evangelist Columbanus, with his countryman Gallus, planted the gospel in Swabia and Switzerland."[2] These countries are next door to Bohemia and Moravia. Columbanus used *The Received Text* in the form of the Celtic Bible, as his scriptural source. *"Both the Keltic and Slavic races... were originally far more independent of the influence of Rome... In our own country* [Bohemia] *Irish and Scotch missionaries... predominated in the north."*[2]

In 863 AD, missionaries to the Slavs were sent from the Greek Church in Thessalonika - two brothers named Cyrillus and Methodius. Cyrillus was sent because he had knowledge of the alphabets being developed in the east, and Methodius because of his knowledge of the Slavonic language. Historians credit them for creating the earliest Slavonic alphabet, called Glagolithic, and translating the Gospels into Slavonic. The two brothers were scholars from the Greek Church, not the Roman Church, and used *The Received Text* of Lucian as their Scripture.

**95 Theses on the Power and Efficacy of Indulgences.* [2]Jane Whately, est. 1850, reprint 2018:p.4, *The Gospel in Bohemia*, Religious Tract Society, London.

"*The Slavonians rejoiced at hearing the greatness of God related in their own tongue!*"[3] The early history of Bohemia and Moravia comes from the *Persecutions Buchlein* (*Book of Persecutions*). "*It is... the history of the oldest pure and evangelical community existing - with the sole exception of the Waldensians - a community kept alive for centuries in the midst of a furnace of persecution, then apparently crushed to death, then arising with new life from the ashes, to win triumphs for the gospel.*"[4]

About 873 AD, Methodius, because of the friction between the Greek Orthodox and the Roman Catholic Churches, felt it necessary to go to the pope in Rome to smooth things out. The pope anointed Methodius as the Metropolitan of Moravia. He returned to the pope again in 879 because others had complained of his use of the Slavonian Scripture and language in his teaching. Methodius "*actually convinced the pontiff of the soundness of his doctrinal views, and the propriety of conducting worship in the language of the people, for the general use of Latin was only beginning to creep in.*"[5]

Later in this Bohemian saga, Jan Hus (John Huss) was born around 1372. He studied at the University of Prague, was ordained - and taught at the Bethlehem Chapel in Prague. "*Services at the Bethlehem Chapel were conducted in Czech, contrary to the common practice of conducting services in Latin. The Bible was read and sermons were preached in the common language.*"[6] Hus was influenced by John Wycliffe, the English reformer who railed against Roman Church abuses and translated the Latin Vulgate into English so all could read it. Hus also criticized the Church, since "*financial abuses, sexual immorality, and drunkenness were common among the priests of Europe. Hus called for preaching and Bible reading in the common language, and for all Christians to receive full communion.*"[6]

Hus also opposed the sale of indulgences and the doctrine of infallibility of the pope. Hus was excommunicated and summoned to the Council of Constance (1414) to defend his beliefs. He was granted safe conduct by Holy Roman Emperor Sisimund. But Hus was not allowed to defend his beliefs. Sisimund was convinced no promise need be kept to a heretic. **Hus was burned at the stake in 1415. The Slavs rose up in open rebellion!**

---

[3] Attributed to Nestor, the oldest Slavonic chronicler, in *The Annals of Nestor*.
[4] Jane Whately, est. 1850:p.vii, *The Gospel in Bohemia*. [5] *Ibid.*, Whately, p.6.
[6] Editors of Kenyon.edu, 2021, *The Moravian Church - Jan Hus*.

The gospel truth espoused by Jan Hus touched the soul of the nation! The resistance of his followers, called the Hussite Wars, continued decade after decade (1415-1457), defeating all the armies of Rome sent to put the genie back into the bottle. The Moravian Church, called the Unity of Bohemian Brethren, was finally authorized by Rome to exist. The Brethren soon swelled to a quarter million congregants. Twenty-five years before the birth of Martin Luther, and sixty years before the Lutheran Church, the Unity Church was a successful and influential reform denomination. They published the Bible, and hymnals, in their own language. Like the Puritans, the Hussites were Neo-Messianic in important ways (restoring the early gospel in the common language) but not in others (the embrace of violence).

There were various other early reformers such as Petr Chelsiky of Bohemia (1390-1460), Arnaldo of Lombardy (aka Arnold of Brescia, 1090-1155), and Girolamo Savonarola of Florence (1494-1498). Most were executed by the Roman Church. Many refugees from oppression fled to Holland.

> In Holland the Reformation Church was... active in promoting an almost Jewish domestic life and faith. Indeed... Jewish ideas were deeply influencing the two great Christian groups, Kabbalism among the Catholics and Propheticism among the Protestants. The Old Testament took a new hold on the religious consciousness. Men began to find in the Law of Moses the divinely appointed rule of conduct, and to study the Prophets for light on the last days. Jew and Christian drew nearer together than they had done for many centuries past.[7]

One of the most important of these early reformers was **Nicolas of Lyra, a Messianic Jewish-Christian**. *"He became Doctor of Theology and taught at the Sorbonne until 1325... well versed in Talmudic literature, he favored the literal interpretation of Scripture after the method of the great Jewish commentator Rashi... He set himself in his chief work*... to explain the Old and New Testaments on what he held to be the corrected principles, not sparing in the course of the work to castigate the abuses prevailing in the Church.* **These commentaries proved of such service to Martin Luther,** *that the Bishop of Naumberg was moved to write his famous couplet..."*[8]

"If Lyra had not written, Luther would not have come forth!"

[7]Hugo Schonfield, 1936, 2009:p.145, *History of Jewish Christianity.* [8]*Ibid*,p.124.
*Nicolas Lyra, *Postillae, Perbetuae, sive Brevia Commentaria Universa Biblia.*

Ulrich Zwingli was the catalyst for the Reformation in the Swiss Confederation. Zwingli was a preacher, and renowned scholar, who moved to Zurich in 1518, one year after Luther's *95 Theses* were published. Zwingli published a tract called *The 57 Conclusions,* remarkably similar to Luther's *Theses.* Zwingli claims to have come to his theology independent of Luther. Although these two sets of doctrines developed into different denominations there was little difference in their beliefs. **Many of Zwingli's followers were among those who believed the Reformation did not go far enough.** Their movement was called the ***Radical Reformation!*** The Anabaptists, Puritans, Amish, Mennonites and Quakers were all religious movements springing from the fountain of the Radical Reformation.

Ulrich Zwingli died in 1531. *"In 1541 John Calvin, a French Protestant who had spent the previous decade in exile writing his 'Institutes of the Christian Religion,' was invited to settle in Geneva and put his Reformed doctrine… into practice."*[9] Although his doctrinal practices are often described as harsh and austere, they took root and spread to Scotland, France, and the Netherlands. Dutch Calvinism became a powerful force during the following four centuries. The Calvinist Huguenots of France once composed as much as 10% of the French population. Over more than a century of continual persecution and slaughter, they were all but eliminated. The end came in the 1670s when Louis XIV began a policy of destroying Huguenot churches and schools. He billeted French soldiers, call dragoons, in Huguenot homes with instructions to abuse and steal from them at will. This kind of persecution was called a *'dragonnade'* and the soldiers got so out of hand, causing such outrage, they finally had to be restrained. The French Protestants who survived either converted to Catholicism, went underground, or emigrated.

"In England, the Reformation began with Henry VIII's quest for a male heir. When Pope Clement VII refused to annul Henry's marriage to Catherine of Aragon so he could remarry, the English king declared that he alone should be the final authority in matters relating to the English church. **Henry dissolved England's monasteries to confiscate their wealth and worked to place the Bible in the hands of the people. Beginning in 1536, every parish was required to have a copy.***"*[10] Henry's church was called the Church of England, or Anglican Church.

---

[9] Britannica.com/event/Reformation.   [10] History.com/topics/Reformation.

Luther began by criticising the sale of indulgences, insisting that the Pope had no authority over purgatory and that the Treasury of Merit had no foundation in the Bible. The Reformation developed further to include a distinction between Law and Gospel, a complete reliance on Scripture as the only source of proper doctrine (***sola scriptura***) and the belief that faith in Jesus is the only way to receive God's pardon for sin (***sola fide***) rather than good works.[11]

Luther claimed his success came from restoring the theology of the Church rather than simply criticizing its abuses. He did, eventually, write about clerical celibacy, the infallibility of the pope, sacraments, ecclesiastical law, excommunication, works versus faith, purgatory, monasticism, and the '*Virgin Mary*.' His theology was critical - but his survival is what allowed the Reformation to continue to thrive. Luther was summoned before the Diet of Worms in 1521 and called upon to recant his writings. Luther defended his beliefs bravely and ably, "*Unless I am convicted by Scripture and plain reason - I do not accept the authority of popes and councils, for they have contradicted each other - my conscience is captive to the Word of God.* ***I cannot and I will not recant anything!***"[12]

Nonetheless, Luther was excommunicated by the Church. He survived because he was protected by powerful German princes. Friedrich, the Elector of Saxony, hid Luther away in his castle at Wartburg during this dangerous period. It was at Wartburg that Luther translated the Gospels into German, published in September 1522. The *Lutherbibel* was completed in 1534 with the addition of the Old Testament. But the most crucial factor was the new power of the printing press.

"*No reformer was more adept than Martin Luther at using the power of the press to spread his ideas. Between 1518 and 1525, Luther published more works than the next 17 most prolific reformers combined!*"[13]

Luther's reforms succeeded in Germany and beyond, causing the Roman Church to war against the Protestants of central Europe. It was called the Thirty Years War. Bohemia/Moravia, a unified country by then, was in the center between the armies of the Protestant north and those of the Catholic south.

---

[11] Wikipedia.com/Reformation/overview. [12] Legends of Luther, https://www.luther.de/en/ws.html. [13] History.com/topics/reformation.

For thirty years the carnage was overwhelming and it was followed by year after year of famine and starvation. As much as 50% of the population of central Europe perished - an estimated eight million people died! Both sides were too depleted to go on. At the peace of Westphalia in 1648, the leaders of each country chose which church they would follow. That acceptance, of Protestant churches by Rome and the other nobles, was considered the endmark of the Reformation period. Bohemia/Moravia fell into the Catholic column. The Moravian Church, and its adherents, had been ground down mercilessly and crushed to death.

The Moravian Revival at Herrnhut

Moravian survivors from the devastation were invited to find refuge on the estate of Nicolas Ludwig, Count Zinzendorf, at Berthelsdorf Castle in Saxony, Germany. **It came to be called Herrnhut - which means '*The Lord's Watch.*'**

Count Zinzendorf was a remarkable young man. He attended the University of Wittenberg, absorbing Lutheran piety at the source of the Reformation. By the time he left Wittenberg he had established seven prayer societies, apparently one for every day of the week so he could attend them all. He had a beautiful love of the Savior since his youngest days. One day, at a pivotal moment in his life, Nicolas viewed a painting, *Ecce Homo* by Domenico Feti. Nicolas was seized with conviction to dedicate his life to Jesus. "*I have loved Him for a long time, but I have never actually done anything for Him. From now on I will do whatever He leads me to do!*"

Count Zinzendorf did not have long to wait. In 1722 he met Christian David, a Moravian refugee, and offered him and others refuge on his estate. David made ten dangerous and difficult journeys to and from Moravia, shepherding refugees to Herrnhut. Count Zinzendorf called Christian David, **"*the Moravian Moses.*"**

Ecce Homo by Domenico Feti

[14] https://en.wikipedia.org/wiki/Nicolaus_Zinzendorf

Christian David also had a pivotal moment in his life when he was given a German *Luther Bible*. Once the Word took root in his life he sought ways to serve the many victims of the wars - which led him to his historic encounter with Zinzendorf. Herrnhut gained a reputation as an asylum from religious persecution and other groups began to gather there. Most were Moravian Church believers, but some others were on opposite sides of the religious divide that transformed the Reformation into the Thirty Years War. The Herrnhut community became embroiled in serious controversy.

At this point of conflict, Count Zinzendorf showed his true depth of character. He started going to each home to pray about the need for unity of prayer. On May 12, 1727, he called them all into assembly for intense Bible study upon how Christians should live in community. The result was the *Brotherly Agreement* - signed by all members of the community. They agreed on a regular prayer - a prayer of intercession for the entire community.

On August 13, 1727, during their regular afternoon prayer session, the spirit of God fell upon the entire assembly! Two members who were working twenty miles away also felt the spirit fall upon them at the same moment. There are various degrees of spiritual visitation. This was a *"blessing corresponding in its signs and affects to the blessing received by the Apostles at Pentecost."*[15] From the evidence this was a visitation of the highest order. **The Shekinah glory of Yehovah descended at once upon the entire assembly at Herrnhut!**

> The Holy Spirit came upon us and in those days great signs and wonders took place in our midst. From that time scarcely a day but what we beheld His almighty workings amongst us. A great hunger after the Word of God took possession of us so that we had to have three services every day, viz 5:00 and 7:30 AM and 9:00 PM. Everyone desired above everything else that the Holy Spirit might have full control. Self-love and self-will as well as all disobedience disappeared and **an overwhelming flood of grace swept us all out into the great ocean of Divine Love!**[16]

---

[15] John Greenfield, 1928:p.8, *Power From on High*, reprint 2017 CTM Publishing, Atlanta, Ga, citing James Elder Cummings. [16] *Ibid.*, p.10.

"They left the house of God that noon 'hardly knowing whether they belong to earth or had already gone to Heaven.'"[17]

The great Moravian Church was started by Methodius in the 9th century, and turned into the first Reform Church under Jan Hus in the 1400s. It had been crushed by the Thirty Years War (1618-1648). Believers were starved by the resulting famine, and oppressed by the Roman Church takeover of the country. Their churches and schools were closed and they were forced to go underground to worship in secret. Many Moravians were martyred for refusing to renounce their faith. *"Before Hus was martyred* [in 1415], *he prophesied that the Bible teaching and praying that he had done with* **these Moravian people would be a 'hidden seed' buried in the ground, and that one day it would spring up into REVIVAL!"*[18]

In 1727 at Herrnhut, that *"Hidden Seed"* sparked the fulfillment of the revival prophesied. Like the outpouring of the Holy Spirit at Jerusalem, **"God poured out His Holy Spirit and imbued them with power from on high**... *Supernatural knowledge and power seemed to possess them.... Therefore they that were scattered abroad went everywhere preaching the Word."*[19] During the following decades, **Herrnhut sent out more than 300 missionaries** from their tiny community to establish churches on every continent resulting in the salvation of more than a million souls! At Herrnhut they resolved themselves to continual prayer and praise. At every hour of the night and day, a group of believers at Herrnhut would be communing with their Maker. **Continual prayer continued for 100 years!**

The Moravian *"English Missionary Magazine - Periodical Accounts, - inspired Dr. William Carey,"* who is known as the father of the Protestant mission field. *"In a meeting of his Baptist brethren he threw a copy of the paper on the table with these memorable and historic words:"*[20]

"See what the Moravians have done! Cannot we follow their example and in obedience to our Heavenly Master go out into the world, and preach the Gospel to the Heathen? **This small [Moravian] Church in twenty years called into being more Missions than the whole Evangelical Church has done in two centuries!**"[20]

---

[17]John Greenfield, 1928:p.11, *Power From on High*, reprint 2017 CTM Publishing, Atlanta, Ga. [18] https://acsirevivals.wordpress.com/other-revivals/the-moravian-prayer-movement. [19] *Op. cit.*, Greenfield, 1928:p.13. [20] *Ibid.*, p.15.

The domino effect of the Moravian Revival would take many volumes to relate. One of the converts from their meetings in England was John Wesley, the founder of the Methodist Church. It was the Methodist Church that followed American migration from Atlantic to Pacific. Two other converts who were inspired by the Moravians through William Carey were William and Catherine Booth, founders of the Salvation Army.

Were the Moravians Neo-Messianic? In spirit they certainly were, carrying salvation through the Holy Spirit to the farthest reaches of the world. In doctrine, not as much. They worshiped on the Lord's Day, Sunday, and celebrated Easter with a sunrise service, originally a pagan ritual. They believed the wine and bread, to some degree, became the actual blood and flesh of Jesus. They did not use the sacred names of Yehovah or Yeshua, nor did they hold to Torah.

It is crucial to know what this teaches us, because we must now follow that golden thread of revival to bring our story up to the present day. It is clear that if one's heart is right towards God, He will bless us with His Holy Spirit regardless of the state of our ignorance. Millions of souls have been saved through the new churches despite their departure from the doctrine of the original Church of the Messiah. **People generally become Bible scholars after their salvation rather than before it.** However, to postulate that this proves Yehovah, and Yeshua, do not care about us following the instructions and commandments in Torah - is unsustainable!

The elements of Revival are these: Participants have chosen to participate in a unity of prayer. The community are all praying for the same thing, the outpouring of the Holy Spirit. It will take some time. At Jerusalem, believers were told to pray and wait for Shavuot, fifty days after Yeshua's death. Herrnhut engaged in unity of prayer for three months before the outpouring of the Spirit. These are not the only revivals. The website Beautiful Feet gives 133 Accounts of Revival. Some take years. Afterward, the group often engages in continual prayer as they did in Jerusalem and in the Celtic Church visitation. **In Ireland, *Laus Perennis* - continual prayer 24/7 - lasted for centuries. When it stops the visitation ends!**

Reformation Bibles

All the principals in our story of revival had *The Received Text* of the Bible. The Waldensians had a Bible that predated the Catholic Vulgate, as did the Cathars, and the Conversos of Spain. The enormous popularity of these early Neo-Messianic movements makes it evident they were revivalist in nature. Count Zinzendorf studied the *Luther Bible* at Wittenburg, and Christian David received a *Luther Bible* as a gift, which turned his life around. Where did these Reformation Bibles come from?

Two sources - we have spoken of the Waldensian texts which survived - but there was another source. *"The greatest treasure accruing to the world by the fall of Constantinople was the recovery of multiple manuscripts of the Greek New Testament. The vast majority of these manuscripts were The Received Text."*[21] The Greek Orthodox Church had kept their treasures away from the prying eyes of the West. Once the Ottoman Sultan Mehmed II took Constantinople in 1453, he was eager to attract western commerce and scholarship. The extensive ancient libraries of Constantinople were opened wide to the West.

It was Erasmus of Holland who rocked Europe, in 1516, with a new edition of the Greek New Testament hailed as *The Received Text* of the Bible. Erasmus was the intellectual giant of the era. It was Erasmus who **"*divided all Greek New Testament manuscripts into two classes:***

***those which followed The Received Text**, edited by Lucian, and those which followed the Vaticanus manuscript, the pride of the Vatican Library* [Eusebius' version].

He [Erasmus] *specified the grounds... upon which he rejected the Vaticanus and received the other...* ***This was the edition which all the Protestant churches of that period used.*** *It became the text for Luther's Bible in German and for Tyndale's translation in English!"*[22]

Erasmus 1466-1536

---

[21] Ben Wilkinson, 1944:p.374, *Truth Triumphant*, Hartland Publications, Va.
[22] *Ibid.*, Wilkinson, p.374.

The Waldensian Source of Reformation Bibles

"The Reformers held that the Waldensian Church was formed about 120 A.D., from which date they passed down from father to son the teachings they received from the Apostles. The [Old] Latin Bible was translated from the Greek [& Hebrew] not later than 157 A.D."[23] [brackets mine] This is the trail of manuscripts that we have been pursuing for so long in this book. *"The noble Waldensians in northern Italy still possessed, in Latin, The Received Text... in the form of a Latin translation,* **the Old Latin or Itala version, which predates the Vulgate**.*"*[24] The Itala was the primary source for *The Received Text - Lucian's Greek Bible*.

> It seems likely that the Old Latin was translated in the Syrian Antioch by missionaries going to the West. Existing manuscripts certainly show a strong Syrian or Aramaic tendency. This being the case, the Old Latin is associated with that city which is the missionary center of the Book of Acts, and had immediate concourse with those cities in Asia Minor which received the Epistles of Paul. History is so unanimous to Antioch being the fountainhead of the Traditional Text that it has been called the *"Antiochan Text."*
>
> *55 or 60 OL [Old Latin] manuscripts... remain for us today. It is the branch of the Old Latin used in northern Italy that attracts our attention the most, and establishes one of the crucial chapters in Bible transmission history!* [25]

Keep in mind that *The Received Text* is referred to by different names over the centuries-long history of this dialog. Some of them are - **Received Text, Traditional Text, Antiochan Text, Authorized Version** and **Lucian Bible**. Lucian (240-312) started a school in Antioch. He was a Hebrew scholar expert enough to correct mistakes in the Greek Septuagint from his knowledge of the Hebrew text of the Tanakh (Old Testament). **This speaks to the definite possibility that Lucian was a Messianic!** There were many Messianics in Antioch. Gentile Hebrew scholars were extremely rare. The Messianic Church had fled to Antioch. Lucian was martyred in the persecution of Emperor Diocletian after nine years in prison and terrible tortures.

---

[23] Ben Wilkinson, 1930, 2014:p.26, *Our Authorized Bible Vindicated*, Teach Services Publishing, Calhoun, Ga. [24] Alan James O'Reilly, 1995:p.731, *The Old Latin & Waldensian Bibles*, chapter 12 of *The Whitewash Conspiracy*, Bethany House Publishers. [25] Jack A. Moorman, 1990, *Early Manuscripts and the Authorized Version, A Closer Look!*, B.F.T. #1825, The Bible for Today.

A number of Bibles produced under Neo-Messianic "Waldensian influence touched... history!"[26] Sometime between 1170-80, the Waldensian leader Peter Waldo commissioned his Bible in Romaunt, or Romance. At the Waldensian synod at Laux, in 1526, two members were sent to make contact with the Reformers. They did so, encountering Guillaume Farel there, a fellow Waldensian and Reformer, who became the contact between the two groups. Pierre Robert Olivetan (1506-1538), a Waldensian pastor, was the first to translate the Bible into French in 1537, using the Waldensian *Received Text*. *"This godly man, Olivetan, in the preface of his Bible recognizes with thanks to God, that since the time of the Apostles… the torch of the gospel has been lit among the Vaudois, dwellers in the valleys of the Alps, and has never since been extinguished."*[27] Later, *"John Calvin* [a relative of Olivetan] *edited a second edition of the Olivetan Bible. The Olivetan in turn became the basis of the Geneva Bible in English, which was the leading version in England in 1611, when the King James appeared."*[28]

The Geneva Bible was also the first and foremost Bible used in America!

John Calvin was recruited by Guillaume Farel to join the Reformers active in Geneva. Theodore Beza, a friend of Calvin, and *"the illustrious group of scholars which gathered around Beza in Geneva,"* in 1588, published a new edition of the *Bezae Codex*, a 5th or 6th century manuscript from southern France, owned by Beza. It was also carefully correlated with the work of Erasmus. *"This later edition of the Received Text is in reality a Greek New Testament brought out under Waldensian influence."*[28] Giovanni Diodati *"takes the same and translates into Italian a new and famous edition* [the Diodati Bible]*, adopted and circulated by the Waldenses. Leger, the Waldensian historian of his people, studied under Diodati at Geneva."*[29] Beza's 1588 Greek N.T. also became the basis of the 1611 King James version of the Bible. The Geneva connection between Reformers and Waldensians had become a hotbed of biblical revival! ***"The two streams of descent of the Received Text, through the Greek East and the Waldensian West, ran together… illustrated by the meeting of the Olivetan Bible and the Received Text!"***[30]

---

[26] Ben Wilkinson, 2014:p.27, *Our Authorized Bible Vindicated*. [27] Jean Leger, *General History of the Vaudois Churches*, p.165. printed at Lycden, 1669.
[28] Wilkinson, p.27. [29] *Ibid.*, p.26. [30] Ibid., p.27.

B.C.	Hebrew Tanakh*	Old Testament	Greek Septuagint
A.D.	**Hebrew Gospels**	**New Testament**	**Greek Gospels**
100	Itala Bible-Old Latin		
200	Lucian Greek Bible		
300	Waldensian Roumant Bible		Eusebius Greek Bible 320
300			Jerome Latin Vulgate 380
400-600			
700-900			
1000 1100	Waldo NT 1175		
1200-1400		Wycliffe English Bible 1382	
1500 1500	Eramus Greek 1516 Tyndale English 1526		
1500 1500	Luther German 1534 Olivetan French 1535		Catholic French 1550
1600 1600	Geneva English 1606 King James 1611		Rheims English 1610
1600 1700	Diodati Italian 1649		Martini Italian 1769

Erasmus Two Streams of Manuscripts - Expanded Version

The progression is simple. *The Hebrew Tanakh* (OT) and *The Hebrew Gospels* **became** > *The Itala Bible* which **became** > *The Received Text of Lucian's Greek Bible*. The Waldensians formed the Italick *See* (*seat* of the church) in northern Italy, in opposition to the Roman See in the south. **Rome tried to destroy them!**

In 2015, Pope Francis went to the Waldensians in Turin and said, "*On behalf of the Catholic Church, I ask forgiveness for the un-Christian and even inhumane positions and actions taken against you historically. In the name of the Lord Jesus Christ, forgive us!*

The Arrested Reformation

> It is a serious error to think of the Reformation era, glorious and fruitful as it was, as if it were the golden age of the church, or as if everything was perfect... at its best. The best is yet to be, the best for which all ages have done their work.[31]

The rallying cry of the Reformation, penned by Luther, was "*sola scriptura - sola fide*" (**Scripture alone - Faith alone**). Is it ungracious of me to point out this is a logical contradiction? If we are saved by faith alone - what need is there of Scripture? If Scripture alone - note that Scripture says three times in the Epistle of James - **we are not saved by faith alone!** (James 2:24)

The Reformation broke mankind out of the iron grip of the Apostate Church! The fact Protestants repeated many apostate errors is rather human - or inhuman - as the case may be. **Thus, there is a need for every Christian and every church to repent of the original apostasy - the declaration of the Messiah's Church as heretic and the ongoing crusade to destroy Messianics and their Church over the millennia.**

We are reminded of the greater lesson of the Inquisition. "*The Inquisition, church and state courts, and the legal codes… taken together, meant that **early modern Europeans inherited a fully fledged apparatus of persecution and an intellectual tradition that justified killing in the name of God!**"*[32] Protestants did not shed this inheritance of warmed-over Greco-Roman evil thinking until centuries later.

"*I think it is grave to kill men, under the pretext that they are mistaken on the interpretation of some point, for we know that even the chosen ones are not exempt from sometimes being wrong... To kill a man is not to protect a doctrine, it is just to kill a man.*" Michael Servetus was a brilliant Spanish theologian and physician who had a heated running debate with the Reformer John Calvin. He wrote a book criticizing the Trinity. As ruler of Geneva, Calvin had him seized and burned alive Oct. 12, 1553.

Michael Servetus
1511-1553

---

[31] William Muir, 2015:p.9, *The Arrested Reformation*, Scholar Select.
[32] Cullen Murphy, 2012:p.188, *God's Jury - The Inquisition & Making of the Modern World*, Houghton-Mifflin, N.Y.

Persecution under Protestantism

> During the reign of Elizabeth I... An act of Parliament in 1571 made it high treason to question the queen's title as head of the Church of England - thus making the practice of Roman Catholicism an essentially treasonable act - and authorized the confiscation of the property of Roman Catholics, many of whom fled to the European continent. In the ensuing persecution, 183 English Catholics were put to death between 1577 and 1603; altogether, some 600 Catholics died in the persecutions of the 16th and 17th centuries. Some were executed for offenses as trivial as obtaining a papal license to marry.[33]

The persecution of Catholics never reached anywhere near the level, extent or consistency over time as the Inquisitions against the Neo-Messianics. Protestant groups were also persecuted by other Protestants where they were competition to the more dominant of the newly-established churches. Anabaptists were severely persecuted, probably because of the perceived threat arising from the Anabaptist uprising and takeover of Muenster in 1534. The principles, arguments and authority applied to the burnings were the same as before Reformation. State churches became the norm. The union of church and state ruled.

Luther and the Jews

Luther believed his theology to be the pure form of Scripture. One must imagine what it is like for a preacher when millions of people everywhere in Europe rapidly embrace his sermons and reforms. Monks left their monasteries, Nuns left their convents to join the bandwagon. Believers were willing to be martyred for the new vision of the kingdom of God which Luther brought to them. Even more were willing to fight to gain independence from the Apostate Church. Luther was convinced the Jews would also embrace this *'pure faith'* and he was gracious in welcoming them. He railed against their mistreatment:

> They have treated the Jews as if they were dogs, not men, and as if they were fit for nothing but to be reviled.
> **They are blood relatives of our Lord, therefore, if we respect flesh and blood, the Jews belong to Christ more than we.**[34]

---

[33] https://www.britannica.com/topic/Forty-Martyrs-of-England-and-Wales.
[34] Martin Luther, 1523, *That Jesus was born a Jew*.

The Reformation had a long way to go to cleanse itself of anti-Semitism. The Christian redemption requires sacrifice. *"The sacrificial reading of the gospel offers Christians their redemption at the expense of the damnation of the Jews."*[35] Christianity had appropriated the mantle of the chosen people. Scripture, seen as a unified doctrine between the Old Testament and the New, would mean the true original heritors are Messianic Jews who embrace both the Hebrew Torah and the Hebrew Messiah. For Christians to be validated as the new chosen people of Israel, the old chosen people, the Jews - and especially the Messianics - must vanish from the scene. To the supersessionist Christians, this is seen as the will of God.

> This sorry plot lies at the very foundations of the long, ugly history of Christian attitudes and actions toward Jews and Judaism. The destruction of their city [Jerusalem] was only a sign. They did not vanish as was their due and thus were there to reap repeatedly the wrath of God in anticipation of the final, apocalyptic resolution.
> **No thinking person can justify this long history, nor doubt that the gospel has justified it in the eyes of Christians!**[36]

The Jews did not flock to the new banner. Remember that in the early church they came to the Messianic Church in large numbers, both in Jerusalem and Hebrew communities throughout the world. The Word then was offered to them via *The Hebrew Gospels* by Messianics who embraced both Torah and Messiah. Twenty-one years later, Luther changed his tune.

> **Burn their synagogues and schools**; what will not burn, bury with earth, that neither stone nor rubbish remain.... In like manner, **break into and destroy their homes**... Take away all their prayer-books and Talmuds, in which are nothing but godlessness, lies, cursing and swearing... Forbid their rabbis to teach on pain of life and limb... Forbid them to travel... [37]

"Protestant Germany took up the tale of persecution in the 16th century where Catholic Germany had left off in the 15th. The Jews were given the alternative of baptism and banishment in Berlin, were expelled from Bavaria in 1553... and the tragedy of oppression was carried on through the ensuing centuries."[38]

---

[35] Burton Mack, 1988:p.375, *A Myth of Innocence*, Fortress Press, PA. [36] Hugh Schonfield, 1936, 2009:p.136, *History of Jewish Christianity*. Duckworth, UK.
[37] Martin Luther, 1544, *Of the Jews and their Lies*. [38] Schonfield, pp.137-138.

This is undoubtedly a subconscious holdover from the pagan era of human sacrifice meant to appease the gods. In the Christian era of the Inquisition, man created the archetype of a Christian god who approved of, if not thirsted for, the blood of those who were not doctrinally pure. Keep in mind this archetype is the creation of evil men seeking the power of a Holy Mother Church - not the creation of the God of mercy in the Bible. One should note, as in the Inquisition, more women than men were accused and executed for witchcraft. Usually, they were single women living apart from the community, tortured into confessing. As such they were the easiest scapegoats. Women and children are easier to sacrifice than men, who have more power. However, men were also targeted and executed.

Witch Trials in Salem

The first witch execution in America was Alse Young in Windsor, Connecticut in 1647. Overall, in Connecticut between 1647-1697 there were 46 people tried for witchcraft, eleven were executed. In Virginia there were about two dozen witch trials, the first in 1626. In 1655 a law was passed, in Norfolk County, making it a crime to falsely accuse someone of witchcraft, so the hysteria was dampened in Virginia. Of the two dozen tried there, some were imprisoned, none were executed.

It is in Salem, in 1692, among supposedly non-violent Puritan Quakers, where 150 were accused of witchcraft. Of those, eighteen were executed - usually by hanging - twelve were female, six male. Five more of the accused died in prison.

> The Salem witch trials began when 9-year-old Elizabeth Parris and 11-year-old Abigail Williams began suffering from fits, body contortions and uncontrolled screaming... As more young women began to exhibit symptoms, mass hysteria ensued, and three women were accused of witchcraft: Sarah Goods, Sarah Osborn and Tituba, an enslaved woman owned by Parris's father. Tituba confessed to being a witch and began accusing others of using black magic.
>
> **On June 10, Bridget Bishop became the first accused witch to be put to death.**[39]

---

[39] https://www.history.com/topics/folklore/history-of-witches.

To the best of our knowledge, none of the accused were actually witches, except possibly Tituba. Accusations, trials and executions lasted little more than a year from February 1692 to May 1693. Other girls exhibited some of the same symptoms as the first two, and joined into their accusations. Eventually the girls moved from accusing marginalized members of the community to pious citizens, especially those that publicly expressed skepticism about the girls' hysterical behavior and accusations. Over time, the girls moved on to accuse prominent members of the power structure. At this point they were strongly challenged and their shenanigans caused their credibility to evaporate.

Witch Trials in Salem 1992-1993

One of the victims was six-year-old Dorothy Goods who was accused and imprisoned along with her mother Sarah Goods and another child, Sarah's infant baby. The infant died in prison. From her cell window little Dorothy watched her mother hanged for witchcraft. It is reported that Dorothy cried from sunrise to sunset - from that point forward. Dorothy was eventually released, although psychologically damaged for life.

The piteous cries of six-year-old Dorothy, along with other victims tortured and executed for heresy and witchcraft, call into question claims of Protestant moral superiority.

**The template of the Inquisition was alive and well!
The Reformation was arrested far too soon.**

The difference is that the Inquisition ground on and on for three and a half centuries, destroying untold lives worldwide. The Protestant heretic burnings in Europe died out almost immediately. Protestants had no stomach for them. One could argue the witch-hunts were the Protestant equivalent of the Inquisition, although they were not targeted against the Neo-Messianic movement. Eventually, they died out as well, slowly in Europe, but rapidly in America due, in part, to the public spectacle of the Salem witch trials covered in every newspaper in the colonies.

The Puritans were branded forever by these travesties!

The Cochin Hebrew Gospels

Claudius Buchanan was a Scottish minister and evangelist to Asia in the 1800s. He was an erudite scholar, prolific writer, and a keen enthusiast in preserving Bible texts of Asia. Buchanan reveled in the discovery of India's early Christian heritage. *"In every church, and in many of the private homes here, are manuscripts in the Syriac language, and I have been successful in procuring some old and valuable copies of the Scriptures and other books, written in different ages and in different characters."*[40] In Cochin, India, Buchanan made his greatest discovery - various manuscripts of *The Hebrew Gospels and Brit Hadashah* (N.T.). *"In this place I have found a good many valuable manuscripts!"*[41]

I obtained copies of four of Buchanan's forgotten manuscripts at Cambridge Library on December 5, 2019:

1) The New Testament in Hebrew (Cambridge MS Oo.1.32)
2) Acts & Epistles of Cor, Gal, Eph. in Hebrew (MS Oo.1.16.1)
3) Revelation in Hebrew (Cambridge MS Oo.1.16.2)
4) The Gospel of John in Hebrew (MS Add.170)
5) Hebrew Gospels & Brit Hadashah (Gaster MS 1616)

Two days later we discovered the fifth manuscript at Rylands Library in Manchester, (#5) Gaster MS 1616, another complete manuscript *of The Hebrew Gospels and Brit Hadashah!* All five manuscripts were recovered from Cochin, India - documents from the St. Thomas Christians - the first of which, probably brought there by the Apostle Thomas in the first century. The manuscript at Rylands (Gaster MS) had this notation: *"This volume contains an exact transcript of the Four Gospels from the Hebrew copy of the New Testament brought from the Black Jews of Travancore by Dr. Claudius Buchanan and deposited in the University Library Cambridge. Done from the original manuscript in Jerusalem characters into the sacred or square characters by T.Y. - 1810."*[42]

<u>Are *The Cochin Gospels* authentic?</u> We will authenticate *The Cochin Gospels* with the same proof used for *The Hebrew Gospels from Catalonia*. That proof is reprinted on the following page. After that, we will compare the same verses in the *Cochin* and the *Catalan Hebrew Gospels*.

---

[40] Claudius Buchanan, 1812, 2019:p.126-7, *Christian Researches in Asia*, Forgotten Books. [41] *Ibid.*, p.140. [42] Written in front cover of Gaster MS 1616.

Authentication of the *Hebrew Gospels from Catalonia**

The most important question concerning *The Hebrew Gospels from Catalonia* is their authenticity. **Do the *Hebrew Gospels from Catalonia* [HGC] come from the original *Hebrew Gospel* of the first century?** The original *Hebrew Gospel* would be Matthew, and probably much of Luke. Historical attestations indicate the other Gospels were available to the Messianic community in Hebrew translation, therefore a compilation of *The Hebrew Gospels* was inevitable. The Hebrew Gospels from Catalonia are proof such a compilation did exist. To simplify matters, a reference to *The Hebrew Gospel* (singular) would be *Hebrew Matthew* and part of Luke, whereas *The Hebrew Gospels* (plural) would denote the compilation of all four Gospels as in the HGC.

In Jerome's *Commentary on Matthew*, he states that, in *The Hebrew Gospel*, another name is used for Bar Abbas, the criminal who is released by Pilate. Jerome cites his name as *"son of their teacher in the Gospel according to the Hebrews."*[43] "Barabbas (בר אב) is an Aramaic name meaning 'son of the father,' whereas 'son of their teacher' would be בר רבן [*Bar Rabban*]."[44] In *The Hebrew Gospels,* he is referred to four times as *Bar Rabban* (Matthew 27:16,17,20,21), *'son of the teacher.'*

So we have external evidence, an historical attestation by Jerome, of the name *Bar Rabban* used in *The Hebrew Gospel*. We also have internal evidence from *The Hebrew Gospels from Catalonia* [HGC] which used *Bar Rabban* all four times his name is mentioned. I can think of no possible way this could have happened by chance or by collusion. One correlation, however, can always be dismissed. **One correlation is a coincidence.**

<u>**Two is a pattern!**</u>

The ideal authentication of *The Hebrew Gospels* [HGC], would have these criteria:

1. A credible ancient source citing events and/or quotations from the original *Hebrew Gospel* that differ from the *Greek Gospel*,
2. Multiple ancient citations of that same event or quotation,
3. Independent historical confirmation of the event or quotation,
4. Confirmation of the same event or quotation from the text of *The Hebrew Gospels* [HGC] that have come down to us.

---

*From excerpts *Sons of Zions vs Sons of Greece*, 2019pp.168-9, Miles R. Jones.
[43] Jerome, *Comm. on Matthew*, 27.16. [44] Edwards, *The Hebrew Gospel*, 2009:88.

Breaking of the Lintel in *The Hebrew Gospels**

In three instances Jerome preserves evidence of a tradition in the early church of the breaking of the Temple *lintel* stone rather than the Temple *curtain* at the crucifixion of Jesus (Matt. 27:51; Mark 15:38; Luke 23:45).[45] *"In the Gospel we often mention, we read that the immense temple lintel fell and broke to pieces."*[46] Again, **"*In the Gospel, however, which is composed in Hebrew, we read not that the Temple curtain was torn but that the Temple lintel of wondrous size fell!*"**[47]

In *The Hebrew Gospels* [HGC], it is the breaking of the stones of the Temple that are cited, which felled the lintel stone above the entry of the Holy of Holies. Compare the verses given in the King James Bible [KJV] to *The Hebrew Gospels* [HGC]:

HGC Matt 27:51
"*And here the Temple was broken on both sides up and down and the earth quaked and the stones split in the middle.*"
KJV Matthew 27:51
"*And, behold, the veil of the temple was rent in twain from the top to the bottom; and the earth did quake, and the rocks rent.*"

HGC Mark 15:38 "*The temple was broken on both sides up and down...*"
KJV Mark 15:38 "*And the veil of the temple was rent in twain from the top to the bottom.*"

HGC Luke 23:45 "*The sun went dark and covered the temple and it was split in the middle.*"
KJV Luke 23:45 "*The sun was darkened, and the veil of the temple was rent in the midst.*"

The earthquake would account for the breaking of the large lintel stone over the entrance to the inner Temple, "*the stones split in the middle.*" Note that the damage would also have torn the veil hanging beneath the lintel. However, the veil alone could hardly be ripped by an earthquake absent other damage. **The first century church tradition of the breaking of the lintel - as preserved by Jerome from *The Hebrew Gospel* - is confirmed in all 3 verses of *The Hebrew Gospels from Catalonia!***

Now we have a pattern!

---

[45] James Edwards, *The Hebrew Gospel & Development of the Synoptic Tradition*, 2009, p.88. [46]Jerome, *Commentary on Matthew* 27:51. [47]Jerome, *Epistle* 120.8.2, *Ad Hedybiam*. *Excerpts, Jones, 2019, *Sons of Zion vs Sons of Greece*.

Authentication of *The Cochin Hebrew Gospels*

Matthew 27:51 in *The Cochin Hebrew Gospels*

הו זה ישו שוב צעק בקול גדול ועזב לרוחו ; 51. ובמהרה פני הדלת של 50
ההיכל נתבצע לשנים מן תחילתו עד סופו וארץ כדעזוע ואבנים נסתרו ; 52

"And suddenly the face of the entry of the Temple was split in
two from the beginning until the end and the earth
shook and the [heavens] were hidden."
<u>Cochin Gospels</u>

"And here the Temple was broken on both sides up and down
and the earth quaked and the stones split in the middle."
<u>Catalan Gospels</u>

Mark 15:38 in *The Cochin Hebrew Gospels*

בקול רם ונוסר נפשו ; 38. ופני הדלת ההיכל נתבקע לשנים מן ת
תחילתנו עד סופו ; 39. פיון שראה זה ההחיילים העומדים אילו שאיך

"And the entry to the Temple cracked
after the start of the earthquake."
<u>Cochin Gospels</u>

"The Temple was broken on both sides up and down."
<u>Catalan Gospels</u>

Luke 23:45 in *The Cochin Hebrew Gospels*

שעות והוא חושך על כל ה'ארץ עד תשיעה שעה ; 45. ושמש חשך ונקרע
פני הדלת על ההיכל מאמצע ; 46. וצעק בקול רם ואמר אבי בידך אני

"It was dark and split the entry of the Temple
down the middle."
<u>Cochin Gospels</u>

"And the sun went dark and covered the Temple
and it was split in the middle."
<u>Catalan Gospels</u>

We have two manuscripts of *The Hebrew Gospels* that have been separated by five thousand miles and two thousand years! There is no possible coincidence or collusion that can explain these nearly identical readings first identified by Jerome. Both these manuscripts come from the early first century church tradition. These are *The Hebrew Gospels* from the first century that both Conversos in Spain and St. Thomas Christians in India were martyred for preserving. Their sacrifice has not been in vain. There is so much more to tell about these manuscripts but our research, analysis and translation has just begun. There is so much potential in these manuscripts!

The Hebrew Gospels Surviving Manuscripts

There are significant differences between *The Hebrew Gospels* and *The Greek Gospels*. These differences do not change the Gospel story - but they do add tremendous depth to the Hebrew perspective never before seen. There is a method to the madness of those who changed things in the Greek and Latin Gospels. The changes were clearly made to support the doctrines of the newly formed Greco-Roman Church. The B'nai Emunah Institute is dedicated to restoring *The Received Text,* the original manuscripts of the New Testament.

For a quick summary; Matthew was originally written in Hebrew. Luke - as well - was originally written in Hebrew but when translated later into Greek much was added to it. Luke is a hybrid. Hebrews, Peter, John, James, Jude and Revelation were originally from Hebrew manuscripts. Acts is in question. The manuscripts of Paul were initially in Greek, except for Hebrews, as far as we know. I do not care if the original manuscript was written in Hebrew or Greek, I just want the truth.

Everywhere I go to teach about *The Hebrew Gospels* - I bump up against the '*expert*' academic opinion that there is "*absolutely zero evidence of The Hebrew Gospels!*" Certainly we will hear this from professors, researchers and pastors but it is also reflected by Christian, and even some Messianic, believers. This opinion is conveyed with the certitude that it is the '*gospel truth!*' I usually carry a copy of *The Hebrew Gospels* so participants can hold the manuscript in their hands and turn the pages, see the Hebrew text and translation notes, etc. In the following pages you will see page views from all the extant Hebrew manuscripts of *The Hebrew Gospels and Brit Hadashah* (N.T).

The Hebrew Gospels from Catalonia [HGC]
Vat. Ebr. 100 (Vaticano Ebreu Manuscrito #100)

The text is 304 pages, including the books of Matthew, Mark, Luke and John in Hebrew along with prefaces to Matthew, Mark & Luke by St. Jerome in Hebrew as well. Jerome, by his own declaration, had translated *The Hebrew Gospel(s)* into Greek and Latin - apparently adding the Hebrew prefaces at the same time. This is a 15th century manuscript which has been validated as coming from a first century source. This was copied by Messianic scribes, believers in the Hebrew Messiah, who used Hebrew conventions such as substituting Adonai, Hashem, Elohim, etc. for the name of Yehovah. They risked being burned at the stake for copying, or even being in possession of *The Hebrew Gospels*. The name of the Messiah is used in Hebrew - Yeshuas Mashiach. Although more work needs to be done to ascertain the journey of this manuscript, historical attestation cites *The Hebrew Gospels* as being extant in the Medieval period in Spain where it was translated into Catalan. A century later it was translated back into Hebrew - probably because the original Hebrew document was no longer available - either lost, destroyed by the Inquisition, or taken into hiding underground. The Hebrew preface to Matthew says, "*The first evangelist wrote this in the holy tongue for his brothers...*" The acknowledgement in the preface that *The Hebrew Gospel* was originally written in Hebrew, the holy tongue ("*lashon hachodesh*"), is one of several markers of the Hebrew Manuscript Tradition.

Luke 1
Luke is missing first 4 verses

"The beginning of their [Hebrew] Gospel has this:

'*In the days when Herod was king of Judaea...*'"

(315-403 AD)

The Cochin Hebrew Gospels
Rylands Library - Manchester, U.K.
Hebrew Manuscript #1616

The manuscript has 584 pages and includes all four Gospels & Acts of the Apostles, all of the Epistles and the book of Revelation. It is a complete text of *The Hebrew New Testament*, one of two complete texts of the New Testament in the Cochin Collection. **These Gospels have been ascertained to have come from a first century source!** It was discovered in 1806 at the Synagogue of the Black Jews of Cochin and recopied from the "*ancient Jerusalem script*" by Claudius Buchanan in 1810.

Cochin, in India, was the territory where the Apostle Thomas evangelized and established a church that continues to this day. Bartholomew was cited by Eusebius, in the early church literature, because he took a copy of *The Hebrew Gospel* to Cochin in the first century. In the second century, Pantaenus was cited as sojourning there and returning to Alexandria with a copy of *The Hebrew Gospel*. Throughout the centuries, the Messianic community of Cochin preserved the Gospels and added Hebrew translations of the Greek epistles in order to have a complete Hebrew compilation of the *Brit Hadashah* (N.T.).

First page says:	
The book of the Gospel	הספר של ואנגילון
Good News of Matthew	סברת מאטיאוס
Good News of Mark	סברת מרקוס
Good News of Luke	סברת לוקס
Good News of John	סברת יוחנן

The Cochin Hebrew New Testament [CNT]
Cambridge Library Oo.1.32 (in the Manuscript Collection)

The manuscript is 373 pages, including all four Gospels, Acts of the Apostles, all of the Epistles - but no book of Revelation. Below is the first page of that document. The manuscript did not have a cover so the first page is discolored and worn from exposure. The rest of the manuscript is in much better condition. It is quite readable, although written in a script somewhat peculiar.

The Cochin Collection also contains another manuscript which is the complete text of Revelation [see next page]. Although it is definitely a different manuscript it has been bound along with the Epistles of the New Testament in Hebrew.

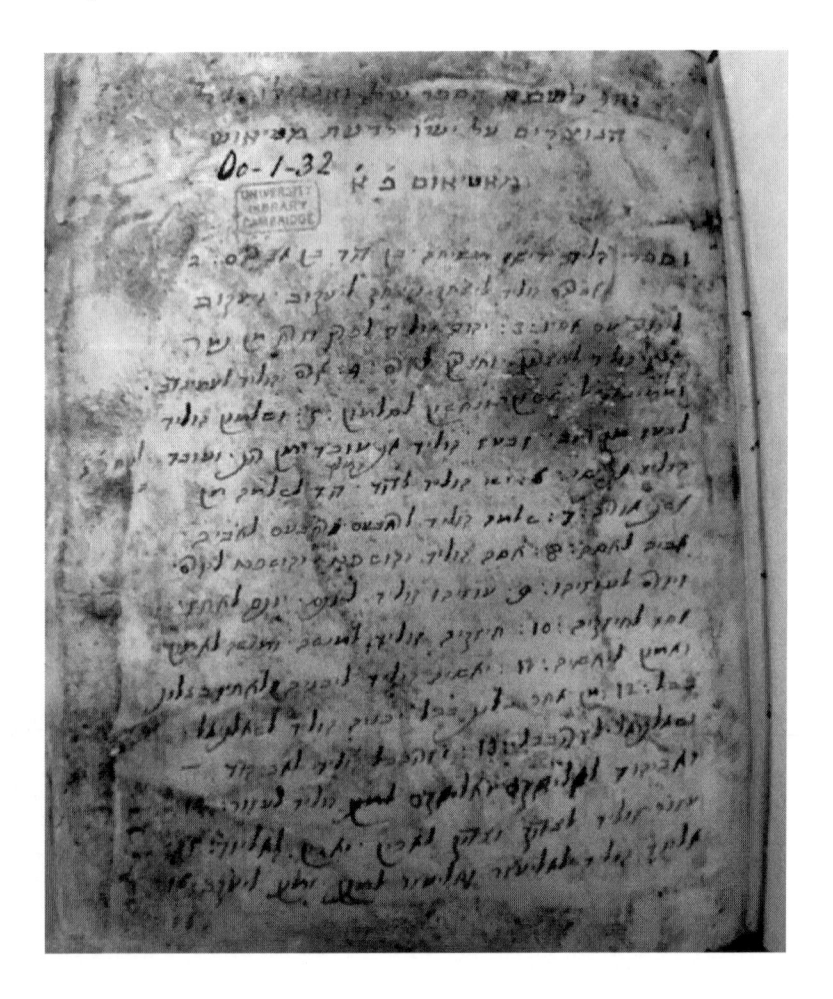

The Cochin Hebrew Gospel of Revelation
Cambridge Library Oo.1.16.2

    This is the first complete manuscript of the Hebrew Book of Revelation ever discovered! The age of this manuscript has yet to be determined. *The Cochin Gospels* are also a complete Hebrew N.T. including Revelation. So that means we have two (early) Hebrew manuscripts of Revelation. However, it has yet to be determined if *The Cochin Gospels* (& N.T.) were, in fact, recopied from the manuscript of *The Cochin Hebrew New Testament.* Nonetheless, having the first complete Hebrew manuscript of Revelation with some claim to authenticity is an enormous discovery! The translation, analysis, and comparison of this manuscript with others such as The Cochin Hebrew N.T. and the Hazon Manuscript of Revelation could help establish the authentic original Hebrew text of Revelation. Many scholars have concluded that Revelation comes from a Hebrew subtext, meaning an analysis of the underlying syntax shows Revelation to be of Hebrew origin.

The Cochin Hebrew N.T. Epistles
Cambridge University Library Oo.1.16.1

This manuscript includes the Hebrew text of Acts of the Apostles, Romans, 1st & 2nd Corinthians, Galatians, and Ephesians. An early presumption about this manuscript is that it contains Hebrew translations of the Greek Epistles in order to compile them with the Hebrew elements to achieve a complete Hebrew New Testament. That remains to be seen. The Hebrew origin of Acts is in question. Luke wrote both the Gospel of Luke and Acts as a two part letter to Theophilus. We know Luke was originally written in Hebrew - so logically Acts was as well. See the complete evidentiary analysis of the Hebrew origin of Luke in *Sons of Zion vs Sons of Greece*. This manuscript of Acts should help to answer that very important question.

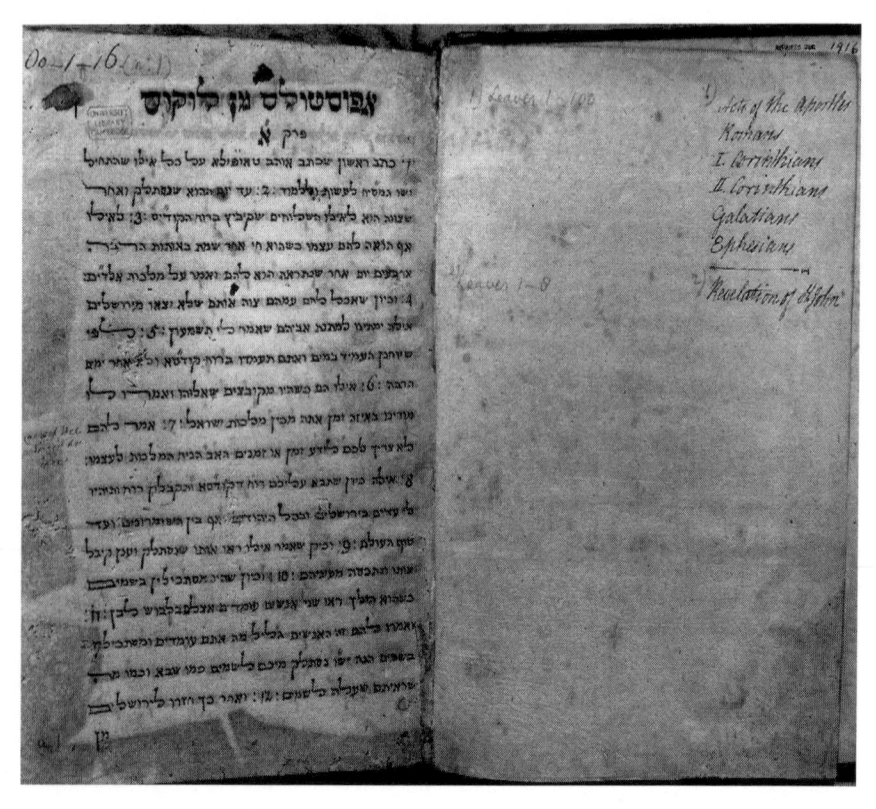

The Cochin Hebrew Gospel of John
Cambridge Oo.Add.170

The Gospel of John raises so many historical questions. Many historians do not believe that it was written by the Apostle John. The early church felt a Greek Gospel by an Apostle was needed to counterbalance the Hebrew Gospel of Matthew - otherwise, the only eyewitness testimony to the Messiah is from Hebrew, not a good thing to the early Greek Church. John had little historical attestation as to its author. It was heavily edited by Greek editors, more than 60 third person insertions are in the text, giving the *"Love Gospel"* the dubious distinction of having the most anti-Judaic statements in the New Testament. This Hebrew manuscript of John may go a long way towards answering those historical questions. See *Sons of Zion vs Sons of Greece* for a detailed assessment of its authorship.

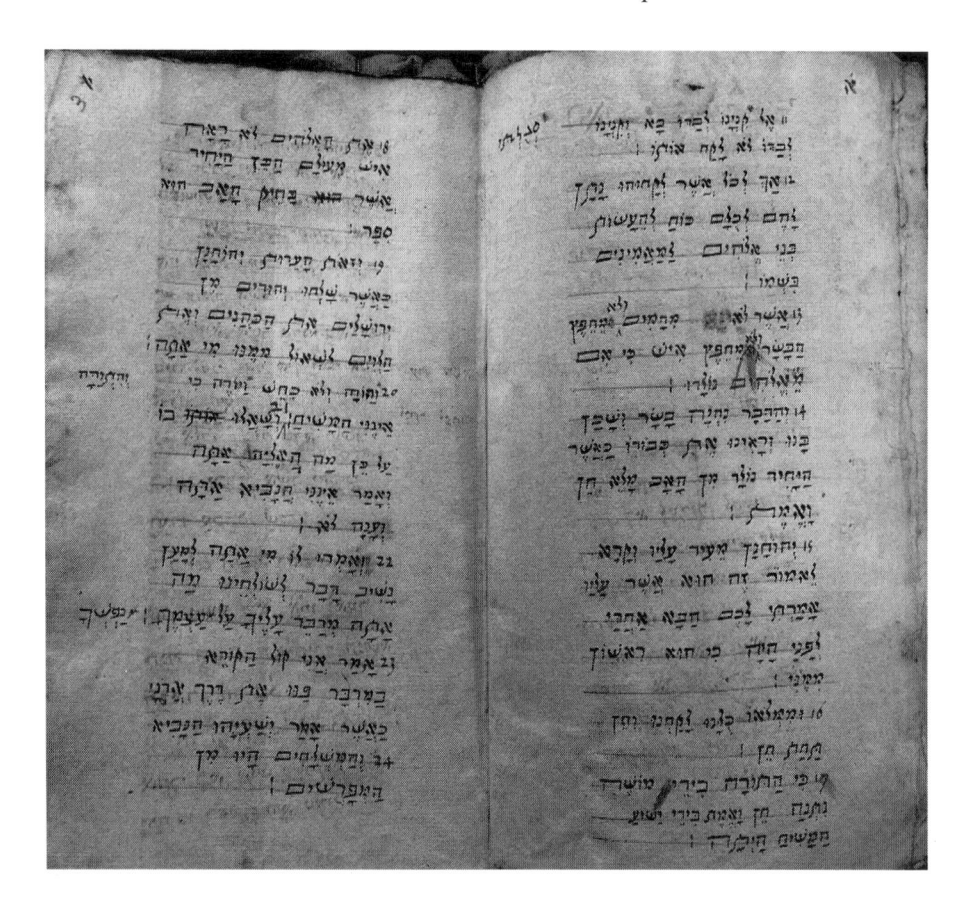

Shem Tov Hebrew Matthew: The Touchstone
Vat. Ebr. 101 (Vaticano Ebreu Manuscrito #101)

The Hebrew Matthew portion of the manuscript is 75 pages. So far this is the only *Hebrew Gospel* that has been translated into English. The translation was done by George Howard - Mercer University Press in 1995. The Shem Tov Manuscript of Hebrew Matthew was entitled *The Touchstone* ['*Evan Bohan'* in Hebrew]. It is an amazing work of twelve chapters only one of which is the Hebrew Matthew. The other chapters discuss differences in the Greek Septuagint translation from the Hebrew text of the Tanakh (Old Testament). This major part of the document has never been translated. The *Shem Tov*, as it is called, was widely copied and recopied among the Messianic communities throughout the centuries. So far we know of 28 manuscripts of the *Shem Tov*. Fourteen of these have been recovered by Nehemia Gordon from Eastern Europe. In 1385, Shem Tov Ibn Shaprut transcribed from *The Hebrew Gospels* - the book of Matthew - in order to add debate annotations. Shem Tov and other Jewish leaders were being forced to debate Christians over the truth of the Gospels. If they lost the debate, they and their whole community would be forced to convert to Christianity. Shem Tov planned to do the same with Mark, Luke and John but never completed them.

Shem Tov Ibn Shaprut
14th century Spain

Vatican Hebrew Manuscript #530
Vat. Ebr. 530 - Framento 11 (Fragment #11)

This fragment is four pages from what was a complete manuscript of *The Hebrew Gospels*. It includes the title pages of both Luke and John. It's importance comes from the fact that it is a new document - although it is clearly from the Hebrew Manuscript Tradition - it does not seem to be copied from the same source document as *The Hebrew Gospels from Catalonia* or *The Cochin Gospels*. If this is true, there was another surviving branch of the original Hebrew manuscript texts of the first century.

Note the small red box in the left margin. In Vat. Ebr. 530 (fragment 11) the name of God - Yehováh - is used throughout including the vowel pointing so there is no doubt as to its correct pronunciation. This partial pageview is from the title page of Luke, the title below says "*First Chapter.*" The first line says "*And it was in the days of Herodos king of Judaea...*" Epiphanius (315=403 AD), the Jewish Christian Bishop of Salamis, cited this as the first line of *The Hebrew Gospel*. This is also the first line in *The Hebrew Gospels from Catalonia* [HGC] in Luke 1:5. Luke verses 1:1-4 are not part of *The Hebrew Gospel*. See *Sons of Zion versus Sons of Greece* for the detailed analysis. Luke 1:1-4, called the prologue to Luke in the *Greek Gospels*, basically says it is a copy of documents from the Apostles. *The Hebrew Gospel of Luke* does not say it is a copy! Therefore, it is more likely to be the original.

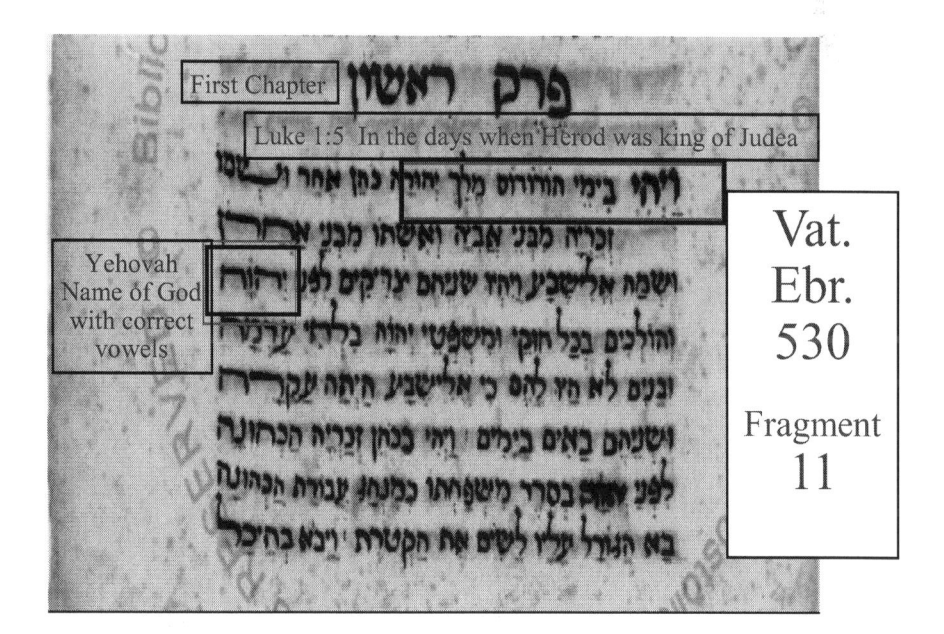

The Hazon Hebrew Manuscript of Revelation
British Library - Sloane Collection Manuscript #273

This manuscript is the first seven pages of Revelation - from chapter one, verse one, to chapter two, verse twelve. Chapter one, verse eight in the red box below reads, *"I am the Aleph and the Tav, said Yehováh Elohim - Who is, Who was, Who is to come, 'HaShaddai' The Almighty."* Note that this manuscript uses the name of God - Yehováh - with the correct vowel pointing, which is often a marker of Messianic scribes. Also, instead of saying the Alpha and Omega, first and last letters of the Greek alphabet, it says Aleph Tav, first and last letters of the Hebrew alphabet. The Aleph Tav (Alpha Omega in Greek) was the phrase used to mean the *'alphabet'* before that word came into use some centuries later. Here, God is literally claiming the alphabet is of Him. See *The Writing of God* for more research evidence of the first alphabet of letter-symbols being given at Mount Sinai.

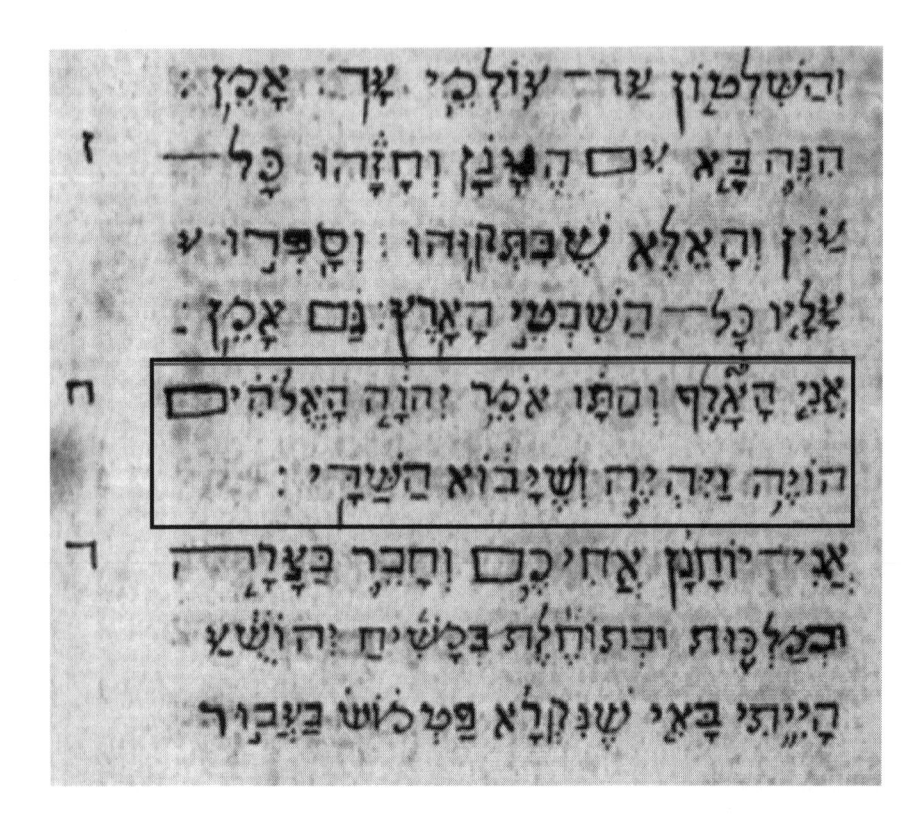

The Hebrew Epistles of James & Jude
British Royal Museum Manuscript #16 A II

These Epistles are Hebrew versions of the Epistles of James and Jude with a Latin dedication to Henry VIII. They are 16th century (est. 1540 AD) manuscripts. They were presented to the British Museum by George II in 1757 from the old Royal Library. They were originally a gift of John Shepreve, the prodigy Hebraist of Oxford, to King Henry VIII. Did they come from original Hebrew manuscripts? Now with the discovery of the Cochin Collection we may be able to ascertain their authenticity, or lack of it, by comparison with the Cochin Hebrew Epistles.

There is also a Hebrew manuscript of 2nd Peter in the British Library. These apostles were Hebrews who did not know Greek (Acts 4:13). They would have written or dictated their letters in Hebrew. There is no reason to dismiss the possibility of original Hebrew Epistles by Peter, James, Jude and John. In fact, that was the most likely outcome. Remember the Messianic Church was predominantly Hebrew during their lifetimes. Their family of faith they would have written to would have been Hebrew. John Shepreve may have had Hebrew sources for his Epistles. Establishing authenticity is the first step for all of these Hebrew manuscripts. That work is now begun.

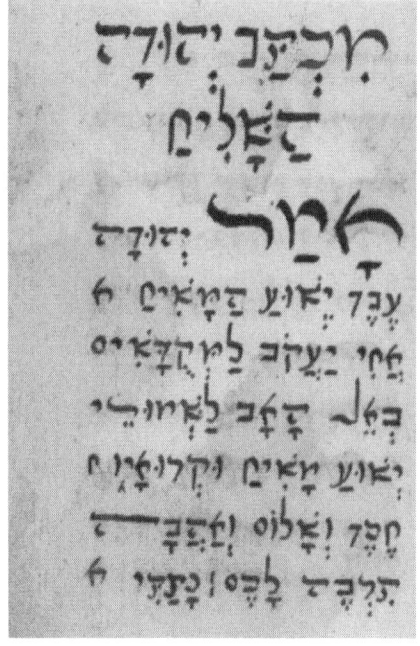

The Received Text of Hebrew Scripture

At the birth of the Reformation, four Messianic Jews played a decisive role that was to impact the Rabbinic Bible, called *The Received Text* of Hebrew Scripture. Hebrew Scripture has the same problems as texts in other languages. Eventually, over time there arise a multitude of manuscripts which do not match. Scribal errors, additions, omissions, translation mistakes and differences all add up to a forest of discrepancies. *"However, there is one text that is accepted in Rabbinic circles and read in synagogues around the world...* **Those behind the final establishment of that Rabbinic Bible were Jews who believed in Jesus!***"*[48]

It was begun by Felix Pratensis. He was born in Italy in the late 1400s, he died in 1539. Pratensis was discovered by Daniel Bomberg who had a Hebrew Press in Venice. Pratensis had an excellent education where he mastered three languages (most likely Hebrew, Greek, and Latin). *"Perhaps due to his prolonged focus on the text of Scripture, he became convinced that Jesus is the Messiah, and trusted in Him for salvation, probably in 1515."*[48] It was Pratensis who *"played a role in introducing his publisher [Bomberg] to his Messiah and instructed him in the faith."*[48] *"The first rabbinic Bible, i.e., the Hebrew text... with full vowel points and accents, accompanied by the Aramaic Targums and major medieval Jewish commentaries - was edited by Felix Pratensis and published by Daniel Bomberg (Venice, 1516)."*[49] **Both Pratensis and Bomberg were Messianics!**

"The second edition, edited by Jacob ben Hayyim ibn Adonijah and issued by Bomberg in four volumes (Venice, 1524/25), **became the prototype of future Hebrew Bibles down to the 20th century.** *It contained a vast text-critical apparatus of Masoretic notes never since equaled in any edition."*[50] *"Building on the labors of Pratensis, Jacob Ibn Adonijah began his preparation for the second edition of the Rabbinic Bible shortly after the first edition had been published. He completed his work in 1524–25. What he was able to accomplish in only seven or eight years is astonishing."*[51]

---

[48]Jim Shibley, 2015, *How Two 16th Century Messianic Jews Impacted Rabbinic Bible Study*, One for Israel website - oneforisrael.org, article presented to the Lausanne Consultation on Jewish Evangelism, 10th Int'l Conference, 2015.
[49]Encyclopedia Britannica, www.britannica.com. [50]*Ibid.* [51]Jim Shibley, 2015.

What is certain is that during the years 1517–1527 Ibn Adoniyah accomplished a truly prodigious amount of work. He edited the whole of the Babylonian Talmud, Rabbi Nathan's Concordance and the *Mishne Torah* of Maimonides. And all the time he was busy traveling, collecting and collating codices preparatory to **publishing the great Rabbinic Bible which was accepted as the authoritative text for four hundred years and more.**[52]

Jacob Ibn Adonijah and his family escaped the Inquisition by fleeing from Spain to Tunisia. After seven years of wandering, Jacob found himself in Venice for his historic encounter with Daniel Bomberg in 1517. As Jacob describes Bomberg: *"God sent a highly distinguished and pious Christian, Daniel Bomberg, to meet me!"*[51] It was said that *"due to the painstaking work of Jacob Ibn Adonijah, the Masoretic Text of the Hebrew Scriptures had been rescued. if not from perdition, at least from centuries of scribal error and neglect."*[53]

Following in the footsteps of his predecessor, Felix Pretensis, **Jacob Ibn Adoniyah, under the influence of the Scripture of *The Received Text in Hebrew*, also became a Messianic believer!** He took a new name after his baptism, Jacob ben Chayim (*Jacob son of Life*). David Ginsburg, editor of the 20th century Rabbinic Bible, said that his work on The Rabbinic Bible, *"was the most powerful auxiliary to the then commencing Reformation!"*[53] *"The Rabbinic Bible of Ben Chayim contained the authoritative text, or Textus Receptus, of the Hebrew Bible and therefore became the basis for most translations from Tyndale until modern times, including the King James version."*[51] **David Ginsburg, the editor, also became a Messianic, changing his name to *Christian* David Ginsburg!**

Some may wonder why the Hebrew Scriptures would be so significant to the Protestant Reformation. Yet, as Felix Pratensis rightly claims in his preface to the first edition, **"the entire superstructure of Christianity rests" on the Hebrew Bible**. This is not even to mention the fact that the New Covenant Scriptures are full of direct quotations and allusions to the Hebrew Scriptures. **The New Testament without the Hebrew Scriptures is like a house without a foundation.**[54]

---

[51] Jim Shibley, 2015, *How Two 16th Century Messianic Jews Impacted Rabbinic Bible Study*. [52] Norman Snaith, 1968, p.viii, Introduction to *The Rabbinic Bible*, Christian D. Ginsburg, ed., KTAV Publishing House, N.Y. [53] *The Rabbinic Bible*, 1968, Introduction. [54] Jim Shibley, 2015

The renewed emphasis on the study of the Old Testament sparked by the Reformation Bibles gave *"rise to the British Restorationist Movement, which later would be known as Christian Zionism.... Ultimately, these ideas found expression in the Balfour Declaration* [by England in 1917], *and this, in turn, ultimately led to the creation of the state of Israel (1948). The role that the translation* [of *The Received Text*] *of the Bible into English played in all of this is undeniable!"*[55] [brackets mine]

Portents for the Future

Despite the triumph of the Reformation we are left with ominous portents for the future! The Roman Church is still clinging to the Inquisition. The Protestant Churches have continued with the same apostasies in the slaughter of those they do not agree with - both heretics and witches. *The Received Text* of Scripture has been recovered, but Martin Luther has come out of the closet as a rabid anti-Semite. Hatred of Hebrews, including Messianics, seems to be baked into the Reformation cake and the soul of Christianity.

The spiritual battle rages with undiminished intensity!

Yet, there is light! The Moravian Revival, a small community of 300 believers at Herrnhut, had changed the world. Can this slender golden thread of Revival save the church? **It is the sole surviving spirit of the Messianic Church!**

---

[55] Jim Shibley, 2015, *How Two 16th Century Messianic Jews Impacted Rabbinic Bible Study*.

Chapter Twelve
Messianic Church Arising!

*The remnant of her seed,
which kept the commandments of Yehovah,
and have the testimony of Yeshua HaMashiach.*
Hebrew N.T. Revelation 12:17

The golden thread of revival weaved itself into the Church throughout the Celtic Revivals, like the Welsh Revival, for example, to the Great Awakening in the American colonies, and many others. We see the blossoming of the seed in the Remnant Church of the Sabbatarians, Puritans, Pilgrims, Seventh-Day Baptists, and Wesley's Methodist Movement sparked by the Moravian Revival now brought to the Americas. Yet the Spirit of God was not the only thing moving.

After the religious wars following the Reformation, an exhausted peace settled upon Europe and, eventually, along with it came an ecumenical effort to establish a version of the Bible that both Catholics and Protestants could embrace. The Codex Sinaiticus had just been discovered by Tischendorf in 1856. That text was hailed as the oldest complete manuscript of Scripture - and therefore the obvious template for the new ecumenical Bible. The Codex Sinaiticus, however, was a copy of the Catholic Bible done by Eusebius in the fourth century. So the Bible Committee of England, followed by those in America and elsewhere, re-romanized the Bible according to the Codex Sinaiticus. **The Reformation Bibles -** *The Received Text* **of the Bible - all were replaced in the twinkling of an eye!**

Many would contest this as unimportant, making a few *'small'* changes to *The Received Text*. Consider the unfolding context of history before making such a judgement. In Germany, we witnessed the rise of German Nationalism - and along with it an intensification of Hebrew hatred - all bolstered by Replacement Theology and Markan Priority - a reworking of the Gospels into an Aryan mold! The result was the Holocaust, a return with vengeance to the hatreds of the past two thousand years. There was no exemption for Messianics in the slaughter of the bHolocaust. They were Hebrews. The Messianic Movement must be seen through the lens of history. **We have created a modern church - schizophrenic in nature - trying to embrace the Messiah and reject him at the same time!**

The Golden Thread of Teshuvah-Revival

"The revival that began with John the Baptist was carried on by Jesus, and even after Jesus' death and resurrection the revival continued through His disciples, beginning on the Day of Pentecost... that revival which carried the Church into the next century."[1] The ministry of Yeshua Ha Maschiach was revivalist, as were most, if not all, of the subsequent Messianic congregations and the Neo-Messianic movements such as the Waldensian, Cathar, and Converso. Revival, or *Teshuvah* - repenting and returning to Yehovah - is a common thread throughout the Bible; occurring in the time of Jacob, Moses, Joshua, Samuel, Asa, Jehoshaphat, Elijah, Jonah, Hezekiah, Josiah, Zerubbabel, Zechariah, Ezra, and Nehemiah. It is also cited many times in *Acts of the Apostles*, in the Epistles and Revelation.

Revival via the Holy Spirit at Pentecost, is the foundation experience of Christianity, *"And suddenly there came a sound from heaven as of a rushing mighty wind, and it filled all of the house where they were sitting. And there appeared unto them cloven tongues like as of fire... And they were all filled with the Holy Spirit"* (Acts 2:1-4). Soon, the multitudes in Jerusalem who had gathered for Shavuot [Pentecost] heard about this. The Apostles spoke to the crowds at the Temple, *"Peter, standing up with the eleven, lifted up his voice and said unto them... This is what was spoken by the prophet Joel... And it shall come to pass... said God, I shall pour out my Spirit upon all flesh"* (Acts 2:14-17). And the people said to the Apostles, *"What shall we do? Then Peter said unto them. Repent, and be baptized every one of you in the name of Yeshua Ha Maschiach for the remission of sins, and you shall receive the gift of the Holy Spirit"* (Acts 2:37-38 from *The Hebrew Gospels*). *"And the same day, there were added unto them about three thousand souls!"* (Acts 2:41). **Teshuvah-Revival was, and remains, the life's blood of the Messianic-Apostolic Church!**

What sparks revival? More importantly - what enables it to change our lives permanently? **The Holy Spirit comes like a high tide lifting all in its path. However, that tide will return from whence it came, stranding us once again on the cold wet shore of our previous life. It does not have to be so!** It is but a stage in making believers the bringers of the light via the Spirit.

---

[1]Chet & Phyllis Swearingen, 2021, from their website https://romans1015.com, *Accounts of Revival: 27 A.D, Revival Under Jesus and His Disciples*.

Yeshua prepared his Apostles before he ascended, saying *"Wait for the promise of the Father... You will be baptized by the Holy Spirit not many days hence"* (Acts 1:4-5). *"They returned to Jerusalem* [where]... *They all continued with one accord in prayer and supplication."* (Acts 1:12,14) At Herrnhut they met together and agreed upon an intercessionary prayer and prayed continually for three months. In the Celtic Revivals sparked by Saint Patrick one can assume that the continual prayer (*laus perennis*) they dedicated themselves to for three centuries after the arrival of the Shekinah glory, was started even before it happened. Unity of prayer is a crucial element of revival not only to spark it, but also to maintain its blessings over time.

Unity of prayer must include consent. In 1662, the English Parliament passed the Act of Uniformity - the state church - the Church of England required a common clergy, common rites, and a book of common prayer. Much of the new approved religion resembled Catholicism. It was an attempt by Queen Elizabeth to find common ground among her subjects. It led to the decertification of more than two thousand clergy who would not conform. Resistance was especially intense in Celtic Scotland where many were martyred. It remains a scar on the public consciousness. This was Protestant against Protestant violence. **This was not unity of prayer. It was oppression!**

> It is to be said, however, that this work to a great extent receded. **The Reformation itself needed reforming**; inherited remnants of the papacy brought forth their... fruits. Persecution acted a painful part! The fires of martyrdom were frequently lighted in France, Holland and Switzerland, while in England the severity of Elizabeth's government was so great that the separatists [like the Puritans] of all classes were scattered, and forced to hold their meetings in the utmost privacy. James I, though affecting zeal for Presbyterianism while in Scotland, was as bigoted and despotic as Elizabeth. *'I will make them conform,'* said he [of the Puritans]. *'or I will hurry them out of the land, or else worse'*...[2] [brackets mine]
>
> This was all the working of the Act of Uniformity, passed in 1662, and in force about 25 years. By it some two thousand ministers were ejected from their pulpits... '***These inhuman decrees but testify to... the persecutions of the saints***, *especially in Scotland, in the attempt to enforce the Uniformity Act.*'[2]

[2] Henry Fish, 1874, 2011:287-310, *Handbook of Revivals*, Counted Faithful Pub.

At Herrnhut, a tiny community of 300, 24/7 continual prayer was maintained for more than a century. In Ireland, it was maintained for more than three centuries. In both cases it was only broken off by military force. Continual praise and prayer at one time happened in the Jerusalem Temple. When we take Yehovah for granted and stop welcoming His Presence - He leaves and goes somewhere where He is wanted. It is a sobering lesson. In Ezekiel, we have the narrative of this happening.

"The hand of Yehovah fell upon me... and lifted me up between the earth and the heavens... And behold the glory of the God of Israel was there" (Ez 8:1-4). *"He said unto me, Son of man,* **'Do you see what they do, the great abominations that the house of Israel commits here, in order that I should go far off from my sanctuary?'***... "Go in, and behold the wicked abominations that they do here. So I went in and saw...* **all the idols of the house of Israel***, portrayed upon the wall round about. And there stood before them [the statues of beasts, idols and pagan images] seventy men of the ancients of the house of Israel... every man in the chambers of his imagery... for they say 'Yehovah sees us not; Yehovah has forsaken the earth'.... Then He brought me to the door of the gate of Yehovah's house... and* **behold there sat women weeping for Tammuz!***... And He brought me into the inner court of Yehovah's house, and behold* **at the door of the temple of Yehovah*** ...* **were about twenty five men** *with their backs toward the temple of Yehovah, and their faces toward the east,* **and they worshiped the sun***..."*(Ez 8:6-16). Ezekiel was taken into the **Holy of Holies** to the Ark of the Covenant, *"Then the glory of Yehovah went up... and stood over the* **threshold of the house***...* **Then the glory of Yehovah departed from off the threshold of the house***... And the cherubims lifted up their wings, and mounted from the earth in my sight... and every one stood at the* **door of the east gate** *of Yehovah's house... Then He said... Son of man, these are the men that devise mischief, and give wicked counsel in this city... this city is the cauldron and we are the meat. Therefore prophesy against them, O Son of man. And the spirit of Yehovah fell upon me, and said unto me, Speak!"* (Ez 10:4-11:5). **"And the glory of Yehovah went up from the midst of the city, and stood upon the mountain which is on the east side of the city.** *Afterward, the Spirit took me up and* **brought me... by the Spirit of God into Chaldea,** *to them of the captivity."* (Ez 11:23-24).

Let me unpack this long passage for you. Ezekiel is told by Yehovah to witness the abominations of the high holy men of Israel. They are worshiping images and statues of sacred beasts like the Egyptians and Babylonians do. The women are weeping for Tammuz, a ritual of Ashtoreth (Easter). The men are worshiping the sun god. All these rituals are part of the counterfeit religion which moved from region to region taking on different names but always the same religion. You have the sun god; Babylonian Nimrod Ba'al, Egyptian Ra, Greek Helios, Roman Sol Invicta. The *'queen of heaven'* called - Semiramis, Easter, Inanna, Isis, Astarte, and Ashtaroth. One also has the son of the sun god; Tammuz, Horus, Phaethon, and Mithra. The leaders of Israel are breaking the first commandment, *"You shall have no other gods before me!"* It was expressly forbidden by Yehovah, **"Do not inquire... How did these nations serve their gods? I will do likewise. You shall not do so unto Yehovah your god!** *For every abomination to Yehovah, which He hates, have they done unto their gods. For even their sons and their daughters they have burnt in the fire to their gods!"* (Deut. 12:30-1).

Yehovah takes Ezekiel even into the sanctuary of the ark of the Covenant. Then as He shows Ezekiel the abominations one by one, Yehovah removes his presence from the Temple. First He detaches from the sanctuary as He first told Ezekiel He must do - to go far away from the uncleanness! Then He hovers over the threshold of the house of Yehovah, then He departs from there and goes to the door of the east gate of the Temple. He shows Ezekiel the evil men of the city and instructs him to prophesy. It is apparently fruitless, and Yehovah rises up from the midst of the city and hovers over the mountain to the east. Then Yehovah transports Ezekiel east to Chaldea, amid the captives of Babylon, from which Daniel will continue Yehovah's work.

So Yehovah sent a prophet, Ezekiel, to warn of His departure. Then He stops at several places in His departure before taking His glory from the Temple, from Jerusalem, and from Israel. Yehovah is waiting to see if the people would awaken to His departure and turn back to Him. There is a remnant that cries over the blasphemies in the Temple. Nonetheless, the image conveyed is one of a spiritually dead city. The Israelites have turned their backs on Yehovah to worship pagan gods. So Yehovah goes to Daniel and the remnant in Chaldea. **Do you live in such a city? Do we live in such a time? Have we adopted pagan feast days and rituals and rejected Yehovah?**

Return to Revival

Often, the spark of Teshuvah-Revival is facilitated by a single person who has been anointed by the Holy Spirit - Peter at Pentecost, Patrick in Ireland, Zinzendorf at Herrnhut, and Jonathan Edwards during the Great Awakening Revivals of the New England colonies (1730-1740s). Rees Howells was just such a spark in the later Welsh Revival of 1904. His narrative serves as a guide to the revival experience.

There have been many revivalist writers, like Jonathan Edwards, who have chronicled the outpouring of the Holy Spirit upon their congregations. Howells, unlike other revivalist writers, narrated the ongoing refinement of the spirit within him after the outpouring of the Holy Spirit from God. The outpouring is only the first step - discipleship is needed to grow the faith of new converts beyond the stage of suckling milk. **The Holy Spirit descends upon those whose hearts are right - it is not a divine sign that their doctrine is right!** Believers generally become Bible scholars after their conversion, not before. Far too many get stuck on the first step, if so then the Spirit comes and the Spirit goes, leaving them with lives that are little changed.

Rees Howells was born in Wales in 1879. He was, by all accounts, an exemplary young man, devout and endowed with a generosity of spirit. He did not receive the baptism of the Holy Spirit until he emigrated to the United States at the age of 22. Rees had a bout with typhoid fever and nearly died. Facing his mortality he realized that his faith, although sincere, was still superficial. As Howells put it, *"I found that I had only an historical Christ, not a personal Savior that would take me to the other side."*[3] From that point on he vowed to search continually, *"to find a man to show him the way to eternal life."*[3]

Maurice Reuben - Messianic Preacher

Rees made a 100-mile journey to Pittsburgh to hear the testimony of Maurice Reuben, who had been a manager of Solomon and Reuben, his wealthy family's huge department store in Pittsburgh. One day Reuben had an encounter with a buyer.

---

[3] Norman Grubb, 1966:p.25, *Rees Howells: Intercessor*, Lutterworth Press, UK.

There was so much joy pouring forth from the man that Reuben had to inquire. The man said that he had been born again. *"In my second birth I accepted the Lord Jesus Christ and was born of God!"*[4] The Holy Spirit was where the joy was coming from! Maurice was deeply impacted. He obtained a New Testament, which was forbidden to Jews by their religion. **For the first time, Maurice Reuben realized that Jesus and all of his followers were Jews!** He read what the Messiah said to the rich young Jew who came to him seeking salvation, *"Sell all that you have and give it to the poor... then come and follow me"* (Luke 18:22). Maurice was under conviction - he was a rich Jew of the twentieth century, *"reading of the Savior's dealings with a rich Jew of the first century."*[4] Maurice had everything to lose - his ancestral religion, his fortune, his family and friends. *"One day, on his way to the store, Reuben heard a voice repeating... John 14:6 'I am the way, the truth, and the life.'* **He accepted Christ and entered into life at that moment!***"*[4]

The will of Reuben's father stipulated that if he changed religion he would lose every penny of his inheritance. His brothers rejected him. His wife left him. Detectives appeared at his door and took him to the Police Station - where doctors came and inquired about the voice he had heard. He was committed to an insane asylum. Maurice prayed to God and was given a vision of Calvary and every stage of the suffering of the Messiah. Then the Messiah spoke to him. *"Must I bear the cross alone?"* From that moment Maurice Reuben was freed. He began to pray for the other patients in the asylum, and his family. Two weeks later his brother came to visit him and offered $70,000, his part of the inheritance - a princely sum in 1904 - if he would leave Pittsburgh so as not to embarrass the family. Maurice refused. He realized his commitment was not about a medical condition. Six weeks later, concerned Christians brought his asylum commitment to court. The judge was a Christian who released him.

Maurice Reuben *"won many converts, but for two years he hardly had a square meal. A year later his wife came to see him at a camp meeting and was converted, and for the first time he saw his little boy who had been born after his wife left him. She was willing to make her home with him again, if only he would earn a living as other Christians did."*[5]

---

[4]Norman Grubb, 1966:p.26, *Rees Howells: Intercessor.*   [5] *Ibid.*, Grubb, p. 27.

Maurice prayed over the request, which seemed so reasonable, but his petition was refused. Yehovah had more in store for him than the life of a wage-earner. He said goodbye to his wife and child with bitter tears. But as the train left the station he was filled with an overwhelming joy for his surrender.

"He did not see his wife for another three years. Then, in another camp meeting, she too had a revelation of the cross... whereas before as a believer she had not been willing to share the sacrificial life of her husband - if it would be for God's glory - she would now be willing to beg her bread from door to door. They were reunited and she became a wonderful coworker for him in his ministry."[6]

Rees Howells' Journey

"One thing that had hindered Rees Howells from coming through before was that while people said they were born again, he could not see that their lives were better than his. How then could he be convinced that they had something that he had not? But he had sometimes said to the Lord, **'If I ever see someone who is living the Sermon on the Mount, I will give in.'** *Before Reuben came to the end of his story,* **the Lord said to Rees, 'Is this your man?'"**[6] At that moment Rees had a vision of the cross and the full realization that the Messiah had died for him.

"Then he spoke to me and said, 'Behold, I stand at the door and knock. May I come into you, as I came into Reuben and took the place of wife and son and home and store and world? Will you accept me?' 'Yes, I replied, and He came in, and that moment I was changed. I was born into another world. I found myself in the Kingdom of God, and the Creator became my Father. That night I received the gift of eternal life, the gift that money cannot buy!'"[7]

Rees received the message to return home to Wales. He spoke of this day as his spiritual birthday, the most outstanding day of his life. **"He never forgot that it was... through a [Messianic] Jew that he found the Savior, and that he owed a debt to God's chosen people!"**[8]

---

[6]Norman Grubb, 1966:p.28, *Rees Howells: Intercessor.* [7]*Ibid,* p. 29. [8]*Ibid,* p. 30.

The Onward Journey

There had been many Celtic Revivals - since the time of Saint Patrick the remnant seed had been sown far and wide in those areas of Ireland, Scotland, Wales, England, even unto Germany and Bohemia. Rees Howells' grandparents had been converted in the Welsh Revival of 1859. In 1904, the later Welsh Revival was called the *'Great Revival!'* Rees Howells had just been equipped by Yehovah to play a great part. *"In a short while the whole of the country was aflame! Every church was stirred to its depths. Strong men were in tears of penitence, and women moved with a new fervor. People were overpowered with the Spirit as on the day of Pentecost... Often they had to first pray out the hindrances to blessing: disobedience and unforgiving hearts were two sins that were constantly dealt with."*[9]

"Under the influence of the Spirit there was an irresistible power... *Whole congregations were melted, and people were crying out in agony of soul, 'What must we do to be saved?' ...But the real problem arose as the revival proceeded and thousands were added to the churches. There were more children born then there were nurses to tend them. The establishing of the converts became the greatest need, which if not met would be the most dangerous weakness of the Revival."*[10] *"As enthusiasm abated there were bound to be many who had depended more upon feelings and had not yet learned to have their faith solidly grounded in the Word of God."*[11]

The experienced believers in the church realized they had not yet been *'imbued with power from on high!'* They did not yet know the secret of the power of service - how to disciple once the Spirit abated. God will equip those he calls, but he must also empower others to be the equippers. This had not yet happened. As Howells later explained, *"The Intercession of the Holy Ghost for the saints in this present evil world must be made through believers filled with the Holy Ghost. (Romans 8:26-27)* **Oh the tragedy, to be helpless in front of the enemy when he was sifting young converts like wheat!"**[11] **Many converts simply returned to their old lives.** *"They had the joy before they had the power, so joy was no proof of that endowment of the Spirit. We had that same joy in the Revival - unspeakable joy - but at the same time we felt the lack of power for service!"*[12]

[9]Norman Grubb, 1966:p.31, *Rees Howells*. [10]*Ibid*,p. 32. [11]*Ibid*,p. 33. [12]*Ibid*,p. 34.

What was Missing?

In a train on the way to a conference in Llandrindod, Wales, Rees heard a voice speak to him, "*'When you return, you will be a new man.' 'But I am a new man,' he protested. 'No,' came the answer. 'You are a child!'* "[13] Rees' dilemma is reflected in the words of Paul in Hebrews 5:12-14, *"For this time you ought to be teachers, but you have need that one teach you again what are the first principles of the oracles of God. And you are become such as have need of milk, and not of strong meat.* **For every one that uses milk is unskillful in the word of righteousness,** *for he is a babe. Strong meat belongs to them that are of full age, even those who by reason of use have their senses exercised to discern both good and evil!"* So Paul is saying what Rees Howells has been seeing, that the milk of the Spirit - as joyous and divine as it truly is - is only the first step, like as we would feed a babe in arms. One must grow in the Word.

Rees listened to the speaker at the conference expound on Ephesian 2:1-6, *"You has he quickened... and has raised us up... and made us sit together in heavenly places with Christ Jesus."* Rees knew that he had been quickened through his baptism of the Holy Spirit, but he had not been raised up to the heavenly place of power referred to in Scripture. At that moment, the Holy Spirit appeared to him offering to indwell in him that he might ascend to those heavenly places. He spoke to him exactly as a person and Rees Howells saw a vision of the Glorified Lord, *"As truly as I had seen the Crucified Christ and the Risen Christ, I now saw the Glorified Christ, and the same voice I had heard on the train said to me, 'Would you like to sit there with Him? There is a place for you.' ... I knew now what it meant to be glorified... and I was dazzled!"*[13] There was only one condition. He had to die to himself for the Holy Spirit to indwell in him. There could not be two wills contending in the same body. There was only one way - unconditional surrender of self! Howells struggled for five days with the decision. For days he cried his heart out for the coveted things he would lose. One by one, the Spirit walked him through the things he would lose, love of money, ambition, reputation, sharing his life with a mate, and other things. *"What is permissible to an ordinary man, will not be permissible to you."*[14]

---

[13]Norman Grubb, 1966:p.36, *Rees Howells: Intercessor.* [14]*Ibid,*p. 39.

The Holy Spirit *"was not going to take any superficial surrender. He put his finger on each part of my self-life, and I had to decide in cold blood. He could never take a thing away until I gave my consent. Then the moment I gave it, some purging took place (Isaiah 5:6-7), and I could never touch that thing again... Day by day the dealing went on. He was coming in as God, and I had lived as a man."*[15]

It came time for the final answer. *"The life I will live in you will be one hundred percent for others... Now are you ready?"*[16] Rees came to the ultimate dilemma. *"How can self be willing to give up self?"*[17] It did not seem possible. This was the moment when the Savior, in his own human body, was sweating blood. *"Then the Spirit spoke again, 'If you can't be willing, would you like Me to help you? Are you willing to be made willing?' "*[17] Howells had been given a deadline of 6 o'clock to make his decision. He would never be offered this choice again. *"It was one minute to six. I bowed my head and said, 'Lord, I am willing.' "*[17] The Holy Spirit entered into him within the hour.

" **'Immediately,' said Rees, 'I was transported into another realm, within that sacred veil where the Father, the Savior, and the Holy Ghost live. There I heard God speaking to me, and I have lived there ever since**.' "[17] *"An eyewitness tells us that no words can describe the little meeting in the house that night, the glory of God came down... Then from 9 pm to 2:30 am it was 'nothing but the Holy Ghost speaking things I had never dreamed of and exalting the Savior.'"*[17] *"The Holy Ghost had come in 'to abide forever.' The feeling I had was 'He brought me to the banqueting house, and His banner over me was love.' It is impossible to describe the floods of joy that followed!"*[18] **"It was the first stream of those promised rivers which Jesus said, flow out of those in whom the Spirit dwells**."[18]

Howells' biographer, Norman Grubb, in his first encounter with Rees Howells in 1928, said of him, *"Light simply poured into my soul as he took time to tell me about some of the Lord's inner dealings with him!"*[19] Rees Howells founded the Bible College of Wales, devoted to discipleship. Howells exemplified the '*remnant seed*' which carries the light of the Spirit wherever it goes, sparking Teshuvah-Revival in its path!

[15]Norman Grubb, 1966:p.39. [16]*Ibid*,p. 41. [17]*Ibid*,p. 42. [18]*Ibid*,p. 43. [19]*Ibid*,p. 7.

Headwaters of American Evangelicalism

"The combined influence of Continental Pietism and Scots-Irish Presbyterianism... joined with New England Puritanism... [formed] *the headwaters of American evangelicalism."*[20] Evangelicalism, often called the *'religion of the heart,'* is a revivalist movement that has not abated to this day. All of these denominational movements contain strains of their Messianic foundations. Lutheran Pietism, an outgrowth of Reformation Revival, was the religion that prepared Count Zinzendorf to spark the Moravian Revival of the Bohemian Reform Church. The Scots-Irish still carried the ingrained beliefs and practices of the Messianic St. Patrick - which sparked not only their primitive revivalist worship but also their unique music, bluegrass gospel. (The word *primitive* is used in the sense of being the *original* form of worship.) Puritanism, strongly based on the Old Testament covenant contract between Yehovah and His people, provided the concepts for the U.S. Constitution. Above all, **the revivalism blossoming periodically throughout the country was, and still remains, the life's blood of the original church!**

The Committee to Rewrite the Bible

On February 10, 1870, the Southern Convocation of the Church of England issued a resolution to revise the King James Version of the Bible. **It was specified that only clear errors were to be changed.** The Northern Convocation of the Church of England, from the Celtic northern areas, refused to participate condemning it as a risky endeavor. Eighteen members of the Southern Convocation were elected, divided into the Old and the New Testament groups. They were authorized to invite other scholars to participate. The New Testament contingent swelled to twenty five members. There was a history leading up to this.

The violent struggle that followed the Reformation had led to a stalemate. Now the spiritual warfare turned covert rather than overt. Many devout English Catholics were recruited for the Jesuit colleges, educated and indoctrinated, then sent back into England posing as Protestants to effect change from within the Church of England and the English universities, especially Cambridge and Oxford.[21]

---

[20] Thomas Kidd, 2007:location 571, *The Great Awakening*, Yale Univ. Press, US.
[21] Edmond Paris, 1983, *Secret History of the Jesuits*, Chick Publications, CA.

By the 1870s, English society had endured centuries of intellectual warfare between Catholics and Protestants. Much of this conflict was initiated through the Tractarian Society and the Oxford Movement. The Reformation was over, but the reform hardly begun. Dissention and debate raged around every religious question. Desire for any sort of peace grew stronger. It was in this atmosphere the Revision Committee was approved.

Among the members of the committee was W.F. Moulton who played an influential and energetic role in selecting the additional scholars who would participate. Dr. Moulton placed more authority on the Latin Vulgate than the Greek texts used in the King James Version. In his own words, *"The Latin translation [of the Vulgate], being derived from manuscripts more ancient than any we now possess... its testimony is in many cases confirmed by Greek manuscripts which have been discovered or examined since the 16th century."*[22] [brackets mine] I am sure it has not escaped the reader that this is a prominent Protestant, in a position of authority to revise the Protestant 1611 King James Version of the Bible, who thinks the Catholic Latin Vulgate version of the Bible is superior. If that is in any doubt, here is Dr. Moulton's opinion of the Catholic Jesuit New Testament in English, called the Rhemish Version, of 1582. *"The Rhemish Testament agrees with the best critical editions of the present day."*[23] Since Moulton was responsible for hand-picking most of the scholars invited to participate - it is easy to see how a Catholic tilt was established on the Revision Committee.

"When the English New Testament Committee met, it was immediately apparent what was going to happen. Though for ten long years the iron rule of silence kept the public ignorant of what was going on behind closed doors, the story is now known. The first meeting of the Committee found itself a divided body [but] **the majority being determined to incorporate into the proposed revision the latest and most extreme higher criticism!** *The majority was dominated and carried along by a triumvirate of Hort, Westcott, and Lightfoot."*[24]

"It was not until the work of revision was all over, that the world awoke..." [25]

---

[22] W.F. Moulton, 1878, reprint 2018:p.184, *The History of the English Bible*, Forgotten Books, London.   [23] *Ibid.*, in the same place, Moulton, p.185.
[24] Benjamin Wilkinson, 1930, reprint 2014:p.103, *Our Authorized Bible Vindicated*, Teach Services Publishing, USA.   [25] *Ibid.*, Wilkinson, p.101.

"Westcott and Hort, who had worked together before this for twenty years - in bringing out a Greek New Testament constructed on principles which deviated the farthest ever yet known from The Received Text."[26] Westcott had already written to Hort, *"the rules though liberal are vague, and the interpretation of them will depend upon decided action at first."*[27] These new members, supposedly bound by the rules of the resolution, *"threw the rules completely aside by interpreting them with the widest latitude."*[28] So much for only correcting clear errors.

The *Received Text* is based on the vast majority of Greek texts extant. These manuscripts are in close agreement with each other even over 1500 years of history. *"These MSS have in agreement with them, by far the vast majority of numbers. So vast is this majority that [even] the enemies of The Received Text admit that ninety nine hundredths (99%) of all Greek MSS are of this class, while 100% of the Hebrew MSS are for The Received Text."*[29] Against this preponderance of evidence we have two Catholic manuscripts, the *Codex Sinaiticus* and the *Codex Vaticanus*, which, it is argued, are the oldest surviving compilations of the Bible.

The fact is that Westcott and Hort, along with their allies, *"came prepared to effect a systematic change in the Protestant Bible."*[28] **Hort wrote back to Westcott referring to,** *"that vile and villainous Textus Receptus!"*[30] Westcott responded that the chairman of the Committee *"seems to me quite capable of accepting heartily, and adopting personally a thorough scheme,"*[31] that is, to rewrite the King James Bible.

In the minority was Frederick Scrivener. Dr. Scrivener was **the foremost scholar of the Greek New Testament** and its history, at that time. There was constant intense debate between Schrivener and Hort over the text. It was a prolonged duel between the two and their backers. In the end it was the vote which determined the changes and *"Dr. Scrivener was continuously and systematically outvoted,"*[32] along with his supporters.

---

[26] George Salmon, 1897:pp.10-11, *Some Thoughts on the Textual Criticism of the New Testament*, John Murray Co., London. [27] Samuel Hemphill, 1906:p.44, *A History of the Received Version of The New Testament*, E. Stock Co, London.
[28] Ben Wilkinson, 2014:p.104, *Our Authorized Bible Vindicated*. [29] *Ibid.*,p.13.
[30] William Sanday, 1897:p.211, *The Life & Letters of Fenton Hort*, Oxford, U.K.
[31] Arthur Westcott, 1905:p393, *Life & Letters of Brooke Westcott*, MacMillan,NY.
[32] Wilkinson, 2014:p.104.

Results of the Revision Committee

"*The **Wescott-Hort** generalship moved forward, changing the divine Word to bear the impress of their doctrines, until they had **changed the Greek in 5,337 places, and the English of the King James in 36,000 places!**"*[33] Let us look at a handful of these issues so it will be evident some are substantive changes.

"*The tradition of celebrating 'Holy Week' - 'Good Friday to Easter Sunday' is the most contentious example of differing interpretation of the Gospel Scriptures.*"[34] It is drawn from the '*sign of Jonah*' in Matthew 12. "***It was the most repeated (3 times), the only prophet Yeshua associates himself with by name (Matthew 12:41), and the sole prophecy upon which Yeshua declared his authenticity may be judged!***" [34]

> An evil and adulterous generation seeks after a sign; and there shall be no sign given to it but the sign of the prophet Yonah: **for as Yonah was three days and three nights in the great fish's belly; so shall the Son of Man be three days and three nights in the heart of the earth.** (Matthew 12:39-40)

The problem of interpretation arises with the use of the phrase, '*on the third day he will be raised to life*" as it is said in various verses. It is even cited as coming from Yeshua himself in Luke 24:46, "*This is what is written: The Messiah will suffer and rise from the dead on the third day...*" In English this could mean 1) Friday, 2) Saturday, 3) Sunday - the third day. But Yeshua said three full days and nights as we see in the chart below.[35]

Passover 31 AD	Wednesday April 25	Thursday	Friday	Sabbath	Sunday
NIGHT					
DAY					

"*The statement in Mark 8:31 that 'The Son of Man must suffer many things... and be killed and <u>after three days</u> rise again,' seems to involve a chronological difficulty, and **some copyists changed the phrase to the more familiar expression <u>'on the third day</u>**,*"[36] which was enshrined in the new Version.

---

[33] Benjamin Wilkinson, 2014:p.138, *Our Authorized Bible Vindicated*. [34] Miles Jones, 2021:p.188, *Sons of Zion vs Sons of Greece*, v.1. [35] *Ibid.*, p.189. [36] Bruce Metzger & Bart Ehrman, 2005:p.264, *The Text of the New Testament*, Oxford.

The *'Good Friday - Easter Sunday'* scenario assumes, for one thing, that Pesach (Passover) was on a Friday. It was in 33 AD - but not in 31 AD. Even in 33 AD, the argument wrongly assumes that Friday and Sunday can be counted as partial days. Yeshua was put into the tomb at twilight, which cannot count as a day. Also, both Matthew (28:1) and Mark (16:2) are clear on Sunday. *"At the end of the Sabbath, as it began to dawn, toward the first day of the week [Sunday], came Mary Magdalene and the other Mary..."* the stone was already rolled away and the angel informed them that Yeshua was already risen and gone. Mark reads the same, *"And very early in the morning the first day of the week, they came unto the sepulcher at the rising of the sun..."* and Yeshua Ha Mashiach was already gone!

Passover 33 AD	Wednesday	Thursday	Friday April 3	Sabbath	Easter Sunday
NIGHT					
DAY			X		X

This is all part of some hugely important controversies about Scripture.[37] It is used to validate changing the Sabbath from Saturday to the *'Lord's Day'* Sunday. It is also used to transform and extend the ministry of Yeshua from *"the acceptable year of Yehovah"* (Isaiah 61:2) to a 3½ year ministry. **The very first act of Yeshua's public ministry was to read from the Isaiah scroll in the Synagogue and call all present as witnesses to the *"year of Yehovah's favor"*[37]** which was changed to *"the acceptable year of the Lord."* Readers may have differing beliefs upon these monumental questions, however we can all agree rewriting Scripture to support a bias is not the answer.

You may remember the impetus for the Reformation was the selling of indulgences. Indulgences were even sold to get the dead out of Purgatory and into Heaven. Martin Luther rightly claimed that the Church had no authority over the afterlife. In the KJV 1st Peter 4:6, it states, *"For this cause was the gospel preached, even to those that are* [now] *dead."* The New Revised Version says, *"For unto this end was the gospel preached even unto the dead,"* claiming church powers *"even unto the dead!"*

---

[37] These arguments are far more adequately covered in *Sons of Zion vs Sons of Greece*, vol 1, ch.10. [38] *"The year of Yehovah's favor'* is the correct translation. *"The acceptable year of the Lord"* is the translation used in the Revised Version.

Other changes range from trivial to highly significant to capricious. *"In many places in the Gospels there is mention of 'prayer and fasting...' In Matthew 17:21 [fasting] is entirely omitted."*[39] This should not be thought of as a small thing. The three principal tools in the Messiah's spiritual tool kit were prayer, fasting, and meditation. Because of omissions like this, modern believers typically only incorporate one of the three, prayer, into their spiritual practices.

In the KJV Luke 9:55-56, it says *"You know not what manner of spirit you are of,* **for the Son of man is not come to destroy men's lives, but to save them!"** The highlighted portion is omitted from the Revised Version. Why is this important? In *Sons of Zion vs Sons of Greece*, ch.11, p.219-222, we discussed insertions by later Greek editors into the parable of the talents in Luke. The parable is detailed in thirty verses in Matthew 25. This was the original Gospel account made by an Apostle who was an eyewitness. In Luke 19, we find elements of a different story inserted into the parable of the talents, causing John Chrysosthom, in the fourth century, to make this incredible statement:

God always hated the Jews. It is incumbent upon all Christians to hate the Jews... *When animals are unfit... they are marked for slaughter, and this is the very thing which the Jews have experienced...* **This is why Christ said, 'As for my enemies, who did not want me to reign over them, bring them here and slay them before me'"** (Lk 19:27).[40]

So the Greek Christ has now become a bringer of hatred and death! This is a transformation of our Savior that I cannot accept! Does this resonate in your soul as the true message of the Messiah? This insertion into the parable of the talents, only in Luke 19:27, has long been used as a justification for oppression, torture, and execution of Messianics and others. It is an entirely different story inserted into the parable in Luke by later Greek editors - which is totally opposite the parable in Matthew! You can see the declaration by Yeshua **"I did not come to destroy men's lives, but to save them!"** does not fit with the Greco-Roman Church's claim of authority to '*slay enemies.*'

[39] Dublin Review, July, 1881. [40] Catholic Encyclopedia, *John Chrysothom.*

The Name of God

I am a text critic, which should be clear to anyone who has read this far. **I always keep in mind that only God's truth is inerrant, not man's truth!** We should be critical of the agendas of those who would change the text of the Word to enforce their doctrinal beliefs. Textual criticism is a good tool, but it can be misused and taken too far. The original 1611 King James Version used the name of God, written *Jehovah*, almost 7,000 times in the KJV Bible. The spelling came from German, where the J letter represents the Y sound, so it is a reasonably correct rendering of the Sacred Name. Look in your Bible today and see if the Sacred Name is represented even once as YHVH, or Yehovah, or Jehovah. This is the result of *higher text criticism*!

The Sacred Name of Yehovah has been erased from the Bible!

The American Committee was *"put in the hands of Dr. Phillip Schaff of the Union Theological Seminary in New York City... The American Committee had no deciding vote on points of revision. As soon as portions of the Holy Book were revised by the English committees, they were sent to the American Committee for confirmation or amendment."*[41] The American Committee was nothing more than a reviewing body, selected by the English Revision Committee. The fact that they offered so few suggestions indicates how similar were the views of Dr. Schaff and Dr. Hort. Dr. Schaff's proclivities were well known.

Hort wrote to Wescott, *"A most singular movement is taking place among the German 'Reformation' settled in America, the center of the movement being Mercersburg."*[42] *"The 'Mercersburg Movement,' or the 'Mercersburg Theology,' made a revolutionary and permanent change in American Theological colleges and American Theology... The outstanding leader... was Dr. Phillip Schaff... It was in 1844 that Dr. Schaff, still a young man, arrived from Germany to assume his duties as Professor of Church History and Biblical Literature in the Theological Seminary of Mercersburg."*[43] **Schaff's textual criticism was condemned as Romanizing, anti-Scriptural, and anti-Protestant!**

---

[41]Benjamin Wilkinson, 1930, 2014:p.103, *Our Authorized Bible Vindicated*.
[42]William Sanday, 1897:vol.1, p.177, *The Life & Letters of Fenton Hort*, Oxford.
[43] Wilkinson, 2014:pp.142-143.

Phillip Schaff's major work was *The History of the Apostolic Church*. It would be hard to write a history more openly admiring of the Papacy. *"In classifying the sources of history, he puts in the first rank the 'official letters, decrees, and bulls of Popes,' pronouncing them 'pure original utterances of history.'"*[44] Schaff avows the authority of the Church as springing from the primacy of Peter as the first Pope. *"The claims of the Papacy are well known to center there!"*[45]

We examined this issue in chapter five. The claim of the Roman Church to Apostolic Succession via Peter as the first Pope has been refuted. The fact is that Peter never set foot in Rome. There is no record of it whatsoever. Scripture certainly does not support that claim. Peter's last letter came from Babylon. Supporters of the *'Peter the Pope'* scenario claim that *Babylon* was a code word for *Rome*. Interesting, but there is a record that Peter was actually in Babylon, not Rome. Paul says he was abandoned by all in Rome, except Luke. Paul does not mention Peter in his last letter from Rome, unthinkable really if Peter - the leader of the Apostles - were there! Neither does Luke mention, anywhere in Acts, that Peter was in Rome. The Catholic Church no longer attempts to defend this claim. So, Schaff's love affair with the Papacy is exposed for what it is, propaganda. *"Cardinal Newman and Dr. Schaff drank their inspiration from the same fountain - the higher critical theology of Germany."*[46]

Higher Textual Criticism in Germany

It is time to take a look at that German higher critical theology, its origin, and the fruits it produced. **For example, modern biblical exegesis teaches the gospels were all written in the second century - therefore none of the gospels were written by the authors attributed to them!**[47] I know this may seem astonishing to the reader but it is truly the sad state of affairs in modern New Testament studies. That distortion originated from German higher textual criticism. The historical validity of the New Testament was challenged by humanist scholars during the Reformation. Higher textual criticism and the Roman Church have one thing in common - they place their traditions above the Word of God.

---

[44] Ben Wilkinson, 2014:p.104, *Our Authorized Bible Vindicated*.
[45] New Brunswick Review, May, 1854, p.23. [46] Wilkinson, p.148.
[47] Bart Ehrman, 2000. *The New Testament* (on DVDs), Great Courses.

The Markan Priority

Markan Priority states that Mark was actually the first gospel and Matthew and Luke were written later from the template of Mark. The Markan Priority resulted from German higher text criticism. German theologians, as torchbearers of the German (Martin Luther's) Reformation, rose to monumental influence in the Protestant Movement. The argument for Markan Priority has more holes than Swiss cheese - but it has become an article of faith among seminarians, theologians, and pastors - who are well indoctrinated in this theory.

The unstated aim of Markan Priority is to knock *Matthew* from the cornerstone of Christianity! *Matthew* is the original gospel, the most detailed gospel, and the only eyewitness account by an Apostle. **It is upon the foundation of the truth of the *Gospel of Matthew* - *The Hebrew Gospel* - that all of Christianity rests!** Replacement Theology claims the Gentile Christian Church has inherited the mantle of the chosen people of Israel. The real heritors are the Messianics who embraced both the Hebrew Son of Yehovah and the Hebrew Torah of Yehovah - and took *The Hebrew Gospels* to the world - long before Gentile Christians came along. Taking *Matthew* out is essential to Replacement Theology. Mark is the ideal gospel for Replacement Theology! That analysis of the Markan Perspective was done in *Sons of Zion -Volume One*, pp. 224-229. It is reprinted here in Appendix C. Read it before proceeding if you wish.

History of the Theory

The first critical theorist to posit that Mark was the first gospel was Gottlob Storr in 1794, *"because it seemed the most 'rational' gospel. Mark leaves off the supposedly mythical infancy stories, including the virgin birth, as well as the resurrection appearances to the disciples."*[48] Although Markan Priority was a fringe position - that was about to change. In 1806, *"Napoleon entered Berlin* [capitol of Prussia at the time], *the proud Prussians had been defeated and the Holy Roman Empire under Francis II in Vienna had formally come to an end. The Prussians felt deeply humiliated by their devastating defeat in Jena on 14 October 1806.* **During that very year a number of militant clergymen took the initiative in rallying the citizens."**[49]

---

[48] Hado Meijboom, 1866, reprint 1993:p.xviii, *A History & Critique of the Origin of the Marcan Hypothesis*, Mercer University Press, GA. [49] *Ibid.*, p.xv.

The most prominent was Friedrich Schleiermacher, who *"used his pulpit for the national cause. He was called the 'first great political preacher of the Germans since Luther!'"*[50] Schleiermacher's prominence as a *'great'* German nationalist preacher made Markan Priority - called the *'Two-Document Hypothesis'* or *'Markan Hypothesis'* - a player in the great conversation. In 1810, the Prussian king, Friedrich Wilhelm III, instituted the Royal University of Berlin with Schleiermacher as its first dean of theology, *"for the purpose of revitalizing the German spirit."*[50] There, Schleiermacher focused on the historical search for the *"Logia"* of Christ testified to by Papias in the second century. It was Papias who wrote that *"Matthew organized the Logia [Words of Jesus] in the Hebrew language."*[51] **The fact that Papias was clearly referring to *Hebrew Matthew* is never acknowledged by proponents of the Markan Priority Hypothesis!** Schleiermacher determined this *Logia* to be the first gospel document, now lost, and that Mark was the second gospel - now the oldest and therefore most authentic. **From the beginning, Markan Priority was inseparably intertwined with German nationalism!**

"The issue of Matthean or Marcan priority entailed a decisive sociopolitical stance hotly debated during the crucial decades preceding the institution in 1870 of **the united German Empire under the chancellor Otto von Bismarck....** *The political and religious conservatives identified with the historical-inductive approach.* [critical text theory] *They **affirmed Marcan priority since it seemed the earliest and most concise of the gospels**."*[52] *"The nationalistic movement was especially strong in the universities."*[53] There were two great schools of thought, the **Tubingen** school which affirmed Matthean priority and the **Gottingen** school which promoted Markan priority.

Otto von Bismarck was a graduate of the Gottingen school.

This political-theological stance intensified during the *Kulterkampf* (Culture War) between Bismarck and Pope Pius IX. *"At issue was whether Catholic* [professors] *were to obey the pope or the Iron Chancellor."*[54] Bismarck's opposition to the pope was quite popular among Germany's Protestant majority.

---

[50] Hado Meijboom, 1866, 1993:p.xv, *A History & Critique of the Origin of the Marcan Hypothesis*, Mercer University Press, GA. [51] Papias cited by Eusebius in *Ecclesiastical History of the Church, Hist. eccl.* 3.39.16. [52]*Op.cit.*, in the work cited, Meijboom, p.xviii. [53]*Ibid.*, in the same work, p.xvii. [54] William Farmer, 1994:p.149, *The Gospel of Jesus*, John Knox Press, KY.

The issue was the infallible authority of the pope, which revolved around the scriptural authority of Peter, considered to be the first pope, in Matthew 16:18, *"upon this rock I will build my church!"* Germany's theological position *"was achieved by denying the foundational role of Matthew."*[55] **Catholic scholars believed in Matthean priority - German scholars in Markan priority.** The battle lines were drawn.

The theological ammunition at the core of the debate came from the universities. *"Germany's state-controlled universities, which dominated biblical research, were financially dependent upon the government... **It is the German university system and more precisely German science... that is to provide the national magisterium in the struggle for salvation of the German state.** How shortsighted this reliance on the German universities was... only began to become clear during the Third Reich."*[56]

Both sides agreed to religious tolerance - there would be no torture or capital punishment. Nonetheless, *"the measures taken by Bismarck to break down Catholic resistance are shocking. By 1876 every Prussian [Catholic] bishop either was in prison or had left the country. It is estimated that at the height of the controversy, as many as 989 Prussian parishes were without priests."*[57] The conflict escalated until, *"136 editors had been arrested, 20 confiscations of newspapers had been executed, 210 Center (Catholic) Party members had been arrested, 74 house searches had been executed, 55 dissolutions of meetings and organizations had occurred, and 103 expulsions and internments had been ordered."*[58] Vatican Council I had begun the *Kulturkampf*. *"By Vatican Council II [Catholics] had come to recognize **who was sovereign in Germany. It was Mark, not Matthew!**"*[59]

*"All professors at German universities, Catholics as well as Protestants, were appointed by the state... **German scholars who would publicly question Markan primacy would be endangering 'the foundation of the state...'** denying a decisive defensive weapon against the use the Vatican was making of **the Peter passage, a Matthean passage** [Matthew 16:18], **notably absent in Mark!**"*[59] The Markan Priority had become a *theologomenon* - serving as a doctrinal truth despite its lack of scriptural authority.

---

[55] William Farmer, 1994:p.152, *The Gospel of Jesus*, John Knox Press, KY.
[56] *Ibid.*, Farmer, p.151. [57] *Ibid.*, p.152. [58] *Ibid.*, p.153. [59] *Ibid.*, p.157.

In 1874, at the height of the *Kulturkampf*, Heinrich Holtzmann was appointed to the prestigious position of professor of theology at the new University of Strasbourg. In 1863, Holtzmann had written a book in support of the Markan Hypothesis, *The Synoptic Gospels, Their Origin and Their Historical Character*.[60] *"The major argument that Holtzman presents as a justification of his hypothesis - repeatedly he points to the fact that **his conclusion is not the outcome of data extraneous to the gospels, but entirely the result of internal criticism**!"*[61] This has been the credo of higher text criticism ever since - only upon the sacred altar of internal text criticism can truth be found. All other sources, such as historical attestations of its existence, contents and provenance - are ignored. **I refuse to play by those rules!**

Holtzman was given false credit for placing the Markan Hypothesis on solid academic ground, so much so that future theologians have asserted the Markan Hypothesis is no longer a theory - but a proven principle - the Markan Priority! Hado Heijboom, a contemporary of Holtzman did an extensive analysis of the Markan Hypothesis in 1866 focusing on Holtzman's work. Meijboom's analysis showed that *"From beginning to end he [Holtzman] **posited the Marcan Hypothesis as a proven fact**, in order then to act as if he was providing a conclusive argument. By this circular reasoning Holtzman revealed how his entire study was nothing else than a commendation of the hypothesis."*[62] **In other words, Holtzman did not prove the Markan Hypothesis to be true, he simply did his entire study assuming it was!** Modern scholars still treat the theory as if it is already proven.

Amazingly, because Markan Priority was such a political mandate it evaded serious academic criticism for a century. *"Most learned scholars in Germany never accepted this conclusion. The scholars who never accepted Markan Priority are a who's who of relevant nineteenth-century scholarship."*[63] *"Once Meijboom's work was rediscovered... it was recognized that the academic sham of Holtzman's case for the Two-Source Hypothesis [Markan Priority] had been exposed as early as 1866."*[64] Heijboom, who did indeed *"prove the weakness of the Marcan Hypothesis,"* called it *"**the swindle of the century**!"*[65]

[60]Heinrich Holtzman, 1863, Die synoptischen Evangelien, Englemann Publishing, Leipzig. [61]Hado Meijboom, 1866, 1993:p.72, *A History & Critique of... the Marcan Hypothesis*, Mercer Univ. Press, GA. [62]*Ibid.*,p.81. [63]William Farmer, 1994:p.146, *The Gospel of Jesus*. [64] *Ibid.*, p.147. [65]Meijboom, 1866, 1993:p.228.

"*The basic concept supporting Markan Priority, in nineteenth-century Germany, its birthplace, was that **the shortest gospel is the earlier**... Reduced to its simplest form, the enduring idea of Markan Priority has been this: **Mark is first because Mark is shortest.***"[66] This flies in the face of everything practiced in historical linguistics. **It seems to be a principle invented solely to make the argument for Markan Priority!** "*Markan Priority was dramatically transformed for Protestants into a fixed idea that... resists rational refutation - an idea in which many people... have come to believe.*"[67]

The memory science behind storytelling over time is clear. If one writes down an account right after it happens, it is rich in both the details of the event and the recall of thoughts and emotions surrounding that event. One can write pages and pages. For example, I have kept a journal during much of my life. If the reader has done so, you will recognize this effect. If you wait until the next day to record an entry, it will be dramatically reduced in detail by half. This can actually occur within a few hours as other thoughts, concerns, and events crowd your mind. If you wait a week, you lose even more detail - you may only be able to capture a half page or less of recollection. A year later, if you remember it at all, you might put together a paragraph. Accuracy is the first casualty of delay in recording events.

Repeated stories can get elaborated but that leads to inaccuracies - which degrade the story - but are fairly easy to detect. That is one good reason we give more weight to first-hand accounts (like Matthew) over second-hand accounts (like Mark). **The practical principle of historical linguistics and memory science is that the longest entry is more likely to be the earliest since more detail is captured!**

In Mark's gospel, we are talking about a second-hand account done decades after events which the author did not witness. Matthew, however, was an eyewitness and disciple of Yeshua who spoke with him daily and traveled with him constantly. Although Matthew published his gospel ten years after the death of the Messiah, it is likely he was writing it all along. Wouldn't you, if you were a highly literate person like Matthew, in the midst of momentous events?

---

[66]William Farmer, 1994:p.127. *The Gospel of Jesus.*   [67]*Ibid.*, Farmer, p.6.

The explanation of Markan Priority is that Mark was taken and elaborated upon later to create the gospels attributed to Matthew and Luke. In the Markan Hypothesis - Matthew and Luke were not the authors of the gospels attributed to them. Markan Priority states that the later authors of Matthew and Luke had another source for the details missing in Mark. Matthew is 28 chapters. Luke is 24 chapters and adds considerable detail not in Matthew. Mark is only 16 chapters. **That is a lot of missing detail!** The Sermon on the Mount, for example, is not in Mark. It was clear, for the first two millennia, that scholars considered Mark a summary of Matthew and Luke - both earlier gospels were available to Mark. Mark is considered a *harmony* of the gospel story - where events are put in order without repetition.

A Harmony of the Gospels

Augustine of Hippo (354-430 AD) published an exhaustive study of the four gospels called *The Harmony of the Gospels*. Hippo's conclusion was that Mark "*holds a course in conjunction... with Matthew in the larger number of passages [but] he is nevertheless at one rather with Luke in some others.*"[68] Hippo is referring to the order of events in the gospels, a phenomenon that has been much studied. Mark uses the order of events in Matthew mostly, but occasionally switches to the order followed in Luke. In other words Mark copied the stories of Matthew word-for-word at times, but when focusing on the parts from Luke, Mark did the same, copying Luke word-for-word or close enough to ascertain which gospel he was citing from. And so concluded Hippo, "*Mark is literally dependent upon both Matthew and Luke.*"[68] This view was shared by theologians for 1500 years.

There are two problems that must be resolved for the rickety argument of Markan Priority to be taken seriously:

One, it must be posited there is another source* from which all the additional details in Matthew and Luke were taken. [*It is called the *Q Gospel* from German for '*source*' - *Quelle*. Keep in mind the *Q Gospel* is entirely theoretical, there is no actual evidence - even fragments of texts - that it ever existed.]

Two, the massive historical documentation from the church fathers - that *Hebrew Matthew* was the original gospel - must be dismissed somehow by the proponents of Markan Priority.

---

[68] William Farmer, 1994:p.17, *The Gospel of Jesus*, citing Augustine of Hippo.

One important line of attack was the attempt to prove that **there was no direct connection between the Apostles and the Evangelists [gospel writers], who were said to belong to a later period when myth rather than fact reigned**. H.S. Reimarus and G.E. Lessing were leading members of this movement that, by degrees, undermined the confidence of many Christians in the historical character of the Gospels.[69]

"As soon as there appeared to be no necessity for dating the Gospels before A.D. 70, the way was open for the advance of the Markan priority hypothesis... Under the influence of Heinrich Holtzman... the cause of Markan priority advanced rapidly and achieved predominance by World War I."[70]

The priority of Mark was effectively established in all the universities belonging to the Reformation tradition, and the **historical evidence for the priority of Matthew had come to be regarded as <u>too problematic</u>** to support the ancient tradition any longer. **After World War I [there was] virtual unanimity in academic circles in favor of Markan priority**.[70]

Chapter Nine of *Sons of Zion versus Sons of Greece - Volume One*, is a synopsis of the historical evidence of Hebrew Matthew. It begins like this: *"Practically every early Christian writer attested to the writing of the first Gospel - Matthew - in Hebrew. There are 76 early attestations of that fact and **80 quotations from The Hebrew Gospel in their writings**."*[71] Even so, this is only the tip of the iceberg of historical documentation of the primacy of *Matthew*, in particular *Hebrew Matthew*. I have further documented that various of the **80 quotations** cited above are in *The Hebrew Gospels* which have survived.

The study and authentication of early manuscripts depend upon **two types of evidence: external** - historical commentary of their existence and contents; **and internal** - the analysis of the text contents itself. These are two sides to the same coin. You cannot ignore the other side of the coin! **The hypothesis of Markan Priority depends upon a complete rejection of all historical evidence external to the contents of the texts.**

This is sufficient reason to discredit the Markan Priority as invalid!

---

[69] Bernard Orchard & Harold Riley, 1987:p.112, *The Order of the Synoptics*, Mercer University Press, Macon, GA. [70] *Ibid.*, p.113. [71] Miles Jones, third edition, 2021:p.165, *Sons of Zion vs Sons of Greece - Volume One*.

The Nazi Connection

The stage was set 60 years before the Nazis took over German universities in the 1930s. In the 1870s there was already totalitarian oppression of free speech and thought, manipulation of Christian minds and beliefs and, of course, anti-Semitism.

> In the debate [on the Markan Priority] between Heinrich Ewald of Gottingen and Ferdinand Christian Baur of Tubingen... as was demonstrated... Ewald's style was most lively and vituperate, personal as well as political, and he vented feelings of strong rejection against Baur:
>
> **"Herr Baur, in my opinion, is neither a Christian... nor one of the better heathen. He is one of the literary Jews, this present-day pest of our poor Germany!"**[72]

The debate was no longer one of ideas but of indoctrination and incrimination, and Ewald made it clear that the Messianic Jewish-Christian Baur had no place in the new Germany.

The Gospel of Matthew was considered:

"the product of a discredited Jewish brand of Christianity that was fated to wane and die!"[73]

"A more virulent strain of anti-Semitism preyed on virtually all aspects of German scholarship during the Nazi period. 'German Christians' - a movement that in the Nazi era numbered three out of every four German pastors - was swept up in the theological alchemy of attempting to construct a 'heroic' Aryan faith by the eradication from Christianity of every possible vestige of Judaism. Several premier German theologians... attempted to justify anti-Semitism on theological grounds!"[73]

> *"The beginnings of such absurd and nefarious ideas were already present in nineteenth-century Germany.*
> ***The Nazis did not invent anti-Semitism.***
> ***<u>They harvested it!</u>"***[74]

---

[72] John Kiwiet, 1866, 1993:p.xxvi, in the Translator's Introduction to Meijboom, *A History & Critique of the Origin of the Marcan Hypothesis*, Mercer, GA.
[73] James Edwards, 2009:p.204, *The Hebrew Gospel & the Development of the Synoptic Tradition*, William Eerdmans Publishing, MI. [74] *Ibid.*, Edwards, p.205.

Burton Mack, and myself, have called this sacrificial view, a harkening back to the blood. *"The life of the flesh is in the blood, and I myself have given it to you upon the altar to make atonement for your lives, for it is the blood, by means of the life, that makes atonement"* (Leviticus 17:11). From the viewpoint of ancient religion: *"The sacrificial reading of the gospels offers Christians their redemption - at the expense of the damnation of the Jews. Their [Christian] righteousness is attested by innocence while **the blame for the violence is laid to the account of the enemy of God!**"*[75] **That would be the Hebrews!**

> This sorry plot lies at the very foundations of the long, ugly history of Christian attitudes and actions toward Jews and Judaism. The destruction of their city [Jerusalem] was only a sign. They did not vanish as was their due and thus were there to reap repeatedly the wrath of God in anticipation of **the final apocalyptic resolution!**[75]

To the German Christians of the Nazi era, this *"final apocalyptic resolution"* was the Holocaust. Although Germans did not necessarily know precisely what was happening to all of the hated Jews who were disappearing, neither were they interested in finding out. *"No thinking person can justify this long history, nor doubt that the gospel has justified it in the eyes of Christians... the documents pile up from the time of the early church, through the 'Adversus Judaeos' [Anti-Jewish] literature, to the crusades, reactions to the plagues, Catholic doctrine, Luther's pronouncements, German tracts of the nineteenth and early twentieth centuries, common clichés in New Testament scholarship, and the anomaly of anti-Semitic attitudes that emerge throughout the third world wherever the gospel is read today."*[75] This is what the manipulation of Scripture does!

> **"The Nazi enactment of the final solution...**
> **may have been tainted by pagan desires,**
> **but the rationale was Christian.**
> **The Holocaust was also a gospel event!"**[75]

It would be nice if Messianic believers had been given a pass from the Holocaust. They were not. To the Nazis and German Christians they were Hebrews, not Christians.

---

[75]Burton Mack, 1988:p.375, *A Myth of Innocence: Mark & Christian Origins*, Fortress Press, PA.

*"We must never forget what happened to the 'quest for truth' in the universities of **the Third Reich**. A 'politically correct' civil religion, pushed by university-trained German Christian theologians like Emanuel Hirsch, **gloried in the idea of Markan priority** with its understanding of Christian theology based on the Two-Source Hypothesis, while **Christians who witnessed unto blood and resisted unto death the Nazi horrors that led to the Holocaust drew spiritual support from a reading of the Gospels that called them to be saints and martyrs..."*[76]
[rather than oppressors]

"...an understanding of Christ called for by any hypothesis that recognizes the primary character of the Matthean text!"[76]

*"This is the difference.
This is what is at stake for the church!"*[76]

*"The saints and martyrs of the church... those who have witnessed unto blood on behalf of the poor and oppressed. **They care very little for our university-based critical tradition**, and ... read the Gospels as they were first read by oppressed Christians in the pre-Constantinian church, and as they have been read by oppressed Christians throughout the ages."*[76]

The Messianic - Jewish Christian Revival!

"Twelve weary centuries had passed since Jewish Christianity lost its corporate existence, twelve centuries in which any suspicion of Jewishness in any convert was condemned as Christian apostasy and punished with all the cruelty of the times!"[77] During those centuries, the goal of outreach to Jews was to offer salvation in exchange for separating from everything Jewish, including family. *"How much suffering would have been spared... Jewish Christians cut off from their racial heritage by the Church's insistence that by acceptance of Christ they had ceased in any sense to be Jews. What agonies of soul, what broken hearts, have resulted from the Gentile fear of Judaizing! How many Jewish homes mourned a lost son or daughter?"*[78]

As far as the converted Jewish-Christian was concerned:

*"**Romanism tortured his body but...
Protestantism tortured his soul!**"*[79]

---

[76] William Farmer, 1994:p.8, *The Gospel of Jesus*. Mercer Univ. Press, GA.
[77] Hugh Schonfield, 1936, 2009:p.157, *The History of Jewish Christianity*, first edition Duckworth, London, UK. [78]Schonfield, 2009:p.150. [79]*Ibid.*,p.151.

"*Missions to the Jews, mainly founded in the nineteenth century, paved the way directly for the reconstitution of Jewish Christianity.*"[80] "*By the end of the nineteenth century there were nearly a hundred agencies working among the Jews in different parts of the world... at least a quarter million Jews were won for Christ during this century.*"[81]

During the Enlightenment period - the Age of Reason - (1685-1815) much oppression was lifted from the shoulders of the Jews and Messianics. As we detailed, much religious liberty and citizenship were regained by the late 1700s. But, by the end of the 1800s anti-Semitism was once again on the rise. The original apostasy of the Christian Church reared its head once more. Sin not confessed, repented, and atoned for - will be repeated! A resurgence of Hebrew-hatred climaxed during World War II.

Sympathy for the suffering of the Jews during the Holocaust led to changes in the mentality of nations and the Church. England had already formalized support for a Jewish nation in the Balfour Declaration of 1917. This had been popularized and promoted in the late 1800s by Theodore Herzel (Herschel). Credit is given to Herzel for the Return to Israel Movement. **There was also a leader who resuscitated the Messianic Movement.**

"*The same spirit which led Theodore Herschel to seek the solution of the Jewish problem in a revived Jewish state had led* **Joseph Rabinowitz to seek a solution in a Jewish... kingdom, with Jesus as the sovereign... The New Testament was a sealed book to...** *Jews, and never having read it they judged the book by the deeds of those who claimed to be bound by its teaching.*" [82]

Rabbinowitz' movement was widespread in the 1800s and echoed by many voices. In the words of Rabbi Isaac Lichtenstein of Hungary, "*I used to think that Christ was the plague and curse of the Jews, the origin and promoter of our sorrow and persecution... It was* [just such] *a blood accusation which first drew me to read the New Testament... The cry re-echoed, 'Death to the Jew!' The frenzy was excessive, and among the ringleaders were many who used the name of Christ and his doctrine as a cloak to cover their abominable doings.*"[83]

---

[80]Hugh Schonfield, 1936, 2009:p.153, *The History of Jewish Christianity*, first edition Duckworth, London, UK. [81]Schonfield, 2009:p.154. [82]*Ibid.*,p.166.
[83]Rabbi I. Lichtenstein, 1896, *Judenspiegel*, L. Schoenberger, Vienna.

Lichtenstein goes on to say that in the New Testament *"Jesus was spoken of as he who brings joy to man, the Prince of Peace, and the Redeemer, and his Gospel was extolled as a message of love and life to all people. I was surprised, and, scarcely trusting my eyes, I took a New Testament... and I began to turn over its leaves and to read. How can I express the impression which I then received? Not the half had been told me of the greatness, glory, and power of this book, formerly a sealed book to me."*[84] Lichtenstein quoted the New Testament from his pulpit and, after admitting his faith in Christ, was forced to resign, although many Jews fought for him to stay. He never ceased to preach the amazing truth that had been revealed to him.

> A sudden glory, a light, flashed through my soul. I looked for thorns and gathered roses: I discovered pearls instead of pebbles; instead of hatred, love; instead of vengeance, forgiveness; instead of bondage, freedom; instead of pride, humility; instead of enmity, conciliation; instead of death... life, salvation, resurrection, and heavenly treasure.[85]

"The position of these New Covenant Jews raised an acute problem in the Christian Church. They would not be absorbed, they would not be assimilated. They claimed the right as Jews to maintain the name and customs of their race! *They held that they had not forsaken Judaism, but crowned it with Jesus, the chief corner stone."*[86] Whereas the Church had been imposing the Greek Jesus on the Jews from without - now we were seeing a reclamation of the Hebrew Messiah from within. Many Gentile Christians found this revival resonating with their own scriptural beliefs. Others cried foul. Messianics were unfairly accused of the heresy of '*Ebionitism*.' [Ebionites rejected the divine birth of Jesus as a contradiction to monotheism.] As a result, *"many a Jewish convert entered the Church in the naïve belief that all Christians were brethren...* [and] *frequently found that they were not wanted in the Church...* [However] *there were Gentile Christians who were friends of Israel in deed as well as in name, and who poured themselves out in love to bring comfort to the stranger."*[87] **In this way, Messianic believers made Teshuvah - returning to the embrace of their Hebrew Messiah, Hebrew Torah, and Hebrew God. Many Gentile believers did the same - creating the modern Hebraic Roots Movement!**

[84]Hugh Schonfield, 1936, 2009:p.167, *The History of Jewish Christianity*, first edition Duckworth, London, UK. [85]Isaac Lichtenstein, est.1900, *Judenthum und Christenthum*. [86] Schonfield, p.167. [87] *Ibid.*, p.169.

On September 9, 1813, in London, the Hebrew Christian Association was formed. It was called *Beni Avraham*, or Children of Abraham. It was a charitable society for Jewish Christians and its good works continued for many decades. On May 23, 1866, Dr. Carl Schwartz, minister of Trinity Chapel in London, initiated the formation of the British Hebrew-Christian Alliance. Other groups formed within Christian denominations. *"A portent of the new era for Jewish Christianity was visible in the consecration to the newly-created Anglican See of Jerusalem of **Bishop Michael Solomon Alexander in 1841, the first Jewish -Christian Bishop of Jerusalem since A.D. 135.**"*[88]

In 1907, Mark Levy, founder of the Christian Jews' Patriotic Alliance, appealed to the General Assembly of the Episcopal Church of the United States. Levy pleaded for *"the restoration of the original Hebrew-Christian branch of the Church, and for the public proclamation of the Scriptural truth: **That the Church does not require its Jewish members to forsake their own people, but leaves them in their Christ-given liberty... according to God's covenant with Abraham... to observe all other customs inherited from their fathers.**"*[89] The General Assembly resolved affirmatively using Levy's exact words. The effects of these changes were far-reaching. Once Christian Salvation was no longer being wielded as *"an axe to sever the Jewish Christian wholly and completely from his former co-religionists..."*[90] we soon see that, *"there was an increase and not a diminution of conversions."*[91] Not only that, but since observance of the Old Testament was no longer prohibited to Jewish Christians, many other Christians - not of Jewish blood - began to seek their Hebrew roots in the Torah and observe its statutes and feast days.

"It remained for Joseph Rabinowitz in 1882 to found the first Jewish Christian communion in modern times which belonged to no definite denomination, but was rather in the nature of a Synagogue of Jewish believers in Jesus. The story of Rabinowitz is a remarkable one. He may, without unfair comparison, be described as the Herzel of Jewish Christianity."[92] Rabinowitz - like so many other Jews, from the first century until the present day - was converted by reading the New Testament.

Can you imagine the impact on Jews of *The Hebrew Gospels* without Greek anti-Judaic insertions and doctrinal changes?

---
[88] Hugh Schonfield, 1936, 2009:p.157, *The History of Jewish Christianity*.
[89] *Ibid.*,Schonfield, 2009:p.171. [90] *Ibid.*,p.153. [91] *Ibid.*,p.155. [92] *Ibid.*,p.163.

The Neo-Messianic - Hebraic Roots Revival!

Once again, *"The tide which had carried Christianity steadily further away from the Jewish apostolic faith was now at its turn, and thousands not of the Hebrew race began to turn their eyes Zionwards, literally and spiritually."*[93]

The Neo-Messianics had also survived! The Waldensians, experienced extreme persecution for centuries culminating in a most brutal massacre April 24, 1655. Many sought refuge in Switzerland. Eventually, they were offered repatriation to Italy. In 1848 they were granted full religious and civil rights. One group of Waldensians migrated to North Carolina, establishing the township of Valdese. The Waldensian Episcopal Church spread throughout northern Italy and beyond. During World War II - they were active in saving Jews fleeing Nazi attempts to exterminate them - often hiding them in the same upper valleys of the Alps that had been the Waldensians' refuge in times past.

The Conversos of Spain and Portugal often maintained their Hebrew covenant in secret as best they could for centuries up until modern times when they have begun to come out of the closet. They were called *Anusim* in Hebrew, *'forced ones.'* Although many chose to convert - they all ended up as victims of the Inquisition. Many Spanish, especially those of Messianic blood, aided fleeing Jews during WWII. Some Jewish organizations have reached out to support them now. The obstacle has been that the Conversos refuse to give up their Hebrew Messiah. Now they are coming together in organizations such as American Anusim in San Antonio headed up by Dr. Dell Sanchez. Their website claims, *"There are over 500 million Latino/Hispanics in the Western Hemisphere. At least 100 million of these Hispanic/Latinos are descendants of Sephardic Anusim Jews."* [94]

Many of the mainstream Protestant denominations have had divergent congregations that followed Sabbath worship on the seventh day - Saturday. The Puritans had a seventh day group called Pilgrims. The 7th Day Baptists had many congregations both in Europe and America. Most of these lay claim to Hebraic influence. These are the enduring threads woven into the modern Neo-Messianic/Hebraic Roots Movement.

---

[93] Hugh Schonfield, 1936, 2009:p.145, *The History of Jewish Christianity*, first edition Duckworth, London, UK. [94] Americananusim.org.

To take one example, the Seventh Day Adventist Church, officially the Church of God: Seventh Day, originated in 1863, from the Second Great Awakening Revival in upper state New York. Their beliefs hold to the Saturday Sabbath and a precise understanding of themselves as the Remnant Church charged with a mission to hold to God's commandments both now and up until the end times.

In 1933, Herbert W. Armstrong was ordained as a minister in the Adventist Church. His ministry began with a radio program and newspaper called *The Plain Truth*. As Armstrong gained more and more followers he began to deviate from the Adventists to the point that his credentials were revoked. His international congregation soon developed into a church in its own right - the Radio Church of God - which became so successful that Armstrong had followers from countries all over the world. Millions of copies of his newspaper *The Plain Truth* were distributed in 187 countries worldwide every week. Soon, Armstrong adopted the name Worldwide Church of God. Although he never had more than about 100,000 congregants, he was reaching millions of listeners and readers. He advocated a return to the feast days of Yehovah and other distinctive traits of the early church. Armstrong's Worldwide Church of God was perhaps the first modern Christian denomination to try and restore the feast days of Yehovah to their doctrine.

Armstrong helped advance a grass roots movement that had been growing for the past century - which advocated returning to the Hebraic roots of Christian faith. There is no central headquarters, no dogma, no noticeable organization at all. Despite this there are an estimated 300,000 congregants in the United States with about ten times that number of sympathetic participants, whom I refer to as *'leaners.'* The numbers of Hebraic Roots congregants are increasing rapidly. There are missions abroad and working in prisons - all without organized backing! There are many televised ministries. At his annual Sukkot (Tabernacles) gathering, Monte Judah draws as many as 7,000 participants - the size of a megachurch. Michael Rood TV reaches worldwide audiences not only in every English-speaking country, but also in Spanish, and other languages, even Chinese. Stephen Pidgeon, Todd Bennett, Jonathan Cahn and numerous other Messianic authors and preachers reach millions.

Know the End from the Beginning

In Israel, in 1993, Derek Prince preached a sermon on the *Sons of Zion versus the Sons of Greece*. In it, he claims that **Humanism will be Satan's tool for raising up the Anti-Christ!**

I was really as much a son of Greece as anyone who is not Greek could ever be. I started learning Latin... when I was 9, and Greek when I was 10, and I spent the next 15 years studying Latin and Greek... the last five years at Cambridge University studying Greek philosophy. I mixed with the people who would be the future leaders of Britain, in every field. Eton College, where I was for 5 years, has contributed 25 prime ministers to Britain. **And I want to say that we were mostly sons of Greece.**

We were all, theoretically, Christians. We respected Christ and Christianity but we also respected the Greek poets, tragedians and philosophers. And I would say Plato was more often quoted than Paul. And we would mention the names of the Greek gods, without exactly believing in them - but certainly not disbelieving in them. They had a really important place in our thinking. We would more often express ourselves in quotations from Greek writers than we ever would think of quoting from the Bible.

So then... we were really sons of Greece!

If you analyze history, Babylon has had very little real influence on western history. Persia has had relatively little influence. Rome has had a great influence but you need to remember that **Rome defeated Greece militarily but Greece defeated Rome philosophically!** So the Romans came under the thinking of the Greeks. The procreative life that issued from that historical background **[Rome] was the life of Greece!**

It is hard for people who are not familiar with it to realize how much the thinking, the culture, of Europe and the countries that have been influenced by Europe, have been under the dominion of Greek thought.[95]

---

[95] Derek Prince, 1993, *Sons of Zion vs Sons of Greece*, www.derekprince.com.

I studied Greek philosophy. The first known Greek philosopher was called Heraclitus...

"Man is the measure of all things!"

Humanism is the denial of any power or moral value superior to that of humanity, the rejection of religion in favor of the belief in the advancement of humanity by its own efforts... Humanism is a very strong negative force! **Atheism pushes God away and says we don't want you. Humanism just walks past as if God was not there.** Really, that is a very conspicuous feature of our contemporary culture.

In Israel [and] the United States... both of them are totally dominated by humanism. That is also true of the majority of European nations; certainly Sweden, Denmark, Germany, France... I am not able to speak in detail about every nation. But the power that dominates their thinking, their culture, their values, and their course of action is the power of humanism.

I believe that humanism is the ultimate tactic of Satan to raise up the Anti-Christ.

The Sons of Greece are humanists.

The greatest single weapon that Satan has against the human race is deception.

<u>The only protection against deception is the love of the truth!</u> [95]

The story of the *Sons of Zion versus the Sons of Greece* is far from over. The Messianic Church and *The Hebrew Gospels* still have a dominant role to play both in the present day and in the end times story.

---

[95] Derek Prince, 1993, a recorded speech, *"Sons of Zion vs Sons of Greece,"* www.derekprince.com.

Conclusion
Chapter Thirteen
The Schizophrenic Church

*A double minded man is unstable
in all his ways... Let not that man think
he shall receive anything from Yehovah.*
James 1:7-8

Derek Prince's comments on the end times had a profound effect on me. He was citing 2nd Thessalonians 2:3-12:

> The coming of the man of sin [son of perdition] will be accompanied by the power of Satan. He will use every kind of power, including miraculous signs, lying wonders, and with all the deception of wickedness... **for those who perish, because they did not receive the love of the truth so as to be saved. For this reason God will send upon them a spirit of delusion so that they will believe what is false, in order that they all may be damned who did not believe the truth, but took pleasure in wickedness.**

I do not believe I have ever read anything so chilling as this in the Bible! Note that it is God, not Satan, who is sending these people a spirit of delusion. They are being culled from the flock! Scripture is clear that not all souls will live on. These are those whose souls will be destroyed. Yehovah does not seem to want to consign them to the fires of hell - these are nominal believers - so he gives them a delusion pill, kind of like Prozac. They have already made their decision. They have deluded themselves. God is simply saying okay - you have chosen to live in your delusion. Your fate is sealed. I call them *Prozac* Christians.

How many have attended sermons faithfully every Sunday but continued their everyday lives as if there were no God? Perhaps politicians who sit in the pews then go out to fight for the right to kill babies in the womb, or the priests who presided over the torture and execution of fellow believers during the Inquisition. These are Christians who participated in pogroms and the Holocaust - or those who have rationalized away, or ignored the truth, whenever faced with crucial moral choices.

For the Love of the Truth

Since the Benai Emunah Institute has begun this work of recovering *The Hebrew Gospels* - translating and publishing them - our work has been shadowed by others! It is appropriate that we critique their efforts since we have done so with every other researcher who has published on *The Hebrew Gospels*.

Al Garza has a website DrAlGarza.org - and a secondary website THISS.org (The Hebrew Institute of Semitic Studies). Many of my readers have emailed me about his videos, on his website and Youtube, which mimic my research results without giving me credit - **in other words Al Garza is claiming credit for my work!** His videos and websites use, as evidence of his claims, numerous photos from my book *The Hebrew Gospels - Do They Exist?* If it were simply a reputation issue I would not bother. The problem is that Al Garza is claiming my work as his own in order to solicit money from his followers. **I will not allow fraud committed, on the basis of my research being falsely claimed by another, for monetary gain.**

On his website, **"Dr."** Al Garza claims to have a PhD in Biblical Studies from the Department of Defense (DoD). The Department of Defense is not a degree-granting institute. So, Al Garza does not have a PhD in Biblical Studies from the DoD. He has a transcript of his PhD program on his website. It is a fake. It has all the course work of Hebrew University's Israel Institute of Biblical Studies on the transcript but it does **not** have the name of the degree-granting university. **It has the seal of the National Academic Higher Education Agency, which was lifted from their website. They are an accreditation bureau, not a degree-granting entity. They do not give PhDs in biblical studies!**

Al Garza claims to be a graduate Associate Scholar of Biblical Studies at the Hebrew University Israel Institute of Biblical Studies. He has an official-looking certificate on his website. However, it cannot be enlarged to examine or investigate the validity of the certificate. I myself attend the Israel Institute, which does online courses in Hebrew. I called the Registrar to inquire, and I was told they had never had an Al or Albert Garza register for classes there. Al Garza does appear to have acquired a lot of knowledge and done some valuable (authentic?) research. However, once fraud is discovered few will take Garza's research seriously. Fraud negates his good work along with the bad.

Other Translations of *The Hebrew Gospels*

My website is **thehebrewgospels.com.** There is another website hebrewgospels.com, which is the work of the Van Rensburg family. I spoke with Piet Van Rensburg and his talented teenage (at the time) children; Justin, Michael and Theone - before they began their project. He informed me a principal reason for their translation was to restore the name of God - **Yahweh** - to the text. I informed them that neither the name Yahweh, nor Yehovah, nor YHVH appear in the text of the HGC anywhere. They could not do a straight translation which gives readers the impression *The Hebrew Gospels from Catalonia* (HGC) validate the name Yahweh. It is dishonest and makes us no different from those who have edited the *Greek Gospels* to suit themselves or their doctrine. We parted ways on this issue.

The Van Rensburgs have done the translation and inserted the name Yahweh into the text. They also expressed their disgust with the research of Nehemia Gordon - who is leading people astray - they said. Their videos attacking Nehemia Gordon smack of anti-Semitism. I haven't watched them all - but the titles of the *Ten Reasons Why Yehovah is Not the Name of God* all start with "*Nehemia Gordon*" as if the evidence is not the issue, Nehemia is the issue. **Yehovah** - with the correct vowel pointing - is found many thousands of times in the Hebrew texts of the Bible, including the earliest and most prestigious manuscripts. **What can one say about "Yahweh?" There is zero evidence of its use in Hebrew texts! It is a Gentile invention - always has been!** The evidence is so out of whack with the Van Rensburg claims - that it has not warranted comment up to now.

Another problem is that some parts of the text of *The Hebrew Gospels from Catalonia* are missing or corrupted. To publish a straight translation is to hold these defects up to public view where they can be, and will be, used to discredit the entire *Hebrew Gospels* project as defective, therefore invalid. Either that or the Van Rensburgs will clean it up - which is, again - to edit the text to suit their ends. There are other issues with their translation but they are not worth going into. Yes, it is a bit amateurish but still a formidable effort for teens to translate *The Hebrew Gospels!* **I did not publish my initial translation of *The Hebrew Gospels from Catalonia* because I discovered more manuscripts which must be included in the compilation!**

Almost all Bible texts in print today are compilations. You take the most authentic manuscripts available and, from them - analyze and compile the most authentic version possible. What difference does that make? We now have at least two Hebrew manuscripts of each book of the New Testament, three for each of the Gospels, four for the Gospel of John. **In many of these Gospels the sacred name of God - Yehovah - is used with the correct vowel pointing!**

For example, *'Yehovah'* (with vowels) is written in the Hazon MS #273 in the Sloane Collection of the British Library, in the Epistles of Peter, James, and Jude in the British Museum, in the fragment of the latest *Hebrew Gospels* to be uncovered at the Vatican (Vat. Ebr. MS 530), and in the *Cochin Hebrew Gospels* (Gaster MS # 1616) which I have recently recovered.

There is now plenty of evidence to justify putting the sacred name of God - Yehovah - back in the Brit Hadashah!

You cannot do that based on one manuscript - or you may end up making a serious error like the Van Rensburgs have made. I will stand before the throne of God for everything I have done in translating these texts. I take that very seriously - like my life depends upon it!

The Schizophrenic Church

We have come a long, long way together in uncovering the greatest story never told. In *Sons of Zion vs Sons of Greece*, we spoke of the earliest artifact with the name of God on it. It is called the YHVH stone, aka the Moses stone, a 14th century BC artifact which was discovered by Dr. Sung Hak Kim from the pilgrimage path to Mount Sinai in Arabia. It was sent to me and I translated it - the earliest inscription we will probably ever find of the name of God - YeHoVaH.

Recently, I attended my Messianic Assembly and an elder read and discussed the *Parashah* (weekly Bible reading). That week it was Exodus 3:14, which speaks of the sacred name of God. The elder discussed restoration of the sacred name, the deeper meaning of the sacred name, its power and primacy, the sanctity and import, of the sacred name - for almost half an hour - without once ever saying the sacred name of God - ***Yehovah!***

Welcome to the Schizophrenic Church!

Schizophrenia is defined as a psychotic disorder where one becomes dissociated from reality, causing delusions - false beliefs; seeing and hearing things - hallucinations; leading to emotional instability and loss of motivation to live - withdrawal. The societal equivalent of these symptoms has been called *existential nihilism*, or more accurately, *existential annihilism!* Carl Jung, the famous psychoanalyst, typified modern Western culture in this way - the psyche of modern man hangs by a slender thread. *"Our world is, so to speak, dissociated like a neurotic!"*[1] In that quote from *Man and His Symbols*, Jung is referring to the standoff between god-believing governments (democratic republics) and god-rejecting governments (communism) and the cultures they spawn. *"With the Iron Curtain marking the symbolic line of division."*[1] Jung, however, is making a much larger point. **He examines man's dissociation from his subconscious, from nature, and from nature's God. <u>We are of two minds</u>!** *"It is the face of his own evil shadow that grins at Western man from the other side of the Iron Curtain."*[1]

I quote Jung because he speaks truths that theologians cannot say - stuck in the belief theirs is inerrant doctrine. Jung speaks about the mind of man separating itself from its roots and its reality. We have become so arrogant in our modern progressivism that we define our world and its history, including religion, as we see fit, rather than as it is. So many '*modern*' minds see themselves as beyond the primitive need for religion. *"Religion is the opiate of the masses!"* as Karl Marx so aptly phrased it.

"Things whose enormity no one could have imagined in the idyllic harmlessness of the first decade of our century have happened and have turned our world upside down. **Ever since, the world has remained in a state of schizophrenia!**"[2] Jung was speaking of the 17 million dead of World War I, the 70 million dead worldwide during World War II, 35 million dead during the communist takeover of the Soviet Union, 75 million dead in the communist takeover of China. The communist death tolls were not in battle but men, women, and children exterminated because they opposed an ideology. This was ideological slaughter - like the Spanish Inquisition - but on a massive scale! It is over now - so we put these horrendous happenings out of mind - as if they were aberrant to the modern progressive mind and could not happen again. **But of course they can - and will - it is foretold!**

[1] Carl G. Jung, 1964:p.85, *Man and His Symbols*, Doubleday, N.Y. [2] *Ibid.,* p.93.

"**Modern man** does not understand how much his *'rationalism'* ...has put him at the mercy of the psychic *'underworld.'* He has freed himself from *'superstitition'* (or so he believes), but in the process **he has lost his spiritual values to a positively dangerous degree... and he is now paying for this break-up in world wide disorientation and dissociation.**"[3]

'Rationalism' is not the logical faculty to seek truth, but rather the mind's ability to construct the reality it wants. We *'rationalize'* an evil deed, for example, by constructing reasons (*'rationales'*) why the evil deed is acceptable, even good. *"As scientific understanding has grown, so our world has become dehumanized!"*[4] That is to say, all things not deemed *'scientific'* are dismissed, even mocked or scorned by the rationalist. That includes religious belief, which is certainly supernatural. The Spirit of God is being challenged by the Spirit of Scientific Enlightenment. There is truth and good in both. They do not need to be in conflict. It is man who paints them at odds.

Back to the Sacred Name

We all gather together on the Sabbath to sing the hymn, *Holy God we Praise your Sacred Name*, without anyone involved being aware they do not even know the *'Sacred Name,'* much less use it or give it any importance in their spiritual life! All the things we willfully ignore get pushed down into our subconscious, Jung's *'psychic underworld.'* As a result we are easily manipulated by those who know how to punch our subconscious buttons. Why does this matter? *"Christians had appropriated the mantle of the chosen people, changed the sacred name of God and His Son to Greek, and proclaimed this new god demanded a doctrine of anti-Semitism that demonized all things Hebrew - including the Sacred Name Yehovah, the Hebrew Messiah, Torah, Sabbath day, Feast Days of Yehovah, and The Hebrew Gospels!* **This new Christian god was a Hebrew-hating god!** *('The suffering of the Jews in which divine justice delights!') Messianics were required to condemn and hate anything remotely Hebrew.* **Many Messianics refused to bow - dying by torture or burning - without saying a word!**"[5] The use of the Sacred Name branded one as a *Judaizer*, and the penalty for *judaizing* was death!

Welcome to the Schizophrenic Church!

[3] Carl G. Jung, 1964:p.94, *Man and His Symbols*, Doubleday, N.Y. [4]*Ibid.*, p.95.
[5] Miles Jones, cited from chapter 7, page 171, of *Messianic Church Arising!*

So, are we still blindly following the mandates of the Medieval Inquisition? In fact, the mandate has been in effect since the creation of the new Greek Church in the fourth century. Theologians have reinterpreted Scripture to rationalize their desire to erase the Sacred Name - and erased it has been! In a recent movie about the Exodus, *Gods and Kings*, Pharaoh calls the God of the Israelites, the *"god-with-no-name!"* Although this is historically incorrect - it is prophetically accurate. Having jettisoned His one true name, all that remains are titles, substitutes, and foreign names. And, of course, endless singing and sermonizing about the Sacred Name, its power and holiness, its vast importance, and its eternal presence in our hearts and minds.

There is no *god-with-no-name* in Scripture! *Yehovah* is the most important word in the Bible. In Psalm 138:1-2 it says:

> I will worship toward your Holy Temple
> I will praise your Name
> **according to** your lovingkindness, and
> **according to** your truth
> **For you have magnified
> your Name above all,**
> *according to* **your say so**.

In the standard translation this has been adjusted just a tad. *"For you have magnified your word - above all your name!"* The word '*amartka,*' 'you*r saying*' or '*your say so,*' has been translated as '*your Word*' and it has been moved in the sentence from the secondary clause into the primary clause - meaning it has been placed in importance before the Name. Even so, it still conveys that the Word has been magnified - but above all is His Name. **Theologians then assure us it means the opposite of what it says - the Word has been exalted above the Name!**

The original meaning of this verse is: *'Wherever I am, I will face toward your Temple in Jerusalem for my daily prayers and I will invoke your Sacred Name - Yehovah - above all, with praise; because of your lovingkindness, your truth, and because you said to do so!'* **How do we know this?** *"Yehovah commands us in His Word to declare His Sacred Name - to speak it, sing it, shout it out joyfully, give glory to it, magnify it, revere the Name, love it, give thanks to it, meditate upon it, ask salvation of it, serve it, bless it, bless others in His Name, to trust in the Name Yehovah, and to swear by it 'As Yehovah lives!'"*[6]

---
[6] Miles Jones, 2021:p.160, *Sons of Zion vs Sons of Greece*, Benai Emunah, TX.

The name of God - **Yehováh** - is given in Scripture almost 7000 times. I did an extensive examination of the evidence of the Sacred Name in *Sons Vol. One*, chapter eight, pages 151-162. That analysis is encapsulated in a free PDF available by emailing **writingofgod.com** and asking for *The Ineffable Name* download. Research on this has been done by Nehemia Gordon and published in his book *Shattering the Conspiracy of Silence*. Gordon's evidence and conclusions are definitive.

So we now observe theologians blindly wandering about, banging their heads against the trees, searching for the forest. The name of God has disappeared! Cannot seem to find it anywhere. Despite hundreds of commands in Scripture to use it - and never to change it or to render it naught - **we have erased the name of Yehovah! It is the greatest abomination imaginable - and we are blissfully unaware!**

Welcome to the Schizophrenic Church!

The name of Yehovah was discarded for the Greek name Theos, Deus in Latin, Dios in Spanish, LORD in English. In the fourth century the new Greek Church demonized and declared heretic the church of the Messiah - the Messianic Church.

It matters not whether you call him Yeshua or Jesus - <u>This was his church</u>!

Its destruction was the Great Apostasy that Greek Christianity was founded upon! I know how harsh that sounds but what choice is there? Having divorced themselves from the Messianic Church - their primary competition - the Greek Church demonized all things Hebrew, including the Sacred Name *Yehovah*! By the end of the fourth century they were burning people at the stake for judaizing. Of course, all of the bloodshed was properly sanctified by Greco-Roman prelates.

The families of the condemned Messianics were required to gather the wood for the burning of their beloved father, husband and provider. They had to gather both dry wood and green wood. If he would still not confess his sin of judaizing at the *auto-da-fe* - then green wood was used - greatly prolonging the agony of his burning at the stake. After placing the wood about his feet, the family were required to stand and watch. Their home and property were seized. They were now reduced to beggary and starvation in their misery. **Apologists appease our discomfort by reminding us that** - *'They were, after all, heretics!'*

Not only has the name of God been changed to a Greek name but all those who hold to the Sacred Name of Yehovah must be culled. They, and often their families, must be subjected to the most degrading humiliation, imprisonment so brutal many die, inhuman torture, and execution made as painful and prolonged as man can devise. **An awful example was made so you - the reader - accept the Sacred Name is Greek, not Hebrew!**

There are consequences to ignoring truth! Modern Christians are not responsible for all of this but that does not mean they bear no burden of apostasy. Have we repented of these things done in the name of Christ? Not simply agreed that it was wrong but repented of it and its consequences which are still with us. If you have not - just do it now in prayer! Churches and denominations will repent of their generational sin once their members have done so and determined that it should stop. **There is no corporate exception for sin! Churches must repent!**

The template of the Inquisition - the authorization - in the name of God, to torture and kill those who disagree with church doctrine, has been bequeathed to the world! Protestants used it not only to burn dissidents, but also to kill and torture tens of thousands of those accused, rightly or wrongly, of witchcraft. If in your heart you agree with that - then you carry the template of the Inquisition inside of you. It justifies violence by any -ism out there that seeks power. They would do violence anyway, but it is nice to have the cover of the Church.

"In accordance with principles established by the Greco-Roman Church itself, adopted in turn by all their offspring churches, even atheists can claim they are ***'justified by a vision of the one true path,'*** *as they destroy all who think differently, whether they be numbered in the hundreds or the hundreds of millions. If the principle is correct then the scope of its reach is like-wise justified."*[7] The Church has yet to repent of the Great Apostasy! Until it does, it has no firm moral ground to stand on.

They were called "*Kulaks*," the Russian farmers and small property owners who resisted giving up their land to the communists in the 1920s and 30s. They were '*resettled*' by being crammed into railroad cars, transported to Siberia, and dumped in the frozen wilderness without food, water, warm clothing, tools or supplies. Left to die in the frigid winter - by the millions!

---

[7] Quoted from this volume, end of chapter seven, page 174.

Humanism took root during the Enlightenment period of the 17th and 18th centuries. The Catholic god was torturing and burning thousands of heretics at the stake. The Protestant god was doing the same to thousands of witches. These gods accepted no moral commandments that applied to heretics, witches, and infidels. They could be dispossessed, deceived and destroyed. They could be tortured in ways so inhumane it scours my soul to read of them! These persecutions were about power, certainly not about salvation, or even doctrine for the most part. An accusation was equivalent to a death sentence. There was no real trial or consideration of evidence. A confession by torture was all that was needed. The '*heretics*' knew not what they had been charged with, nor who had made the charges, nor did they have the chance to testify against the charges. They were imprisoned, often for years, and only on the day of the auto-da-fe were they informed, as they stood before the court, of the charges and their sentence.

In comparison to this Christian god, Humanism looked pretty good. Humanism believed that all humans were intrinsically good, and therefore both Catholic and Protestant persecutions against all mankind were evil. **Hard to argue that!** When compared to the blood-thirsty, Hebrew-hating god which the Apostate Church had created - Humanism appeared as a shining light. **Plenty were willing, and still are, to dispense with religion and the horrific way it played god and practiced evil!**

Humanism rejected God! Despite the impetus it gave mankind to shut down the Inquisitions and other evils of the Church - **Humanism is a dead end**! Bertrand Russell offers the defining philosophy of Humanism in his essay, "*A Free Man's Worship.*"

> Man... his origin, his hopes and fears, his loves and his beliefs, are but the outcome of accidental collocations of atoms... No heroism, no intensity of thought and feeling, can preserve an individual life beyond the grave... All the labors of the ages, all the devotion, all the inspiration, all the noonday brightness of human genius, are destined to extinction in the vast death of the solar system, and that the whole temple of man's achievement must inevitably be buried beneath the debris of a universe in ruins... **Only within the scaffolding of these truths...**
> <u>**Only on the firm foundation of unyielding despair, can the soul's habitation henceforth be built!**</u>[8]

---

[8]Bertrand Russell, 1903, "*A Free Man's Worship*," & 1985, Routledge, London.

Is this all ancient history to you? Look around you. Do you see a world adhering to truth - or do you see a world that distorts truth to its own ends - not even trying to be consistent from one moment to the next? All Americans must soon be vaccinated to fly, re-enter the country, attend public events, or eat out in restaurants. Yet millions of the unvaccinated are encouraged by the same power brokers to pour over our border - no vaccination required! There are endless contradictions of truth occurring as we speak. We are dancing ever closer to the brink of collapse. It is growing worse. Things are falling apart and most are caught like deer in the headlights - uncertain, confused and afraid! **It is a painful awakening!** As William Butler Yeats predicted in *The Second Coming*:

> Things fall apart, the centre cannot hold;
> Mere anarchy is loosed upon the world,
> The blood-dimmed tide is loosened and
> everywhere the ceremony of innocence is drowned;
> **The best lack all conviction, while the worst
> are filled with passionate intensity!**[9]

The unvaccinated are the new Kulaks. I myself am unvaccinated. I have had Covid and recovered, gaining natural immunity. That does not matter to those pulling the strings. All must be vaccinated! I don't need it. I also have a heart condition. The vaccine(s) have been proven to cause myocarditis, pericarditis, and stroke even in healthy recipients. For those with a heart condition, it could be a death sentence. None of this matters. All must be vaccinated! I will not take the vaccine. Once one is forced to take an experimental vaccine, or anything else (such as a chip), against their will, they have accepted the state's right to impose it.

**This, my friend, is the mark of the beast!
The options for behavior control are endless.
We may win this battle but the war will rage on.**

The rule of law is being selectively enforced. In 1930s Germany, Nazi brownshirt rioters vandalized businesses nationwide, committing arson and even murder - and they were neither arrested nor prosecuted. In America 2020, Antifa/BLM rioters vandalized businesses nationwide, committing arson even murder - and they were neither arrested nor prosecuted! **We think it cannot happen to us... but it is happening!**

[9]William Butler Yeats. 1920, *The Second Coming*, The Dial Magazine, Ireland.

Yehovah's Renewed Covenant

A Messianic friend recently turned down an invitation to partake in a Christmas day feast and celebration. My friend thanked her acquaintance and declined. She said she was doing the feast days of Yehovah. The sender took offense and unloaded a full artillery barrage of Scripture in response. It boiled down to the judgement that - you are Old Testament and we are New Testament! We have a new covenant - new wine that calls for new wineskins. Others simply asked if she had become a Jew.

The new covenant mentioned is in Jeremiah 31:31-37:

> Behold the days are coming, **declares Yehovah**,
> when **I will make a renewed covenant with**
> **- the house of Israel and with the house of Judah -**
> not like the covenant which I made with their fathers…
>
> This is the covenant I will make with the house of Israel
> after those days, **declares Yehovah**,
> **I will put My Torah within them,**
> **and on their heart I will write it.**
> **And I will be their God and they will be my people!**

This Renewed Covenant is with the house of Israel and the house of Judah. So why do Christians think they are included? *The Hebrew Gospels* declare that "You *are all sons of God through faith in Yeshua Ha Mashiach…. There is neither Jew nor Greek… For you are all one in Yeshua…*" (Gal 3:26-28). Those who embrace the Son of Yehovah "*are grafted into*" the family tree of Israel equal to anyone else, with the caution that we not be boastful, or become "*wise in our conceits,*" because we can be removed just as easily (Rom 11:16-25). "***This is the only new covenant in the Bible. It is the only one to which the LORD God [Yehovah] is committed. He is not committed to what he has not promised!***"[10] 'LORD' is the translators' convention for '*Yehovah.*' So there are two requirements for being part of this Renewed Covenant. **One**, we must accept Yehovah's Son - Yeshua - the Hebrew Messiah - as our Savior. **Two**, we must accept Yehovah's Torah - His law - written upon our hearts.

It must be said that Yeshua was a Hebrew Messiah, and…
- no matter how much we may want it to be so -
Yeshua will never be Greek!

[10] Daniel Gruber, 2005:p.225, *Separation of Church & Faith,* v.1, Elijah Pub, NH.

Many have petitioned to Jesus Christ for their salvation and it was given. I could not be happier that Yeshua will answer to that name! Jesus and Yeshua are the same historical person. However, their archetypes are quite different. An archetype is our perception of who they are, what is their message, and what are their goals. **Many want to reject the Hebrew Yeshua - who upholds Torah - and embrace the Greek Jesus - who has done away with Torah! Welcome to the Schizophrenic Church!**

The remarkable truth is, there is no '*Christianity*'[11] in the New Testament, neither in word, nor concept! Yeshua was not calling for a new religion but for *Teshuvah* - a return to Yehovah and His Torah. Does that mean Christianity is bad?

> Some of the greatest humanitarians and humanitarian actions have come out of Christianity. Some of the greatest servants of God and Man, and some of the greatest servants to Israel, did what they did because of what their Christianity taught them. They produced some of the most beautiful events in mankind's rather ugly history. God produced in them works of great beauty and love. But it was God working in them, not **Christianity... All it did was provide a new name, a name which proclaimed separation from the Jewish people.**[12]

Yehovah answers to Theos, Deus, Dios, and LORD - Yeshua answers to the name Jesus. Good! But Yehovah and His Son Yeshua want you to know them on a deeper level. Intimacy without knowing the real names of Yehovah and Yeshua is much harder than it need be! The reason is simple enough.

We are grafted into the tree of Israel and the blessing of Abraham. **We are one with the chosen people!** The problem is that **Christianity - as a 'New Covenant Religion,'** "*has defined itself in opposition to the Jewish people for seventeen hundred years. All Jewishness has been removed from the major Church creeds.*"[13] "*After countless attempts to annihilate the Jewish people and any connection with them, after almost unceasing Catholic, Protestant, Orthodox, and Evangelical theological denunciation of the Jewish people and what God has given them -*

***Such an understanding of '*Christianity*' is not possible!*"**[14]

We want to embrace the Renewed Covenant and redefine it!
Welcome to the Schizophrenic Church!

---
[11] The word "*Christians*" in Acts is not in any of the earliest Greek manuscripts!
[12] Gruber, 2005:p.190, *Separation of Church & Faith.* [13]*Ibid.,p.191.* [14]*Ibid.,p.190.*

I know that many believe the tragedies of anti-Semitism are all behind us now. Think again. The Great Apostasy is not just the declaration to destroy the Messianic Church and Messianics but the Judaic Church and Jews as well. It is religious bigotry which has fueled and condoned anti-Semitism throughout the ages, including today. *"The recent spate of vicious attacks against Jewish Americans shouldn't surprise anyone. The fact is, anti-Semitism has been comfortably housed inside the Black Lives Matter movement. And just like attacks against police officers are tolerated and even celebrated by BLM activists, so are attacks against Jews."*[15] It is starting all over again - just as it has so often in history. **Welcome to the Schizophrenic Church!**

What Can We Do?

We can rejoice that *The Hebrew Gospels* and the Messianic Church have survived the long travail of the ages for a reason - to restore our understanding of the unity and balance of the Old Covenant and the Renewed Covenant! They are not set against each other. It is man who has made them so. This covenant is the key to our walk with our Creator and our Savior. The Messianics had tremendous success in bringing their brethren to Teshuvah. **What if we stopped encouraging Jews to become good Christians and embrace our Greek Jesus? What if we encouraged them to become better Jews and embrace their Hebrew Messiah - Yeshua?** *"Israel is going to turn to the Lord and be restored, but Israel is not going to come to Christianity!"*[16] Is truth so fearsome? The Hebrews - who are now mostly a highly secularized society - may choose to return to Yehovah as Messianics rather than Baptists or Catholics!

It will happen soon enough. We must awaken to the reality that we are not earthly creatures having a temporary spiritual experience. **We are spiritual creatures having a temporary earthly experience!** Trouble is coming - like in times past we must gird our loins. This is boot camp - not Club Med! We are created to be spiritual warriors. We are in the midst of a spiritual battle which cannot be understood in the spirit of scientific rationalism. Yehovah will anoint us and empower us. He will open our spiritual eyes - then it will make sense - and we will know what we have to do. Many will want to ignore - or escape - the truth anyway possible, even by hiding under the bed.

---

[15] Laura Ingraham, lauraingraham.com, May 21, 2021. [16] Daniel Gruber, p.192.

I do not want to miss this! I do not want to be sitting on the sidelines - or curled up in a fetal position - hiding under my bed. Yehovah is going to pour His spirit out on His anointed ones like never before! I want to be wherever I can do the most good. Millions upon millions of people will be making *Teshuvah* - returning to Yehovah and His Word of Truth in Torah - finding Salvation through His Son Yeshua! Yehovah will protect His own or take them home.

**We will fight the spiritual battle -
not as martyrs but as conquerors!
The spiritual battle is not over...
It has only just begun!**

*For your sake we are killed all the day long,
we are accounted as sheep for the slaughter.*
**<u>Nay</u>, in all these things we are more than conquerors
through him that loved us!**
Romans 8:36-37

This prophecy is from Psalms 44:22
& Zechariah 11:4-7.

End

| Little Lord Fauntleroy | The Fairy Princess |

Appendix A

In Memoriam:

*This book is dedicated
to my parents
Orlan & Wini Jones
who inspired me to be
a writer &
taught me their craft,
and to my beloved daughter
Firen Michelle
the best a father could have!*

Orlan Roger Jones
born Jan 22, 1928
Wilkesbarre, PA
died Oct 19, 2006
Kerrville, TX
Writer, Editor

Winifred Main Jones
born Jan 17, 1924
Hamilton, TX
died Feb 7, 2008
Kerrville, TX
Writer, Poet

Ladder to Heaven
by Miles Jones
2017

In our last memories they were not in their prime.
But we must never forget that, once upon a time…
The maiden Wini was The Fairy Princess,
And Orlan the boy, Little Lord Fauntleroy.

And I was The Midnight Rider of the Purple Sage,
By danger unfazed, my six guns blazed
To defend the good and vanquish evil.

We must never regret nor ever forget
These seeds of imaginings,
These magic beans, these day dreams
Shape the greater dream that is our lives.

For when I planted them, they thrived
And grew a stout and leafy vine, a ladder,
That reached all the way to heaven.

The Midnight Rider

The Intrepid Explorer

I bequeath these magic beans to you
My beloved… and to...
Your children and, in turn, their own.

For you are The Intrepid Explorer
Who round the whole wide world did roam
In search of adventure with me.

And I would not trade that memory of you,
To be a happy little cowboy again
Playing in the sunshine of youth.

One day, from this dream I will awaken
And climb that ladder to heaven…
Up to the greatest adventure of all.

And The Fairy Princess and The Little Lord
Will be waiting there to help me through,
As one day… The Midnight Rider
Will be there awaiting you too.

Appendix B

Review of Books by Dr. Miles Jones

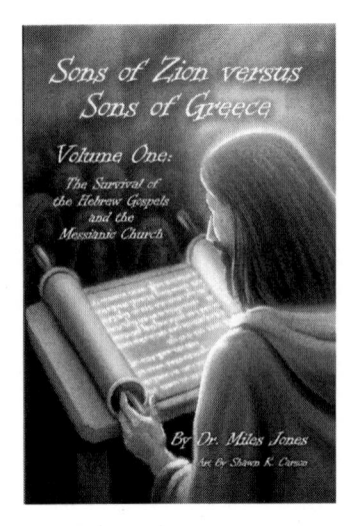

Reader Reviews of

Sons of Zion versus Sons of Greece

Volume One

My mind has been continuously blown/thrilled by what I've read and I have no doubts it will be blown many more times before this final chapter is complete! There is such a beautiful mixture of historical/scientific fact & incredible spiritual revelation in this book! Yehovah bless you for writing this and sharing this information, and bless the writing of Volume 2! Knowing the history of the early church, the history of the Messianic believers is something everyone who follows Yeshua needs to know!   Logan

I purchased this book and left a five star review! I'm 2/3s of the way thru it and found it hard to put down. The review was tough to do as there is so much good info, it was hard to describe to the public. A great "Hebrew Roots Primer" or a "Messianic Church Foundational Basics." Your book is truly many things covering cutting edge material for today's Hebraic Messianic Church. I can not imagine the hours of research and effort you put into this book. I can say well done!   Eric

Truth is being made flesh. You are giving me a greater understanding of my roots, a case of lost or mistaken identity. I am excited & can hardly wait for your second volume!   Douglas

Impressive and thought provoking. A confluence of significant biblical issues. Your work and investment to produce this is appreciated. He is Risen!   Ed

I have found your new book extraordinary, amazing & thoroughly scholarly. It has "blown me away"!!!   Paul

The author, by the Grace of God, has produced a valuable work for believers and non believers alike in these end times and has revealed a rare commodity by todays standards, THE TRUTH. Do not think that this book is a boring, dry, "Religious" dissertation- it is not. It is a fascinating read!   Arik

You know how a veil can drop, and one can see something in a whole new way, while wondering how it had been there all along and be unseen - the way you explained the reality and impact of the alphabet being given to humanity at Horeb.   Henry

Raises the standard for research!
Edward

Dr. Miles Jones has earned three degrees in languages and linguistics, culminating in a doctorate from The University of Texas at Austin in 1985. He is the author of *The Writing of God*, in which he translated the ancient Hebrew inscriptions from Mount Sinai in Midian, in Arabia. Their story speaks of events straight from the pages of Exodus. These inscriptions provided physical proof of the location of the real Mount Sinai, and that the *"writing of God"* from Exodus 32:16 - was the original alphabet of letters!

Dr. Jones doing field work in Arabia 1990

Sons of Zion versus Sons of Greece
Survival of the Hebrew Gospels & the Messianic Church

Dr. Jones has uncovered the earliest Hebrew manuscript of the Gospels - and authenticated their first century origin! The translation of ***The Hebrew Gospels*** of Matthew, Mark, Luke, and John - reveal a new depth of knowledge of our Hebrew Messiah, Yeshua Ha Mashiach. Heretofore, every thing we know about our Hebrew Messiah has come down to us through the Greek filter of a different language, culture, and thought. *Sons of Zion* reveals a secret power given to the Hebrews upon Mt. Sinai, and transferred in some degree to the Greeks. The subsequent history of the transmission of the Word has been the story of the war between the ***Sons of Zion vs Sons of Greece. The Hebrew Gospels*** were carefully preserved, and spread, by the original Messianic Church. Both *The Hebrew Gospels* and the Messianic Church were targeted for extinction by the Greco-Roman Church of Constantine.

**This is the untold story
of their miraculous survival!**

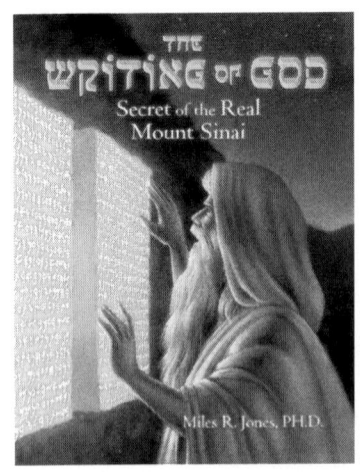

THE WRITING OF GOD
Secret of the Real Mount Sinai
Dr. Miles R. Jones

The Writing of God presents proof of the seminal event of the Old Testament, the Sinai Covenant, when God handed down to Moses the Word and the *"writing of God"* (Ex 32:16). The location of the real Mount Sinai has long been debated. Scripture states definitively that it is in Midian in Arabia (Galatians 4:26) where **researchers have found stunning archeological evidence of the events of the Exodus, including inscriptions from the base of Mount Sinai!**

These inscriptions reveal an incredible secret of the Bible. The ***"writing of God"*** written by *"the finger of God"* (Ex 31:18) is the first alphabetic writing! The Sinai Covenant was an educational covenant calling the Israelites to read, write, and *"diligently"* educate their children.

The evidence taken from the latest linguistic and archaeological research reveals the origin of the alphabet, the context of writing in the ancient world of 2nd millennium BC, the accurate timeline of Bible history, and the validation of the Old Testament as an historically accurate source.

The Writing of God explains the decline of modern education, especially literacy, as a result of abandoning the moral and the alphabetic principle of God in our schools. The call from Sinai is the spiritual clarion call for today's home-schoolers.

To order your copy go to *writingofgod.com*.

The Writing of God is the fascinating culmination of years of research by Dr. Miles Jones. His book on the writing covering the rocks at Mount Sinai in Arabia is nothing short of profound. Backed up by definitive evidence, it is an ancient puzzle coming together in our day.
This is a must read!
Jim & Penny Caldwell
Split Rock Research Foundation
authors, *God of the Mountain*

Miles Jones tackles a vital facet of New Chronology research – a revised timeline for the development of the first alphabetic script, from its beginnings in Egypt to the earliest scratchings of Proto-Semitic on desert rocks, through to Proto-Hebrew, Phoenician and Greek. The invention of our ancient alphabet – the alphabet used to write the Ten Commandments and the Book of Genesis – a fascinating story with major implications for world history!
David Rohl, author of *Pharaohs and Kings*,
From Eden to Exile, *Lords of Avaris*, and *Exodus*

Dr. Miles Jones is one of the few language experts exploring the link between the origins of the alphabet and the early writing of the Bible. This investigation for new evidence is both controversial and fascinating. The numerous connections brought to light in this new book demand further consideration by all thinkers.
Timothy Mahoney, documentary film maker,
Patterns of Evidence - The Exodus

"The stones will cry out!" Dr. Miles Jones has taken the inscriptions at Mount Sinai in Midian and made the stones speak! *The Writing of God* clarifies where and when God came to earth and what He said to the world.
I cannot wait for your book to be published!
Dr. Sung Hak Kim, author of *The Burning Bush*

This is the book that ties it all together! The discovery of the real Mount Sinai in Arabia makes real God's deed - to Abraham's seed - of the Promised Land. Here in Israel, the *"writing of God"* and the mapping of the footprints of the Israelites are the hope of this generation.
Michael Rood, author of *The Chronological Gospels*

The Coming Crisis
Answering the Call from Sinai in a time of Chaos

This book is not only a prophetic voice of what is facing us in the near future, but also how we got into this crisis in the first place and how we can rectify our lives and the future of our nation. Dr. Jones traces the roots of the crisis as it has been brewing in our educational system and society for many decades. For those who want the truth and facts you will not get from the media - **this is the time to heed the prophetic voice. It may be the only time we have left!**

Dr. Miles Jones has earned three degrees in languages and linguistics, culminating in a doctorate from the University of Texas at Austin in 1985. Dr. Jones has lived the stories he relates in The Coming Crisis as a long-time classroom teacher and an Associate Professor of Education. He has researched the topic of educational effectiveness and reform for decades. His description of the corruption and challenges we face in reforming the educational system come from the inside out.

Dr. Jones is the author of *The Writing of God*, in which he translated ancient Hebrew inscriptions from Mount Sinai in Midian, in Arabia. They tell a story straight from the pages of Exodus! These inscriptions provided physical proof of the location of the real Mount Sinai, and that the *"writing of God"* was the original alphabet. The call from Sinai was a mandate for universal education. Dr. Jones recovered the earliest Hebrew manuscripts of the Gospels - and authenticated their first century origin! He translated them and wrote their story in *Sons of Zion vs Sons of Greece: Survival of the Hebrew Gospels and the Messianic Church*.

To order your copy go to *writingofgod.com*

The Epistle of James from the Hebrew

James (Ya'kov), the brother of Yeshua the Messiah was one of the most critical players in the early history of what we now call Christianity. According to Paul (Shaul) and *The Hebrew Gospels*, Yeshua, after his resurrection, appeared to James and Cleopas and anointed his brother James as the leader of the Nazarenes. This is a story left out of the Greek Gospels and Church history. The emerging Greek Church did not want to sanctify a Yeshua dynasty. The Greeks wanted a Greek dynasty not a Hebrew one. They wanted a Greek Church and to make it authoritative they needed Greek Scripture, Greek doctrine, a Greek God, and a Greek Jesus. They also wanted the mantle of the chosen people. Christians typically have no idea that four of Yeshua's Apostles were relatives - nor that his brothers James and Jude, and his cousin Simeon, led the Messianic Church during its spread throughout the world. Little note is made of **James' thirty years of leadership of the Nazarenes during the most dynamic and dangerous period of its existence!**

James' vibrant message in his Epistle is made to sit in the back of the bus, rather the back of the Bible, with the other Hebrew Epistles - Hebrews, James, 1st-2nd Peter, 1st-3rd John, Jude and Revelation. James' message is one that rocks the Greek Church on its heels. **It is not by faith alone that we are saved!** If you claim faith but take no action then you did not get the complete message! Most importantly, James puts the Torah back in Scripture making it crystal clear - he that slanders the Torah is trying to be the Torah - to assume the role of Yehovah. As the Messiah did, James also declares the Sacred Name of Yehovah.

In July of 2021, the Epistle of James (Ya'akov) from the Hebrew was the first translation from the Hebrew Gospels & Brit Hadashah (New Testament).

This is the first publication of The Hebrew Gospels Publication Project!

To order your copy go to *writingofgod.com*

Appendix C

The Markan Perspective

Reprinted from:
Sons of Zion vs Sons of Greece - Volume One
Chapter 12 - The Acculturation Principle

"To understand the *Markan Perspective*, one must imagine it as the only Gospel.

If there were no other Gospels, what picture would Mark paint for us of the disciples?"[1]

---

[1] Miles R. Jones, 2019:p.226, *Sons of Zion vs Sons of Greece: Volume One*.

| 40 AD | 50 | 40-60 | 60 | 90-100 |

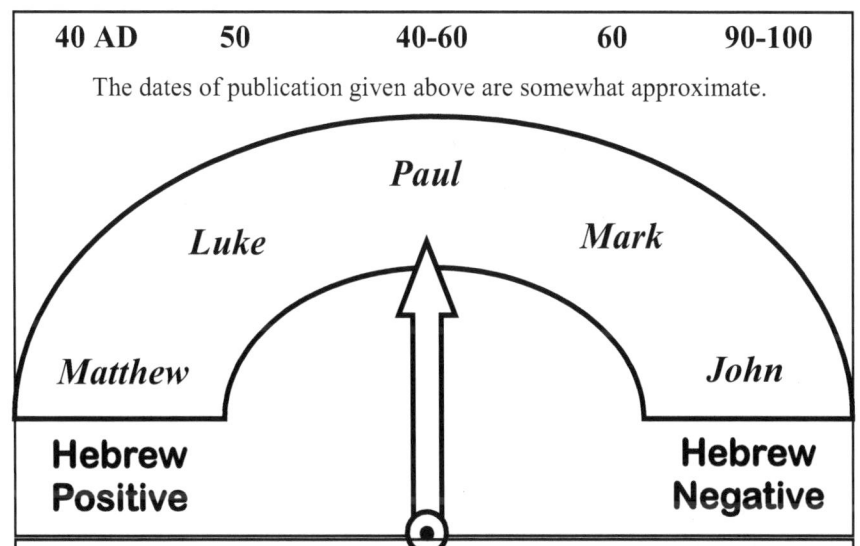

The dates of publication given above are somewhat approximate.

```
          Paul
   Luke          Mark

Matthew                John

Hebrew                 Hebrew
Positive               Negative
```

The Acculturation Principle - Any text transported, translated, copied and recopied into another language and culture will tend to take on elements of that culture. The distance from its origin across time, place & culture will usually determine what degree of acculturation differences will be integrated into the text.

The Principle of Acculturation is well known in linguistic practice.[2] As applied to language learning it is the major causal factor in success in learning another language in the cultural context - living and learning in the culture - as opposed to the classroom. A language learner achieves mastery via cultural assimilation - becoming part of that culture. **The acceptance of a textual tradition, along with its ideas, into a new culture, typically mimics that cultural assimilation.** A Gentile Church growing increasingly distant from its Hebrew roots over time, over distance, and over culture - would expect to see that reflected in the texts it produced. **As many Gentiles, including Christians, became more anti-Semitic - so did their religious writing!**

<u>**The Gospels are no exception to this principle!**</u>

Matthew is the most Hebrew positive of all the Gospels, followed by Luke. Paul straddles the fence, *"I have become all things to all men, that I might by all means save some"* (1st Cor 9:22). **Mark depicts the Hebrew characters of his Gospel (other than Jesus) - especially the disciples - in a negative light!** John, however, has the most glaring anti-Judaic declarations of any book in the New Testament. (See chart above)

[2] John Schumann, 1979:pp.27-107, *"The Acculturation Model,"* in Gingras.

The Gospel of Mark

Mark was half Jewish, his mother was reported to be the widow of a Roman. Mark is a man straddling the divide between his mother's Hebrew worldview and his father's Hellenistic one. Mark's conflict of identity is a defining factor in his gospel perspective. "*Mark wrote in a predominantly Gentile milieu.*"[3]

Within the Greek Church a new archetype of the Messiah was emerging - **a Greek Jesus who rejects Torah is overshadowing the Hebrew Yeshua who upholds it!** Mark is a Grecian - writing in Greek for the Greeks. Mark portrays the Greek Christ, an archetype very different from Yeshua.[4] Mark's depiction of the Apostles is dramatically different from the Hebrew positive Gospels of Matthew and Luke.

Mark's Polemic Argument Against the Disciples

Mark's portrayal of the disciples must be seen as a literary device in the service of a polemic against a conservative Jewish Christian group in Palestine which placed no positive meaning in Jesus' death, held to the long-established Jewish practices, and rejected the necessity of the Gentile mission.[5]

Theodore Weeden describes three progressive stages in Mark's "*polemic against the disciples.*" In Stage One, which occupies the first half of the Gospel, the disciples cannot perceive the true identity and power of Jesus. To cite one example, in Mark 4:3-9 Jesus preaches the Parable of the Sower.

Some seeds fall on bad ground and wither away or are eaten, while some fall on good ground and bring forth fruit, some thirtyfold, some sixty and some one hundredfold. Jesus ends by saying, "*He that has ears to hear, let him hear.*" He tells the disciples that it is given unto them "to *know the mystery of the kingdom of God*" (Mk 4:11-13) and then he asks: "*Know you not this parable? And how then will you know all parables?*" And so it goes, Jesus speaks to the people in parables and each time he must explain them to his disciples (Mk 4:34).

---

[3] Bernard Orchard & Harold Riley, 1987:p.97, *The Order of the Synoptics*.
[4] I use '*Jesus*' or '*Christ*' when the context reflects the Greek archetype and '*Yeshua*' or '*Messiah*' when the Hebrew archetype is reflected or referred to.
[5] Theodore Weeden, 1971:p.25, *Mark: Traditions in Conflict*, Fortress Press.

The people flocked to Jesus as a miracle worker and when one such crowd had gathered, he asked his disciples to feed his flock. They replied they had only five loaves and two fish. Jesus blessed them and the people all ate and they took up 12 baskets of leftovers when they were done. *"And they that ate of the loaves were about five thousand men. And straightaway he constrained his disciples to get into the ship and go..."* Jesus departed unto a mountain to pray. A storm soon arose and they rowed desperately. Then they saw Jesus *"walking upon the sea."* As soon as he went up into the boat - the wind ceased - and the disciples were *"amazed... beyond measure, and wondered.* **Yet they considered not the miracle of the loaves: for their hearts were hardened**" (Mark 6:43-52). Having seen miracles of nature, healing, and provenance - still they did not understand! In Matthew 14:33, after Jesus walked on water and calmed the storm, they *"came to him and worshiped him, saying, of a truth you are the Son of God."*

The multitudes of the Jews understand that Jesus was a miracle worker - but in Mark - His disciples show no signs of knowing who he is for many months. Strangers get it, foreigners get it, even the demons know who he is, but his disciples seem perplexed, obdurate. A week after the feeding of the 5,000 - another multitude gathers to hear Jesus, many, after following him for days, are famished. Again Jesus wants to feed them and again the disciples are hapless, *"From where can a man satisfy these with bread here in the wilderness?"* (Mk 8:4). After feeding this new crowd of 4,000, Jesus says, *"Beware the leaven of the Pharisees, and of the leaven of Herod"* (Mk 8:15).

> Now the disciples had forgotten to take bread... And they reasoned among themselves, saying, **It is because we have no bread.** And when Jesus knew it, he said unto them, Why reason you, because you have no bread? Perceive you not yet, neither understand? **Have you your heart yet hardened?** Having eyes, see you not? And having ears, hear you not? And do you not remember? When I broke the five loaves among 5,000... And then the seven among 4,000... **How is it that you do not understand?** (Mark 8:14-21)

Right after the second miraculous feeding of bread to thousands - the disciples are concerned over their lack of bread! Jesus explains again but the disciples do not understand and Jesus reproaches them, *"How is it you do not understand?"* (Mark 8:21)

There are some passages in Matthew and Luke where the disciples are uncomprehending but they are minor compared to the big picture. In Mark, the narrative of the disciples' unyielding bewilderment is the whole picture!

In Stage Two the disciples are awakening to Jesus as the Messiah, but they misconceive his mission. When Peter responds to Jesus' query, *"Whom say you that I am? Peter answered... You are the Christ"* (Mark 8:29). It seems like progress, but *"any assumption the disciples have received a complete understanding of Jesus is soon proven false."* [6] Jesus then *"began to teach them, that the Son of Man must suffer many things... and be killed"* (Mark 8:32). *"And Peter took him and began to rebuke him."* The disciples in Mark were not able to accept what Jesus was telling them about his coming martyrdom.

The Markan disciples wanted a conquering-king messiah not a suffering-servant messiah. *"Consequently, throughout the rest of the Gospel one finds the disciples and Jesus locked in a continuous conflict over the characteristics of authentic messiahship."*[7] Jesus is thorough in teaching his disciples the meaning of his sacrifice and their own place in it (see Mark 8:31, 9:31, 10:33-43). Yet they argue. James and John want to sit on his right hand and his left as heirs to his kingdom (10:35). This is not so odd if you remember they are relatives, the grandsons of Jesus' uncle Cleopas. Nonetheless, it is not about mounting a throne - but about mounting a cross!

Repeatedly, the disciples fail to absorb this teaching. Weeden gives other passages illustrating the disciples' misconception of Jesus' mission in Mark 9:39-40 and 10:13-16. In Matthew and Luke these discordant passages are either not present or the conflicts are softened and explained, presenting a net neutral picture of the disciples at this stage. Stage One: Misperception - Stage Two: Misconception - now we move into the final Stage Three of the Markan Perspective: Rejection.

To understand the *Markan Perspective*,[8] one must imagine it as the only Gospel. If there were no other Gospels, what picture would Mark paint for us of the disciples? Stage Three of the Markan Perspective - Rejection - begins with the betrayal of Jesus by his disciple Judas Iscariot.

---

[6] Weeden, 1971: p.33, *Mark: Traditions in Conflict*, Fortress Press. [7] Ibid, p.34.
[8] The *'Markan Priority'* theory that Mark was actually the first Gospel, became predominate only in the 1900s and will be discussed at length in Volume Two.

At Gethsemane, Jesus asks Peter, James, and John to stand vigil with Him and pray - yet three times he finds them asleep! Later, when Jesus was seized, *"they all forsook him and fled"* (Mark 14:50), despite Peter's insistence that *"Even if all fall away, I will not!"* (Mark 14:29). To this Jesus responds, *"Even this night, before the cock crows twice, you shall deny me thrice"* (Mark 14:30). And so it goes, Peter followed the soldiers to the Palace and was identified three times as a follower, and three times he denied it, finally *"he began to curse and to swear, saying, I know not this man of whom you speak"* (Mark 14:71).

Total renouncement of Jesus by Peter, the acknowledged leader of the disciples, is the climax of Stage Three in Mark. The other Gospels contain a kinder narrative - including redemptive passages. Luke, for example, *"You are they which have continued with me in my temptations. And I appoint unto you a kingdom, as my Father has appointed unto me"* (Luke 22:28-29). In the other Gospels the disciples are redeemed. The resurrection erases their blindness, the risen Christ re-embraces them with the knowledge that what he, and they, have been through was necessary and foretold. He takes them up on the mountain in Galilee to teach them and they come down very clearly as changed and courageous men. As I have previously written, *"they went up as lambs and came down as lions."* The Holy Spirit descends upon them at Pentecost (Shavuot) and in this baptism of the Spirit they receive their divine anointment as Apostles.

From the Markan Perspective none of this happens! Jesus arose from the grave and appeared to them, *"and upbraided them with their unbelief and hardness of heart because they believed not them which had seen him after he was risen"* then immediately commands them to *"go into all the world, and preach the gospel"* (Mark 16:14-15).

Mark's Gospel is tremendously challenged by the fact that **the last twelve verses are nowhere to be found in the earliest Greek manuscripts - leaving out entirely the great commission!** It ended with the discovery of the angel at the empty tomb by the women, who went away and told no one because they were afraid (Mark 16:1-8). These last verses of Mark are in ***The Hebrew Gospels from Catalonia*** [HGC] so it is possible they were recovered from *The Hebrew Gospels*.

I have reviewed the evidence in great detail and I agree *"that we should consider the question of the last twelve verses of Mark 'still open'"* including the possibility that *"Mark 16:9-20 was written by a later writer..."*[9] I think that it is far more likely the final page of the widely copied Greek manuscript was simply lost or that Mark himself later added the final verses - because his Gospel obviously had no ending, no closure.

The Markan Perspective of Stage Three - Rejection - comes from what is <u>not</u> in Mark - rather than what is. The disciples are never redeemed! After Judas' betrayal, and Peter's denial, of the Messiah - the disciples fled and were absent from most all subsequent events. They were not at the cross. They were not at the tomb. Jesus returns to rebuke them then sends them out. They receive no forgiveness, no enlightenment, no transformative teaching upon the mount in Galilee, no baptism of the Holy Spirit - no final anointment *"given to know the mystery of the kingdom of God"* (Mk 4:11) which had been offered. **From the Markan Perspective the disciples have failed completely!**

The Markan Perspective interprets Mark as the Gospel of Replacement Theology. It is a rejection - not only of the Judaic religion blamed for the crucifixion of Jesus - but also a rejection of the Messianic Church in Jerusalem led by the failed disciples. In Mark - for abandoning the Son of God - the disciples were rejected by God! From the Markan Perspective, they fall back into rabbinic law - the commandments of men. *"Howbeit in vain do they worship me, teaching for doctrines the commandments of men"* (Mark 7:7). From the Markan Perspective the Apostles have turned away from Jesus' teachings! A view I do not share.

In this way, the Markan Perspective separated Jesus from his Hebrew disciples - who have ALL - not only failed him, but also rejected him! The divine Son of God is seen as being above the Hebrew race, religion and language. Yeshua is no longer a Hebrew. Jesus is now a Greek Christian!

> With the separation of Christianity from Judaism… Jesus' Jewishness was forgotten; he became a "Christian" and was understood to be criticizing Judaism from without. This tendency became normative in Christianity.[10]

---

[9] William Farmer, 1974:p.109, *The Last Twelve Verses of Mark*.
[10] William Farmer, 1999:p.4, *Anti-Judaism and the Gospels*.

Redemption of the Gospel of Mark

Let me make it perfectly clear that as a Bible scholar and believer - I utterly and unequivocally reject this interpretation of the Markan Perspective! Mark contributed little that was new to the Gospels. Thankfully, we have the witness of the earlier Gospels of Matthew and Luke to balance our knowledge of the Apostles. If those Gospels had edited out all positive references to the Apostles the result might be something similar to the viewpoint from Mark. I suspect the tailoring of this perspective in Mark may have been done by later Greek editors. It is difficult to believe Mark held this Hebrew negative perspective. Nonetheless, it should not be the perspective of believers.

Like so many Christians I have been taught to anchor my faith upon the inerrancy of the Word. It is inescapable, and highly disturbing to me, that Mark, the first Gospel originally and entirely written in Greek, is Hebrew negative! The Church declared the Gospels divine and inerrant for two reasons. First, to put them on a par with the Hebrew Old Testament. Second, the claim of inerrancy prevents any challenge to church dogma. It also makes it easier to manipulate the text. **Always keep foremost in mind that only God's truth is inerrant, not man's!**

Much has been made of the statement in 2nd Timothy 3:16, *"All Scripture is given by inspiration of God..."* This refers to the Torah, the Old Testament, vetted for centuries. At the time, most of the New Testament had yet to be written, compiled and canonized. In my view, however, the Old & New Testament both are the sacred Word of God - and it is our sacred duty to be vigilant about changes made by later agenda-driven editors!

Should we not want to know this truth about Mark? As Yeshua Ha Mashiach said repeatedly to his disciples, *"He who has ears to hear, let him hear."* Do we have ears to hear the truth or do we hear only what we want to hear? If so, then we are deaf to the truth. Do we have eyes to see the truth or do we see only what we want to see? If so, then we are blind to the truth. Hebrews 13:8 says, ***"Jesus Christ is the same - yesterday, today and forever."*** **If so, Yeshua the Messiah is still the Son of God *and* a Hebrew rabbi welcoming all - Hebrew, Greek, and Gentile - equally into the love and grace of Yehovah!**

Appendix D

Bar & Bat Mitzvah Accelerated Learning Programs of the Benai Emunah Institute

בְּנֵי אֱמוּנָה

Benai Emunah Institute for Accelerated Learning

B'nai Emunah - Household of Faith

Let us do good to all, but especially to those of the household of faith. Galatians 6:10

B'nai Emunah is a non-profit educational & religious institute dedicated to restoring the original Messianic Church of the first century through research and education. 121 Mountain Way Drive, Kerrville, Tx 78028 - phone 214 546 7893, writingofgod.com

HEBREW INSCRIPTIONS DISCOVERED !

The first photographic and video evidence was brought out by Jim & Penny Caldwell in 1992. Since then dozens of books and documentaries have been done on the discovery of the real Mount Sinai in Midian. In 2002, Dr. Miles Jones contacted the Caldwells and they shared with him photographs of ancient inscriptions from the base of Mount Sinai and from Rephidim. The inscriptions from Rephidim were the footprints of the Israelites traced into the stones with an alphabetic caption which said they were the *"soles of their feet,"* written in the oldest alphabet known to linguistic science, the Thamudic alphabet. Four other inscriptions were deciphered by Dr. Jones, all funerary. One said *"Died Amalek"*, another *"Died Hagar"* and another *"Died Amiah daughter of Hagar"* - all written in ancient Hebrew - telling a story from the pages of Exodus!

Dr. Jones doing field work in Arabia 1990

Order Dr. Jones' book *The Writing of God* for the exciting story!
Go to *writingofgod.com*.

Jones Geniuses
in the news

For more information
on B'nai Emunah Institute
for Accelerated Learning
go to jonesgeniuses.com
or call 817 718 8822

The Call from Sinai - Ten Keys - Scriptural Basis of Home Schooling

From *The Writing of God* by Dr. Miles Jones

1) The call from Sinai is **a sacred Covenant which God intended to reach the whole world**… *"Now therefore, if you will obey my voice indeed, and keep my covenant then you shall be a peculiar treasure unto me above all people, for all the earth is mine. And you shall be unto me a kingdom of priests…"* (Ex 19:5-6)

2) **It is written by God's own hand**, it could be important… *"And He gave unto Moses, when he had made an end of communing with him upon Mount Sinai, two tablets of testimony, tablets of stone, written with the finger of God."* (Ex 31:18)

3) **The Sinai Covenant is a teaching Covenant**… *"And the LORD said unto Moses, come up to me into the mount, and be there: And I will give you tablets of stone, and a law, and commandments which I have written; that you may teach them."* (Ex 24:12)

4) God stipulates **two purposes of the Covenant, His word and His writing**… *"And the LORD said unto Moses, write these words, for after the purpose and character of these words I have made a covenant with you and with Israel"* (Ex 34:27 Amplified Bible).

5) **God provided the Israelites with a system of writing**… *"And Moses turned, and went down the mount, and the two tablets of the testimony were in his hand: the tablets were written on both their sides; on the one side and on the other were they written. **And the tablets were the work of God, and the writing was the writing of God…**"* (Ex 32:15-16) God specified the writing of God, the alphabet, is of Him. *"I am Alpha and Omega, the beginning and the ending… the first and the last: what you see, write in a book…"* (Rev 1:8-11). The Covenant included numeracy - letters were also used for numbers. *"Take you the sum…and divide…"* and multiply, measure, do fractions, etc. (Numbers 1:1-2).

6) **The Covenant bestows a blessing** on those who answer the call from Sinai… *"And He has filled him with the spirit of God, in wisdom, in understanding, and in knowledge…"* (Ex 35:31) *"And He has put it in his heart that he may teach…"* (Ex 35:34). God specified the power of this Covenant blessing to His believers… *"Behold I make a covenant… I will do marvels, such as have not been done in all the earth… with you"* (Ex 34:10). (continued on next page)

(continued from previous page)

7) **The Covenant is for men... and women...** *"And every able and wise-hearted man in whose mind the Lord had put wisdom and ability, everyone whose heart stirred him up to come to do the work..."* (Ex 36:2) ***"And they came, both men and women, as many as were willing-hearted..."*** (Ex 35:22), **and children...** Daniel and his cohort were learning the word & the writing of God. *"God gave them knowledge and skill in all learning and wisdom..."* (Dan 1:17 also Ex 35:31).

8) **Scripture specifies a Godly Yardstick** - a measure for those receiving the blessing of the Covenant... *"In all matters of wisdom and understanding, that the king inquired of them, he found them **ten times better than all the** [wise men] **that were in his realm**"* (Dan 1:20).

9) **The Covenant commanded believers to teach the word & the writing of God to their children...** *"Said the Lord, I will put my law in their inward parts, and write it in their hearts; and will be their God, and they shall be my people"* (Jer 31:33). *"You shall read this law..."* (Deut 31:11) *"And you shall write them* [words of the law] *upon the posts of your house, and on your gates"* (Deut 6:9). *"And you shalt teach them diligently unto your children, and shall talk of them when you sit in your house, and when you walk by the way, and when you lie down,* and when you rise up" (Deut 6:7).

10) **There is a curse to those who do not obey the Covenant...** *"Behold, I set before you this day a blessing and a curse, a blessing if you obey... and a curse if you will not obey..."* (Deut 11:26-28) *"My people are destroyed for lack of knowledge: because you have rejected knowledge, I will also reject you, that you shalt be no priest to me: seeing you have forgotten the law of your God, I will also forget your children"* (Hos 4:6).

The Mensa Contest

In 1995 inner-city Dallas 2nd graders took on MENSA PhDs in a contest of speed and accuracy calculating powers and roots. The 2nd graders did all the math mentally, the PhDs were allowed to use calculators. Teams had to answer first, and correctly to win. We spoke of the Godly Yardstick of Daniel 1:20, where the king stated Daniel and his fellows were *"ten times better than all the wise men in his kingdom."* You be the judge whether Mensa PhDs are some of the most knowledgeable men in the kingdom - and whether these children were *"ten times better!"*

Jones Geniuses Beat Mensa PhDs 14 to 6!

Some of the contest problems!

$107^2 = 11{,}449$

$1025^2 = 1{,}050{,}625$

$(\sqrt[3]{5832})^2 = 324$

$\sqrt[3]{2{,}887{,}174{,}368} = 78$

$10{,}035^2 = 100{,}701{,}225$

$(\sqrt[3]{373{,}248})^2 = 5184$

$1{,}000{,}455^2 = 1{,}000{,}910{,}206{,}025$

$\sqrt[3]{681{,}472} = 88$

$75{,}500^2 = 5{,}700{,}250{,}000$

$1{,}000{,}955{,}000^2 = 1{,}001{,}910{,}912{,}025{,}000{,}000$

Initial Results of Jones Geniuses Accelerated Learning Program

1993-94 L.K. Hall Elementary - Out of 22 second graders, 13 read at or above 3rd grade reading level - 10 read at or above 4th grade, 7 read at or above 5th grade, 5 read at or above 6th grade and 1 read at or above 8th grade. Average - grade 3, 8th month.

1994-95 Sam Houston Elementary - First Grade, 75% were above the 50th percentile on the SABE, 25% above the 90th percentile.

1995-96 John F. Kennedy Learning Center - Sixth Grade, after only 7-10 days of Accelerated Learning, students went from 46% passing on math basic skills tests to 95% passing.

1997-99 Rogers Elementary - First Grade, 95% of students were above the 50th percentile in reading, 53% in the top quartile. In math 90% of students above 50th percentile, 56% in top quartile.

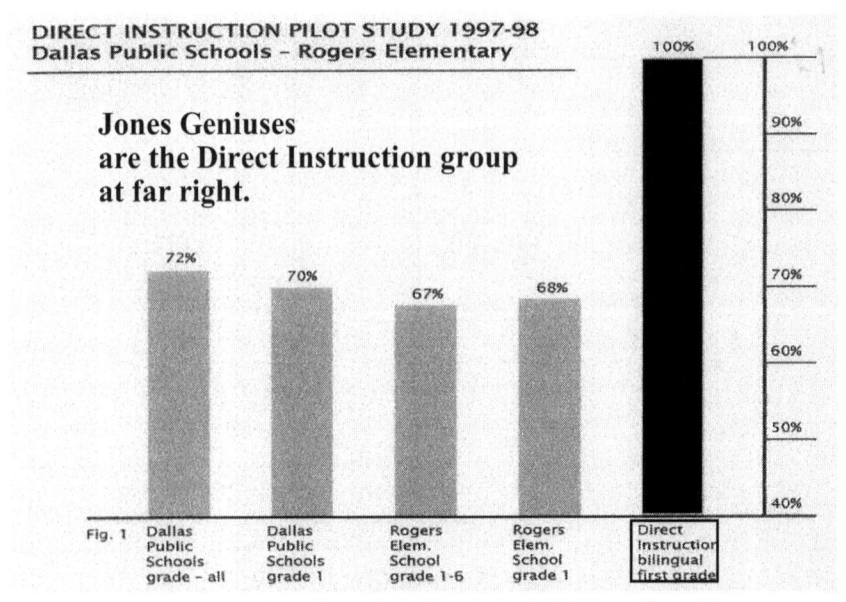

DIRECT INSTRUCTION PILOT STUDY 1997-98
Dallas Public Schools - Rogers Elementary

Jones Geniuses are the Direct Instruction group at far right.

Fig. 1	Dallas Public Schools grade - all	Dallas Public Schools grade 1	Rogers Elem. School grade 1-6	Rogers Elem. School grade 1	Direct Instruction bilingual first grade
	72%	70%	67%	68%	100%

Percent Passing Standardized SABE Reading Test

JONES GENIUSES ACCELERATED EDUCATION

So Many Can't be Wrong!

For more info, go to: jonesgeniuses.com or call 817 718 8822

"Dr. Jones' math curriculum is the most advanced, exciting and easy to implement program I have ever found. The kids excelled quickly and came to enjoy a subject they had only tolerated before. My 3-year-old learned the basic of reading and math. My 17-year-old is doing cube roots in her head. What more can you ask of a course of study?" **Cindy Camp, Garland, Texas**

"The *Genios* regularly stun observers with lightning-fast mathematical calculations. Children are zipping through problems most educated adults would have trouble solving even with a calculator."
Rebecca Rodriguez, Dallas Observer

"I was in my first college math course with students who were several years older than me. On the first day the teacher asked what was the fifth root of 32. Of course, to a Jones Genius that is an easy question, but when I answered it everyone turned to look at me in awe." **Meredith Escobar, Lancaster, Tx**

"Dr. Jones speed reading class definitely helped me obtain a better score on my college entrance exams. Since I have used time-compressed speech for the past three months my reading speed has increased by leaps and bounds. While I was taking the test I was able to skim the reading material quickly and answer the questions correctly. The Speed Reading Lab has definitely helped my reading ability, comprehension and speed." **Cameron Cooper, Austin, Texas**

"Nine months ago none of these children spoke English... Now they are reading Tom Sawyer. First graders now do fourth, fifth, and sixth grade work... A teacher who is making a difference!"
Doug Wilson, Channel Eight News, Dallas

"Kevin is surging into addition and subtraction and phonics. And Maureen 'loves' math. They both love the ribbons. Wow! I'm impressed. Being a math kind of guy myself, I can see the incredible depth of understanding of how the mind learns and the amount of tedious work that has gone into this. I want to encourage you because you are really on to something."
Randle McCaslin, Austin, Texas

"When we first met Dr. Jones, Kristen was in 6th grade and needed a jumpstart in math. She was suffering from math phobia and was very behind, barely able to add and subtract, let alone multiply and divide. Within that year she became a Grand Facts Master and her math phobia disappeared. She went on to be on the demonstration team and eventually became captain of the team. I tell people that she went from not being able to multiply to finding the cube root of six-digit numbers. Amazing!" **Tara Rose, DeSoto, Texas**

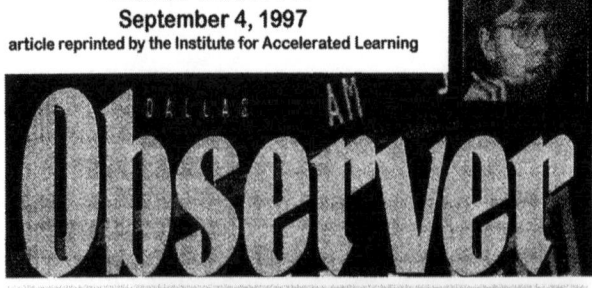

Dallas Observer
September 4, 1997
article reprinted by the Institute for Accelerated Learning

Are "Jones' Geniuses" too smart for DISD?

Observer

TOO SMART FOR THEIR OWN GOOD

"JONES' GENIUSES" CAN CALCULATE DIFFICULT MATH PROBLEMS IN THEIR HEADS. BUT DISD HASN'T ALWAYS LIKED THE ANSWERS.

BY REBECA RODRIGUEZ

PHOTOGRAPHS BY MARK GRAHAM

DISD accelerated learning expert Miles Jones teaches his "geniuses" in after-school math sessions, which he sometimes holds in his Oak Lawn apartment. Here he uses handmade flashcards to pose yet another challenge to his elementary-school pupils.

Eight-year-old Veronica Martinez is calculating the cube root of 474,552 in her head. At the same time, she is attempting to devour a cheese sandwich - between gulps of water from a tan-rimmed coffee cup.

It takes less than eight seconds to consume the mathematical problem, slightly longer for the sandwich. She wriggles a hand free and slams it down hard on her bell. "Seventy-eight!" she yells out.

"Seventy-eight what?" asks Miles Jones, her teacher. "Seventy-eight feet," she answers coyly.

Veronica continues to ignore the scratch pad in front of her as she moves on to other problems. Like 75,500 squared. (Answer: 5,700,250,000.) Or the fifth root of 2,887,174,368. (Answer: 78.) Sometimes, as she's working through the numbers in her mind, her eyes glaze over a little through pink plastic glasses. But eventually, the pigtails start swinging, and she smiles again. She's got the answer.

To read the complete article and others, or watch videos of Jones Geniuses go to jonesgeniuses.com.

Bibliography of Messianic Church Arising!

Bibliography

Adams, Susan M. *et al.* 2008. *"The Genetic Legacy of Religious Diversity..."* American Journal Human Genetics. 83(6):p.75.
Adler, Elkan. 1987. *Jewish Travellers in The Middle Ages.* Dover, N.Y.
Akins, Jimmy. 2018. *"Does Luke Contradict when Jesus was Born?"* Catholic Answers online at strangenotions.com.
Akenson, Donald Harmon. 1998. *Surpassing Wonder.* Harcourt Brace, N.Y.
Allen, H.R. 1976. *Buccaneer Admiral Sir Henry Morgan.* Barker Publishing, London.
Allen, Jarette K. 2011. *La Bible en Occittan.*
Al-Ansary, Abdul-Rahman & Majeed Khan et al. 2002. *Al-bid: History & Archaeology.* Saudi Arabian Ministries of Education, Antiquities & Museums.
Arnaud, Henri. 1827. *Glorious Recovery by the Vaudois.* Murray, London.
Asbury, Herbert. 1936, reprinted 1984. *The French Quarter.* Alfred A. Knopf. Reprint by Mockingbird Books, GA.
Ashdown, A. G. *The Evangelical Library Bulletin.* Spring 1986, #76, p.3.
Augustine. 354-430 AD. *The City of God.*
Baer, Yitzhak.1966. *A History of the Jews in Christian Spain.* Duke University Press. US.
Baity, Elizabeth Chesley. *"Archaeoastronomy... So Far."* Current Anthropology, Oct 1973, vol. 14, no. 4.
Baker, R.A. 2015. *"The First Century,"* churchhistory101.com.
Barc, Bernard. 2015, *"Siméon le Juste: L'auteur oublié de la Bible hébraïque,"* in Paul-Hubert Poirier, *Judaïsme Ancien et Origines du Christianisme.* Turnout, Brepols Online.
Barnes, A.S. 1905. *"The Gospel According to the Hebrews."* Journal of Theological Studies, vol. 6, p.361.
Barreto, Mascarenhas. 1988. English ed. 1992, The *Portuguese Columbus: Secret Agent of John II,* McMillan Press, N.Y.
Baus, Karl. 1965. *The Apostolic Community to Constantine.* Herder and Herder, New York.
Beauregard, Cosa de. 1816. *Memoires Historiques.*
Beinart, Haim. 1981. *Conversos on Trial.* Magnes Press. Hebrew University. Israel.
Bennett, Todd. 2016. *The Christian Conundrum.* Herkimer, NY.

Bethune-Baker, J.F. 1998. *Nestorius and His Teaching: A Fresh Examination.* Wipf & Stock Publishers, Eugene, OR.

Boase, Roger. 1978. *The Troubadour Revival.* Routledge & Kegan Paul, London.

Bovon, Francois & John Duffy. 2012:pp.457-465. "*A New Greek Fragment of Ariston of Pella's Dialogue of Jason and Papiscus.*" Harvard Theological Review, vol 105, issue 4.

Boyarin, Daniel. 2012. *The Jewish Gospels: The Story of the Jewish Christ.* The New Press, N.Y.

Bradford, Will editor, 1850. *Correspondences of Charles V*, Bently Publishers, London.

Brague, Remi. 2011. *The Legend of the Middle Ages.* Univ. of Chicago Press, Chicago.

Broadbent, Eric. *The Pilgrim Church.* 1931, reprinted 2014 by Resurrected Books, U.S.

Brown, Michael. 1990. *Our Hands are Stained with Blood.* Destiny Publishers, PA.

Blenkinsopp, Joseph. 1992. *The Pentateuch.* Doubleday, N.Y.

Buchanan, Claudius. 1812, 2019. *Christian Researches in Asia*, Forgotten Books.

Bütz, Jeffrey. 2005. *The Brother of Jesus.* Inner Traditions, Rochester, Vermont.

Cassuto, Humbertus. 1956. *Codices Vaticani Hebraici 1-115*, Bibliotheca Vaticana.

Caiger, Stephen. 1936. *Bible and Spade.* Oxford University Press, London, UK.

Caldwell, Penny. 2008. *God of the Mountain.* Bridge Logos Publisher, Alachua, Florida.

Cantor, Norman. 1995. *The Sacred Chain: The History of the Jews.* Harper Collins Perennial books, N.Y.

Capellanus, Andreas. 1150, 1960. *Art of Courtly Love.* Columbia University Press.

Carroll, J.M. 2003. *The Trail of Blood.* Challenge Press, Emmaus, PA.

Carroll, James. 2001. *Constantine's Sword: The Church and the Jews.* Houghton Mifflin, Boston.

Casanellas, Pere & Harvey Hames, 2014. "*A Textual and Contextual Analysis of The Hebrew Gospels translated from Catalan.*" In Melilah: Manchester Journal of Jewish Studies, 2014, Volume 11, pp. 68-81.

Cary, Max. 1939. *The Cambridge Ancient History, vol VI.* Cambridge University Press.

Castro, Americo. 1971. *The Spaniards: Introduction to their History*. California Library Reprint Series.
Ceram, C.W. 1951, 1967, 1994. *Gods, Graves and Scholars*. Alfred A. Knopf, N.Y.
Ceram, C.W. 1955. *Secret of the Hittites*. Phoenix Press, U.K.
Charles, Robert H. 1920, reprint 2017. *A Critical & Exegetical Commentary on the Revelation of Saint John*. Charles Scribner's Sons, N.Y. Reprint by Forgotten Books, KY.
Chrysostom, John. 2nd century AD. *Homilies on Matthew*.
Clement of Alexandria (2nd century A.D.). *Stromata*, bk 1. Quoted in Owen.
Clement of Rome. *First Epistle of Rome to Corinthians*, 5:15.
Clover, R. 2002. *The Sacred Name YHWH*. Qadesh La Yahweh Press, Garden Grove, CA.
Cohen, J.M. ed. 1969. *Four Voyages of Christopher Columbus*, Penguin Books, U.K.
Columbus, Christopher. *The Book of Prophecies*. Reprinted in 2004, in *Repertorium Columbianum*, Roberto Rusconi, editor, Wipf & Stock Publishers, Eugene, Or.
Columbus, Fernando. 1540, 1992. *Life of Admiral Christopher Columbus by His Son Fernando*. Rutgers U. Press, New Brunswick, N.J
Conybeare, Fred. 2012. *The Key of Truth: Manual of the Paulician Church of Armenia*. First edition 1898, Clarendon Press, Oxford, U.K. Reprint by Forgotten Books, London.
Fr. Cornelius a' Lapide. 1681. *The Great Commentary*.
Costa de Beauregard. 1816. *Memoires Historiques*. Pierre Joseph, Turin
Cross, Frank Moor. 1998. *From Epic to Canon: History and Literature in Ancient Israel*. Johns Hopkins University Press, Baltimore, MD.
Crossland, Ronald. 1971. "*Reconstructing Languages and Cultures*" in Polome & Winter, eds. Trends in Linguistics, #58.
Cundall, Frank & Joseph Pietersz. 1919. *Jamaica Under the Spaniards*. Archives of Seville. Jamaica.
Danielou, Jean & Henri Marrou. 1964. *The Christian Centuries*. Datton, Longman & Todd, London.
Daniels, Peter & William Bright. 1996. *World's Writing Systems*. Oxford University Press.
Dankenbring, William. 2014. "*Mysterious Events of the Year 30 AD.*" https://ensignmessage.com.

Davis, Tamar. 1851. *The General History of the Sabbatarians.* Lindsay & Blakiston. Philadelphia, US.

Deakin, Michael. 2007. *Hypatia of Alexandria: Mathematician and Martyr.* Prometheus Books, Amherst, N.Y.

Delcor, Matias. 1981. "Un manuscript hébraïque inédit des quatre évangiles conservé a la Bibliothéque Vaticane" (Vat. Ebr. 100), *Anuario de Filología,* volume 7, pp.201-219.

Dimont, Max. 1981. *The Indestructible Jews.* Penguin, USA.

Dourson, Michael. 2014. *Messiah's Star.* messiahstar.com. Middletown, DE.

Downey, Kirsten. 2015. *Isabella: The Warrior Queen.* Anchor Books. N.Y.

Dungan, David Laird. 1999. A *History of the Synoptic Problem.* Doubleday, N.Y.

Dunkelgrün, Theodor. 2020. *Bastards and Believers.* University of Pennsylvania Press. Philadelphia, PA.

Durant, Will. 1926, 1961. *The Story of Philosophy.* Simon & Schuster, N.Y.

Edwards, James R. 2009. *The Hebrew Gospel & Development of the Synoptic Tradition.* Eerdmans, Grand Rapids, MI.

Ehrman, Bart. 2005. *Misquoting Jesus: The Story Behind Who Changed the Bible and Why.* Harper Collins, N.Y.

Ehrman, Bart. 2003. *Lost Christianities: The Battle for Scripture and the Faiths We Never Knew.* Oxford Univ. Press.

Emhardt, William & George Lamsa. 1926, reprint 2013. *The Oldest Christian People: A Brief Account of the History and Traditions of the Assyrians People and the Fateful History of the Nestorian Church.* Wipf & Stock Publishers, UK.

Epiphanius. 2nd century AD. *Panarion.*

Epiphanius. *Weights and Measures.*

Esposito, Don. 2001. *The Great Falling Away.* Morris Publishing, Kearney, NE.

Esposito, Don. 2007. *Who is the Messiah of Israel.* Morris Publishing, Kearney, NE.

Esposito, Don, ed. 2012. *Hebraic Roots Bible with Study Notes.* Word of Truth Publications, NJ.

Eusebius of Caesaria. *Praeparatio Evangelica.*

Eusebius of Caesaria. *The Last Days of Constantine.*

Eusebius of Caesaria. *History of the Church.*

Eusebius of Caesaria. *In Praise of Constantine.*

Fabricius' *Bibliotheca Graeca,* volume 14, p.166.

Farmer, William R. 1964. *The Synoptic Problem: A Critical Analysis.* McMillan Publisher, N.Y.
Farmer, William R. 1974. *The Last Twelve Verses of Mark.* Cambridge University Press, London.
Farmer, William R. 1994. *The Gospel of Jesus.* John Knox Press, Louisville, KY.
Farmer, William R., ed. 1999. *Anti-Judaism in the Gospels.* Trinity Press, Harrisburg, PA.
Ferguson, Everett. 1987. "Persecution in the Early Church." https://www.christianitytoday.com.
Fernandez-Morera, Dario. 2016. *The Myth of the Andalusian Paradise.* ISI Books, Wilmington, Del.
Fernandez de Oviedo y Valdez. 2000. *Batallas y Quincuagenas.*
Ferrell, Vance. 2003. *Christmas, Easter and Halloween -Where Do They Come From?* Altamont, TN: Harvestime.
Findlay, Adam Fyfe. "Byways in Early Christian Literature," vol. 50 (The Kerr Lectures 1920-21).
Finegan, Jack. 1998. *Handbook of Biblical Chronology.* Hendrickson Publishers. Peabody, MA.
Finkelstein, I. & N. Silberman. 2001. *The Bible Unearthed: Archaeology's New Vision of Ancient Israel and the Origin of Its Sacred Texts.* New York.
Finn, James. 1841, 2012. *Sephardim: History of the Jews in Spain and Portugal.* First edition Rivington Pub. 1841, London. Reprinted by Forgotten Books 2012, London.
Fish, Henry. 1874, 2011. *Handbook of Revivals.* Counted Faithful Publications.
Fitzgerald, Edward. 1952. *The Rubaiyat of Omar Khayyam.*
Frend, W.H.C. 1984. *Rise of Christianity.* Fortress Press, Philadelphia.
Fjordman, B. 2012. *Assyrian Contributions to Islamic Civilization.*
Fritz, Glen A. 2006. *The Lost Sea of the Exodus: A Modern Geographical Analysis.* Instant Publisher, U.S.
Fournier, Jacques. *The Inquisition Record of Jacques Fournier - Bishop of Pamiers 1318-1325.* San Jose University, CA.
Fowler, Everett W. 1981. *Evaluating Versions of the New Testament.* Strait Street Incorporated, Cedarville, IL.
Gadalla, Moustafa. 1996. *Untold Story of Ancient Egypt.*
Galil, Gershon. 2010. "Most Ancient Biblical Inscription Deciphered." University of Haifa.

Garza, Al. 2020. *New Testament in Hebrew*. Sefer Press. US.
Gassendi, Pierre. 1970. *Peiresc & His Books*. David Godine Publisher, Boston, MA.
Gerber, Jane. 1992. *The Jews of Spain: A History of the Sephardic Experience*. The Free Press, New York.
Gibbons, Cardinal James. 1876. *The Faith of Our Fathers*. Baltimore, MD.
Gilly, William Stephen. 1844. *Vigilantius and His Times*. Seeley & Burnside, London.
Gilly, William Stephen. 1848. *The Roumant Version of the Gospel according to St. John*. John Murray Pub., London.
Glinert, Lewis. 2017. *The Story of Hebrew*. Princeton University Press, N.J.
Goldman, David. 2011. *How Civilizations Die*. Regnery Publishing, Washington, D.C.
Goldwasser, Orly. 2010. "*How the Alphabet was Born from Hieroglyphs.*" Biblical Archaeology Review, 36:2, Mar/Apr.
Gordon, Janet. 1896. *The Spanish Inquisition*. Nimmo, Hay & Mitchell Publishers. Edinburgh, Scotland.
Gordon, Nehemia. 2005. *The Hebrew Yeshua vs The Greek Jesus*. Hilkiah Press.
Gordon, Nehemia. 2008. *The Naming of Jesus in Hebrew Matthew*. Makor Hebrew Foundation.
Gordon, Nehemia & Keith Johnson. 2009. *APrayer to Our Father: Hebrew Origins of Lord's Prayer*. Hilkiah Press.
Gordon, Nehemia. 2012. *Shattering the Conspiracy of Silence*. Hilkiah Press.
Grant, Michael. 1914, reprinted 1982. *From Alexander to Cleopatra*. Charles Schribner's Sons, N.Y.
Green, John. 1890. *A Short History of the English People*, Macmillan, London.
Green, Peter. 1991. *Alexander of Macedon*. University of California Press, Berkeley, CA.
Greenfield, John. 1928. *Power From on High*, reprint 2017. CTM Publishing. Atlanta, GA.
Grimme, Hubert, 1896. *Grundzüge der Hebraeischen: Akzent und Vokallehre - mit Anhang - Ueber die Form des Namens Jahwae* [Guidelines of the Hebrew: Accent and Vocal Teaching - with Appendix - Concerning the Form of the name Yahweh]. Freiburg Universitaes Buchhandlung, Freiburg, Germany.

Grimme, Hubert, 1923. *Althebräische Inschriften vom Sinai* [Ancient Hebrew Inscriptions in Sinai]. Orient Buchhandlung Heinz Lafaire, Hannover, Germany.

Grubb, Norman. 1966. *Rees Howells: Intercessor.* Lutterworth Press, UK

Gruber, Daniel. 2005. *The Separation of Church & Faith, Volume One - Copernicus and the Jews.* Elijah Pub. N.H..

Gruber, Daniel. 2011. *The Messianic Writings.* Elijah Publishing. Hanover, NH.

Gruber, Daniel. 2014. *Torah and the New Covenant.* Elijah Publishing. Hanover, N.H.

Guirand, Jean. 1913. *Saint Dominic.* Duckworth Publishing.UK.

Hagee, John. 2013. *Four Blood Moons.* Worthy Publishing, TN.

Halberstadt, Haimo. 14th century AD. *Commentary on Isaiah.*

Hall, Christopher. May 2018. "*How Arianism Almost Won,*" in Christianity Today, issue 85.

Hames, Harvey J. 2012. *Translated from Catalan: Looking at a Fifteenth-Century Hebrew Version of the Gospels.* In *Knowledge and Vernacular Languages in the Age of LLull...* Publicacions de l'Abadia de Montserrat, Barcelona.

Handemann, Rudolf. 1888. *Das Hebraer-Evangelium.* Leipzig.

Handschrift, Sammel. 14th-15th century, f.65r, *Historia Passionis Domini*; MS: Theology.

Haring, Ben. 2015. "*Earliest Abecedary.*" https://phys.org/news/2015-10-earliest-abecedary.html.

Harris, Nathaniel. 2000. *History of Ancient Greece.* Octopus Publishing, London.

Hays, Jeffrey. 2008. "*Christianity and the Mongols.*" http://factsanddetails.com.

Harris, William. 1989. *Ancient Literacy.* Harvard University Press, Cambridge, MA.

Hebrew Gospels from Catalonia [HGC], Vat. Ebr. 100.

Heggesipus. 2nd century AD. *Five Books of Memoir.*

Heidler, Robert D. 2006. *The Messianic Church Arising.* Glory of Zion Ministry, TX.

Hemphill, Samuel. 1906. *A History of the Received Version of The New Testament.* E. Stock Co. London.

Hierapolis, Papias. 70-163 AD. *Exposition of the Sayings of the Lord - Fragment X,* earlychristianwritings.com.

Hillel the Third (1st century A.D.). "*The Hillel Letters*", in Mahan, W.D. *The Archko Volume.* 1887, reprinted 1975:174). Keats Publishing, New Canaan, CT.

Hilpetha, R. Jose ben. 3-4th century. *Order of Time.*
Hilton, Michael. 2014. *Bar Mitzvah: A History.* University of Nebraska Press. Lincoln.
Historia Passionis Domini. MS: Theology. Sammel Handschrift Publisher. 14-15th century, foll. 65r.
Hitti, P.K. 1961. *The Near East in History: A 5000 Year Story.* Van Nostrand Co., Princeton, N.J.
Homza, Lu Ann. 2006. *The Spanish Inquisition: An Anthology of Sources.* Hackett Publishing. Cambridge.
Hoffman, Joel M. 2004. *In the Beginning: A Short History of the Hebrew Language.* New York University Press, N.Y.
Hoffman, Joel M. 2010. *And God Said: How Translations Conceal the Bible's Original Meaning.* St. Martin's Press, N.Y.
Hoffmeier, James K. and Alan Millard, eds. 2004. *The Future of Biblical Archaeology.* Eerdmans, Grand Rapids, MI.
Holtzman, Heinrich Julius. 1863. *Die synoptischen Evangelien, Ihr Ursprtung und geschichtlicher Charakter.* Englemann Publishing. Leipzig.
Hooker, Richard. 2018. *The Hebrews: A Learning Module.* Washington State University, online.
Hooks, Walter F. 1846. *An Ecclesiastical Biography: A Brief History of the Church in Every Age*, Rivington. Oxford. UK.
Howard, George. 1995. *Hebrew Gospel of Matthew.* Mercer University Press, Macon, GA.
Howard, Kenneth. 1993. *Jewish Christianity in the Early Church.* Honors Thesis. Virginia Theological Seminary.
Houwelingen, P.H.R. 2003. "The Departure of Christians from Jerusalem to Pella," WTJ vol. 5, 2003:pp.181-200.
Hippolytus of Rome (170 – 235 AD). *De Duodecim Apostolis.* [Testimony of the Twelve Apostles].
Hutchison, Dwight. 2015. *The Lion Led the Way.* Editions Signes Célestes, France.
Irizarry, Estelle. 2009. *Christopher Columbus: The DNA of His Writings.* Ediciones Puerto.
Ironside, H.A. 2017. *The Real St. Patrick.* Crossreach Pub.
Irving, Washington. 1828. *Life and Voyages of Christopher Columbus*, volumes 1 & 2.
Jacobs, Janet Liebman. 2002. *Hidden Heritage: Legacy of the Crypto-Jews.* Univ. of California Press, Berkeley.
Jaume, Casanellas & Tarrech. 2004. "*Catalan Bibles of 15th century Spain.*" Corpus Scriptorum Calaloniae, vol.3, Barcelona: Publicaciones de L'Abadia de Montserrat..

Jehovah's Witnesses. 1990. *Mankind's Search for God.* Watch Tower Bible Society, New York.
Jerome. 4th century AD. *Commentary on Galatians.*
Jerome. *Hebrew Questions on Genesis.*
Jerome. *Illustrious Men.*
Jerome. *Commentary on Matthew.*
Jerome. *Commentary on Micah.*
Jerome. *Vulgate Bible.*
Johnson, Ken. 2008. *Ancient Book of Jasher.* Biblefacts Ministries, U.S.A.
Johnson, Keith. *His Hallowed Name Revealed Again.* Biblical Foundations, Minneapolis, MN.
Jones, Christopher. 2014. *Mashiach and the Sign of Yonah.* Amazon Books.
Jones, Christopher. In publication, est. 2020. *The Quartodeciman Controversy.*
Jones, Miles R. 2010, third edition 2016. *The Writing of God.* Amazon Books, U.S.
Jones, Miles R. 2019. *Sons of Zion versus Sons of Greece: Vol. One - Survival of The Hebrew Gospels & Messianic Church.* Benai Emunah Institute. Kerrville. TX.
Jones, Miles R. 2022. *Messianic Church Arising! Recovery of the Received Text. Volume Two of Sons of Zion vs Sons of Greece.* Benai Emunah Institute. Kerrville. TX.
Jones, Miles R. *"Evidence of the Exodus."* Faith for All of Life, March 2013, pp. 4-10.
Jones, Miles R. *"The Stones Will Cry Out."* Faith for All of Life, May 2013, pp. 4-11.
Jones, Miles R. *"The Call from Sinai."* Faith for All of Life, July 2013, pp. 12-17.
Josephus, Titus Flavius (born Yosef ben Matthias). 1st century AD. *Antiquities of the Jews.*
Josephus, Titus Flavius. *Against Apion.*
Josephus, Titus Flavius. *The Jewish War.*
Jost, J.M. 1859. *Geschicte des Judentums und seiner Sekten, vol.2 [History of Judaism and its Sects].* Reprinted 2017 by Forgotten Books, London.
Jung, Carl G. 1964. *Man and His Symbols.* Doubleday. N.Y.
Kamen, Henry. 1997. *The Spanish Inquisition: An Historical Revision.* Yale University Press. US.
Keller, Werner. 1909, reprinted 1981. *The Bible as History.*

Kelly, J.N.D. 2001. *Early Christian Doctrines*. Continuum Publisher.
Kenyon, Kathleen. 1960. *Archaeology in the Holy Land*. Routledge, N.Y.
Kerkeslager, Allen. 1998. "*Jewish Pilgrimage and Jewish Identity in Hellenistic and Early Roman Egypt*," pp. 99-225 in *Pilgrimage and Holy Space in Late Antique Egypt*, edited by David Frankfurter, *Religions in the Graeco-Roman World*, 134: Leiden, The Netherlands: Brill, 1998.
Khayyam, Omar. Edward Fitzgerald, translator. 1952. *The Rubaiyat of Omar Khayyam*. Doubleday & Co., N.Y.
Kidd, Thomas. 2007. *The Great Awakening*. Yale Press. US
Kilpatrick, G.D. 1978. "*The Itala*." The Classical Review, vol.28, no.1, pp. 56-58.
Kim, Sung Hak. 2006. *The Burning Bush*. (in Korean) tpress@duranno.co.kr. ISBN 978-89-531-0839-4.
Kitchen, Kenneth. 1973. *The Third Intermediate Period in Egypt*. Warminster Publishing, U.K.
Kitchen, Kenneth. 1982. *Pharaoh Triumphant*, Warminster.
Klimczak, Natalia. 2016. "*Who is buried at the Shrine of Santiago de Compostela?*" Ancient-Origins.net.
Kiwiet, John. 1993. Translator's Introduction to Meijboom. *A History & Critique of the Origin of the Marcan Hypothesis*, Mercer, GA.
Koester, Craig. 1989. "*The Origin and Significance of the Flight to Pella Tradition*." Catholic Bible Quarterly 51, #1, Jan 1989:pp. 90-100.
Kraemer, Joel L. 2008. *Maimonides: The Life and World of One of Civilization's Greatest Minds*. Doubleday, N.Y.
Kreis, Steven. 2016. The History Guide: thehistoryguide.org.
Kyeyune, Stephen. 2010. "*The New Generation of Worshipers*," https://www.tmf-fdn.org/outcome-stories.
Kritzler, Edward. 2008. *Jewish Pirates of the Caribbean*, Doubleday. NY.
Ladurie, Emmanuel LeRoy. 1978. *Montaillou: Portrait of a Medieval Village*. Penguin Books, NY.
LaGrange, M.J. 1922. "*L'Evangile selon les Hebreux.*" Revue Biblique, vol. 31.
Lamsa, George M. 1931, reprinted 1985. *Idioms in the Bible Explained and a Key to the Original Gospels*. Harper Collins, N.Y.

Landstrom, Bjorn. 1966. *Columbus*, MacMillan. New York.
Lapide, Pinchas. 1984. *Hebrew in the Church*. Eerdmans, Grand Rapids, MI.
Lappin, David. 2002. *"The Decline of Sothic Dating."* Journal of Ancient Chronology, v.9.
Larson, Rick. 2009. *The Star of Bethlehem* [documentary film]. MPower Pictures. Go to bethlehemstar.com.
Latourette, Kenneth. 1884, reprinted 1937. *A History of the Expansion of Christianity: The First Five Centuries*, vol. 1. Harper & Brothers, New York and London.
Lea, Henry Charles. 1908. *A History of the Inquisition in Spain*, volume 1. McMillan Publishing. NY.
Lendering, Jona. 2017, *"Trajan's War,"* livius.org/roman-jewish-wars.
Levine, Amy Jill. 2006. *The Misunderstood Jew: The Church and the Scandal of the Jewish Jesus*. Harper Collins, N.Y.
Lichtenstein, Isaac. 1896. *Judenspiegel*. L. Schoenberger Publishing. Vienna.
Lichtenstein, Isaac. Est.1900. *Judenthum und Christenthum*.
Liebman, Seymour. 1970. *The Jews in New Spain*. University of Miami Press.
Lindsay, Phillip. 1951. *The Great Buccaneer*. William Funk Publishing Co. N.Y.
Litfin, Bryan. *After Acts: Exploring the Lives and Legends of the Apostles*. Moody Publishers, Chicago, IL.
Logan, Robert K. 1986. *The Alphabet Effect*. William Morrow & Co., New York, NY.
Loofs, Friedrich. 1914. *Nestorius: His Place in the History of Christian Doctrine*. Cambridge University Press, U.K.
Lowney, Chris. 2005. *A Vanished World: Muslims, Christians, and Jews in Medieval Spain*. Oxford U. Press.
Lüdemann, Gerd. 1980. "The *Successors of Pre-70 Jerusalem Christianity: A Critical. Evaluation of the Pella Tradition*," Jewish and Christian Self-Definition, ed. E. P. Sanders; Philadelphia: Fortress Press, 1, pp.161-73.
Lüdemann, Gerd. 2002. *Paul: The Founder of Christianity*. Prometheus Books, Amherst, N.Y.
Lüdemann, Gerd. 2003. *Primitive Christianity*. T & T Clark, London, New York.
Lüdemann, Gerd. 2005. *The Acts of the Apostles*. Prometheus Books, Amherst, N.Y.

Lumpkin, Joseph B. 2011. *The Books of Enoch.* Fifth Estate Publishers, AL.
Luther, Martin. 1523. *That Jesus was born a Jew.*
Luther, Martin. 1544. *Of the Jews and their Lies.*
Lynch, Hannah. 2014. *Toledo: The Story of an Old Spanish Capital.* EBook #46301.
Lyra, Nicolas. Est. 1340. *Postillae, Perbetuae, sive Brevia Commentaria Universa Biblia.*
Maccoby, Hyam. 1993, *Judaism on Trial.* Littman Library.
Mack, Burton. 1988. *A Myth of Innocence: Mark and Christian Origins.* Fortress Press, Philadelphia, PA.
Mack, Burton. 1995. *Who Wrote the New Testament.* Harper Collins, N.Y.
Maddox, Maeve. 2011. "*Alaric the Visigoth was Christian,*" americanenglishdoctor.com.
Maier, Paul. 2011. *The Constantine Codex.* Tyndale House, NY.
Maimonides, Moses (1135-1204 AD). 1952 translation, 1995 reprint. *The Guide to the Perplexed.* Hackett Publishing, Indianapolis, IN.
Mann, Charles. 2011. *1493:Uncovering the New World...* Random House Audio Books, N.Y.
Marshall, Peter & David Manuel, 1977. *The Light and The Glory.* Revell Publishing, Grand Rapids, MI.
Martinez-Davila, Roger; Diaz, Josef & Hart, Ron. 2016, *Fractured Faiths*, from the New Mexico History Museum, printed by Fresco Books, Italy.
Marx, Alexander. 1929. *The Polemical Manuscripts.* Vienna. Jewish Theological Seminary of America.
Mastin, Luke. 2010. *The Story of Mathematics*, www.storyofmathematics.com.
Mariani, Mike. 2014. "A Brief History of the Christmas Controversy." Pacific Standard, https://psmag.com.
Martin, Earnest. 1988. *Secret of Golgotha.* ASK Publications, Alhambra, CA.
McBirnie, William. 1973. *The Search for the Twelve Apostles.* Tyndale House, Carol Stream, IL.
McRay, Ron & John Eoff. 2013. *Was Jesus Three Days and Three Nights In the Heart of the Earth?* New Bible Concepts, Charleston, SC.
Medved, Michael. August 9, 2006. "*Why the World Hates Jews.*" Townhall.com.

Meijboom, Hado. 1866, reprint 1993. *A History & Critique of the Origin of the Marcan Hypothesis.* Mercer University Press. GA.

Metzger, Bruce & Bart Ehrman. 2005. *The Text of the New Testament.* Oxford University Press, Oxford, U.K. & N.Y.

Metzger, Bruce. 1987. *The Canon of the New Testament.* Oxford University Press, N.Y.

Meyers, E.M. 1988. "*Early Judaism and Christianity*", Biblical Archaology v.51(2).

Meyerson, Mark. 2004. *A Jewish Renaissance in 15th century Spain.* Princeton Press.

Millard, A.R. 1983. *Essays on the Patriarchal Narratives.* Eisenbrauns Publishers, Winona Lake, Indiana.

Missick, Stephen. July 2012. "*Mongols, Christianity, Nestorians and the Silk Road.*" Journal of Assyrian Academic Studies.

Mitchell, Wayne. 1990. *"Ancient Astronomical Observations and Near Eastern Chronology"* in Journal of Ancient Chronology Forum, vol. 3, pp.18-20.

Möller, Lennart. 2008. *The Exodus Case.* Scandinavia Publishing House, Copenhagen, Denmark.

Monastier, Antoine. 1859. *The History of the Vaudois Church.* The Religious Tract Society, London.

Monmouth, Geoffrey of. 1136. *History of the Kings of Britain.*

Moorman, Jack. 1990. "*Early Manuscripts and the Authorized Version: A Closer Look!*" Bible for Today, #1825.

Morrison, James. 2007. *The Astrolabe*, Classical Science Press.

Mosheim, John. 1856. *Historical Commentaries on the State of Christianity in the First Centuries...* Converse, N.Y.

Moulton, W.F. 1878, reprint 2018. *The History of the English Bible.* Forgotten Books. London.

Müller, William M. 1888. *Encyclopedia Biblica*, vol. IV, col. 4486, no. 5. In Cheyne & Black (eds.), London.

Muir, William. 2015. *The Arrested Reformation.* Scholar Select.

Murphy, Cullen. 2012. *God's Jury.* Houghton Mifflin. Boston.

Muston, Alexis. 1875. *The Israel of the Alps, vols. I & II.* Ingram Cook, London.

Neale, John Mason. 1850. *A History of th Holy Eastern Church*, vol 1, MacMillan & Co. London.

Nestle, Eberhard & Kurt Aland. First ed. 1514. *Novum Testamentum Graece.* Nestle-Aland 27th Edition (New Testament) / Edition 27, 1998, American Bible Society.

Netanyahu, Benzion. 2012. *The Founding Fathers of Zionism.* Geffen Publishing, Jerusalem & Balfour Books, OK.
Netanyahu, Benzion. 1999. *Marranos of Spain.* Cornell Press.
Newgrosh, Bernard. 2007. *Chronology at the Crossroads: The Late Bronze Age in Western Asia.* Troubador Publishing.
Nissenbaum, Stephen. 1996. *The Battle for Christmas.* Knopf Publishers, New York
Nizam ul-Mulk. Reprint 1960. *The Book of Government or Rules for Kings.* Yale Univ. Press, New Haven. .
Nongbri, Brent. 2014:pp.1-35. "*Date and Provenance of P. Bodmer II (P66),*" in *Museum Helveticum*, vol. 71.
Odoric, Friar. 1330. *Eastern Parts of the World.*
Oppenheimer, Mike. 2013. "*The Churches Past and Current History with the Jews.*" letusreason.org/juda15.htm.
O'Leary, Lacy. 1909. *The Syriac Church & Fathers.* Society for Christian Knowledge, London.
O'Leary, Lacy. 1949, 1964. *How Greek Science Passed to the Arabs.* Routledge & Kegan Paul Ltd, London.
O'Reilly, Alan James. 1995. *The Whitewash Conspiracy.* Bethany House Publishers.
Orchard, Bernard & Thomas Longstaff. 1978, reprinted 2005. *J.J. Griesbach: Synoptic and Text-Critical Studies 1776-1976.* Cambridge University Press, London & N.Y.
Orchard, Bernard & Harold Riley. 1987. *The Order of the Synoptics: Why Three Synoptic Gospels?* Mercer University Press, Macon, GA.
Oviedo y Valdes, Fernandez. 1878. *Batallas y Quincuagenas.*
Owen, John. 1661, translated from Latin and reprinted 1994. *Biblical Theology.* Soli Deo Gloria Publications, Grand Rapids, MI.
Pack, David. *The True Origin of Easter.* Real Truth magazine, rcg.org
Paris, Edmond. 1983. *Secret History of the Jesuits.* Chick Publications. CA.
Parker, Pierson. 1940. "*A Proto-Lukan Basis for the Gospel According to the Hebrews.*" Journal of Biblical Literature, #59, p.478.
Parks, James. 1974. *Conflict of the Church and the Synagogue.* Atheneum Publishers, New York, NY.
Petrovich, Douglas. 2016. *The World's Oldest Alphabet.* Carta, Jerusalem.

Rood, Michael. 2013. *The Chronological Gospels*. Aviv Moon Publishing. Fort Mill, S.C.

Rohl, David. 1995. *A Test of Time*. Century, London, UK. Reprinted in U.S. as *Pharaohs and Kings*. Crown, N.Y.

Rohl, David. 2007. *The Lords of Avaris*. Century, Random House, London, UK. In 2008 by Arrow Books, London.

Rohl, David. 2009. *From Eden to Exile*. Century, Random House, London, UK.

Rohl, David. 2015. *Exodus: Myth or History*. Thinking Man Media, St. Louis Park, MN.

Rolfe, Frederick. 1901. *Chronicles of the house of Borgia*, Sagwan Press, openlibrary.org.

Romer, John. 1988. *Testament: The Bible and History*. Konecky & Konecky Publishers, CT.

Rorenco, Marco. 1630. *History of the Waldenses*.

Roth, Cecil. 1932. *History of the Marranos*. Jewish Publication Society, Philadelphia. & 1966 Harper Torchbooks.

Roth, Cecil. 1959. *The Jews in the Renaissance*. Jewish Publication Society of America, Philadelphia, PA.

Ruffin, C. Bernard. 1984, 1997. *The Twelve: Lives of the Apostles after Calvary*. Our Sunday Visitor, Huntington, IN.

Runciman, Steven. 1994. *The Medieval Manichee*. Cambridge University Press.

Russell, Bertrand. 1903. *"A Free Man's Worship."* Reprinted 1985, Routledge, London, U.K.

Russell, Jeffrey. 1965. *Dissent & Reform in the Middle Ages*. University of California Press.

Salmon, George. 1897. *Some Thoughts on the Textual Criticism of the New Testament*. John Murray Co. London.

Salomon, H.P. 1982. *Portrait of a New Christian*. Centro Cultural Portugués. Paris.

Samuel, Judith. 1982. *Your Jewish Lexicon*. Union of American Hebrew Congregations, N.Y.

Sanders, E.P. 1996. *The Historical Figure of Jesus*. Penguin.

Sanders, E.P. 2015. *Paul: The Apostle's Life, Letters, and Thought*. Fortress Press.

Sanchez, Dell F. 2014. *Crypto Jews: Anusim*. Jubilee Publications, San Antonio, TX.

Sanday, William. 1897. *The Life & Letters of Fenton Hort*. Oxford. U.K.

Sandoval, Prudencio de. 1792. *Historia de los Reyes de Castilla y de Leon*.

San Francisco, Luis de. *Globus Arcanorum Linguae Sanctae*, volume 14, p. 709.

Sharma, Jai. 2015. *Portuguese Inquisition - A Brief History*. Indiafacts.org.in.

Shibley, Jim. 2015. *"How Two 16th Century Messianic Jews Impacted Rabbinic Bible Study."* One for Israel website.

Schaeffer, Francis A. 1976, 2005. *How Should We Then Live?* Crossway Publishing. Wheaton, IL.

Schlain, Leonard. 1998. *The Alphabet versus the Goddess: Conflict between Word and Image.* Penguin, NY.

Schonfield, Hugh. 1937:pp.13-18. *According to the Hebrews: A New Translation of the Jewish Life of Jesus.* Duckworth Publishers, London.

Schonfield, Hugh. 1936. *The History of Jewish Christianity.* Duckworth Publishers, London. 2nd edition, 2009. Bruce R. Booker, editor. Messianic Bible Institute.

Schumann, John. 1979:pp.27-107, *"The Acculturation Model,"* in R. Gingras, ed. *Second Language Acquisition and Foreign Language Teaching.* Center - Applied Linguistics, Arlington, VA.

Schurer, Emil. 1890. *History of the Jewish People in the Time of Jesus Christ.* T & T Clark, Edinburgh.

Schrivener, Frederick. 1894. *Criticism of the New Testament.* George Bell & Sons, London.

Skarsaune, Oskar & Raidar Valvik. 2007. *Jewish Believers in Jesus: The Early Centuries.* Hendrickson, Peabody, Mass.

Scott, R.B.Y. 1899, reprint. *The Original Language of the Apocalypse.* ICG testing.com.

Snaith, Norman. 1968. Introduction to *The Rabbinic Bible.* Christian D. Ginsburg, ed. KTAV Publishing House. N.Y.

Snodgrass, A.M. 2001. *Dark Age of Greece.* Routledge, N.Y.

Socrates Scholasticus. *"Ecclesiastical History,"* Nicene and Post-Nicene Fathers.

Spiro, Rabbi Ken. *Crash Course in Jewish History.* Targum Press, also online.

St. Cher, Hugo. 13th century AD. *Liber Isaiah* [Book of Isaiah].

Stark, Rodney. 1997. *The Rise of Christianity.* Harper Collins Publishers & Princeton University Press.

Stokes, G. T. 1892. *Ireland and the Celtic Church.* Dublin.

Swetschinski, Daniel. Dec, 1982. *"The Adventure of Caribbean Jewish Settlement,"* American Jewish Historical Society.

Szpiech, Ryan. 2007. *"Bibles from Catalan,"* The Medieval Review. Indiana University.

Tabor, James. 2006. *The Jesus Dynasty*. Simon & Schuster, N.Y.
Tcherikover, Victor. 1977, reprinted 2001. *Hellenistic Civilization and the Jews*. McMillan Publisher, USA.
Thiele, Edwin. 1983. *The Mysterious Numbers of the Hebrew Kings*. Zondervan Publishing Co. Grand Rapids, MI.
Thomas, Sarah-Mae. 2013. *"The Convivencia in Islamic Spain."* The Fountain Magazine, Issue 94.
Thompson, Thomas L. 1999. *The Bible in History*. Pimlico Publishing, London, U.K.
Todhunter, Andrew. *"The Journey of the Apostles"*. National Geographic Magazine, March 2012.
Tolkowsky, Samuel. 1964. *They took to the Sea: A Historical Survey of Jewish Maritime Activities*, German edition.
Triesch, Gene. 2009, second edition 2015. *Truth or Consequences: The Church in a Rearview Mirror*. Menorah Ministry, TX.
Trimm, James Scott. 2012. *"Historical Evidence that Yeshua is Messiah."* http://nazarenespace.com.
Ullman, B.L. 1927. "The Origin and Development of the Alphabet." American Journal of Archaeology, vol. XXI.
Ul-Mulk, Nizam. 1960. Hubert Darke, translator. *Book of Government or Rules for Kings*. Yale University Press.
Vaticano Ebreo 100, *The Hebrew Gospels of Catalonia*, [HGC].
Virga, R. Solomon ben. 13th century, *Sceptre of Judah*.
Wakefield, Walter & Austin Evans. 1991. *Heresies of the High Middle Ages*. Columbia University Press.
Wagner, Clarence. 1997. *"Metal-Working in the Bible."* Jewish Bible Quarterly, May/June 1997.
Wasson, Don. 2015. *"Fall of the Roman Empire."* Ancient History Encyclopedia.
Wedgwood, C.V. 1938. *The Thirty Years War*. New York Review of Books, N.Y.
Weeden, Theodore. 1971. *Mark: Traditions in Conflict*. Fortress Press, Philadelphia, PA.
Westcott, Arthur. 1905. *Life & Letters of Brooke Westcott*. MacMillan, N.Y.
Westcott, Brooke & Fenton Hort. 1896. *New Testament in the Original Greek*. MacMillan & Co., New York.
Whately, Jane. 1850, reprint 2018. *The Gospel in Bohemia*. Religious Tract Society. London.

Wiesenthal, Simon. 1973. *Sails of Hope: Secret Mission of Christopher Columbus*, McMillan Press, N.Y.

Wilmhurst, David. 2011. *The Martyred Church: History of the Church of the East*. East & West Publishing, London.

Wilkinson, B. G. 1944. *Truth Triumphant: The Church in the Wilderness*. Hartland Publications, Rapidan, VA.

Wilkinson, B. G. first ed. 1930, 2014. *Our Authorized Bible Vindicated*. TEACH Publishing.

Wilson, Marvin R. 1989. *YHWH in the Bible: Divine Titles, Names & Attributes*. Pilgrim Publishing, TX.

Wilson, Marvin T. 1997, 2001. *Our Father Abraham: Jewish Roots of the Christian Faith*. Eerdmans, Grand Rapids, MI.

Winsham, Willow. 2017. *Sex & Citadel: Eleanor of Aquitaine & Courtly Love.*

Whiston, William. 1998. *Josephus: The Complete Works*. Thomas Nelson Publishers, Nashville, TN.

White, Ellen G. *The Great Controversy*. Pacific Press, ID.

Wilmshurst, David. 2011. *The Matyred Church: A History of the Church of the East*. East-West Pub. Limited, London.

Wood, Michael. 2008. *The Jerome Conspiracy*. iUniverse, Bloomington, IN.

Yardeni, Ada. 2014. *Understanding the Alphabet of the Dead Sea Scrolls*. Carta, Jerusalem.

Yeats, William Butler. 1920. *"The Second Coming!"* The Dial Magazine, Ireland.

Yonge, C.D. 1993. *The Works of Philo*. Hendrickson Publishers, U.S.A.

Xanthapoulos, Nicephorus. *circa* 1320, *Chronographia Brevia*.

Printed in Poland
by Amazon Fulfillment
Poland Sp. z o.o., Wrocław